Metaphors in the Mind

Abstract concepts are often embodied through metaphor. For example, we talk about moving through time in metaphorical terms, as if we were moving through space, allowing us to 'look back' on past events. Much of the work on embodied metaphor to date has assumed a single set of universal, shared bodily experiences that motivate our understanding of abstract concepts. This book explores sources of variation in people's experiences of embodied metaphor, including, for example, the shape and size of one's body, one's age, gender, state of mind, physical or linguistic impairments, personality, ideology, political stance, religious beliefs and linguistic background. It focuses on the ways in which people's experiences of metaphor fluctuate over time within a single communicative event or across a lifetime. Combining theoretical argument with findings from new studies, Littlemore analyses sources of variation in embodied metaphor and provides a deeper understanding of the nature of embodied metaphor itself.

JEANNETTE LITTLEMORE is Professor of Applied Linguistics in the Department of English Language and Linguistics at the University of Birmingham. She is the author of multiple books, including *Metonymy: Hidden Shortcuts in Language, Thought and Communication* (Cambridge University Press, 2015) and *Figurative Language, Genre and Register* (with Alice Deignan and Elena Semino, Cambridge University Press, 2013).

Metaphors in the Mind

Sources of Variation in Embodied Metaphor

Jeannette Littlemore

University of Birmingham

CAMBRIDGE
UNIVERSITY PRESS

CAMBRIDGE
UNIVERSITY PRESS

University Printing House, Cambridge CB2 8BS, United Kingdom

One Liberty Plaza, 20th Floor, New York, NY 10006, USA

477 Williamstown Road, Port Melbourne, VIC 3207, Australia

314–321, 3rd Floor, Plot 3, Splendor Forum, Jasola District Centre,
New Delhi – 110025, India

79 Anson Road, #06–04/06, Singapore 079906

Cambridge University Press is part of the University of Cambridge.

It furthers the University's mission by disseminating knowledge in the pursuit of
education, learning, and research at the highest international levels of excellence.

www.cambridge.org
Information on this title: www.cambridge.org/9781108416566
DOI: 10.1017/9781108241441

First published 2019

Printed in the United Kingdom by TJ International Ltd, Padstow Cornwall

A catalogue record for this publication is available from the British Library.

Library of Congress Cataloging-in-Publication Data
Names: Littlemore, Jeannette, author.
Title: Metaphors in the mind : sources of variation in embodied metaphor / Jeannette
    Littlemore.
Description: New York, NY : Cambridge University Press, 2019. | Includes
    bibliographical references and index.
Identifiers: LCCN 2019008018 | ISBN 9781108416566 (hardback) |
    ISBN 9781108403986 (paperback)
Subjects: LCSH: Metaphor. | Figures of speech. | BISAC: LANGUAGE ARTS &
    DISCIPLINES / Linguistics / General.
Classification: LCC P301.5.M48 L58 2019 | DDC 401/.43–dc23
LC record available at https://lccn.loc.gov/2019008018

ISBN 978-1-108-41656-6 Hardback
ISBN 978-1-108-40398-6 Paperback

Cambridge University Press has no responsibility for the persistence or accuracy
of URLs for external or third-party internet websites referred to in this publication
and does not guarantee that any content on such websites is, or will remain,
accurate or appropriate.

For Dan, Joe, Oscar, Mum and Dad

Contents

List of Figures   *page* x
Preface   xiii
Acknowledgements   xv

1   'I Am Trying to Climb Everest in Flip-Flops.' What Is
    Embodied Metaphor and Where Does It Come From?   1
    1.1   Introduction   1
    1.2   Embodied Cognition   3
    1.3   Embodied Metaphor   10
    1.4   Where Do Embodied Primary Metaphors Come From?   16
    1.5   Conclusion   19

2   'Would You Prefer a Pencil or an Antiseptic Wipe?' What
    Evidence Is There for Embodied Metaphor and Why Is It
    Important to Consider This Variation?   21
    2.1   Introduction   21
    2.2   Evidence from Behavioural Studies   22
    2.3   Evidence from Neurological Studies   33
    2.4   Evidence from Naturally Occurring Data   37
    2.5   Variation in Embodied Metaphor   48
    2.6   Outline of the Rest of the Book   51

3   'I'm Running on This Soapy Conveyor Belt with People
    Throwing Wet Sponges at Me.' Which Metaphors Are Embodied
    and When? Variation According to Type, Function and Context   54
    3.1   Introduction   54
    3.2   Intrinsic and Co-Textual Features That Render Metaphors More Likely to
          Evoke Sensorimotor Activation   56
    3.3   Contextual Factors That May Render Metaphors More Likely to Evoke
          Sensorimotor Responses: The Influence of Genre and Register   69
    3.4   Conclusion   75

4   'This One Sounds Like A Bell and This One Sounds Like
    When You're Dead.' Age, and the Developmental Nature of
    Embodied Metaphor   77
    4.1   Introduction   77

4.2 The Development of Embodied Metaphor Comprehension in Infants
     and Children   77
4.3 Metaphors That Are Particularly Strong in Infancy   81
4.4 Maths, Music and Metaphor: A Comparison of Young Children's
     Representations of Number, Valence, Music and Time with Those of Adults 89
4.5 Embodied Metaphor and Older Adults   102
4.6 Conclusion   103

5 'I Did Not Know Where I Started and Where I Ended.' Different
   Bodies: Different Minds? How Handedness, Body Shape and
   Gender Affect the Way We Experience the World through
   Metaphor   105
   5.1 Introduction   105
   5.2 How Does Handedness Affect One's Embodied Experience of Metaphor? 106
   5.3 How Do Body Size and Shape Affect One's Embodied Experience
        of Metaphor?   108
   5.4 How Does Gender Affect One's Embodied Experience of Metaphor?   113
   5.5 Conclusion   121

6 'Those Cookies Tasted of Regret and Rotting Flesh.' Sensory
   Metaphor and Associated Impairments and Conditions   123
   6.1 Introduction   123
   6.2 Sensory Language and Impairments   124
   6.3 Synaesthesia   137
   6.4 Conclusion   148

7 'Things Come Out of My Mouth That Shouldn't Be There.' 'Altered
   Minds': The Impact of Depression and Psychological Disorders
   on the Way People Experience the World through Metaphor   150
   7.1 Introduction   150
   7.2 Depression   152
   7.3 Pregnancy Loss   157
   7.4 Schizophrenia   163
   7.5 Autistic Spectrum Disorders and Asperger Syndrome   169
   7.6 Conclusion   174

8 'This Is My Body Which Will Be Given Up for You.' Individual
   Differences in Personality, Thinking Style, Political Stance and
   Religious Beliefs   176
   8.1 Introduction   176
   8.2 Internally Driven Individual Differences   176
   8.3 Externally Driven (Social) Sources of Variation   185
   8.4 Conclusion   190

9 'Malodorous Blacksmiths and Lazy Livers.' Cross-Linguistic and
   Cross-Cultural Variation in Embodied Metaphor   192
   9.1 Introduction   192
   9.2 Different Language, Different Embodied Metaphor?   193
   9.3 Does Speaking a Second Language Affect the Way in Which We
        Understand and Use Embodied Metaphors?   201

9.4 Are Bodily Based Word–Colour Associations More Likely to Be Universal Than Less Bodily Based Associations? 208
9.5 Are Bodily Based Word–Colour Associations More Likely to Be Adopted by Second Language Learners? 210
9.6 Conclusion 212

10 Conclusion 214
10.1 Introduction 214
10.2 Sources of Variation in the Experience of Metaphor 215
10.3 What Does This Variation Tell Us about Embodied Metaphor? 222
10.4 What Remains to Be Explored? 223
10.5 Conclusion 225

Notes 227
References 229
Index 266

Figures

1.1 'High notes and low notes' *page* 12

1.2 'T'ai chi' 13

2.1 'Sorting out' 45

2.2 'Fit in' 45

2.3 'Adjust yourself' 46

3.1 Extract from class on the meaning of 'units' 72

4.1 Arrangement of stickers used by a five-to-six-year-old child to represent time horizontally 94

4.2 Sticker configuration produced by a five-to-six-year-old child to represent pitch without making use of the vertical axis 95

4.3 Sticker configuration produced by an adult to represent pitch, making use of the vertical axis 96

4.4 Drawing produced by a six-to-seven-year-old child to represent staccato notes as 'an angry girl' 97

4.5 Drawing produced by a five-to-six-year-old child to represent legato and staccato notes as 'a girl walking with a boy' and 'a volcano', respectively 98

4.6 Drawing produced by a seven-to-eight-year-old child to represent legato and staccato notes as 'a house' and 'somebody creeping up', respectively 98

4.7 Drawing produced by an adult to represent legato and staccato notes as a series of lines and a series of dots, respectively 99

4.8 Drawing produced by a seven-toeight-year-old child to represent major and minor chords as a 'sunny meadow' and 'jagged shapes', respectively 100

4.9 Drawing produced by a seven-to-eight-year-old child to represent major and minor chords as 'a piano' and 'bears', respectively 100

4.10 Drawing produced by a five-to-six-year-old child to represent major and minor chords as 'a good day' and 'a scary day in the night', respectively 101

4.11 Drawing produced by an adult to represent major and
      minor chords as a high line with a rising incline and a low
      horizontal line, respectively   101
9.1 'Rigidity'   205
9.2 'Knitting together'   205
9.3 'Cross-disciplinary approach'   206
9.4 'Growth'   207
9.5 'Focusing'   207

Preface

I would like to begin this book on a personal note. When I was eighteen years old, my father died. I was ill-equipped to deal with the emotional fallout that ensued. My over-riding memory of the time involves the sound of bagpipes. Not the sound of real bagpipes, but of bagpipes in my mind. I lived my life with the constant drone of bagpipes in the background. This became both the bass line and the baseline of my everyday experience. On bad days the tunes would start to play, and they would get louder and louder until they became unbearable and I would have to cover my ears. I have never been a fan of the bagpipes, metaphorical or otherwise. As this example shows, in addition to being something that we encounter, metaphor can also be something that we *experience* on a physical and emotional level whether we like it or not. In other words, metaphor can be 'embodied'.

The fact that we often experience meaning through our bodies is well established. According to the Embodied Cognition hypothesis (Rosch et al., 1991), our bodies, and the ways in which we use them to interact with the world and people around us, serve as a basis for the way in which we form ideas and communicate these ideas to others. In other words, our perceptual, motor and emotional experiences play a fundamental role in shaping how we talk about, think about and interact with people, objects and the world around us. Knowledge, therefore, is not acquired or processed in a vacuum. When we perceive an action taking place, we do not simply see or hear that action; we also 'experience' it bodily. More specifically, seeing an action leads to activation of parts of the brain that are involved in movement, processing of sensory stimuli and emotion.

Abstract concepts are also, to a large extent, embodied, often through metaphor, and our bodily interactions with the world around us provide motivation for the metaphorical ways in which we talk about abstract concepts and emotions. We learn to associate certain bodily experiences with particular abstract concepts and emotions, and this allows us to use one to metaphorically represent the other. This is why we often talk about moving through time as if it were moving through space, allowing us, for example, to 'look back on what happened'.[1] It is why we talk about 'feeling down' when we are depressed, and why we talk about emotional closeness as if it were physical closeness. As we will see in this book, expressions such as these have the potential to provoke sensorimotor responses that correspond to the physical action of 'looking back' and to the physical experience of 'closeness'. This is what is meant by 'embodied metaphor' in its purest sense. Weaker versions of embodied metaphor involve the activation of our memory for, or knowledge of, felt, physical experiences that are then used to make sense of metaphors that draw on these experiences.

Much of the early work on embodied metaphor tended to assume a single set of universal, shared bodily experiences that motivate our understanding of abstract concepts. In recent years, it has been acknowledged that the culture we live in can impact on the ways in which embodied metaphors are extended and exploited, and research has shown that they vary across cultures. However, beyond this, there has been little investigation of other sources of variation. Factors such as environment and context, the shape and size of body, age, gender, physical or linguistic impairment, personality, ideology, political stance, religious beliefs and cultural and linguistic background all have the potential to impact on the way in which we form and use embodied metaphor. The aim of this book is to bring together all these different factors, and to combine theoretical argument with findings from studies that I have conducted alone and in collaboration with others, to explore how the variety of 'human experience' shapes the ways in which and the extent to which we acquire and use embodied metaphor. Throughout the book, I emphasise the dynamic interactive and contextual nature of embodied metaphor, and consider the ways in which it develops over time and in different contexts of use. By analysing the ways embodied metaphor varies across different individuals and contexts of use, my aim is to provide a deeper understanding of the nature of embodied metaphor itself.

Eventually, the bagpipes quietened down but they would still resurface from time to time, reflecting the fact that although our felt experience of embodied metaphor is unavoidable and ubiquitous, there are times when we are more aware of it than others: embodied metaphor ebbs and flows over time. A second aim of this book is to offer explanations for this ebb and flow of embodied metaphor. In other words, as well as considering the ways in which the experience of metaphor varies across individuals, I will also look at the way in which it fluctuates over time within a given communicative event and across a lifetime.

Acknowledgements

This book is the product of many fun, informative and productive research collaborations with fantastic colleagues who are also great friends. I would particularly like to thank Satomi Arizono, John Barnden, Marianna Bolognesi, Meera Burgess, Lynne Cameron, Gareth Carrol, Vanliza Chow, Matthew Collins, Alice Deignan, Sarah Duffy, Samantha Ford, Danielle Fuller, Matteo Fuoli, David Houghton, Susan Hunston, Nina Julich, Tina Krennmayr, Karolina Kuberska, Rico Kwong, Danny Leung, Fiona MacArthur, Sheelagh McGuiness, Kate Rumbold, Rawan Saaty, Elena Semino, Paula Pérez-Sobrino, Penny Tuck, Kirsty Wilson and Bodo Winter for being such excellent research collaborators. Special thanks go to Sarah Turner, who has been a fantastic research fellow, research associate and friend these last three years. We have had many inspiring conversations, bounced all sorts of ideas off one another, and had some great moments analysing our data. I would also like to thank Michael Whitby, Andrzej Gasiorek and Suganthi John for providing a huge amount of institutional support and advice on how to balance my work with the rest of my life. In a similar vein, I am as ever indebted to Susan Hunston for her continued guidance and support in all matters, academic, personal and professional. I am grateful to all staff in the Department of English Language and Linguistics at the University of Birmingham for providing such a rich and stimulating environment in which to work – many of those 'kitchen conversations' have played a huge role in shaping my ideas. Much of the work in this book could not have been conducted without the valuable input from my colleagues from outside academia who work in teaching, marketing, communications and pregnancy loss support. These include Chris Arning at Creative Semiotics, Ruth Bender-Atik at the Miscarriage Association, Caroline Browne at the Human Tissue Authority, Dmytro Byelmac at Verilogie, Hannah Davies and Anthony Tattum at 'Big Cat' Marketing, Design and PR Agency, Jane Fisher at Antenatal Results and Choices, Helen Hackett at Parkfield Community School, Ross Jones at the Stillbirth and Neonatal Death Charity, and members of the UK Synaesthesia Association. I have also benefitted hugely from working with my students, particularly Mai Salem Alsubhi, Brian Birdsell, Phil Brown, Samantha Ford, Isabella Fritz, Amanda Hilliard, Fraser Heritage, Tara McIlroy, Kris Ramonda, Rawan Saaty, Joe Tomei and Greg Woodin, who have been a constant source of inspiration. I would like to thank the British Council, the European Union and the UK Economic and Social Research Council for funding much of the research that is reported in this book. As ever, I am grateful to Andrew Winnard at Cambridge University Press for his support and encouragement. Finally, and most importantly, I am forever grateful to Dan, Joe and Oscar for all their love and support, and to whom this book is dedicated.

1 'I Am Trying to Climb Everest in Flip-Flops.'
What Is Embodied Metaphor and Where Does It Come From?

1.1 Introduction

Metaphor is a device through which we perceive or experience one entity in terms of another, but what is 'embodied metaphor' and where does it come from? In order to begin to answer this question, I would like to consider the following extract from a blog written by a woman who had recently experienced the loss of her baby, at birth:

This process of *moving through* his death, and the life we had already *built* around his too-short existence, is our own to deal with; I know this. But like all of us, *I look for insight; some key that will unlock the endless hallway of doors now closed in front of me.*

The problem is, *I don't actually look at grief as a series of doors to unlock over time.* Rather, *it feels much more like I'm standing behind a wall.*

It's a wall without a door and without a key. There are no keys in the online forums, the medical and mental health websites, from the grief counsellors, in the support groups, or from the wisdom of family or friends. No one tells you what to do *when you lose yourself.*

What I hold onto, I guess ... is the hope that I'll *wake up* and *the wall will have finally crumbled.* https://whatsyourgrief.com/loss-of-identity-after-stillbirth/

As we can see in the italicised parts of this extract, the writer makes substantial use of metaphor to describe her experience. She talks about '*moving through* his death', her need to '*unlock* the endless hallway of doors', the fact that she '*feels*' like she is '*standing* behind a wall', her hope that she will one day '*wake up*' from this nightmare. What is striking about all of these metaphors is the fact that they involve bodily actions and senses. It is as if she is not only describing her grief through these metaphors, but that she is actually, on one level, 'experiencing' it through these metaphors.

Metaphors that draw on physical experiences can be found in all languages. They are not uncommon, and many are highly conventional. For example, in English, 'understanding' is often talked about in terms of 'seeing' ('I can *see* why Jim is confused'[1]), 'time' is often talked about in terms of 'space' (e.g. 'He had *come a long way* since his early days as a security guard'), achieving professional advancement is often talked about in terms of upward movement (e.g. 'He *rose* through the ranks to become head inspector'). Many metaphors make reference to the senses, allowing people to say, for example, that an experience 'leaves a *bad taste* in their mouths', that '*sharp* words were exchanged' or that one can '*smell* out bad practice'.

It is now widely accepted that metaphors such as these shape our understanding of the world. They are part of our conceptual system, and without them, we would find it virtually impossible to reason and communicate about abstract concepts. For example, we think about affection as warmth, importance as size, intimacy as closeness, difficulties as burdens, categories as containers, similarity as closeness, organisation as physical structure, time as motion, purposes as destinations, causes as physical forces, knowledge as sight and understanding as grasping (Lakoff and Johnson, 1999). In each of these cases, an abstract concept is understood in more concrete, physical terms via metaphor.

There is now a substantial body of research showing that metaphors such as these are not just part of our language but that at times they are actually 'experienced' albeit at a subconscious level. In other words, when we encounter them, subconscious sensorimotor responses are triggered that are similar to those that would be triggered if we actually observed or experienced these actions and senses in the physical world (Gibbs, 2006a). These metaphors therefore have the potential to be experienced on a physical level, rather than being purely an external, objective phenomenon. Gibbs (2006b) refines this argument by suggesting that part of our ability to make sense of metaphors such as these 'resides in the automatic construction of a simulation whereby we imagine performing the bodily actions referred to in these excerpts' (ibid., 435). He goes on to argue that key areas of the brain, such as the motor cortex, are involved in the processing of metaphors such as these but 'as importantly, people's intuitive, felt, phenomenological experiences of their own bodies shape large portions of metaphoric thought and language use' (ibid., 436). For this reason, metaphors such as these are often described as 'embodied', though the degree of embodiment can range from full-on sensorimotor activation through to the use of bodily knowledge in shaping our metaphorical thought processes. The fact that metaphors can be experienced in this way is not a trivial observation for, as we have just seen, physical human experiences form the basis of a very large number of metaphors, and most, if not all, abstract phenomena are understood through metaphors, many of which are based on bodily experiences.

The majority of humans inhabit roughly the same types of bodies and use them to do roughly the same sorts of things, so there is a great deal of universality in the ways in which we experience metaphor. For this reason, as we will see in Chapter 2, much of the literature on embodied metaphor has focused on the homogeneous nature of human experience and has de-emphasised possible sources of variation. It has been argued that many of the aforementioned metaphorical relationships are universal because they are based on correlations between bodily experiences such as that between affection and warmth or visual perception and understanding, and these are experienced by all humankind (Grady, 1997a, b). There has been a substantial amount of work on cross-cultural variation (e.g. Kövecses, 2015; Musolff, 2017) but the impact of other sources of variation, such as gender, personality, body shape and disability has received very little attention. Notions of universality are prevalent in the world of embodied metaphor.

The aim of this book is to challenge these notions of universality by identifying and exploring sources of variation in human experience that affect the ways in which people make sense of the world through embodied metaphor. I take the position that because people's experiences with the physical world differ in important ways, in physical, emotional and social terms, our experiences of embodied metaphor are also susceptible to variation. By understanding these sources of variation, we will gain deeper insights into the different types of world views that people develop, why they develop them and the mechanisms through which they develop them. We can also use this knowledge to further our understanding of embodied metaphor, or, in other words, what it means to 'experience' the world through metaphor.

1.2   Embodied Cognition

The idea that metaphor is embodied rests on the more fundamental premise that much of cognition itself is embodied. According to the embodied cognition hypothesis (Rosch et al., 1991), the ways in which we interact through our bodies with the world and with people around us serve as a basis for the way in which we form ideas and communicate these ideas to others. In other words, our perceptual, motor and other experiences play a fundamental role in how we talk about, think about and interact with people, objects and the world in general. In Gibbs' words: 'people's subjective, felt experience of their bodies in action provides part of the fundamental grounding for language and thought' (Gibbs, 2006a: 2). Stimuli are thus not just seen or heard, but 'experienced' in the body, leading to the activation of parts of the brain that are involved in movement, processing of sensory stimuli and emotion. So, for example, when we watch a footballer score a deciding goal in the final minute of a football match and then express his jubilance by sliding through the mud on his knees, we mentally simulate both his actions and his state of mind as if they were actually happening (Gallese, 2006) and this is the reason why we empathise with and enjoy the experience.

The embodied cognition hypothesis is inspired, at least in part, by Barsalou's (1999) perceptual systems theory, according to which the simple perception of a stimulus leads to the simulation of actual perceptual, motor and emotional responses that one would experience if one were to interact with the stimulus directly (Barsalou, 2008, 2010). For example, if we see someone drinking a cup of tea, or even hear someone talking about drinking tea, this is interpreted by the brain via a partial recreation of what it would be like for us to actually drink a cup of tea ourselves. Even the sight of a teapot can trigger the firing of neurons that are actually involved in pouring and drinking a cup of tea. Crucially for this book, the embodied cognition hypothesis has important implications for our understanding of how *language* is understood and processed. Like other higher mental functions, proponents of the embodied cognition hypothesis see language as being fundamentally linked to more basic cognitive and neurobiological mechanisms (Feldman and Narayanan, 2004). Reading and hearing about actions, sensations and emotions leads us to recreate those same actions, sensations and emotions in our minds and bodies.

Evidence for the embodied cognition hypothesis and for perceptual simulation comes from large amount of empirical work on the way we understand actions, which is beginning to show that the mechanisms used in interpreting others' actions share a common representational space with mechanisms used during real action execution (Avanzini et al., 2012; Avenanti et al., 2013; Rizzolatti et al., 1996). These studies have employed a variety of research methods, including reaction time studies, neurological studies, eye tracking studies, gesture studies, questionnaires, discourse analysis and interviews. Many of these studies focus on the link between bodily action and cognition. It has been shown, for example, that parts of the frontal cortex normally associated with language processing are activated during sensorimotor action and when actions are being observed (Bonda et al., 1994). Performance on linguistic tasks has been shown to improve when participants are invited to perform corresponding physical actions (Rieser et al., 1994), words with high 'body-object interaction' ratings (such as 'scissors' and 'spoon') are recognised faster than those without (such as 'tree' and 'house') (Saikaluk et al., 2008), and the verbalisation of memories has been found to be facilitated when people assume the same body posture during recall that they had assumed when the memories were first formed (Dijkstra et al., 2007). There is increasing evidence from behavioural psychology to suggest that areas of the brain that were formerly thought to be purely sensorimotoric play important roles in language processing, and that language processing makes significant use of spatial, perceptual and visual imagery (Coslett, 1998; Coslett et al., 2002; Hauk and Pulvermüller, 2004; Rizzolatti and Buccino, 2005). On a very basic, non-linguistic level, it has been observed that when we see a person performing a particular action, such as running, gripping a pencil, laughing or crying, the same neural motor circuits that are recruited when we ourselves perform that action are concurrently activated. Simply watching the performance of an action thus triggers corresponding motoric mental imagery. The neurons thought to be responsible for this have been referred to as 'mirror neurons' (Gallese and Goldman, 1998). Mirror neurons are thought to be partly responsible for our ability to imitate, communicate with and empathise with others (McGlone, Howard and Roberts, 2002; Stamenov, 2002).

Further support for the embodied cognition hypothesis can be found in studies showing that in word and sentence comprehension tasks, people conceptualise perceptual and motor details that go well beyond the propositions that are explicitly presented (Kok and Cienki, 2014). For example, Stanfield and Zwaan (2001) found that when participants read the sentence 'the man hammered the nail into the wall', they were quicker to recognise a picture of a nail in a horizontal orientation than a vertical one as this was compatible with the orientation of the nail in the sentence they had read. Conversely, when they read the sentence 'the man hammered the nail into the floor', they were quicker to recognise a picture of a nail in a vertical orientation. Zwaan et al. (2002) found that when people had heard the sentence 'the ranger saw the eagle in the sky' they were quicker to recognise a picture of an eagle with its wings spread, whereas when people had read the sentence 'the ranger saw the eagle in its nest', they were quicker to recognise a picture of an eagle with its wings folded. Finally, Glenberg and Kashak (2002) found that when people had been asked to read a sentence such as 'you handed Courtney the notebook', they were quicker to make a movement away from their bodies than towards them, which is consistent with the situationally appropriate movement. This evidence suggests that people construct holistic mental simulations in which they 'immerse' themselves into the scene (Zwaan, 2003).

Another set of studies that is often cited as evidence for embodied cognition are those that have shown that people use gesture to help them think. Extensive evidence exists to support the contention that gestures 'activate, manipulate, package and explore spatio-motoric information for thinking and speaking' (Kita et al., 2017: 245) and that this includes thinking and speaking with metaphor (ibid.). Kita et al. refer to this as the 'Gesture-for-Conceptualization Hypothesis'. There is substantial evidence to support this hypothesis. For example, it has been demonstrated that when people are encouraged to use gesture, they are significantly better at solving spatial problems (Chu and Kita, 2011), remembering lists of verbs (Macedonia, 2014; Macedonia and Klimesch, 2014) and performing complex statistical tasks (Rueckert et al., 2017). Finally, there is evidence to suggest that mirror neurons are involved in gesture perception, which means that mental simulation is likely to be involved in the interpretation of gestural meaning (Skipper et al., 2007). The neural networks that are involved in understanding gesture have been shown to be sensitive to contextual factors such as the cultural background of the speaker (Molnar-Szakacs et al., 2007) and the communicative relevance of the gesture (Skipper et al., 2007). Related to this, the 'action-sentence compatibility effect' (Glenberg and Kaschak, 2002) provides evidence for the idea that language and bodily movements are related. For example, Bergen and Wheeler (2010) showed that progressive sentences about hand motion facilitated manual action in the same direction, while perfect sentences that were identical in every way except their aspect did not facilitate such action. The progressive aspect thus appears to focus attention on the nature and direction of the movement. The idea that gestures can provide insights into the embodied nature of thought is encapsulated well in Mittelberg's (2013) notion of the 'exbodied' mind.

The idea that gestures emerge from perceptual and motor simulations that underlie embodied language is particularly well developed in Hostetter and Alibali's (2008) *Gestures as Simulated Action Framework*. This is a theory of language production that attempts to account for the central role that is often played by gesture. Hostetter and Alibali argue that when people are planning to talk about an action, they simulate the action in the premotor cortex, the cerebellum and other subcortical areas, and that this simulated action activation has the potential to spread to other motor areas. When this spreading activation happens, a gesture results. Several factors are thought to affect the extent to which the activation will spread and whether the simulation will thus be realised through an overt gesture. A first factor is the extent to which the simulation involves action. Motor imagery, by definition, involves simulated action as it involves picturing the body in motion, but simulated action may also be evoked by mental imagery if one is talking about how a scene changes over time, viewing it from different perspectives, or evoking its affordances. A second factor is character viewpoint or perspective. The extent to which a speaker simulates actions using motor imagery or animated visual imagery is likely to vary according to whether the speaker is describing his or her own actions. Hostetter and Alibali (2010) found that participants gestured at a higher rate when they were describing a pattern that they had actually made than when describing a pattern they had only viewed. A third factor is individual differences. Individual differences have been observed in people's propensity to gesture: speakers who typically rely on simulations of perception and action are particularly likely to use gesture when speaking. Hostetter and Alibali argue that these individual differences may depend on the strength of the neural connections between the premotor and motor areas, and that the strength of these connections can result from genetic factors, experience or individual differences in the functioning of the nervous system. In support of this claim they cite their finding that speakers with stronger spatial skills tend to gesture more than speakers with weaker spatial skills (Hostetter and Alibali, 2007). A fourth factor is the communicative setting. Studies have shown that teachers increase their use of gesture when teaching particularly difficult concepts or when they believe that their interlocutor may have difficulty understanding them (Alibali and Nathan, 2007). Finally, the nature of the material being discussed and the speaker's attitude towards that material are also likely to affect the use of gesture. McNeill (2005) has shown that speakers are particularly likely to gesture when expressing contrast or when conveying information that is more newsworthy or crucial to the ongoing conversation in general, a feature that he labels *communicative dynamism*. To sum up, the fact that meaningful gestures often accompany speech and that gesture use varies according to different communicative contexts provides compelling support for the idea that cognition is often embodied.

Indirect evidence for the embodied nature of thought can also be found in everyday language. For example, canonical word orderings in English reflect the ways in which we interact with the world through our bodies. As we have eyes in our head, not our feet, look forward rather than backward and stand upright, elements of language that are in front, above and vertical tend to be foregrounded and are mentioned first. For these reasons, it is more conventional to talk about things being 'high and low', 'above and below' and 'front and back' rather than 'low and high', 'below and above' and 'back and front' (Benor and Levy, 2006). Thus words to do with being upwards and forwards are more likely to precede their counterparts in canonical expressions. Using the Web IT 5-gram corpus as his data source, Louwerse (2008) calculated the raw and relative frequencies of iconic and non-iconic word orderings of seventy-one word pairs that have been widely studied in the literature, and found that they were significantly more likely to occur in their canonical (more 'embodied') order than in their non-canonical (less 'embodied') order.

Support for the embodied cognition hypothesis can also be found in the results of eye tracking studies. Huette et al. (2014) had participants look at a blank screen while listening to stories that contained either past progressive sentences or simple past sentences. They found that participants who heard past progressive sentences moved their eyes around the screen significantly more than participants who heard simple past sentences, who fixated on a single spot. This finding is in line with the fact that the past progressive focuses attention on the unfolding aspects of an event, whilst the simple past focuses attention on its end point. Their findings thus provide support for the idea that grammatical aspect alters the way in which events are construed. Huette et al. conclude that 'there is nothing passive about passive listening' and that 'the eyes are actively moving in a way that reflects subtle grammatical differences in the linguistic input' (ibid., 7). Similarly, other studies have found that the speed with which people move their eyes towards a particular target varies according to the amount of speed that is encoded in the verb that they hear. For example, people have been found to move their eyes more quickly towards a target after having heard sentences such as 'the lion dashed toward the balloon' than after having heard sentences such as 'the lion ambled toward the balloon' (Lindsay et al., 2013; Speed and Vigliocco, 2014).

An important feature of the embodied cognition hypothesis is that it emphasises the role played by emotion in cognitive processing. Emotional involvement has been shown to be an integral, indispensable part of much so-called logical or abstract reasoning. It facilitates cognition, supports understanding and enhances long term memory (Storbeck and Clore, 2008). Evidence for this comes from a number of empirical studies. The comprehension of sentences describing emotional situations (Havas et al., 2007) has been found to be affected by the listener's bodily state, and it has been shown that when people engage emotionally with a piece of information, they are more likely to understand it and remember it (Webb, Miles and Sheeran, 2012). In one's first language, words with high emotional content are better retained than more neutral ones (Kensinger and Corkin, 2003). Based on his study of patients who had both decision-making defects and emotional disorders, Damasio (2006) advanced what he refers to as the 'somatic marker hypothesis'. 'Somatic markers' are physical responses that are associated with emotions, such as the association of rapid heartbeat with anxiety or of nausea with disgust. He found that in some of his patients, flawed reasoning, emotional impairment and a reduction in the activation of somatic markers stood out together as consequences of a specific brain lesion. He concludes from this that emotion plays a key role, albeit a subconscious one, in what he refers to as 'the loop of reason' (ibid., xvii), arguing that increased levels of emotion increase the saliency of a premise and in so doing, bias decision-making in favour of that premise. He also argues that heightened emotional engagement helps us to hold in mind multiple facts that must be borne in mind during a decision-making process (xviii). For Damasio, emotion also plays a key role in intuition, which he describes as the speedy cognitive process through which we reach a conclusion without being aware of all the logical steps. To use his words, intuition is 'rapid cognition with the required knowledge partially swept under the carpet' (ibid., xix). A full account of embodied cognition must therefore include consideration of the way in which we interact emotionally with our surroundings as well as physically. Although embodied cognition cannot account for all aspects of cognitive processing (Goldinger et al., 2016), it does explain a number of features of human cognitive and communicative behaviour, which, as we will see later, include the ways in which we understand and use metaphor.

Embodied cognition is not always a conscious process. Lakoff and Johnson (1999) propose three levels at which embodied cognition operates: *neural embodiment* involves the neurological architecture that underpins embodied thinking; the *cognitive unconscious* concerns the rapid underlying mental operations that we use automatically, without being aware of them; and the *phenomenological level* concerns our awareness of our bodies, mental states, our environment and our physical and social interactions. Gibbs (2005) makes the important point that in order to acquire a full understanding of the nature of embodied cognition, we need to focus on all three levels of embodiment, and most importantly, the interactions between them.

In response to the growing number of theories that have been proposed pertaining to embodied cognition, Meteyard et al. (2012) conducted an extensive review of the literature and concluded that there is no empirical support for either strongly embodied theories of cognition or for completely disembodied theories of cognition. They suggest that the remaining theories of embodied cognition are best viewed as sitting along a continuum. This goes from 'secondary embodiment', where semantic content is independent but associated with sensorimotor systems, through 'weak embodiment', where semantic content has partial dependence on the sensorimotor system, to 'strong embodiment', which asserts that there is complete dependence on the sensorimotor system. One of the aims of this book is to explore the ways in which people's experiences of embodied metaphor position themselves along this continuum and then identify factors that contribute to this positioning.

Embodied Cognition and the '4E' Approach

Human cognition is not confined to the individual. Rather, it is shaped by one's physical and social environment as well as one's personal and social history. It is thus environmentally, socially and temporally 'distributed' (e.g., Jensen, 2013; Semin and Cacioppo, 2009). The notion of distributed embodied cognition emphasises the fact that we operate in a world populated by other people and things, and that this world changes over time.

The '4E' approach to cognition emphasises the fact that as well as being *embodied*, cognition is also *extended*, *enactive* and *embedded*. The term 'extended' emphasises the relationship between internal embodied cognition and the physical and social environment. It takes as its starting point the fact that we understand things in terms of what they mean to us and how we can best make use of them or interact with them (Glenberg, 1999; Glenberg and Kaschak, 2002) and what it is that they afford us (Gibson, 1977). The term 'enactive' emphasises the active nature of thinking and foregrounds the role played by gesture and other types of bodily movement in the thinking and communication. The term 'embedded' emphasises the fact that all cognition takes place in a context and that contextual features very much shape the way we think. There is considerable overlap between the 4Es but taken together, they emphasise the fact that both language and cognition are:

materially embodied, culturally/ecologically embedded, naturalistically grounded, affect-based, dialogically coordinated, and socially enacted. (Thibault, 2011: 211)

As we will see later in the chapter, the 4E approach also allows us to see metaphor as a more dynamic phenomenon than traditional embodied approaches. This is the position that I adopt in this book.

1.3   Embodied Metaphor

In recent years, discussions of embodied cognition have been extended to metaphor, in particular to those metaphors that relate abstract content to more concrete referents, such as, for example, AFFECTION IS WARMTH, DIFFICULTY IS WEIGHT or IMPORTANCE IS SIZE.[2] Metaphors such as these are often referred to as 'primary metaphors' (Grady, 1997a). Primary metaphors are metaphorical correspondences or 'mappings', for which there is thought to be an experiential basis as they are derived from real-world experiences, so the three metaphors that I have just mentioned can be accounted for by the facts that: when we think about someone we are close to it can make us feel warm inside; heavy objects are harder to carry; and important things and people tend to be bigger than us, at least when we are children. Primary metaphors are thought to develop in early childhood as a result of correlations between different yet related experiences, and are therefore sometimes referred to as 'correlational' metaphors. For example, as infants, when we experience affection from our parents, it usually takes the form of closeness and warmth, and as adults, we continue to describe affection metaphorically, describing our relationships as 'close' and 'warm', leading to the AFFECTION IS WARMTH metaphor that has just been mentioned. Another primary metaphor is the TIME AS MOTION ALONG A PATH metaphor (Ibid., 294). When we walk along a path, the section of the path where we have already walked is behind us and the section of the path where we have yet to walk is in front of us. We thus perceive of the past as being metaphorically 'behind' us and the future as being metaphorically in front of us. We can see from these examples that there is no clear-cut distinction between 'the body' and 'the mind' and that physical actions influence abstract thought. It is thus argued that abstract concepts originate in our experiences of our bodies as they interact with the physical world, and these experiences constitute our primary, most basic source of understanding (Bergen, 2012).

Relationships that we perceive in our environment are internalised, and this is thought to lead to the formation of 'cross-domain mappings' (Lakoff and Johnson, 1980). These mappings are formed between 'source domains' and 'target domains'. Source domains are concrete concepts that we experience through sensorimotor interactions with the world. In the aforementioned examples, these would be WARMTH, WEIGHT and SIZE. Abstract domains are the less-concrete concepts that are being considered or discussed. In the aforementioned examples, these would be AFFECTION, DIFFICULTY and IMPORTANCE. The theory of neural metaphor (Lakoff, 2008, 2012) goes one step further than this and suggests that primary metaphors emerge from repeated co-occurring activations of the two brain regions involved (i.e. those that correspond respectively to the source and target of the metaphor), and that this results in the development of physical neural connections between the two regions. As we will see in Chapter 2, there is a significant body of empirical evidence in support of the view that primary metaphors are embodied in that they evoke motoric and/or sensory responses in the body, and behavioural studies have revealed strong relationships between people's posture, body movement, the environment and their use of metaphor.

In language, we often find that primary metaphors combine to make more complex 'conceptual metaphors', which in turn underlie many, but not all, 'linguistic metaphors'. In order to illustrate this hierarchical relationship, consider this quotation from Piper Chapman, the main protagonist in the American television series 'Orange is the New Black'. She is a middle-class woman who has been sent to a very rough prison, and unsurprisingly, she is having a terrible time, which she describes to her mother in the following way:

I am not going crazy. I am surrounded by crazy, and *I am trying to climb Everest in flip-flops*.

By using the metaphor 'trying to climb Everest in flip-flops' she manages to convey to her mother just how difficult a time she is having by describing her experience in terms of a physical action. 'Trying to climb Everest in flip-flops' is a linguistic metaphor. Underlying this metaphor is a conceptual metaphor DEALING WITH DIFFICULT PROBLEMS IS CLIMBING A MOUNTAIN. Underlying this conceptual metaphor there are at least three primary metaphors, all of which relate to fundamental physical experiences: CHANGE IS MOTION, ACHIEVING A PURPOSE IS ARRIVING AT A DESTINATION and THE EXPERIENCE OF TIME IS MOTION ALONG A PATH.

Not all linguistic metaphors, however, have clear associations with primary metaphors, or even conceptual metaphors. Some are based purely on perceptual resemblance. For example, when Philip Larkin asks, in his poem 'Toads', 'why should I let the toad work squat on my life?', he is making use of a comparison with a toad to say that he finds work unpleasant and difficult to get rid of. Similarly, the complex road network just outside Birmingham which is known as Spaghetti Junction is called so simply because, from above, it has the tangled, intertwined appearance of spaghetti. It is difficult to see any clear use of primary metaphor in either of these examples.

Primary metaphors are, however, not the only metaphors that involve embodiment. People sometimes accompany resemblance metaphors with gestures that suggest that these metaphors are being experienced on a physical level as well as on a linguistic level. We can see an example of this in this extract, from Deignan, Littlemore and Semino (2013: 144–145), in which a

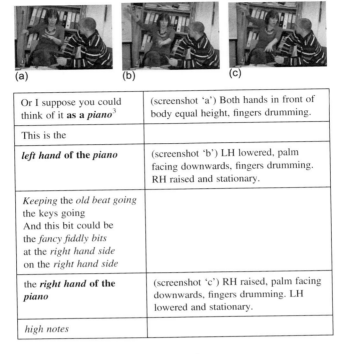

Or I suppose you could think of it **as a _piano_**[3]	(screenshot 'a') Both hands in front of body equal height, fingers drumming.
This is the	
**left hand** **of the** _**piano**_	(screenshot 'b') LH lowered, palm facing downwards, fingers drumming. RH raised and stationary.
Keeping the _old beat going_ the keys going And this bit could be the _fancy fiddly bits_ at the _right hand side_ on the _right hand side_	
the _**right hand**_ **of the** _**piano**_	(screenshot 'c') RH raised, palm facing downwards, fingers drumming. LH lowered and stationary.
high notes	

Figure 1.1 'High notes and low notes'

specialist in business management is explaining to a novice how various organisational management models work. In this extract, she is comparing the complexities of running an organisation to playing a piano (Figure 1.1).

Here, the speaker is using a piano-playing metaphor to convey the idea that different, complementary skill sets are needed in a large organisation, and that they work together like the left and right-hand parts of a piece of piano music. Although this is not a primary metaphor, it does involve reference to bodily action and this is expressed both in language and gesture. The speaker's use of gesture suggests a degree of bodily activation and brings the metaphor to life. As we saw previously, it has been demonstrated that the sight of someone engaging in action triggers motoric responses that resemble those that would be triggered if we were to engage in the action ourselves. This means that her interlocutor may well have experienced a perceptual simulation of playing the piano, which he could have used to help him understand what she is talking about. Müller (2008a), whose work I discuss in detail later, would describe this example as a case of 'activated metaphoricity'.

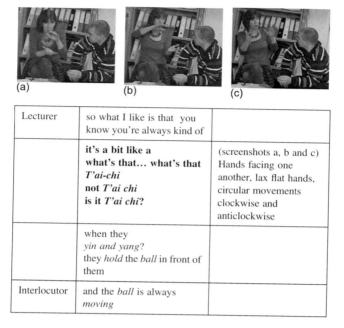

Lecturer	so what I like is that you know you're always kind of	
	it's a bit like a what's that... what's that *T'ai-chi* **not** *T'ai chi* **is it** *T'ai chi?*	(screenshots a, b and c) Hands facing one another, lax flat hands, circular movements clockwise and anticlockwise
	when they *yin and yang?* they *hold* the *ball* in front of them	
Interlocutor	and the *ball* is always *moving*	

Figure 1.2 'T'ai chi'

Thus, although discussions of embodied metaphor tend to be limited to primary metaphors, we can see from this example that some resemblance metaphors may also be embodied in a broader sense. For this reason, the definition of 'embodied metaphor' adopted in this book is somewhat broader than the definition that has been employed by other authors in that it includes physical enactments of action-based resemblance metaphors. Another interesting feature of this 'piano' example is that the resemblance metaphor is interwoven with a primary metaphor, through which musical pitch is described in terms of height. This metaphor is expressed through the positioning of the speaker's hands; she raises her right hand up into the air when she talks about the 'high' notes and lowers her left hand when she talks about the 'low' notes. This gesture is metaphorical, and it does not reflect what one does with one's hands when playing the piano. This example can thus be said to contain two kinds of embodied metaphor: one is an enacted resemblance metaphor and the other is a gestural representation of a primary metaphor.

A similar example, from the same exchange, can be seen when the same speaker refers to 'T'ai Chi', in an attempt to explain the need for balance within an organisation (Figure 1.2).

As Deignan, Littlemore and Semino point out, there is a marked build up to this metaphor ('it's a bit like a what's that... what's that'), which indicates either that the speaker is trying hard to think of a useful way of presenting this concept, or that she is trying to signal her use of a figurative description to the interlocutor so that he will understand it. The gesture that the lecturer uses here conveys the idea that she is holding and manipulating a large imaginary ball in front of her, as one might do in a T'ai chi class. Interestingly, the gesture begins to appear before the words, indicating that it may be helping her to scaffold her thinking processes, and perhaps those of her interlocutor. There also appears to be a mixed metaphor in this example. The lecturer refers to both T'ai chi and yin and yang to convey the idea of intuitive balance that she believes to be necessary in business. These metaphors have different, yet strongly related, source domains, which contribute the meaning of the exchange. The fact that she is holding the ball in her gestures indicates that the T'ai chi metaphor is to some extent embodied.

These two examples call into question the clear-cut distinction between primary metaphor and resemblance metaphor. Ureña and Faber (2010) also reject this distinction. They argue that both primary metaphors and resemblance metaphors involve imagery that can be visual, kinaesthetic, somaesthetic or haptic, that both can have a metonymic basis (see later), that both can involve fictive motion and that both can be productively extended. The only difference between the two types of metaphor is that, unlike primary metaphors, resemblance metaphors do not arise from cases of literal co-occurrence. So, although we may experience affection as warmth in a literal way, we would never actually experience running an organisation as playing the piano or attending a T'ai chi class. However, both types of metaphor have the potential to be embodied in that they can be experienced and enacted rather than simply encountered.

Finally, I would like to mention Kövecses' (2015, 2019) hierarchy of metaphorical schematicity, which has been shown to be useful in the analysis of metaphor. Kövecses argues that metaphors operate within a four-level hierarchy, with each level incorporating an additional degree of specificity, thus becoming less schematic. At the most fundamental, schematic and 'stripped-back' level we have the 'image schema' (in which, for example, 'intensity' might be metaphorically conceptualised as 'heat'). The next, more specific, level is the 'domain' (in which, for example, 'emotion' might be metaphorically conceptualised as 'temperature'), then, as more specificity is added, we move to the level of the 'frame' or 'Idealised Cognitive Model' (in which 'love' might be metaphorically conceptualised as 'fire'), and we finally move to the most specifically enriched level of the 'mental space' (in which, for example, 'fluctuation in love' might be metaphorically conceptualised as 'fluctuation in the experience of heat'). To this hierarchy, we should also add the notion of the 'scenario' (Musolff, 2004, 2017). Scenarios emerge in discourse and can involve more than one metaphor. Scenarios often contain a strong narrative element and frequently perform one or more evaluative functions. In this book I move between all of these levels as the focus is on the different roles that are played by our bodies and our knowledge of our bodies in all kinds of metaphoric formulations, regardless of the level at which they occur. I argue that at each of these levels, the metaphor has the potential to be experienced in a physical way, though it will not always be experienced in such a way or indeed even noticed as a metaphor. The extent to which a metaphor is experienced as embodied will likely fluctuate over time and across individuals and contexts. That is to say, the metaphor can be 'experienced', 'conceptualised' or merely 'expressed linguistically', depending on the context in which it occurs and the characteristics of the person who is using or interacting with it.[4]

Embodied Metaphor and the '4E' Approach

We saw previously that under the '4E' approach to cognition, cognition is at once embodied, embedded, enacted and extended. In other words, cognition is neither 'skull-bound' (Di Paulo, 2009) nor individual. In recent years, there has been increased appreciation of the fact that this also applies to metaphor. Extending this approach to metaphor highlights the fact that metaphor can be something that we 'do' and not something that simply 'exists'. Recent metaphor research has seen much more of an emphasis on the roles of dynamism and interaction. It has been shown that metaphor can be identified empirically in whole-body behaviour. It not only appears in speaking and writing but also in gesture, gaze, movement, posture and dance. This dynamic perspective views embodied metaphor as a dynamic system, in which our sensorimotor experiences are associated in complex, nonlinear ways with cultural models and with the broader and more specific contexts in which people find themselves (see El Refaie, 2014). This means that we need to move beyond the idea of static source-target domain mappings if we are to gain a fuller understanding of the ways in which metaphor is embodied in real-life settings.

In a similar vein, Kok and Cienki (2014) point out that any theory of embodied cognition, and by extension, of embodied metaphor, must take account of the role played by the social, contextual, distributed and pragmatic aspects of communication. By doing so, it will acknowledge the role played by a person's ability to predict, anticipate and recognise the communicative intentions of their interlocutor; identify common ground and relevance; and integrate multimodal cues in real time. It also means that the metaphor analyst must be very aware of the role played by genre and register, as well as the affordances offered by mental simulation in context.

One of the key proponents of this more dynamic, interactive, multimodal view of embodied metaphor is Müller (2008). She argues that conceptual metaphor theory tends to underplay the experiential side of metaphor and focuses too much on conceptualisation. In her view, metaphoric meaning-making involves seeing and *experiencing* one domain in terms of another. For Müller, metaphors are principally a matter of use; they exist in the moment when someone is experiencing one domain in terms of another. They can therefore be both 'dead' and 'alive' at the same time. Their vitality depends on their context of use. Following this line of argument, metaphor is most appropriately considered an intersubjective process; the response of the inter-locutor can help determine the salience of the metaphors produced and the metaphors may become stronger if they don't get a response. The salience of the embodied experience of metaphor can therefore vary over the course of a single communicative event.

Müller (2008) goes on to argue that speakers can have different levels of awareness of the 'metaphoricity' of what they are saying. She describes this awareness as 'activated metaphoricity', and outlines three factors that affect the extent to which metaphoricity can be activated. The first relates to the degree of conventionality of a conceptual metaphor in a given culture ranging from fully conventional to fully novel. The second is the degree of convention-ality of a metaphoric expression in a given culture, also ranging from fully conventional to fully novel. The third is the degree to which attention is drawn to a particular metaphoric expression in use, making it cognitively more or less salient. One's awareness of metaphor can thus vary along all three clines at once, and it will not always be the same for all speakers and listeners. I return to Müller's work in Chapter 2, where I discuss evidence that can be found for embodied metaphor in the field of gesture studies.

1.4   Where Do Embodied Primary Metaphors Come From?

There is no real consensus on the origin of embodied primary metaphors. A number of theories have been proposed, with differing amounts of explana-tory power for different embodied metaphors in different settings. The original hypothesis, proposed by those who first worked on embodied metaphor, is that they result from one's interactions with the environment. A commonly used example in support of this theory is the AFFECTION IS WARMTH metaphor (Grady, 1997: 299). As infants, when we experience affection from our parents, it usually takes the form of physical closeness and warmth, and, as adults, we continue to describe affection metaphorically, describing our rela-tionships as 'close' and 'warm'. Thus, it is argued that the use of these expressions has a physical origin, and is not arbitrary. It has been suggested that for infants these are one and the same, but that as we grow older, we extrapolate via metonymy to more general settings where the source domain (warmth) may not actually be being activated. We use warmth to metonymically stand for the sorts of human relationships that may cause us to experience warmth or that have caused us to experience warmth in the past. A convincing theoretical account of the metonymic basis of embodied metaphor can be found in Radden (2002). His fully embodied account works well to explain the origin of a great many mental metaphors but it cannot fully explain the different ways in which they are extended, elaborated and employed in everyday communication by people from different cultures. To understand this, we need to consider the impact of language and culture.

According to more usage-based accounts of embodied primary metaphor, some of the correspondences reflect the internalisation of statistical regularities in the linguistic environment. At a very basic level, children are exposed to repeated correspondences between literal and metaphorical meanings and as such may have no basis for distinguishing between literal and metaphorical senses of the same word. For example, exposure to the word 'see' can refer both to physical manifestations (e.g. 'let's see what's in this box') and to metaphorical ones (e.g. 'let's see what Mummy thinks'). This idea is summed up in Grady's (1997) 'conflation hypothesis' (see also Johnson, 1997), according to which literal and metaphorical uses are initially associated by children in scenes that conflate their literal and metaphorical meanings. Johnson cites the following example from the Brown (1973) corpus of child language in the CHILDES archive of child language, in which an adult is responding to a child's request for a toy:

Oh, I see what you wanted (CHILDES)

This sentence can be interpreted literally to refer to the speaker's visual experience or it can be interpreted metaphorically to refer to the speaker's new state of awareness. Under this interpretation, it is an example of the UNDERSTANDING IS SEEING metaphor. However, to understand what is meant here it is not necessary to decide whether the use of 'see' is literal or metaphorical. A child may therefore have an initial understanding of the meaning of 'see' which conflates the literal and metaphorical senses and only later might he or she separate out the two meanings so as to understand one as being literal and the other as being metaphorical.

Under this 'usage-based' account (Tomasello, 2003), as the child is exposed to more and more language, he or she will acquire form-meaning pairings through a natural sensitivity to the distributional features of the language that he or she is learning. There is an increasing amount of evidence to suggest that language is acquired in this intuitive, probabilistic manner and there is no reason to expect that metaphors would not be acquired in the same way. In other words, metaphors are likely to be acquired through a combination of active embodied simulation and usage-based learning. I will return to this idea in Chapter 4 when I discuss the acquisition and development of embodied primary metaphors in more detail.

Finally, increasing attention is being given to the role played by cultural artefacts (e.g. clocks, calendars and writing systems) in the development of metaphorical thinking. Our conceptual systems are shaped by the ways in which we witness and interact with these artefacts (Winter and Matlock, 2017). For example, the left-to-right orientation of western writing helps us process time as moving from left to right. There is now a growing body of literature exploring the role of cultural artefacts in scaffolding primary metaphors (Hutchins, 1995, 2005) and it has been suggested that some primary metaphors are shaped as much by culture and writing systems as by embodiment *per se* (Casasanto, 2014, 2017).

In order to explain how the use of one's body and one's exposure to language and culture work together to develop metaphorical models, Casasanto (2014) proposes a theory, which he labels the 'Hierarchical Mental Models Theory' (HMMT). Casasanto offers this theory in order to account for a paradox that has been observed for primary metaphors: if they originate in bodily interactions with the world and are grounded in universal experience, why are they not universal? He points out that despite the fundamental bodily basis of primary metaphors, there is considerable cross-cultural variation in the way they are manifested. For example, in English, time moves along a horizontal sagittal (front/back) trajectory, with the past behind and the future in front. This is thought to reflect the fact that when we move forward in space we are also moving forward in space. However, despite the embodied status of this metaphor, it is by no means universal. In many languages, including English, time also moves along a transverse axis which can be left-right or right-left, in line with different writing systems (Fuhrman and Boroditsky, 2010). In Chinese, time can have a vertical orientation where the past is above and the future below (Fuhrman et al., 2011).

Casasanto argues that to explain this variation, one needs to accept that primary metaphors are constructed hierarchically. That is to say, they develop in two stages. The first stage involves learning from regularities in our experiences of the physical and social world. So here, for example, we might have the development of the idea that CLOSENESS IS WARMTH, MORE IS UP etc. The second stage involves learning from regularities in linguistic and cultural input. He illustrates his model through reference to his work on primary metaphors involving left-right axis. This axis can be used to refer to valence (left is 'bad' and right is 'good'), time (left is the past and right is the future), and politics (where 'Left' is Socialist and 'Right' is Conservative). He shows how each of these metaphors has a different origin. His extensive work on the relationship between handedness and left-right valence (with right handers preferring the right field and left handers preferring the left field) suggests that this metaphor is strongly embodied. In contrast, the time axis displays considerable variation across cultures, with some cultures employing a sagittal axis, others employing a vertical axis, and others different patterns altogether. These findings suggest that this metaphorical relationship is more likely to be influenced by both embodiment and culture. The association of 'left' and 'right' with different kinds of politics is almost entirely culturally based and is therefore not universal.

One somewhat problematic aspect of Casasanto's proposal is that his use of the word 'stages' suggests some kind of linear order. Infants are exposed to the physical world, the language that is used to talk about it and cultural understandings of that world from birth, so all of these inputs are likely to be having an effect on the way they understand their world, from the day they are born. There is also a huge amount of interaction and overlap between these sources of information, which is perhaps under-emphasised in Casasanto's model. However, HMMT provides a useful explanation of the co-existence of both universality and variation in embodied metaphor. My aim in this book is to conduct an extensive analysis of a wide range of sources of variation in embodied metaphor, going beyond those discussed by Casasanto and colleagues, in order to better understand the phenomenon of embodied metaphor and to gain deeper insights into the different ways in which people experience the world through metaphor.

1.5   Conclusion

In this introductory chapter, we have seen that metaphor is not just something that we encounter; it is also very often experienced or 'lived'. Many of the metaphors that we use are derived from the relationships that we have with our bodies and the ways in which we perceive our bodies and can thus be said to be 'embodied'. The fact that for the most part, we all inhabit similar bodies and use them in similar ways means that there is a high degree of universality in the experience of metaphor. This means that in many respects, humans speak a common language when it comes to the conceptualisation and expression of abstract concepts. However, one issue that has been overlooked to date is the extent to which humans vary in terms of the relationships that they have with their own bodies and the ways in which they perceive them, which means that with the exception of some work on linguistic and cultural variation, there has been relatively little work on the ways in which people's experiences of embodied metaphor vary. I believe that it is important to understand the ways in which humans differ in their experiences of embodied metaphor as these differences can explain the existence of disparate and deeply held viewpoints that are difficult to reconcile. In this book, I will show that variation in the experience of embodied metaphor can be found in a wide range of situations beyond language and culture and that by exploring these differences we can learn more about embodied metaphor and gain deeper insights into why it is that people view the world in such different ways and find it hard to perceive things from another's perspective. My aim is therefore to provide the first wide-ranging account of variation in embodied metaphor, and to discuss the theoretical, practical and social implications of this variation.

2 'Would You Prefer a Pencil or an Antiseptic Wipe?'

What Evidence Is There for Embodied Metaphor and Why Is It Important to Consider This Variation?

2.1 Introduction

The focus of this book is on variation in people's experiences of embodied metaphor, but before turning to this variation, it is necessary to consider the vast amount of evidence that provides support for embodied metaphor. This evidence comes from behavioural studies, neurological studies and naturally occurring data. In this chapter, I discuss the evidence for and against embodied metaphor and then explain why it is important to look at the ways in which people's experiences of embodied metaphor vary. Variation in embodied metaphor will form the basis of the remaining chapters of the book.

In a study that took place back in 2006, Zhong and Liljenquist invited participants into a room. There, they were told that they were taking part in a handwriting study and were asked to copy out a story. For half of the participants, the story described an ethical, selfless deed (helping a co-worker) and for the other half, it involved an unethical act (sabotaging a co-worker). On their way out of the room, the participants were invited to select a small token of thanks for having participated in the study. They were given the choice between a pencil or a packet of antiseptic wipes. Those participants who had copied out the 'immoral' story were significantly more likely than those who had copied out the 'moral' story to choose the antiseptic wipes. Why might this be? Zhong and Liljenquist argue that this study (and other studies like it) provides support for the idea that people experience the metaphorical MORAL-ITY IS CLEANLINESS metaphor in a physical way. In other words, exposure to moral indiscretions (either one's own or those of others) poses a moral threat and stimulates a need for physical cleansing. The use of expressions such as 'a dirty business' (BNC) to refer to an immoral activity thus appear to have a physical underpinning. They describe this as the 'Macbeth' effect; after having murdered King Duncan, Lady Macbeth is unable to wash away her bloodied conscience, despite engaging in excessive handwashing. Whilst trying to remove the imaginary blood stain that represents her guilty conscience, she utters the well-known lines: 'Out damn spot! Out I say!' In the end, it drives her mad.

This is just one of over a hundred studies that have found statistically significant support for the embodied nature of metaphor. In recent years, there has been a wealth of experimental evidence demonstrating that metaphor is embodied to various degrees and in various ways. As we will see later in this chapter, this evidence shows that when a word has both a literal and a metaphorical meaning, this is not just a linguistic coincidence: people experience its literal meaning and its metaphorical meaning in very similar ways. The evidence comes from a range of sources employing a variety of research methods, including reaction-time studies, neurological studies, gesture studies, questionnaires, discourse analysis and interviews. These studies can be roughly divided into three broad types: studies involving behavioural evidence (such as the one we have just seen), studies that make use of neurological evidence and studies that draw on evidence from naturally occurring data in different forms of expression (e.g., language, gesture, expressive dance and art). Here I look at each of these different sources of evidence in turn, evaluating the findings from the research and the implications that are proposed by the researchers.

2.2   Evidence from Behavioural Studies

Behavioural studies of embodied metaphor have tended to focus on primary metaphors. These studies have found strong relationships between people's posture, body movement and environment and their use of these metaphors. Some studies show that our bodily position or environment can affect the way we use metaphor to think, whilst others show that the converse is also true: having people engage in types of metaphorical thinking can affect their physical behaviour during or after the experiment. In this section, I present some of this evidence, focusing on the metaphors whose embodied nature it supports. All of the results presented are statistically significant.

Moving Forwards in Time is Moving Forwards in Space

It has been suggested that we understand time metaphorically in terms of space and that, at least in English, the future lies in front of us and the past lies behind us. This relationship is thought to underlie linguistic metaphors such as 'looking ahead to this evening' (BNC) and 'thinking back to earlier that afternoon' (BNC). Relationships have been found between people's bodily position and their propensity to employ metaphors such as these. For example, it has been shown that if people are leaning forwards it is easier for them to talk about the future than if they are leaning backwards, and vice versa (Lempert and Kinsbourne, 1982). The converse is also true: Miles et al. (2010a, b) found that thinking about future events makes people lean or move forwards and thinking about past events makes them lean or move backwards. They concluded that spatiotemporal processing appears to be grounded in the same sensorimotor systems that regulate human movement, and suggested that the embodiment of time and space 'yields an overt behavioural marker of an otherwise invisible mental operation' (Miles et al., 2010b: 223). In a similar vein, people have been found to walk further towards a target when reading a scenario about a positive, successful relationship, which was 'making good progress', than when reading a scenario about a negative, unsuccessful relationship (Gibbs, 2013). Also, Casasanto and Boroditsky (2003) found that spatial displacement can bias temporal judgements: longer movements are perceived as having lasted longer, even when they have not actually done so.

As an extension to this metaphor, the front-back orientation also constitutes a metaphor for success and failure; people often speak of success (e.g., 'advance') and failure (e.g., 'setback') as if they were forwards versus backwards movements through space. Robinson and Fetterman (2015) had participants categorise 'success' versus 'failure' words by moving a joystick forwards or backwards. They found that participants were faster at categorising failure when asked to indicate it by moving the joystick backwards and that they were faster at categorising success when asked to indicate it by moving the joystick forwards. These findings suggest that the relationship between the front-back orientation and the abstract notions of success and failure has a physical basis as well as a linguistic one.

One of the most widely cited pieces of work on the metaphorical relationship between time and space is Boroditsky et al.'s (2002) study of 'moving time' versus 'moving ego'. In English, there are two contrasting ways in which a person's spatial relationship with time can be expressed: the *moving time* metaphor conceptualises time as moving forwards towards the person and the *moving ego* metaphor conceptualises the person as moving forwards towards the future. The *moving time* metaphor is thought to underlie expressions where events move towards us in time (e.g., 'with term approaching fast' [BNC] or 'local government review is coming up fast' [BNC]). The *moving ego* metaphor is thought to underlie expressions where a future event or situation is seen as being on the path in front of us (e.g., 'The situation was rapidly heading towards the ultimate confrontation' [BNC] or 'a number of countries are heading towards recession' [BNC]). People have been shown to vary in terms of which formulation they favour. When people are asked 'Next Wednesday's meeting has been moved forwards two days; when is the meeting now that it has been rescheduled?', people employing a 'moving time' metaphor will report that it has been moved to Monday, whereas people employing a 'moving ego' metaphor will report that it has been moved to Friday. According to Boroditsky et al. (2002), these two conceptualisations are equally likely to be evoked in a 'neutral' context; some people will reply that it is on Monday, whereas others will reply that it is on Friday. However, the manipulation of contextual information can change people's perspectives. For example, they found that people who have been primed to think about objects travelling towards them are much more likely to think about time moving towards them and are thus likely to adopt a 'moving time' perspective. People standing at the front of a queue rather than at the back were found to be more likely to think of themselves moving through time, thus adopting a moving ego perspective, and the same was true of people at an airport who had just flown in (as opposed to those who were waiting to pick up friends) and people at a racecourse who had betted on a number of horses (as opposed to those who had not). These findings suggest a strong interaction between one's thoughts about the experience of physical movement and the metaphorical construal of time in terms of different types of movement.

Finally, there is evidence from eye tracking studies to support the idea that moving through time is mentally simulated as moving through space. When people hear sentences about future activity their eyes move upwards and to the right. Hartmann et al. (2014) asked participants to mentally displace themselves into the past or future while measuring their spontaneous eye movements on a blank screen. Eye gaze was directed more rightwards and upwards when thinking about the future than when thinking about the past. The right movement corresponds to the left-right time line and the upwards movements correspond to findings from visual perception studies showing that objects lying ahead of the speaker are observed to be higher with increasing distance even when in reality, they are not higher, but simply further away (Ooi et al., 2001). The participants in Hartmann et al.'s study thus appear to be mentally projecting a sagittal axis that extends into the computer screen, and looking further along this axis when they think about future events.

More/Positive/Powerful Is Up and Less/Negative/Lacking Power Is Down

There is a rich seam of behavioural evidence for the embodied nature of metaphors that involve the up-down orientation. Linguistic expressions that reflect an underlying MORE IS UP metaphor include, for example, 'rising populations' (BNC) and 'falling prices' (BNC). Behavioural evidence for the embodied nature of the MORE IS UP/LESS IS DOWN metaphor can be found in studies of reading speed. Langston (2002) presented participants with sentences referring to larger and smaller amounts of substance (e.g., 'coffee contains a lot of caffeine' versus 'tea contains little caffeine'). The sentences were positioned above or below each other on a computer screen. He found that participants read the sentences more quickly when they appeared in their canonical position (i.e., with the 'more' sentence at the top of the screen and the 'less' sentence at the bottom of the screen). Thus, the violation of the MORE IS UP/LESS IS DOWN metaphor significantly slowed down reading speed. Body posture also appears to activate the MORE IS UP and LESS IS DOWN metaphor; when asked to generate numbers, people looking up have been found to generate higher numbers than people looking down (Winter and Matlock, 2013).

As well as numerical concepts, positivity and negativity also correlate with the UP/DOWN orientation, as is shown in linguistic expressions such as 'you'll feel on top of the world' (BNC), or 'she was feeling down' (BNC). These metaphors also appear to have an embodied motivation; participants remember emotionally positive images better when they appear at the top of a computer screen, with negative images being recalled better when they are seen towards the bottom of the screen (Crawford et al., 2006). Meier and Robinson (2004) found that participants are significantly more likely to recognise positive words when they appear high on the screen, and negative words when they appear low on the screen. This again is thought to be due to the implicit association of positivity with upwards movement and negativity with downwards movement. There are thought to be parallels in bodily behaviour in that we slouch when we are feeling depressed and stand tall when we are feeling happy.

The up-down orientation is also used to represent power, as we can see in expressions such as 'high ranking officers' (BNC) or 'a position at the bottom of the organisation' (BNC), and again this metaphorical relationship appears to have an embodied motivation: people have been found to judge a group's social power to be greater when these judgements were made at the top of a computer screen than when presented in the lower part of the screen (Schubert, 2005). Lakens et al. (2011) found the association between social hierarchy and the vertical schema to be strongly affected by the roles of the people involved. They took Schubert's (2005) study as their starting point and expanded it in order to assess whether simple contextual cues such as the relative spatial positions of stimuli would influence the results. They were interested in investigating whether the presence or absence of relational differences in the power dimension moderate the extent to which power is represented in the vertical dimension. They found that participants placed powerful groups (e.g., professors) higher in vertical space when powerless groups (e.g., students) were co-present in the same task, compared to when powerless groups were absent. Finally, Zanolie et al. (2012) found that participants were faster at identifying a target at the top of a computer screen when they had just seen a power-related word (e.g., 'king') and were faster at identifying a target at the bottom of the computer screen when they had just seen a word associated with a lack of power (e.g., servant). Taken together, these findings suggest that the up-down orientation is used to form embodied metaphorical representations of quantity, positivity and power.

Affection Is Warmth

In terms of one's interaction with the environment, metaphors relating affection to physical warmth (e.g., 'Goldie is a very warm, honest person' – BNC) have also been found to have an embodied basis. Researchers have found that having people hold warm, as opposed to cold, cups of coffee, for a few minutes led them to judge another person's interpersonal traits as being warmer (Williams and Bargh, 2008). In a follow-up study, they had participants feel and evaluate either a hot therapeutic gel pack, or a cold one. Following the evaluation, participants were asked to say whether they would prefer to offer it to a friend or keep it for themselves. Those who had evaluated the warm heat pad were more likely to say that they would offer it as a gift and those who had evaluated the cold pack said that they would be more likely to want to keep it for themselves. They concluded from these findings that physical feelings of warmth translate metaphorically into greater interpersonal warmth. Caution needs to be exercised regarding this study as various scholars have attempted to replicate it and have failed to do so (see, for example, Lynott et al., 2014). Lynott et al., in attempting to explain why they failed to replicate the study, suggest that the effect observed by Williams and Bargh may have been due, in part, to unconscious cues given by the researcher. In the Williams and Bargh study, the research assistant interacted directly with participants as they received their hot or cold packs, and so it is possible that subconscious cues were transmitted during this brief exchange. In Lynott et al.'s replication study, the research assistant was deliberately kept unaware of the aims of the study.

Some linguistic metaphors relate coldness to social and/or emotional exclusion (e.g., 'you ask me to help you at one moment and leave me out in the cold the next' – BNC). Behavioural studies have shown that this relationship also has an embodied basis. Zhong and Leonardelli (2008) found that participants who were asked to recall a time when they had experienced social exclusion were likely to give lower estimates of the temperature in the room than participants who had been asked to recall an inclusion experience. They also found that when social exclusion was directly induced through an online virtual interaction activity, those participants who had been 'excluded' from the activity reported a greater desire for warm food and drink than those who had not been excluded. They argue from these findings that social perception involves perceptual content and that the psychological experience of coldness is integral to the experience of social exclusion. Writers' choices of temperature-related metaphors also appear to be affected by seasonal factors. In his study of seasonal metaphors used in the *Economist* magazine, Boers (1999) found that significantly more metaphors that have illness-related source domains are used in winter editions of the Economist, and that correspondingly more metaphors with heat-related source domains are used in summer editions.

Morality Is Cleanliness

We saw in Section 2.1 that metaphorical expressions relating morality to cleanliness and a lack of morality to dirt (e.g. 'a dirty business it was too' – BNC) have an embodied basis, with research showing that making the notion of physical purity more salient can affect the way people make moral judgements. In addition to the Zhong and Liljenquist study cited earlier in the chapter, Schnall, Benton et al. (2008) found that having people make judgements about people's behaviour in a dirty work area caused them to rate the behaviour as more immoral than when the same judgements were made in a clean work area. The same result was found after participants had physically cleansed themselves after experiencing disgust. Thinking about moral or immoral deeds can have an effect on subsequent actions. These findings provide support for the embodied nature of the MORALITY IS CLEANLINESS metaphor.

Other studies have found the metaphorical relationship between morality and cleanliness to be modality specific. For example, lying by speaking has been found to prompt people to select a gift of mouthwash rather than hand sanitiser, whereas when people have lied with their hands, they are more likely to select a hand sanitiser over the mouthwash (Lee and Schwarz, 2010). The source domain of CLEANLINESS has also been found to map onto other aspects of human behaviour via embodied metaphor. Lee and Schwartz (2012a) found that the presence of an unpleasant smell in the room can increase the harshness of the moral judgements that a person is likely to make. Personal cleanliness has also been found to shape the strength of one's morality judgements via the embodied metaphor linking physical cleanliness and moral purity. Zhong et al. (2010) found that individuals who had recently been involved in a physical cleansing task or who had been asked to visualise a cleaning task offered much more severe judgements on morally contested issues, such as abortion and pornography. Moral behaviour has also been shown to be shaped by ambient lighting. Chiou and Cheng (2013) found that participants seated in a well-lit room were more likely to engage in ethical behaviour. More specifically, in a business simulation game they found that participants were more likely to return undeserved money, and in response to a fake request from a 'researcher', participants offered to code more data sheets.

Importance Is Weight

Importance is often talked about in terms of weight, as we can see in expressions such as 'heavyweight interviews' and 'lightweight movies' (BNC) which refer, respectively, to interviews that deal with important subjects and films that do not. This embodied metaphor also appears to have a degree of psychological reality. Jostmann et al. (2009) found that having participants hold a heavy clipboard rather than a light one made them consider fair decision-making procedures to be more important. It also led to more elaborate thinking. They thus concluded that the metaphorical relationship between weight and importance exists not only on a linguistic level but also on a conceptual level. In a subsequent study, Schneider et al. (2011) found that when participants were told that a book contained important information, their estimates of the book's weight were significantly higher than those given by participants who had been told that the book contained less important information. They concluded from this that the activation direction from weight to importance can be reversed, suggesting that the connection between weight and importance goes beyond metaphorical mappings and is more in line with an embodied simulation account. Remaining with the subject of weight, Chandlera et al. (2012) found that participants evaluated a book as more important when it weighed heavily in their hands (due to a concealed weight), but only when they had substantive knowledge about the book. Those who had read a synopsis, had read the book or knew details about its plot were influenced by its weight, whereas those unfamiliar with the book were not. Ackerman et al. (2010) found that having participants who held heavy clipboards rated job candidates as more important than participants who held lighter clipboards. These researchers argue from these findings that the relationship goes beyond simple parallels between the words used for the different meanings of heavy and light, as the information is purely perceptual.

Difficulty and Guilt Are Weight

Related to the idea that important things are 'heavy' is the idea that difficult things and guilt are also 'heavy'. Evidence for the physical basis of the DIFFICULTY IS WEIGHT metaphor is provided by Brdar et al. (2015), who found that participants who were asked to wear a heavier rucksack reported that a computer-based task was significantly more difficult than participants who were asked to wear a lighter rucksack, despite the fact that both groups performed equally well on the task and the rucksack did not actually hamper them in any way. Evidence for the physical basis of the WEIGHT IS GUILT metaphor is provided by Kouchaki, Gino and Jami (2014), who found that wearing a heavy backpack generates feelings of guilt. They argue that the physical experience of weight is associated with the emotional experience of guilt and thus that weight intensifies the experience of guilt. They found that participants who wore a heavy backpack experienced higher levels of guilt compared to those who wore a light backpack. Additionally, wearing a heavy backpack led participants to cheat less in a simulated game that they were subsequently asked to play, and participants processed guilty stimuli more fluently when experiencing physical weight. Thus at some level, when we talk of feeling 'weighed down by events' or of things 'weighing on our mind' (BNC), we activate the physical experience of bearing weight.

Positive and Negative Affect Are Lightness and Darkness

There is a well-established metaphor that links positive emotions with light ('he had a sunny disposition' – BNC), and negative emotions with darkness ('sometimes a dark mood ambushed him' – BNC). This link can be found in literature, film and art, where negative emotions are often accompanied by reference to or the actual appearance of dark colours, dingy weather, night time and so on (Winter, 2014). There is evidence from behavioural studies indicating that this metaphorical link is implicit and automatic. Meier, Robinson et al. (2007) found participants rated the level of brightness of a square as being greater when they had been primed with words associated with positive affect and darker when they had been primed with words associated with negative affect. They also found that the brightness of a word affected the speed with which participants were able to identify it as being associated with positive or negative affect; when words that are associated with positive affect were presented in brighter hues, they were more rapidly identified as being positive than when they were presented in darker hues, and vice versa. These findings suggest that the link between affect and brightness goes beyond language.

Resemblance Is Proximity

Evidence has also been found for the embodied nature of the metaphorical relationship that allows us to express similarity as closeness (e.g., '[he] bears a close resemblance to our school janitor' BNC [Radden and Mathis, 2002]). Casasanto (2008) presented participants with a number of pairs of words (e.g., 'duty' and 'pride') on a screen and asked them to rate how close they were in meaning. Some words were presented physically closer to each other on the screen than others. Participants were more likely to rate the words as being similar in meaning if they were presented physically closer to one another than if they were presented far apart. Thus the metaphorical link between resemblance and proximity extends beyond language into the physical domain.

Fictive Motion

Fictive motion is a form of embodied metaphor which allows us to experience a road or a path 'travelling' across terrain as well as just describing it in this way. In fictive motion sentences, stationary objects are talked about as if they are moving (e.g., 'the path travels beside the River Wharfe' – BNC). They are sometimes metonymically extended to refer, for example, to human actions that might be associated with static objects (e.g., 'the single window looked out onto the narrow street' – BNC). The idea of fictive motion was first proposed by Talmy (1996), but it has since been studied widely in relation to mental simulation and embodied cognition.

A substantial amount of evidence for the idea that fictive motion is embodied and that it involves mental simulation comes from work conducted by Teenie Matlock and colleagues. In her 2004 paper, Matlock describes a self-paced timed reading task where participants read short stories containing fictive motion sentences that for the most part involved co-extension paths (e.g., 'the road travelled over rough ground'). Half of the sentences involved difficult terrain and half involved easy terrain. After each story, she then asked participants a question about the story. She found that the participants took significantly longer to read the sentences where the terrain was rough, even though the sentences were matched for length, and that it took them significantly longer to answer the questions pertaining to these sentences. In a later study, Richardson and Matlock (2007) had participants listen to sentences involving fictive motion, where again the going was either easy or difficult. While the participants were listening to these sentences they were asked to look at pictures that corresponded to the scenes, and the movements of their eyes were recorded using an eye tracker. Richardson and Matlock found a significant increase in the amount of eye movement when the participants were listening to fictive motion descriptions where the terrain was described as 'difficult' compared to sentences where the terrain was described as 'easy'. Together, these studies provide strong evidence to suggest that the participants created a mental simulation of the route covered by the roads and paths and that this mental simulation involved different types of movement, although in reality the roads and paths were stationary.

Talmy (2000) noted that listeners and readers display wide variation in terms of the extent to which fictive motion sentences evoke an actual sense of motion, which he termed 'experienced fictive motion'. In other words, some individuals will report that they actually experience feelings of motion, while others say that they do not. Furthermore, individuals differ in terms of what they perceive to be moving in fictive motion sentences. For example, in a sentence such as 'the bypass stretches from here to Ipswich' (BNC), some individuals may simply perceive the bypass itself to be moving, others may perceive a car travelling along the bypass, whereas others simply experience an abstract feeling of movement. Others perceive and experience no movement at all.

The idea that fictive motion triggers mental simulation has been questioned by Blomberg and Zlatev (2014), who argue that the term 'mental simulation' is too simplistic as it does not stipulate what movement is being simulated (e.g., it could be the road itself that is perceived as moving, or simply a person moving along the road). They believe that it blurs conscious processes of imagination with subconscious mechanisms. They claim that it conflates experiential motivations with conventional semantics. Instead they propose the more multifaceted term: 'non-actual motion' and argue that it is important to pay more attention to the ways in which the role played by conscious and subconscious mental processes varies according to the different types of non-actual motion encountered. They identify three different types of experience that may be triggered on encountering non-actual motion: (i) enactive perception, (ii) intentionality and (iii) imagination, and argue that the type of non-actual motion encountered and the context in which it is encountered will determine the extent to which each of these experiences are evoked. I will pick up their work in Chapter 3 and explore it in more depth, when I look at contextual factors that shape people's experiences of embodied metaphor.

Embodied Idioms

Finally, there is evidence to suggest that some metaphorical idioms can provoke sensorimotor responses and thus appear to be embodied. For example, Wilson and Gibbs (2007) found that people comprehend figurative idioms, such as 'It's easy to *grasp* the concept' (BNC) more quickly when they first make, or imagine making, a relevant bodily action, such as a grasping motion. A particularly intriguing study with English speakers examined whether smelling something fishy would raise people's suspicions about others when playing a trust game. This study was motivated by the use of the word 'fishy' to mean 'suspicious' (e.g., 'there was something kind of fishy going on' – BNC). People were led into a room that had been sprayed with fish oil, methane gas or odourless water. When people smelled the fish oil, as opposed to the other smells, they were less willing to contribute money towards a publicly shared resource, indicating greater social suspicion in the fishy smelling condition (Lee and Schwarz, 2012). Finally, Hellmann et al. (2013) investigated whether the sensation of a sweet taste informs judgements of harmful acts via indirect activation of the metaphoric idiom 'revenge is sweet'. They found that when participants had been primed with the idiom 'revenge is sweet' and then given something sweet to taste, they were more likely to make lenient judgements concerning criminal behaviour than participants who had not been primed in this way. Of all the findings discussed so far, the findings from studies involving idioms are the hardest to explain, as the motivation for the meanings of many of these idioms is by no means transparent. I pick up on the subject of embodied idioms in Chapter 3, when I look at the role of novelty in shaping the extent to which a metaphorical relationship is embodied.

Limitations of Behavioural Evidence

Although the behavioural evidence that we have just reviewed is, for the most part, highly compelling, it must be noted at this point that some of these studies do have limitations. One criticism that has been made of some of the studies is that the responses that have been found may have been due to a training effect. To investigate this possibility, Slepian and Ambady (2014) taught participants two novel metaphors: PAST IS HEAVY and PRESENT IS LIGHT, in a controlled setting. They hypothesised that teaching the participants a novel embodied metaphor would lead to them providing social judgements based on these novel metaphors, thus questioning the results of embodiment-based research. In their study, two groups of students were indirectly taught to associate degrees of heaviness with either past or present time. The first group read passages supposedly written by a philosopher with sentences like 'the decisions of your past carry no weight', while the second group read passages with sentences like 'the decisions of your present carry no weight'. After the training sessions, the two groups judged the weight of old and new books that were in fact identical. The group that had been trained in the PAST IS HEAVY condition judged old books as being heavier, while the group that were trained in the PRESENT IS HEAVY condition judged the new book as being heavy. Slepian and Ambody (2014) argue that the results for the novel HEAVINESS metaphor may not be as constant as those found in studies that have investigated bodily-based embodied metaphors, but they do call into question the results of behavioural psychology research. I would argue, however, that Slepian and Ambody's findings do not cast serious doubt over the embodied metaphor hypothesis, as most of the studies whose findings support this hypothesis do not involve any procedures that might be construed as training. Furthermore, many of the metaphorical relationships that have been identified can be found in a wide range of languages and cultures, suggesting that there is more involved than exposure to one's own language.

Another behavioural study whose findings appear to call into question the embodied metaphor hypothesis is Maglio and Trope's (2012) work, which compared the way in which one's temporary physical state impacts upon judgements made about concrete facts, and upon judgements made about abstract concepts. They found that contextual bodily information affected visual length estimates and importance ratings for people who had been led to think concretely, but not for those who had been led to think abstractly. They went on to conclude that embodied cognition works best at a basic, literal level and does not operate well with abstract concepts. However, given the abundance of studies listed about that deal with the metaphorical understanding of abstract concepts, it appears to be the case that embodied metaphor can operate at all levels of abstraction, albeit to different degrees. It is important to note that people do not always need to conduct a full analysis of an embodied metaphor every time they encounter one, in many cases, they simply create representations that are 'just good enough' for the purpose at hand (Gibbs, 2017: 461).

2.3   Evidence from Neurological Studies

As well as behavioural evidence, there is also extensive neurological support for the idea that metaphors can be embodied. For example, it has been found that metaphorically used words with sensorimotor properties recruit sensorimotor regions of the brain, which provides evidence for the neurological grounding of embodied metaphor (Rohrer, 2006). Much of the neurological evidence for the embodied nature of metaphor comes from studies that employ functional Magnetic Resonance Imaging (fMRI). This technique measures brain activity by detecting changes associated with blood flow. In one such study, Lacey et al. (2012) had participants lie in a scanner and read pairs of sentences such as the following:

> 'Sam had a bad day'
> 'Sam had a rough day'

They were asked to push a response button as soon as they understood each statement. In their analysis of the fMRI data, Lacey et al. found that reading the figurative sentences (such as the second one) activated selective sensory areas that are related to the source domain from which the metaphors originated (e.g., 'rough' is related to touch or texture). The fMRI results for texture metaphors revealed activation in both the verbal areas of the brain and the somatosensory cortex, an area which is activated when perceiving tangible textures through haptic and visual stimuli. The results, however, did not show a similar activation with the non-metaphorical sentences, which suggests that the processing of texture metaphors activated the motor areas responsible for tactile perception. This finding, which links the literal and metaphorical meanings of the word 'rough', is in line with experimental evidence provided by Ackerman et al. (2010), who found that having participants manipulate rough or hard objects made them experience more difficulty in social interactions and behave more rigidly in negotiations. Thus these basic tactile sensations appear to influence higher social cognitive processing in metaphor-specific ways.

In an extension to Lacey et al.'s study, Wehling et al. (2015) were able to establish that the findings made for the metaphorical use of words such as 'grasp' also extended to negated uses of the word. Simulation-based models of negation suggest that negation is the product of a comparison between a simulation of the affirmative situation and subsequent simulation of the actual state of affairs (Kaup et al., 2007). Studies have shown that this comparison involves the simulation and subsequent suppression of the affirmative situation (Hasson and Gluksberg, 2004; Kaup, 2001). In other words, in order to imagine someone *not* performing a particular action, people first have to imagine them actually performing it. Wehling et al. investigated whether this processing pattern also holds for metaphoric language. In order to do this, they investigated the processing of literal and metaphoric uses of 'effector-specific' motion verbs (i.e., verbs involving motion that is performed by a particular part of the body) in both negated and affirmative metaphoric and literal sentences (e.g., 'He's (not) crushing the worker unions' versus 'He's (not) crushing the garlic'). They found decreased activity for negated hand-action metaphors compared to affirmative hand-action metaphors in the primary motor and premotor cortex. These results add to previous findings showing that the processing of conventional metaphors activates sensorimotor representations in the brain. They also show that these representations can be modulated by the linguistic context (affirmative vs. negative), suggesting a functional role of embodied representations in metaphor processing. Their results provide further evidence for the neural and cognitive validity of embodied metaphors.

Similar support comes from a study by Gamez-Djokic et al. (under review), who conducted an fMRI study to investigate whether the neural substrates involved in the processing of impure or disgusting things in an abstract, metaphorical sense (e.g., 'that was a rotten thing to do') were the same as those involved in literal descriptions of pathogen disgust inducers (e.g., maggots). They tested participants by having them look at disgust-inducing images and by having them read a series of sentences that contained metaphorical references to disgust. They also showed their participants a series of controls that took the form of both images and sentences. They found that metaphorically used disgust-related language recruited the same brain areas that were involved in the recognition and/or experience of actual disgust.

Another study employing fMRI techniques to find evidence for the sensorimotor processing of embodied metaphors was conducted by Desai et al. (2011), who compared mental activation for literal, abstract and metaphoric sentences. Participants were instructed to think of the meanings of sentences as they read them. Desai et al. compared neural responses to sentences containing action metaphors (e.g., 'the jury grasped the concept' or 'the council bashed the proposal') with sentences containing the literal equivalents of those physical action words (e.g., 'the daughter grasped the flowers' or 'the thief bashed the table'). Their fMRI results showed that both literal and metaphoric sentences activated the left anterior inferior parietal lobe, which is usually activated when people are planning concrete actions. In addition, the metaphoric sentences also activated the left superior temporal regions, which are activated when abstract sentences are being processed. Findings from this study again support the idea that the understanding of metaphorical actions draws on the same cognitive resources as the understanding of literal actions.

Boulenger et al. (2009) compared fMRI images of participants processing idiomatic and literal sentences involving hand and leg actions, such as 'grasp the concept' and 'kick the habit'. They found that the precentral and middle frontal gyri including the premotor and motor cortex were activated when the words were used both literally (e.g., grasp a piece of wood) and metaphorically (e.g., grasp a concept). This study lends support to the idea that the motor and premotor cortices are involved in idiom processing, which indicates the sensorimotor grounding of the metaphorical idioms. Using event-related potentials analysis (i.e., measures of brain responses that are the direct result of a specific sensory, cognitive or motor event), Bardolph and Colson (2014) showed that asking people to move their arms upwards or downwards affected their responses both to words that were associated in a literal way with vertical space (e.g., ascend, descend) and to words that were associated in a metaphorical way with vertical space in line with the GOOD IS UP/BAD IS DOWN metaphor (e.g., inspire, defeat). They found that congruency effects emerged 200–300 ms after word onset for the literal words, but not until after 500 ms post-onset for the metaphorically related words. They conclude that, although their findings do not support a strong view of embodied metaphor where early, bottom-up sensorimotor contributions would have been apparent, they do support a weak version of the embodied metaphor hypothesis.

Finally, there is neurological evidence to support the idea that fictive motion is embodied. It has been shown that the processing of both sentences involving fictive motion and sentences involving literal motion leads to activation in areas of the inferior temporal cortex that are involved in motion detection. This does not hold true for static control sentences, thus providing neurological evidence for the embodied status of fictive motion sentences (Saygin et al., 2010).

To sum up, neurological evidence appears to lend support to the embodied metaphor hypothesis. Although the embodied simulations that are generated for primary metaphors may be less detailed than those generated in response to more literal language, they are no less motor or perceptual (Bergen, 2012: 208).

Limitations of the Neurological Evidence

Casasanto and Gijssels (2015) are somewhat sceptical that the evidence from many of these neuro-imaging studies supports the theory of embodied metaphor. Their main disagreement is with Barsalou's (1999) embodied simulation hypothesis, which argues that thinking involves the construction of 'simulations' of bodily experiences (1999) and that modality-specific brain areas are activated during metaphor processing. They argue that for an experiment to support the simulation claim, it must provide clear evidence that an observed behaviour (e.g., the comprehension of a word) corresponds to modality-specific neural activity. It is over the issue of *modal specificity* where most of the experiments fall down. The neurological studies of metaphor tend to find that source domain representations are implemented in multimodal or a-modal regions of the brain. Although the findings from these studies are consistent with the idea of image schemas (which are a-modal and highly abstract), they do not, according to Casasanto and Gijssels, support the claim that metaphor is embodied. However, Casasanto and Gijssels' position is somewhat problematic, as they appear to be suggesting that in order to count as 'embodied', embodied simulations need to be modality specific (i.e., only involve one sense). In reality, it is rare for one's interaction with any entity (be it concrete or abstract) to be restricted to a single sense: if we taste something, we will often smell it; if we hear something, we will often see it. It is the norm for stimuli to be processed in a multimodal manner and this should, in theory, extend to the way in which they are embodied. There is ample evidence for multimodal simulation in the behavioural studies literature. For example, when reading sentences about object distance, language comprehenders have been found to store the information both visually and auditorily (Winter and Bergen, 2012).

A more compelling case for limiting the role of sensory and motor activation in the understanding of abstract concepts is made by Mahon and Caramazza (2008). Their focus is on embodied cognition, rather than on embodied metaphor per se. They acknowledge the fact that sensory and motor activation accompanies conceptual processing, but point out that patients with sensory and/or motor impairments do not necessarily suffer from conceptual deficits. In order to reconcile these findings, they propose an account of conceptual processing that occupies a middle ground between the embodied and disembodied cognition hypotheses. They suggest, in their 'grounding by interaction' hypothesis, that both sensory and motor information contribute to conceptual processing, but that it is possible to abstract away from these types of processing in order to form more abstract, symbolic representations of concepts. Thus the instantiation of a concept involves the retrieval of relevant sensory and motor information, and the removal of this process would result in an impoverished concept. The activation of sensory and motor representations contributes to the fleshing out of a concept and builds on the more schematic knowledge that one might have of that concept in a very general sense. Thus it appears that embodied cognition plays a role in, but does not fully explain the processing of, abstract concepts.

The main problem with the majority of both the behavioural and the neurological studies is that, because of the research conditions under which they are carried out, they cannot accord sufficient importance to the context-sensitive and interactive nature of metaphor in the real world. The metaphor examples that are used are often highly artificial and are nearly always decontextualised. This fact alone may draw a person's attention to their metaphorical nature and artificially inflate the extent to which they are experienced as embodied. So, although the evidence that they provide does suggest that metaphor comprehension can be highly embodied, at least when it takes place in these highly decontextualised contexts, it does not tell us anything about the way metaphors are processed when they appear in communicative contexts. Such contexts may reduce the salience of the metaphors, as the interlocutors are likely to be focusing on the overall meaning and communicative intent rather than on the language used to express that meaning. The relative salience of a given metaphor is likely to impact upon the sensorimotor and emotional responses that it evokes. One might expect that the more salient the metaphor, the more embodied the response, but we do not know whether this is indeed the case. This theme will be picked up again later in this chapter and in subsequent chapters. To date, we know little about how embodied metaphor works in communicative contexts. Let us begin therefore by looking at metaphor in naturally occurring data .

2.4   Evidence from Naturally Occurring Data

There is evidence in naturally occurring data to suggest that linguistic expressions corresponding to primary metaphors, such as those discussed previously, are frequently employed in language and in other forms of communication. Examples of metaphors, such as GOOD IS UP, MOVING FORWARDS IN TIME IS MOVING FORWARDS IN SPACE and EMOTIONAL CLOSENESS IS WARMTH can be found in language, gesture, art, music and film. However, what we do not have thus far is evidence to suggest that people have any kind of 'bodily experience' of these metaphors when they encounter them in authentic communicative contexts, outside of the laboratory. As we saw previously, one drawback of laboratory studies is that they rely heavily on decontextualised, artificial examples of metaphors, which may well affect the way in which they are processed. Their embodied nature may therefore be more salient in the laboratory than it would be if they were simply encountered in naturally occurring, everyday communication. In an ideal world, studies of embodied metaphor would factor in the interactive, situated nature of human communication, but this is a very difficult thing to do.

Despite the difficulties involved in incorporating real-world focus into controlled experiments, there is a small amount of neurological support for the role played by sensorimotor systems in discourse comprehension. For example, Speer et al. (2007) found that patterns of brain activity mapped onto the boundaries between narrative events, and Wallentin et al. (2011) found that motion verbs triggered activation in the left posterior middle temporal gyrus during storytelling. This area of the brain is involved in the processing of motion. However, there is nothing in discourse studies to parallel the extensive laboratory investigations that have been conducted in order to find evidence for the embodied nature of decontextualised words and sentences. Moreover, to the best of my knowledge there have been no laboratory-based studies of the potentially embodied nature of metaphor in discourse, let alone in multimodal or interactive settings. This is understandable given the intrusive nature of the procedures involved, and the practical difficulties that would be involved in, for example, having participants engage in authentic, interactive, multimodal communication inside an fMRI scanner. There are also difficulties in combining authentic communicative tasks with procedures such as eye tracking, neurological and reaction time studies. As technology develops, some of these difficulties may be surmounted. In the meantime, we need to make use of less direct, more observational data, and accept the limitations that are inherent in this approach. With this caveat in mind, let us now explore the potential that this data has to offer. Because the limitations of real-world data vary according to the type of data under discussion, they are discussed within the context of each data type. For this reason, this section is structured somewhat differently from the previous two sections. Whereas in those sections I included a discussion of limitations at the end, in this section I discuss the limitations of the data as I go along and suggest ways in which these limitations might be addressed.

Linguistic Evidence

Linguistic instantiations of the primary metaphors proposed by Grady (1997a) abound. Not only can analyses of language corpora provide evidence of linguistic expressions that correspond to primary metaphors but they can also reveal how these primary metaphors interact to create more complex metaphors and how their meanings slide into one another. In order to illustrate this, let us look in detail at how three words that have been shown to relate to primary metaphors behave in the 'News on the Web' (NOW) corpus.[1] Let us begin by taking the primary metaphor, EMOTIONAL INTIMACY IS PROXIMITY. Of the one hundred first hits of the adjective 'close', eighty-three are metaphorical. Of these, thirty-seven involve relational closeness. This closeness sometimes has an emotional component (e.g., *his **close** friend; I'm afraid to get **close** when dating*), and sometimes it involves a mutually cooperative relationship (e.g., *a **close** connection with Romania*). Twenty-four are related to similarity, and reflect the primary metaphor, SIMILARITY IS PROXIMITY (e.g., *their perspective may be too **close** to yours*). This also includes examples of numerical similarity (e.g., 'a market valuation of close to $28 billion') and examples of ranking (e.g., *a **close** second*; *'a **close** game'*). It is interesting to note that in examples such as *a **close** game*, metonymic extension is also in evidence, with the metaphorically 'close' scores of the game standing for the game as a whole. Ten are related to the primary metaphor MOMENTS IN TIME ARE OBJECTS IN MOTION ALONG A PATH, wherein people can be conceptualised as moving towards a situation or event in the future (e.g., *how **close** are we to a world without cancer?*; *the town may also be **close** to getting a grocery store back*; *pretty **close** to when Hell freezes over*). Finally, twelve are related to the primary metaphor KNOWING/UNDERSTANDING IS SEEING and its corollary CONSIDERING IS LOOKING AT, with the extension that taking a 'close look' would therefore mean better understanding. This is seen in such examples as *Maria Taylor has seen the sports world up **close*** and *the focussed investigator will pay **close** attention*. Thus all eighty-three of the metaphorical instances of the word 'close' appear to be motivated by primary metaphors.

To take another primary metaphor, AFFECTION IS WARMTH, a search for the first one hundred hits for the adjective 'warm' reveals that thirty-five are metaphorical. Of these, all but three involve the idea of emotional rather than physical warmth (e.g., *Modi was very **warm** and receptive*; *a **warm** welcome*; *a **warm**, cordial and positive meeting*). The remaining three metaphorical examples of 'warm' are used to describe colours (e.g., *A **warm** colour*) and thus do not strictly correspond to any of Grady's primary metaphors. However, it could be argued that they have a physical basis in that warm colours (e.g., red, orange and yellow) tend to evoke objects in the physical world that make us feel warm (e.g., fire and the sun) and can thus be viewed as 'embodied'.

As a final example, of the first one hundred hits for the adjective 'hard', ninety-one examples can be considered metaphorical. Of these, fifty-nine refer directly to the primary metaphor DIFFICULTY IS HARDNESS (e.g., *it's **hard** to see how the economy will recover*; *trying to learn movements that are too **hard***; *he was still having a **hard** time believing it*). Seven refer to its corollary, SYMPATHY IS SOFTNESS (e.g., *by taking a **hard**, unified stance*; *no **hard** feelings*; *he's **hard** on himself about it*). Some of the examples appear to involve more than one primary metaphor. For example, let us consider the examples ***hard** evidence* and *a **hard** Brexit*; while there may be some relation to 'lack of sympathy' in these examples, this primary metaphor cannot be said to capture the whole meaning. The use of the word 'hard' in these examples also refers to the unambiguous, uncompromising and unyielding nature of the subject under discussion. These metaphorical uses of the word 'hard' appear to be motivated by the physical properties of materials, and human interaction with those materials. Thus, two different embodied metaphors appear to be at play. Of the nine remaining examples, there is only one example where it is being used in its most basic, sensory sense: *wearing **hard** hats*. Other examples that can be considered non-metaphorical are the six examples of **hard** *drive*, and the two examples of 'hard' being used in a sporting context: *another* **hard** *hit*. These can be considered metonymic given their close relationship to physical objects or bodily action.

We can conclude from this short analysis that primary metaphors motivate the majority of metaphorical usages of these words but that they do not always do so in straightforward ways. Although in many cases only one primary metaphor is evoked, some instances involve the instantiation of more than one primary metaphor, whereas others involve metonymic extensions and pragmatic elaborations of the metaphorical meaning. Primary metaphors thus appear to provide only a partial motivation for these metaphorical expressions. The expressions themselves appear to operate within radial categories (Taylor, 2003), with more prototypical examples towards the centre and examples towards the periphery taking on more complex, context-specific meanings, occasionally drawing on other primary metaphors.

Although these examples indicate that the primary metaphors have corresponding linguistic expressions, the presence of these linguistic expressions does not prove that the primary metaphors are actively evoked by the writer at the time of writing, or indeed that they are evoked in the reader. It is therefore impossible to comment on the level of embodied activation caused by these expressions. Despite the limitations of corpus data, however, there are two corpus-based studies that do appear to have found indirect support for the embodied metaphor hypothesis. Both studies combined an analysis of corpus data with psycholinguistic experimentation. The first of these studies is Akpinar and Berger's (2015) study, which showed that metaphoric expressions that reflect an underlying embodied relationship are significantly more likely to remain in the language than their literal counterparts. Akpinar and Berger explored the development of sensory embodied metaphoric expressions over the course of 200 years in a corpus of 5 million books written in English. They found that embodied metaphoric expressions were more likely to remain in the language and were thus deemed 'more culturally successful' than their literal counterparts. For example, the term 'sharp increase' is more likely to remain in the language once it has entered it than the 'severe increase' and the term 'warm smile' is more likely to remain than the term 'kind smile'. Akpinar and Berger also tested 365 participants on their ability to recall the different terms and found that they were significantly better at recalling the sensory embodied metaphors than their literal equivalents.

The second study is Johansson-Falck and Gibbs's (2012) investigation into the relationship between the mental imagery that people have for roads and paths in the real world and the ways in which these two words are used metaphorically in corpora. They first collected people's intuitions about their embodied experiences of paths and roads, focusing specifically on what it is that roads and paths afford their users in terms of their possible, relevant bodily actions (Gibson, 1979). They then used this data to make predictions about the ways in which the two words would be employed metaphorically in the British National Corpus. They found that their predictions were largely correct; when people thought of roads, they thought in terms of straightness, width and the ultimate destination, whereas paths evoked a focus on the nature of the (often difficult) terrain and foregrounded a certain aimlessness. In line with these findings, they found that in the corpus data, roads were more likely to be used metaphorically to talk about purposeful activity and political/financial matters, whilst paths were used metaphorically to talk about difficult step by step procedures. Furthermore, metaphorical roads rather than paths were more likely to be taken by large groups of people in an organisation as they moved towards well-defined courses of action; Johansson-Falck and Gibbs argue that this is reminiscent of a vehicle full of people travelling down an actual road.

Studies such as these, which combine a corpus-based approach with a more psycholinguistically oriented approach provide the most promising line of investigation and have the most potential to provide evidence for the psychological reality of embodied metaphor in authentic discourse and in genuinely communicative situations.

Visual Evidence from Film, Advertising and Art

Manifestations of primary metaphor can also be found in non-linguistic data. For example, Winter (2014) finds that horror movies consistently reflect metaphorical associations between verticality and affect, and between brightness and affect. His study of several films in this genre reveals that bad events tend to occur when the characters are moving downwards, or when the lights go off. Monsters and villains tend to emerge from below and from the darkness, and characters tend to get lost and stuck in dark underground caves, dungeons, tunnels and mines. Even in films that are primarily set above ground or in bright light, the most frightening scenes tend to occur below ground and in the dark. Winter comments on the striking consistency with which the two metaphors 'EVIL IS DOWN' and 'EVIL IS DARK' are used within this genre. These reflect the two primary metaphors: BAD IS DOWN and BAD IS DARK. Evidence of primary metaphors can also be found in musical theory, where notes can be 'high' or 'low' and there can be 'depth' of sound. Music itself is often conceived as motion (Larson, 2012), with musical entities being viewed as objects in motion along a path (Johnson and Larson, 2003).

Again, although these studies show that images and music encode primary metaphorical relations, they do not provide evidence to suggest that people actively engage in embodied simulations or experience sensory activations when they encounter them. In other words, they do not prove that individuals are activating the source domains of embodied metaphors when they encounter or use them in these contexts. To demonstrate this, we would need to look at people's sensorimotor and emotional responses to metaphors in film, art and music. Although no studies to date have provided direct evidence of the ability of metaphors in these forms of expression to evoke bodily responses, indirect evidence of sensitivity to primary metaphor in visual modes of expression has been provided by El Refaie (2009). She had participants explain two political cartoons which employed embodied primary metaphors, and analysed the transcripts of their explanations for evidence of awareness of embodied metaphor. She found that primary metaphorical mappings, such as those between size and power and between movement through space and the passage of time, were understood even by participants who had very little background knowledge. In contrast to this, complex structural metaphors could only be read in the way intended by the cartoonist if respondents had an appropriate level of general knowledge and current affairs. It would be interesting to look at the gestures produced by participants in El Refaie's study, as these may have provided an indication of the level of activation that these metaphors provoked in the minds of the viewers. Indeed, of all available methods, the study of gesture is the most promising in terms of its potential to provide insights into the physical nature of metaphor. It is to this subject that we now turn.

Gestural Evidence

As we saw previously, findings from gesture studies provide support for the idea that even very conventional metaphors can be experienced physically. Most researchers in gesture studies would agree that gesture and cognition are inextricably linked, that much gesture simultaneously serves both a communicative and a cognitive function, and that the communicative and cognitive functions of gesture cannot easily be separated. Gesture and speech are usually 'co-expressive'. In other words, they express the same underlying idea unit, but do so in their own ways, often highlighting different perspectives on the same event. The same neural networks (i.e., the bilateral middle temporal regions) are involved in the processing of metaphor in both speech and gesture (Gentilucci and Volta, 2008). The role played by actual bodily movements in the embodiment of abstract concepts is crucial. As Gibbs puts it: 'embodiment is more than physiological and/or brain activity, and is constituted by recurring patterns of kinaesthetic, proprioceptive action that provide much of people's felt, subjective experience' (Gibbs, 2005: 12).

The link between language, thought and gesture is emphasised by McNeill (2005), who argues that by focusing on a person's use of language and gesture during discourse, we can gain insights into the ways in which they formulate their ideas. His argument is that through gesture we see the unification of two modes of thought: imagery and language. For McNeill, the starting point of a thought, the point at which imagery and linguistic content are combined, is referred to as the 'growth point'. This has much in common with Slobin's (1996) 'thinking-for-speaking' hypothesis, according to which the language that we speak forces us to package our ideas in particular ways, and our ideas only thus become fully solidified when we actually need to put them into words. Researchers working in the area have identified a significant role for gesture in the process of packaging ideas into specific language constructions (see, for example, Kendon, 2004; Kita, 2000).

A second and complementary way of viewing the relationship between gesture, language and thought is Kita et al.'s (2017) 'Gesture-for-Conceptualization Hypothesis', which grew out of Kita's original 'Information-Packaging Hypothesis' (Kita, 2000). As we saw in Chapter 1, the Gesture-for-Conceptualization Hypothesis accords a central role to gesture in both thinking and speaking. According to this hypothesis, we employ gesture to help schematise spatio-motoric information, which in turn helps us to activate, manipulate, package and explore that information. In other words, while making the gesture, the speaker is working out, both conceptually and linguistically, what information needs to be conveyed and how this can best be done. Four facts lend support to the idea that the use of gesture helps people to shape their ideas and put these ideas into words. These are that: even people who have been blind since birth use gesture when talking to other blind people, so gesture does not always serve an overtly 'communicative function' (Iverson and Goldin-Meadow, 2001); people who have lost the ability to use gesture instrumentally to explain physical processes and shapes still make use of meaningful gesture when speaking (McNeill, 2005); people with 'phantom limbs' (that is to say people who have no arms but feel the presence of arms all the same) claim that the phantom arms gesture spontaneously when they speak (Ramachandran Blakeslee and Shah, 1998); and people start to gesture before they speak, particularly when the information they are conveying is conceptually challenging (Kita et al., 2017). The intricate relationship among gesture, thought and language is also manifested in studies of the use of gesture by children. These studies have shown that in children speech and gesture only begin to synchronise with each other towards the end of the single-word period when children are beginning to speak in phrases. The use of gesture thus appears to accompany a child's awareness of constructions (Tomasello, 2003). This is an important finding, as it suggests that we use gesture to help us package our thought processes into grammatically formed constructions. It thus provides strong evidence for a link between gesture and grammar. Gesture also plays a crucial role in interaction, as it is above all a collaborative action. As Gallagher (2008: 449) puts it, when people interact with each other, '[their] actions and reactions help to constitute that meaning'. As we will see later, embodied metaphorical meaning is often co-constructed in gesture.

A third view of the relationship between gesture and thought is Hostetter and Alibali's (2008) 'Gestures as Simulated Acton' framework, which was discussed in Chapter 1. This framework is particularly useful here, as it has embodied cognition at its core, claiming to offer an account of 'how gestures make embodiment visible' (Hostetter and Alibali, 2008: 511). The framework sees gestures as relying on visuo-spatial images, views gesture and speech as a single system and views gestures as stemming from imagistic representations that have close ties to action. Of most relevance to this volume is Hostetter and Alibali's contention that their framework applies to the formulation and expression of metaphorical concepts as well as literal ones, as metaphoric gestures arise from perceptual or motor simulations of the spatial images on which those metaphors are based.

There is abundant evidence for the presence of primary metaphor in published gesture studies, with gestures being used to represent primary metaphors such as: KNOWING IS SEEING, CHANGE IS MOTION, ORGANIZATION IS PHYSICAL STRUCTURE, ANALYSING IS CUTTING and EMOTIONAL INTIMACY IS PROXIMITY (see for instance, the edited collection by Cienki and Müller, 2008). For example, in their study of the use of gesture in the US TV News Archive, Winter et al. (2014) found that newsreaders and the people they interviewed consistently employed high gestures to indicate higher numbers. They also found that a precision grip often accompanied the term 'tiny numbers', whilst more open hand gestures were used to accompany the term 'huge numbers'. In her study of a series of television interviews with the French Prime Minister Lionel Jospin, Calbris (2008) found extensive gestural evidence to suggest that speakers were using the transverse axis to measure value (dis-preferred entities were to the left and preferred entities were to the right), quantity (lower numbers were to the left and higher numbers were to the right), time (past events were to the left and future events were to the right) and cause-effect relationships (causes were to the left and effects were to the right). There is now an extensive body of literature on these 'metaphoric' gestures which convey physical representations of abstract concepts (Andric and Small, 2012). During the processing of these gestures, the brain recruits regions that are similar to those involved in the processing of language (Willems and Hagoort, 2007).

In our own data (Littlemore and Kwong in prep.), we have found evidence of people using gesture to illustrate what others might see as highly conventional, but ultimately highly embodied metaphors. We can see this in the following two examples, where the speaker is describing her relationship with family members, which formed part of a wider discussion of the relative roles of men and women in society. She uses gesture to accompany the phrasal verbs

*I have to spend more time with her, doing things, sorting things, **sorting out** money, sorting out stuff, all kinds of things, so that's my time.*
Left hand: curled palm moving out from the center towards the periphery in an arc

Figure 2.1 'Sorting out'

*I started working part time when my family were young, you know, just **fit in** with them.*
Left hand: open hand palm up horizontal, moving towards the center in an arc, with hand rotation

Figure 2.2 'Fit in'

'sort out' and 'fit in'. Many people might describe these as 'dead' metaphors; however, in both cases, the use of gesture brings the embodied origin of the metaphors to the fore (Figures 2.1 and 2.2).

Although the same metaphor is often expressed in speech and gesture, Cienki (2008) cites instances where a metaphor may be expressed in gesture, but not in the corresponding speech, and cases where different yet complementary metaphors are expressed in speech and gesture, both of which relate to the same target domain. For example, he (Cienki, 2008: 13) reports a case where the speaker is talking about truth while making a small chopping gesture in the air with his left hand flat in the vertical plane. Cienki argues that this gesture corresponds to the primary metaphor in which truth is characterised as being 'straight'. In another example (Cienki, 2008: 14), he cites a speaker who describes honesty as being clearly demarcated as 'black or white'. Whilst uttering these words, she makes a chopping gesture as if dividing space.

what kind of training	Hands wriggle upwards
what kind of education	(body wriggling slightly too)
what kind of degrees do people want	
and then you kind of **adjust yourself**	
to produce that sort of product or service	

Figure 2.3 'Adjust yourself'

He argues that this gesture reflects the distinction between the moral categories of right and wrong as if it were a clear distinction separating two distinct spaces.

As well as providing insights into the way people use metaphor to conceptualise abstract concepts, gesture can also shed light on the role of metaphor as a dynamic activity, heavily involved in the process of formulating thoughts. Cienki and Müller (2008b) argue that gesture can provide evidence for the embodied basis of thought, which as we saw previously, suggests that many of our abstract thought processes have their basis in everyday bodily functions and movements (Gibbs, 2006a, b). Metaphorical gestures can involve other parts of the body besides the hands, as we can see in Figure 2.3, which is taken from the exchange referred to in Chapter 1, where a specialist in business management was explaining to a novice how various organisational management models work.

In this example, the speaker is using a personification metaphor to talk about companies as individuals who need to adapt to change. The inclusive 'you' in this extract refers to organisations and those who work for them. She evokes the primary metaphor CHANGE IS MOTION, and illustrates it through her use of gesture. She uses not only her hands but her whole torso to represent this metaphor, by wriggling it to represent the idea of 'adjustment'. For these few seconds, her body becomes a metaphorical representation of the behaviour of the organisation. This is an example of what Müller (2008a) might describe as 'strongly activated metaphoricity' (see Chapter 1).

There are a number of studies showing how changes in the use of gesture, either by the experimenter or by the participant, can actually change the way in which people conceptualise abstract ideas through metaphor. A good example of a study involving gestural manipulation by the experimenter is provided by

Jamalian and Tversky (2012). They conducted four studies, each of which tested the impact of gesture observance on metaphorical reasoning about abstract concepts. In the first study, three groups of participants were informed about a cycle of four events. When the experimenter explained the cycle to the first group of participants, they made four discrete slicing gestures from right to left. When they explained it to the second group, they made four pointing gestures at 12, 9, 6 and 3 o'clock. When they explained it to the third group, they employed no gesture. They then asked the participants to draw the cycle. Those who had seen the discrete slicing gestures were more likely to draw the events in a straight line, whereas those who had seen the cyclical gesture were more likely to draw the events in a circle. In their second study, they repeated this procedure leaving out the 'no gesture' condition. The participants were then asked to say what comes after the last step. Those who had seen the cyclical gesture were significantly more likely to respond with the first step of the procedure than those who had seen the linear gesture, which provides further evidence of the impact of the gestural metaphor on their thinking processes.

In their third study, Jamalian and Tversky added a gesture component to Boroditsky et al.'s (2002) aforementioned study on 'moving time' versus 'moving ego'. Jamalian and Tversky had two conditions. In the first condition, the experimenter made a slice in space in front of her body and then moved her hand forwards, away from her body. In the second condition, after having made the slice in space, she moved her hand backwards towards her body. The majority of the participants who had seen the 'forwards' gesture answered that the meeting had been moved to Friday, whilst the majority of participants who had seen the 'backwards' gesture answered that the meeting had been moved to Monday. In their fourth study, participants were asked to listen to a speaker explaining four stages of the process of essay-writing. Again, there were two conditions. In the first condition, when the participants heard about the second and third stages of the process, the experimenter's gesture suggested that the two stages took place at the same time, whereas in the second condition, the gestures implied that they were sequential. The participants were then asked what happened in these subsequent stages. Those in the first condition reported two actions, whilst those in the second condition reported just one, a finding which shows how gesture can help shape the concrete structures that people use to metaphorically represent an abstract process. Changing the metaphorical structure of a process fundamentally alters the way in which we conceive of that process.

In a similar vein, Ibáñez et al. (2011) found that participants are sensitive to the use of metaphorical gestures by their interlocutor, and use them to help them determine the meanings of their interlocutors' utterances. They played four types of video clips, which contained either a literal or metaphorical expression accompanied by either a congruent or an incongruent gesture. Participants were instructed to classify the gesture accompanying the expression as congruent or incongruent by pressing two different keys. Whilst they were performing the task, participants had their brain activity recorded via an electroencephalogram (EEG). This procedure involves attaching small sensors to the scalp in order to pick up the electrical signals that are produced when the brain cells send messages to one another. It is particularly useful in detecting responses to stimuli that are perceived to be semantically anomalous. Such stimuli disrupt the neurological processing. They found that incongruent metaphorical gestures were significantly more disruptive than incongruent literal gestures, which suggests that metaphorical gestures play a more fundamental role than literal gestures in conveying meaning. Gesture therefore appears to be a rich source of evidence for embodied metaphor.

'Spoken' Gestural Studies

Perlman and Gibbs (2013) extend the idea of metaphorical iconicity in gesture to the realm of 'spoken' gesture, a term that they employ to refer to a phenomenon whereby spoken words and phrases take on prosodic patterns that reflect aspects of their semantic meaning. Some of these relationships involve metaphor. For example, they cite a study by Ohala (1994) in which it was observed that high frequency vocalisations are often used to refer to smallness and by extension to non-threatening, submissive and subordinate attitudes, whereas low frequency vocalisations are often used to denote largeness, and by extension threat, dominance and self-confidence. They also cite a study by Shintel et al. (2006) which found that when people talked about objects moving up, they used rising intonation and when they talked about objects moving down, they used falling intonation. Perlman and Gibbs argue that these correspondences result from sensorimotor simulations and, like Hostetter and Alibali (2008), suggest that there are certain sets of circumstances that lead to an intensification of this kind of behaviour. Perlman is currently conducting investigations into the proposed co-occurrence of increased vocal gesture and increased manual gesture. Their work builds on Hostetter and Alibali's work, as it emphasises the importance to perceptual imagery and the emotional aspects of embodied cognition.

2.5   Variation in Embodied Metaphor

In this chapter we have seen that there is abundant support for embodied metaphor from a wide variety of sources. However, one issue with much of the embodied metaphor work to date is that it takes a somewhat normative approach to human behaviour and cognition, emphasising homogeneity over heterogeneity. This approach is clear in the following extract from Lakoff and Johnson's (1999) book *Philosophy in the Flesh: The Embodied Mind and Its Challenge to Western Thought*:

If you are a *normal* human being, you inevitably acquire an enormous range of primary metaphors just by going about the world constantly moving and perceiving. (Lakoff and Johnson, 1999: 57)

Their focus on homogeneity is also present in their earlier book, *Metaphors We Live By*, which contains references to the '*prototypical* person' (p. 132), the '*normal* conceptual system' (p. 115) and '*natural* kinds of experience' (p. 117). Lakoff and Johnson (1980) are careful to acknowledge the role played by cultural values in shaping the way in which people experience the world through metaphor, but there are many other possible sources of variation that they do not consider. One might, for example, question who these 'normal', 'prototypical' people actually are. In Western society, the word 'prototypical' when applied to humans tends to refer to adult, white, male, middle-class, right-handed individuals who do not experience any kind of physical or mental disability, are of unexceptional height and weight, and who are heterosexual. It is important to consider how embodied metaphors are experienced by people who do not fit this profile because by doing so, we will gain a deeper understanding of the different ways in which people perceive the world and, more importantly, the reasons for these different world views and the mechanisms through which they develop. Such an investigation would also reveal more about the nature of embodied metaphor itself and go some way to addressing current controversies in the metaphor literature concerning the extent to which metaphors are experienced, as opposed to being simply encountered (Gibbs, 2017). The aim of this book is therefore to explore the extent to which people's experiences of embodied metaphor vary across different contexts of use and according to people's own individual characteristics. Let us now consider some of these potential sources of variation.

People with **different bodies**, which do not correspond to the so-called norm, may experience embodied metaphor in very different ways. For example, left-handed individuals may not share the GOOD IS RIGHT/LEFT IS BAD metaphor to quite the same extent as right-handed individuals (Casasanto, 2014). Other sources of variation, such as height, weight, physical and mental disability also need to be considered if we are to gain a fuller understanding of the nature of embodied metaphor. The body itself is constantly constructed and reconstructed on the basis of social and cultural assumptions about class, gender, sex, race, ethnicity, age, health and beauty (Weiss, 1999) and **people's perceptions of their own bodies** may lead them to use information about their bodies differently when processing abstract content.

In recent years, some scholars have begun to focus attention on differences in the way people make metaphorical use of their bodies to understand their emotions and their abstract thoughts. The bulk of this work has been conducted in **cross-cultural variation**, where differences have been found in the ways in which people employ embodied metaphors to reason about time, magnitude and emotion, amongst other things (e.g., Gibbs, 2006a; Johnson, 2007; Kövecses, 2005; Maalej, 2004; Maalej and Yu, 2011).

The way in which metaphor relates to bodily experience is also likely to be shaped by the **immediate context** in which they find themselves. As Gibbs (2015: 171) observes, 'people in different geographical and social contexts are attuned to different aspects of their body experience, which partially motivates differences in the ways in which people express themselves metaphorically'.

In recent years there has been increased recognition of the need to integrate embodied approaches to metaphor with more **situated and interactive** approaches to communication that entail a recognition of the importance of factors such as the ability to read and predict communicative intent, and variation according to genre and register (Gibbs, 2017; Jensen and Cuffari, 2014). In Gibbs' words:

metaphors are 'soft assembled' spontaneously given the present state of the system, the wider context, and the task at hand. (Gibbs, 2013: 30)

There is also a **temporal dimension** to embodied metaphor which has been insufficiently emphasised. Much of the work on embodied metaphor to date has taken a somewhat deterministic view of culture and society, and has not taken account of the ways in which our experiences change over time. The underlying supposition appears to be that we experience our physicality in a way that is stable, straightforward and permanently fixed in early childhood. Embodied metaphor is by no means stable, straightforward or permanently fixed in early childhood. It is more appropriately viewed as a highly complex, dynamic and developmental process, whose nature varies according to the specific situations in which we find ourselves, and the extent to which we are consciously aware of our bodies at any given moment. The nature of our embodied cognition is also likely to develop as we grow older. The **dynamic/ developmental** view of embodied metaphor therefore encapsulates its characteristics as both a developmental and an adaptive process. When studying embodied metaphor, we need to consider how it changes over time and in accordance with changing circumstances. By doing this, we can begin to gain an insight into the ways in which embodied metaphors are experienced in the real world, outside the laboratory.

Embodied metaphor is thus more appropriately conceptualised as a highly complex, ever-shifting process, which involves not only our social and cultural background but also the specific situations in which we found ourselves, including the extent to which we are consciously aware of our bodies at any given moment. In any study of the way embodied metaphor impacts on the way we think and use language, we need to consider how it changes over time and in accordance with changing personal circumstances. In addition to looking at how embodied metaphor varies within and across different contexts of use, it is important to explore how it varies from individual to individual. These are the aims of this book.

2.6   Outline of the Rest of the Book

The remaining chapters of this book explore the ways in which people's experiences of embodied metaphor vary between different individuals and different contexts of use, according to factors such as the characteristics of the body that they inhabit, the ways in which they view their bodies, their position in society, the personal experiences that they undergo, their states of mind and the languages that they speak. In each chapter, I take one overarching source of variation and explore how it shapes (or has the potential to shape) the ways in which people experience the world through embodied metaphor, and the intensity of their embodied experiences. I combine analyses of the work that has been conducted with reports of findings from studies that I have conducted both alone and with colleagues.

Not all metaphors that refer to the human body will be experienced as 'embodied' all of the time. Before embarking on an investigation into individual differences in the experience of embodied metaphor, it is important to consider intrinsic features of the metaphors themselves that render them more likely to be experienced in an embodied way and to look at contextual factors that influence the degree of potential embodiment. Chapter 3 therefore focuses on intrinsic features and contextual factors that are likely to shape the degree to which a metaphor is experienced on a physical level. The intrinsic features are the degree of novelty of the metaphor, the amount of emotion that is involved, the extent to which the metaphor describes motion and the perspective from which it is viewed. I show how these factors have been found to shape the extent to which the motor cortex and the emotional centres of the brain are stimulated. The contextual factors include the physical environment and the genre and register in which the metaphor is used.

In order to fully understand how embodied metaphor works, it is important to examine how it develops in infancy and at how it changes over the course of a lifetime. Age is therefore a critical factor when looking at variation in the experience of metaphor. Chapter 4 therefore takes a more developmental perspective. I begin by looking at how embodied metaphors develop in infants and at how the ways in which they are experienced by infants and children differ from the ways in which they are experienced by adults. I then explore the ways in which they are experienced by older adults. I include some of my own work that has looked at how young children (aged 5–8) make use of embodied metaphor to reason about mathematics and music, and how their embodied metaphorical reasoning behaviour differs from that of adults.

In Chapter 5, I continue to challenge the homogeneity of embodied metaphor by looking at the ways in which having a different kind of body can shape the way in which one uses embodied metaphor. The focus is not only on physical differences but on how those physical differences are viewed by society. The main areas of focus in this chapter are body size and shape, handedness and gender. Gender is particularly important, as many of the embodied metaphors that frame our thinking are based on male experiences, which means that women may find themselves living by men's metaphors. In this chapter, I introduce some of my own work on the ways in which one's own gender and/or one's perceptions of gender roles shape the use of embodied metaphor.

Chapter 6 focuses on people's experiences of sensory metaphor, which is a particularly strong form of embodied metaphor. I begin by looking at how sensory impairments affect the ways in which people employ the senses in metaphorical ways, considering for example, how blind people make use of UNDERSTANDING IS SEEING metaphors and how deaf people make use of HEEDING IS HEARING metaphors. I also look at the cross-sensory metaphorical affordances that are offered by sign languages. I then discuss the condition of synaesthesia, which involves the generation of novel cross-sensory associations, and present findings from my own work that has investigated the unique ways in which synaesthetes experience cross-sensory metaphor.

Chapter 7 looks at the distinctive ways in which people whose states of minds have been altered by traumatic events and psychological disorders make use of embodied metaphor. The experience of a traumatic event can re-shape the way in which one views the world, and one way in which it can do this is through metaphor. In the first part of the chapter I look at how stress, anxiety and depression affect the ways in which people experience and interact with embodied metaphor, and introduce some of my own work that has explored how people's experience of embodied metaphor is shaped by the experience of pregnancy loss. In the second part of the chapter, I focus on psychological conditions, including autistic spectrum disorders, Asperger syndrome and schizophrenia, introducing some of my own work looking at the ways in which individuals with schizophrenia employ embodied metaphor. I draw parallels between these different states of mind and conditions and identify common traits in terms of how they impact on the types of metaphors that people employ and the ways in which they employ them.

Individual differences in personality, cognitive style and political and religious viewpoint have the potential to alter not only the embodied metaphors that people employ but also the ways in which they process these metaphors. Chapter 8 focuses on individual differences in personality, cognitive style, political stance and religious beliefs, and looks at how they shape the ways in which people engage with embodied metaphor. The first half of the chapter focuses on individual or 'internal' traits that are captured under the umbrella terms, cognitive style and personality. The second part of the chapter focuses on more social or 'group-based' sources of variation, namely political and religious beliefs. In both cases, I show how individual differences shape not only the metaphors that people use but also the ways in which they use them. I explore the markedly different ways in which people experience the world through metaphor, depending on their thinking styles and belief systems.

Language and culture have been shown to have a significant impact on the ways in which people interact with embodied metaphor, which again challenges its universality. Chapter 9 focuses on cross-linguistic and cross-cultural variation in embodied metaphor. I begin by looking at how embodied metaphors are experienced differently by people who speak different languages. I then move on to discuss whether, and if so how, speaking a second language affects the way in which one experiences embodied metaphor in that language. In the context of this debate, I discuss my own work on the use of gesture by second language speakers and the ways in which word–colour relationships work in different languages. Through this work, I explore the fundamental issue of whether the strength to which a metaphorical relationship is embodied predicts the likelihood that it will be universal.

Finally, in Chapter 10, I sum up the main findings from the book, draw together the threads that run through the various chapters book and present a set of conclusions outlining what this analysis of variation has told us about the nature of embodied metaphor. In this chapter, and indeed throughout the book, I discuss the societal implications of variation in the experience of embodied metaphor.

3 'I'm Running on This Soapy Conveyor Belt with People Throwing Wet Sponges at Me.'
Which Metaphors Are Embodied and When?
Variation According to Type, Function and Context

3.1   Introduction

So far, we have seen that there is a wealth of evidence from a range of sources showing that metaphor can be experienced as an embodied phenomenon. However, the main aim of this book is to challenge the homogeneity that is inherent in much of the work on embodied metaphor and to explore the ways in which people's experiences of embodied metaphor vary according to factors such as their age, the nature of the body that they inhabit, their gender, the society in which they live and the languages that we speak. By doing so, I hope to develop a richer understanding of the nature of embodied metaphor.

Before embarking on an investigation into individual differences in the experience of embodied metaphor, it is important to consider intrinsic features of the metaphors themselves that render them more likely to be experienced in an embodied way and to look at contextual factors that influence the degree of potential embodiment. Some metaphors are more likely than others to be experienced in an embodied way and there are likely to be contexts which are more likely than others to give rise to such metaphors (Bergen, 2015; Kövecses, 2015). The potential for embodiment is also likely to fluctuate over time, even within an individual communicative event. Moreover, the extent to which the source domain of a primary or conceptual metaphor is activated at any point in time is likely to be due to the complex interplay between different factors, which may include: cultural models, language evolution, levels of entrenchment, the presence of conventional expressions in the language, the speaker's knowledge of real-world concepts and word meaning and the communicative setting (Gibbs, 2011).

In this chapter, I focus on the metaphors themselves and the contexts (and co-texts) within which they are used. I ask whether there are some types of metaphor that are more likely than others to evoke sensorimotor responses (i.e., to be embodied in the physical sense) than others, whether there are certain contexts in which these embodied metaphors are particularly likely to be employed, and whether there are certain conditions that provide fertile ground for the production of creative embodied metaphor. I look at variation according to the type of metaphor, the function that it performs and the context in which it appears. I take as my model work that has been done in gesture studies, and apply it to embodied metaphor. We have already seen that according to Hostetter and Alibali's (2008) 'Gesture as Simulated Action' framework, a number of factors are likely to influence the amount of gesture that is produced to accompany any given utterance. These include: the extent to which the message to be conveyed involves action; the perspective of the narrator; aspects of the communicative setting, such as the speaker's perception of their interlocutor's understanding; the nature of the material being discussed; and the speaker's attitude towards that material, with more gestures tending to accompany material that is perceived to be particularly newsworthy or crucial to the ongoing conversation. Hostetter and Alibali refer to this last feature as *communicative dynamism*. In this chapter, I build on their ideas by discussing factors that are likely to affect the extent to which sensorimotor imagery is evoked by metaphor more generally (not just expressed through gesture) and use findings from the literature to extend the range of factors beyond this list.

In addition to focusing on features of the metaphors themselves, it is also important to consider the contexts in which they occur. Consider, for example, the following extract from an interview with a British Civil Servant who is describing his workplace. This extract is analysed in depth by Littlemore, Turner, Tuck and Cassell (in prep.) in our discussion of the use of metaphor in a series of interviews with British Civil Servants[1]:

I mean, I've described my role here as a bit like an It's a Knockout game. Over here I'm sort of running towards setting the future in the finance function, big change initiatives where finance can really make a difference, but I'm sort of running on this soapy conveyor belt with people throwing wet sponges at me and I've got this sodding great elastic band attached to my back.

This speaker is employing a highly creative, striking, embodied metaphor to express dissatisfaction with his role in the organisation. The metaphor is based on the 1970s television programme *It's a Knockout*, which featured teams who competed in a series of absurd, undignified and humiliating challenges, often dressed in large foam rubber suits. During these challenges (which were often impossible to complete), contestants would sometimes have soft projectiles and water thrown at them. By alluding to this programme, the speaker manages to convey a number of negative evaluations of his current position, namely that he finds the day-to-day challenge virtually impossible, that all sorts of impediments are thrown in his way, that he feels frustrated and that he is deliberately being set up to fail and to look ridiculous. The fact that the speaker uses such a creative, bodily based metaphor is likely to have been influenced by the communicative purpose and the tenor of the exchange. He was being asked to evaluate his workplace in a confidential 1-1 conversation, and we can assume that he talked so openly because he felt comfortable with his inter-locutor. They are not the sort of words that would be uttered in a more formal setting.

In the first part of this chapter, I consider a number of features that are intrinsic to the metaphors themselves as well as co-textual features that may make them particularly likely to evoke sensorimotor responses. I focus on five features in particular: novelty, emotional expression, the role of motion, perspective and signalling (or foregrounding). In the second part of the chapter, I take a more contextualised view and consider the communicative context in which the metaphors are employed. The approach that I employ is dialogistic in that it not only takes account of the interactions between interlocutors but also considers the dynamics of the communicative setting within which the interaction is taking place (Linell, 1998), I thus explore the ways in which the likelihood of an embodied metaphor being used is affected by genre (Swales, 1990) and register (Halliday, 1978; Halliday, Hasan and Hasan, 1985; see also Deignan, Littlemore and Semino, 2013).

3.2   Intrinsic and Co-Textual Features That Render Metaphors More Likely to Evoke Sensorimotor Activation

As we have just seen, there are some intrinsic and co-textual features of the metaphors themselves that render them particularly likely to evoke sensorimotor activation. These are novelty, the presence of emotion, the presence of movement, first person perspective and overt signalling. These factors are not always taken into account in laboratory-based studies of embodied metaphor, but they should be, as they are important. Here I look at each feature in turn.

Novelty

There is evidence to suggest that novelty is a key factor in determining the extent to which a metaphor is experienced as 'embodied' at a neurological level. Findings from neuroimaging studies have shown that there is a relationship between metaphor novelty and sensorimotor activation. These studies have found evidence for the recruitment of sensorimotor representations in response to primary metaphors (Boulenger, Hauk and PulverMüller, 2009), and the engagement with these regions has been found to increase with the novelty of the linguistic metaphor that is used to evoke them (Desai et al., 2011). Thus the engagement of motor regions appears to be inversely correlated with metaphor familiarity; the more familiar the metaphor, the less likely the access to embodied representations. Many of these studies are framed around the 'career of metaphor' hypothesis (Bowdle and Gentner, 2005).

According to this hypothesis, as people are exposed to metaphors, the metaphors gradually become less novel and more conventional and are processed in a different way. More conventional metaphors are likely to be understood more directly with less recourse to overtly 'figurative' processing.

One such study is Cardillo et al.'s (2012) investigation, which uses fMRI data to investigate whether there is a qualitative shift in cognitive processing as metaphors become more conventional. They developed a long list of novel metaphors, and normed them extensively. They then simulated the gradual experience of metaphor conventionalisation over time by exposing the participants repeatedly to the different metaphors. They found that as the metaphors became more familiar, four areas that had been involved in the processing of the novel metaphors were increasingly less used. The first of these was the inferior frontal gyrus (in both hemispheres). This region is involved in tasks that require one to choose between two competing semantic representations. The finding that its involvement in metaphor comprehension declines with familiarity is in line with the career of metaphor hypothesis, as it suggests (unsurprisingly) that when one is familiar with a particular metaphor one can extract its meaning straight away. The second region that exhibited a decline in activation as the metaphors became more familiar was the right pre-frontal cortex. This area plays a supportive role when cognitive demands on the left-lateralised language system are too high. It is therefore unsurprising that as the metaphors become more familiar and fewer processing demands are placed on the linguistic system, the area exhibits reduced levels of activation.

Crucially, the third region to show declining levels of activation as the metaphors became more familiar was the postero-lateral temporal cortex, an area which is activated by tasks that involve the processing of action pictures and videos or the words that are used to describe them. This was true for both metaphors involving action verbs (e.g., to slump) and metaphors that are based on the metaphoric extension of nominalised action verbs (e.g., a slump), a finding which can be attributed to the fact that both types of metaphor entail abstract senses of action events. Cardillo et al. argue that the proximity of this area to motion-sensitive parts of the brain indicates a close relationship between the neural substrates for motor perception and the words that are used to describe motion events. This makes the finding that this area was activated for novel metaphor significant, as it suggests that novel metaphor is more embodied than conventional metaphor. The fourth area whose activation decreased with familiarity was the right postero-lateral occipital cortex, which is generally associated with the processing of visual forms. Thus, as metaphors become more familiar, there is less of a need to access concrete sensory details referring to the visual details of the word's referent. It is these last two areas that are most relevant to the issue of embodiment. Taken together, the findings with respect to these two regions suggest that as metaphors become more familiar there is less of a tendency among listeners to activate their real-world referents, or to enact a motoric response, which suggests that the responses are less embodied on a neurological level.

A similar result was found by Cacciari et al. (2011), although the methods they used in their analysis were somewhat different, and their focus was on the semantics of different types of figurative sentences rather than on conventionality per se. They employed Transcranial Magnetic Stimulation (TMS) (a neurological research method that measures motor responses in the brain) to investigate whether the reading of literal, fictive-motion, metaphorical and idiomatic sentences modulates activity in the motor system. The aim of their study was to investigate whether the degree of metaphoricity/conventionality influences the degree to which motoric responses are activated. They found activation in the motor system for the literal, fictive motion and metaphorical sentences but not for the idioms. They attributed this finding to the fact that in literal, fictive motion and metaphorical sentences, the semantic motion of the verb is maintained, whereas it is not in idiomatic sentences. In other words, in literal sentences motion verbs convey actual movement, in fictive motion sentences the reader mentally scans the described space and in metaphorical sentences the motion is retained albeit at a more abstract level. In contrast, in idioms, the meaning often has little to do with the original motion sense of the verb. They concluded that 'the excitability of the motor system is modulated by the motor component of the verb, which is preserved in fictive and metaphorical motion sentences' (Cacciari et al., 2011: 149).

We can therefore conclude from these studies that novel metaphors are more likely than conventional metaphors to evoke embodied simulation. These findings are important with respect to the overall argument presented in this book, as the cline from novelty to familiarity is likely to interact with other individual differences that affect metaphoric processing.

Emotion

A second important factor which has the potential to impact upon the extent to which metaphors evoke sensorimotor responses is the level of emotion that is involved. It is well documented that when talking about emotional experiences, people employ more metaphor than when talking about less emotional experiences (Gibbs, 1994, 2002; Semino, 2011; Semino et al., 2018). Fainsilber and Ortony (1987) found that participants used significantly more metaphors for describing *how they felt* during a specific event than when describing *what they did* in the same circumstances. Moreover, people have been found to use significantly more metaphor when asked to describe emotionally intense events than mildly intense ones (Fainsilber and Ortony, 1987; Fussell and Moss, 1998). People use metaphor in particularly vivid ways when they want others to experience on a visceral level what they have experienced. Thagard and Shelley (2006) refer to these metaphors as 'hot' analogies. Hartman and Paradis (2018) suggest that metaphors such as these are more likely to be experienced by the hearer in a physical way than more objective, or 'cold' analogies. Finally, people have been found to produce more novel metaphors when writing about their own intense feelings than when writing about the feelings of others (Williams-Whitney, Mio and Whitney, 1992). It has been proposed that it is the first-hand experience of these intense emotions which provides the motivation for creative metaphor production (MacCormac, 1986).

There is also evidence to suggest that the processing of metaphor itself triggers emotion. In their wide-ranging review of brain-imaging evidence, Bohrn, Altman and Jacobs (2012) showed that the reading of metaphorical sentences leads to stronger activation of emotional centres in the brain than literal sentences. In order to test this link explicitly, Citron and Goldberg (2014a) had participants read sentences with metaphorical content (e.g., 'she looked at him sweetly') and their corresponding literal counterparts (e.g., 'she looked at him kindly'). For the metaphorical sentences, they found increased activation in the left amygdala, an area known for its role in processing emotions and emotional language. Left amygdala activation facilitates the successful encoding of emotional verbal material in the hippocampus (Phelps, 2004; Richardson, Strange and Dolan, 2004), and concurrent activation of these two regions has been associated with the successful retrieval of emotional memories (Dolcos, LaBar and Cabeza, 2005). All the stimuli used in Citron and Goldberg's study involved reference to one of the senses, which suggests that there may be a link between metaphor, emotion and sensory activation.

The idea that there is a link between emotion and sensory activation has already been proposed by Damasio (2006), in his discussion of anosognosia. This is a condition in which patients who are suffering from paralysis are unaware of the paralysis and, in some cases, even refuse to admit to the existence of any paralysis at all. This is because they have experienced damage to the somatosensory system, which the brain uses to create an integrated map of the current state of the body. Crucially, anosognosics are unable to make appropriate decisions on personal and social matters, which involve emotional reasoning. There is a complex of somatosensory cortices in the right hemisphere, whose damage compromises reasoning/decision making and emotion/feeling, and, in addition, disrupts the process of basic bodily signalling. One area of the brain that has a particular responsibility for these processes is the anterior cingulate cortex. This area is involved in movement, emotion and attention. Patients with lesions in this area tend to exhibit emotional problems and have problems with metaphor (Miall, 1987). There is thus a neurological link between physical movement and one's experiences of being emotionally 'moved'. Indeed the strong link between motion and emotion is the subject of extensive research, which will be discussed in detail in this chapter.

Another line of research that appears to suggest a symbiotic relationship between emotion and metaphor is the work on metaphor and empathy. In an intriguing study, Horton (2007) explored readers' sensitivity to the interpersonal function of metaphor use, by exposing them to brief stories describing interactions between two ambiguously related characters. In the course of these conversational narratives, one character always used either a metaphoric or literal referring expression to refer to some antecedent information from the story. Horton found that readers consistently judged these characters as knowing each other better when their interactions contained metaphoric references. Moreover, this occurred even when addressees failed to give explicit evidence of having understood the critical expressions. Bowes and Katz (2015) conducted a follow-up study in which they found that when participants had been exposed to exchanges involving metaphor, as opposed to literal language, they were significantly more likely to say that the interlocutors were close to, and emotionally intimate with, one another. In addition, they also found that participants who had been exposed to the metaphorical language performed better on a subsequent 'Reading the Mind in the Eyes Test' (RMET) (Baron-Cohen et al., 2001). This test consists of thirty-six black-and-white photographs of the eye region of thirty-six men and women. Participants are asked to choose from four mental state descriptions the one which best describes what the person in the picture is thinking or feeling. The test is thought to provide a behavioural measure of a person's ability to infer the internal mental state of a person from their facial expression. They conclude from their findings that metaphor plays a key role in orienting people to the mental states of others, making them more aware of the emotions that others are experiencing. Interestingly, performance on the RMET has been found to be positively related to levels of oxytocin, a neuropeptide that is associated with interpersonal closeness, affiliation and attachment (Domes et al., 2007). Emotion appears to be an important mediator in this process.

There is some evidence that emotional arousal during metaphor comprehension is affected by the novelty of the metaphor. Bohrn et al. (2012) showed twenty-six participants a series of familiar proverbs (e.g., Rome was not built in a day') alongside a series of proverbs that had been creatively adapted (e.g., 'Rome was not destroyed in a day'). They measured the fMRI responses of the participants to these proverbs and found that the creatively adapted idioms triggered activation of several areas of the brain that are associated with affective processing as well as the motor and pre-motor cortex. Although the adapted proverbs contained a novel element, they also displayed a sufficient degree of conventionality to render them meaningful and, as such, were 'optimally innovative' (Giora et al., 2004). These findings suggest that optimally innovative uses of figurative language trigger emotional, motoric responses in the brain, and are thus understood in an embodied way at a neurological level.

Tentative evidence to suggest that primary metaphors are more likely to evoke emotion than other types of metaphors comes from a recent study (Houghton and Littlemore, in prep.) in which we investigated the role played by figurative operations (metaphor, metonymy, hyperbole and irony) in promotional videos that appear online. We were interested in studying the relationship between the figurative operations that the videos contained, the reported emotional response that people had to the videos, and the likelihood with which people said they would go on to share the videos on social media. We found a statistically significant relationship between the amount of primary metaphor an advertisement contained and the likelihood that it would promote feelings of joy, happiness and sadness. We also found these emotional responses to be significant predictors of Facebook sharing. Interestingly, no such relationship was found for 'resemblance metaphors' that are based simply on perceptual similarities. This finding suggests that primary metaphor resonates with humans on a more fundamental level than resemblance metaphor because it reflects basic embodied human experience. Our findings suggest that it is the emotional responses that people experience when they interact with primary metaphors (rather than the metaphors themselves) that result in these metaphors being shared and distributed across society as a whole. This helps to explain why primary metaphors are so widespread across cultures.

The role of emotion is an important factor to consider in any discussion of the ways in which the experience of embodied metaphor varies across individuals. There are several ways in which metaphor, sensorimotor activation and emotion might interact, each of which would lead to different patterns of variation. One possibility is that, by virtue of their being processed in the same part of the brain, sensorimotor activation always triggers emotion and vice versa. The implication of this would be that all embodied primary metaphors evoke an emotional response. A second possibility is that emotional pleasure is derived from the act of reconciling the two domains of experience, in which case, we would expect more emotional involvement in the processing of novel metaphors. A third possibility is that the emotional response may arise from the fact that greater processing effort is required for novel metaphor. It has been shown that when a reader or listener has to draw the conclusion for themselves, this leads to an increased sense of ownership of the message (Stayman and Kardes, 1992). This preference for things associated with oneself is known as the 'instant endowment effect' (Kahneman et al., 1991). A fourth possibility is that it is the subject matter of the metaphor itself that triggers emotional response. There is some evidence to suggest that sensorimotor simulation is stronger for metaphors involving emotion. In their study of affective and psycholinguistic norms for 619 German idiomatic expressions, Citron et al. (2015) found that arousal ratings correlated significantly with metaphoricity ratings, which suggests that metaphorical expressions are more emotionally engaging than literal expressions. They also found that arousal correlated positively with concreteness, which was measured by participants' indications of the extent to which the metaphorical meaning could be experienced through one or more of the senses. This finding suggests that more concrete metaphorical idioms trigger stronger sensory representations and that this provokes a stronger emotional response.

Another important source of variation in neurological arousal is the emotional context within which the metaphor occurs. Samur et al. (2015) investigated whether in a more emotionally charged environment metaphors containing motion-related verbs would be more likely to trigger a sensorimotor response than their literal equivalents. Participants in their study were asked to read stories that ended with ambiguous action/motion sentences (e.g., he got it), in which the action/motion could be interpreted metaphorically (he understood the idea) or literally (he caught the ball) depending on the preceding story. The stories were either high or low in terms of emotional content. The results showed that metaphors presented in emotional contexts were more likely than metaphors presented in non-emotional contexts to trigger a neural response in the visual motion areas of the brains. This difference was not found for the literal sentences. These findings suggest that the emotional context leads to a more concrete, more embodied representation of the metaphorical motion. They took their findings as evidence of an 'emotional boost' in the embodiment of metaphorical language (Samur et al., 2015: 109), by which they mean that sensorimotor cortex activation in response to motion-based metaphors is enhanced by emotional contexts.

The degree of emotional engagement may also affect the extent to which metaphor is embodied in gesture. Individuals have been shown to use both more metaphors and more gestures when they are emotionally involved with the subject matter, with basic emotions such as happiness and sadness being more metaphorically productive than so-called higher level emotions such as pride and anger (Fussell and Moss, 1998; Pollick et al., 2001). Further evidence highlighting the multimodal nature of the interaction among emotion, embodiment and metaphor is provided by Horstmann and Ansorge (2011), who found compatibility between tones, head movements and facial expressions. They found that happiness expressions and upwards head tilts were imitated significantly faster when paired with high rather than low tones, while anger expressions and downwards head tilts were imitated significantly faster when paired with low rather than high tones. In a similar vein, Crawford (2009) conducted an extensive review of the literature on conceptual metaphors of affect. She concluded from this review that in line with theories of embodied metaphor, the associations between affect and physical domains such as spatial position, musical pitch, brightness and size which one can find in linguistic metaphors also influence performance on experimental attention, memory and judgement tasks.

A final consideration is the valence of the emotion that is expressed. Studies have identified a human bias to give greater weight to negative entities (Rozin and Royzman, 2001), with people paying more attention to and remembering negative entities and events than positive entities and events. It has also been suggested that metaphors are often used to express and mitigate negative evaluation (Cameron, 2003), although this proposal has not been tested empirically. This leads to the hypothesis that metaphors that are used to express negative emotions may be more likely than those that are used to express positive emotions to evoke sensorimotor imagery. This would be worth exploring in future work.

To sum up, the amount of emotion appears to have a direct effect on the extent to which metaphors are experienced as embodied at a neurological level, with more emotional contexts leading to more embodied metaphor. This is important, as it provides further support for the idea that metaphor is something that is actively experienced and engaged with on an emotional level. It is a 'lived experience', rather than being simply encountered.

Motion

The presence of motion in the source or target domain is also likely to make a metaphor more likely to be experienced on an embodied level. Indirect evidence for this contention can be found in gesture studies. For example, metaphors involving verbs, which imply movement, have been found to attract more gesture than metaphors involving adjectives, which imply an absence of movement (Woodin et al., forthcoming). We constructed a large corpus taken from the TV News Archive and used it to compare the use of gestures accompanying metaphors involving the vertical orientation that were expressed either in the verbal form ('raising and lowering standards') or in the adjectival form ('high and low standards'). We found that the verbal formulation attracted more gestures than the adjectival formulation. This finding suggests that formulations involving movement appear to trigger more 'activated metaphoricity' (Müller, 2008a) than static formulations.

Similar findings have also been made with respect to the metaphorical relationship between time and space, with particular reference to aspect. It has been shown that the spatial responses speakers have to sentences presented in the progressive aspect differ from those that they have when presented with sentences in the simple past. Huette et al. (2014) found that participants who heard past progressive sentences describing an image presented on a computer screen moved their eyes round the screen significantly more than participants who heard simple past sentences, who fixated on a single spot. Past progressive verbs thus appear to shift attention to the ongoing nature of the movement of the verb. Anderson et al. (2010) found that participants listening to a sentence in the progressive aspect moved a computer mouse more slowly along the path as they simulated the motion details associated with the ongoing action. These studies provide support for the idea that the progressive aspect focuses listeners' attention on details of the activity itself rather than on its end point, a proposition that is also supported by the finding that participants are able to answer more questions about the details of an event when it has been reported in the progressive aspect than they are when the event has been presented in the simple past. Embodied simulation of an action is therefore likely to be stronger when it is expressed through the progressive aspect.

We saw in the previous section a brief allusion to the idea that motion and emotion are closely related, as their etymology suggests, and that the neurological substrates involved in the processing of movement are also recruited in the understanding of emotion. Emotions are expressed through movement (Wallbott, 1998) and increases in movement can lead to increases in emotion (Zlatev, 2012). The relationship between the two has been studied at length and is the subject of two edited volumes (Bråten, 2007; Foolen et al., 2012). The contributors to these volumes emphasise the ways in which movement and the expression of emotion work together to help develop empathy and intersubjectivity in infants and adults. The so-called higher emotions, such as love, guilt, pride, shame, embarrassment and envy, are, by definition, interpersonal experiences. The *expression* of more basic emotions, such as joy/pleasure, distress, anger, disgust, fear and surprise (Ekman, 1992) is also a primarily social activity and, as such, plays an important role in the development of empathy. In recent years, our understanding of the relationship between movement and emotion and the role that they play in the sharing of experience has been enhanced by work on 'mirror neurons'. This work has shown that when we perceive others engaged in a particular action, we experience the activation of neural networks that would be involved if we were to act out those movements ourselves (Gallese, 2001). The same applies to emotion; brain areas such as the amygdala have been found to be active in a similar way both when we experience emotions and when we observe others experiencing those same emotions (Adolphs, 2003). Thus, both motion and emotion evoke 'bodily resonance' (Gallagher, 2008).

To sum up, metaphors that involve some kind of bodily movement, be it metaphors that describe movement, metaphors that have movement in their source domain or metaphors that are expressed through movement (e.g., through gesture), have more vitality and are more likely to evoke sensorimotor experiences in both the producer and the perceiver. Again, these findings indicate that metaphor is a 'lived experience' and that its vitality is enhanced by the presence of motion, emotion and empathy. 'In moving ourselves, we move others; in observing others move – we are moved ourselves' (Zlatev, 2012: 2). This quote applies to both the literal and the metaphorical sense of movement and therefore refers both to shared movement and shared emotion.

Perspective

A fourth factor that has the potential to affect the extent to which a metaphor evokes sensorimotor responses in the reader or listener is perspective. Reaction time studies have shown that readers embody an actor's perspective when the pronoun 'you' or 'I' is used, but adopt an external perspective when the pronoun 'he' or 'she' is used. For example, Brunyé et al. (2009) found that people are faster to respond to images taken from an internal perspective when the images have been described in the second person, and they are faster to respond to images taken from an external perspective when the images have been described in the third person. This suggests that readers perform covert motor simulations of the actions that are performed by a protagonist. The pronoun 'you' has also been found to promote the active mental simulation of events from the perspective of an immersed protagonist as opposed to a passive onlooker (Borghi et al., 2004; Ruby and Decety, 2001). Readers are more likely to react to the emotional valence of narratives that embody the affective states of protagonists when the narrative is told with the pronoun 'you' than when it is with the pronoun 'I'. For example, Brunyé et al. (2011) observed that when participants read stories from a second-person perspective, they formed more accurate mental representations of the spatial organisation of the environments in the stories and were more likely to have internalised the emotions experienced by the protagonists in the stories. These findings have implications for embodied metaphor, as they suggest that metaphors presented from the perspective of the reader, listener or viewer will provoke stronger mental simulations and emotional reactions.

The idea that perspective shapes people's responses to embodied metaphor is supported by work conducted by Blomberg and Zlatev (2015) on the perception of non-actual motion (i.e., 'fictive motion'), which was discussed in Chapter 2. They had participants look at a number of pictures that invited the perceptual simulation of movement. These included bridges, paths, fences and walls. Half of the pictures were presented from the first-person perspective (e.g., a picture of a rope bridge stretching out in front of one's eyes) and half were presented from the third-person perspective (e.g., a picture of a rope bridge stretching between two mountains, seen from the side). Some of the objects (e.g., the paths) afforded motion by inviting the viewer into the scene (e.g., they might picture themselves walking along the path), while others did not (e.g., the scene containing a picture of a fence would not immediately afford motion though one might picture oneself walking alongside the fence). Blomberg and Zlatev asked participants to describe the pictures and then coded each description according to whether it contained a non-actual motion sentence. They found that their participants produced significantly more non-actual motion sentences in their descriptions of those pictures that had been presented from the first-person perspective and in their descriptions of pictures that afforded motion. Pictures that combined these two features were significantly more likely to provoke non-actual motion sentences than the three other types.

Perspective has also been found to shape the way people respond to the metaphorical relationship between movement in time and movement in space. Employing the 'next Wednesday's meeting' paradigm, which was discussed in Chapter 2 (i.e., in which participants are told that 'next Wednesday's meeting has been moved forwards two days' and are then asked whether the meeting will now be on Monday or on Friday), Feist and Duffy (2015) found that when the question was posed in the second person, participants were significantly more likely to say that it had been moved to Friday than when it was posed in the third person. Feist and Duffy conclude that when the question was presented in the second person, the respondents inferred more agency, adopting a moving ego perspective rather than a moving time perspective, and thus moved the meeting in a direction that was consistent with their direction of travel.

To sum up, in this section we have seen that people are more likely to experience an active simulation of a metaphor when they experience it from a first-person perspective. When this is the case, they experience more agency and may develop a closer emotional connection with the metaphor.

Signalling and Foregrounding

A final co-textual variable that may affect the extent to which a neurologically embodied response is evoked by a metaphor is the extent in which the metaphor is signalled or foregrounded. Work on metaphorical framing has shown that when metaphors are overtly signalled as such and when more than one reference to same metaphorical domain is included in the text, the metaphors are more likely to shape people's opinions, because they are made more salient (Steen et al., 2014). What we do not know at this stage is whether this increased level of efficacy is related in any way to the triggering of sensorimotor responses in the reader. The use of metaphor signalling devices and extended repetition of elements from the same source domain may serve to increase the salience of the source domain and thus increase the likelihood of an experiential response, but more work is needed to establish whether this is in fact the case.

If we look beyond the linguistic code for signals of metaphoricity, then there may be more scope for postulating a link between signalling/foregrounding and sensorimotor activation. When we look at spoken language for example, the potential cues can be extended to include gesture, bodily position, intonation and facial expression. As we saw in Chapter 1, a more fully-rounded theory of embodied metaphor must take account of the role played by gesture, as it provides evidence of what Müller (2008) refers to as 'activated metaphoricity'. It has been argued elsewhere that gestures provide evidence that the body is involved in thinking and speaking about the ideas expressed in those gestures, and that their presence therefore serves as a good indicator of embodied mental representations (Alibali and Nathan, 2012; Nunez, 2005).

Müller's (2008) work on gesture shows that embodied metaphor is a dynamic phenomenon in that it fluctuates in intensity over time in response to the communicative needs of the situation. Müller (2008) proposed three broad ways in which the source domain of a metaphor can be foregrounded through gesture. These are: iconicity (where more material means more meaning), interaction (which includes, for example, the degree to which people look at the gestures used by their interlocutor or draw attention to their own use of gesture) and syntactic and semantic integration (where, for example, a gesture might replace a word or add more meaning). She argued that the presence of these features (preferably in combination) can be taken as an indication of deeper and richer metaphoric experience.

In order to illustrate this idea, Müller and Ladewig (2013) combined a form-based linguistic approach to gesture analysis with metaphor foregrounding analysis in their study of a ballet class and a tango class. They focused on the gestural part of the metaphoric expressions because they argued that 'gestures in and of themselves are embodied and dynamic conceptualizations of movement' (298). They chose to focus on dance lessons because they provide a suitable context for the grounding of meaning in bodily movement, and contain a number of embodied 'waking' metaphors. Some of these metaphors are indicative of the differences between these two styles of dancing. For example, in the ballet class, the notion of 'finding balance' is expressed (both verbally and gesturally) as feeling a silk thread pulling the navel towards the spine. In the tango class, it is expressed (again, both verbally and gesturally) as the experience of being pulled down by an anchor chain. In the tango class, the teacher illustrates how the anchor chain stabilises the boat. He shapes the chain with his hand, shows the ship bobbing on the water and then points to his leg. The leg then becomes the anchor chain and he uses movement to emphasise the weight of this chain. The students pay close attention to his movements as he enacts the metaphor. Müller and Ladewig argue that at this point, the activated metaphor becomes highly salient, as it is at once embodied, experienced, attended to and ultimately 'lived'.

The work of Müller and her colleagues on the 'activation' of metaphoricity and the ways it can be identified offers potential for the study of embodied metaphor in context. What is now needed is more work on the nature of the relationship between foregrounding, embodiment and awareness. In their paper on metaphor foregrounding analysis, which develops Müller's earlier work on activation, Müller and Tag (2010) claim that:

> [The] foregrounding of metaphoricity also implies an embodied experience of metaphor and thus activation comes with an affective or experiential quality. The core assumption is: if metaphoricity is being foregrounded it is also activated – ideally for both the speaker and the listener. (ibid., 85)

As Johansson-Falck (2010) points out, however, it may not always be appropriate to simply equate the number of activation cues with the degree of metaphor activation. Although it is highly likely that the more activation cues there are, the more likely it is that metaphoricity has been activated, the number of activation cues alone will not be enough to tell us this. Individuals, and indeed cultural groups as a whole, vary in terms of the amount of gesture they use, and this does not mean that they are more actively aware of their embodied metaphors.

One way of addressing this issue would be to examine the number of activation cues that an individual uses at a particular point in a conversation in relation to the amount he or she uses at other points within the conversation. Such an analysis may provide an indication of the extent to which he or she is actively accessing the source domains of the metaphorical concepts that he or she is discussing. The sensorimotor imagery may be more active as these source domains are 'seen' (or even felt), as well as heard. However, we need to be very careful not to make any claims about *conscious* activation of metaphoricity at this point. Although metaphorical concepts may shape the way in which we process and express our ideas, as well as the ways in which those around us understand our ideas, there is no evidence to suggest that this needs to be a conscious or deliberate process. For example, a speaker may employ a gesture reflecting the ANALYSING IS CUTTING metaphor, without being consciously aware of the fact that they are doing so, and without that particular metaphor being present in the linguistic component of what they are saying. Their interlocutor may consciously or subconsciously pick up on these metaphoric gestures and use them to decode the message that is being conveyed. Having said this, attending to gesture and other forms of expression over the course of a single communicative event may provide insights into the extent to which metaphoric processing (be it conscious or subconscious) is taking place. Metaphoricity is ultimately tied to the shared processes of action and interpersonal metaphorical thinking (Wibsen, p.c.). The simultaneous expression of the metaphor through several modalities at once is likely to enrich one's experience of metaphor.

Taken together, the findings from these five areas suggest that novel metaphors that describe emotion and/or motion and that are expressed in the first person, and that are explicitly signalled or foregrounded may be more likely to evoke a sensorimotor response in the listener than metaphors that do not have these qualities. Like humans, metaphors have a tendency to become more 'alive' when emotion, movement and creativity are involved, and when the spotlight is upon them.

3.3 Contextual Factors That May Render Metaphors More Likely to Evoke Sensorimotor Responses: The Influence of Genre and Register

We have just seen that certain sorts of metaphors, and certain sorts of conditions in which they occur that render them more likely to be processed in an embodied way rather than simply being witnessed. The degree to which metaphor evokes sensorimotor responses is likely to vary according to its degree of novelty, its associations with movement and emotion, the perspective of the listener and the extent to which it is signalled. The presence or absence of all these factors is likely to vary according to the context in which a metaphor is employed or encountered. For example, in an animated argument or debate there is likely to be more emotional content, so metaphors that are employed in this context may be experienced more viscerally than those that are used in, say, an academic essay. There are other contextual features that may affect the likelihood with which a metaphor is 'felt', 'lived' and 'experienced' rather than simply encountered.

The range of ways in which language use varies according to context is encapsulated by the notions of 'genre and 'register', and these have been found to have a significant effect on the ways in which linguistic metaphor is used (Deignan et al., 2013; Semino et al., 2018). Deignan et al. propose a framework for analysis, which allows for an accurate and complete description of the ways in which metaphor use is shaped by the genre and register in which it appears. They illustrate the effectiveness of this framework by applying it to a range of datasets that vary in terms of genre and register. In this section, I extend this framework to focus specifically on embodied metaphor. I provide examples to illustrate how the transparency of the role played by embodied cognition in metaphor might be shaped by both genre and register. I focus on the three defining characteristics of genre (communicative purpose, staging and discourse community) and the three defining characteristics of register (field, tenor and mode).

Genre

The three defining characteristics of a genre are its discourse community (i.e., the people who use it), its communicative purpose(s) (i.e., what the communication is for) and the way in which ideas are staged (i.e., the order in which ideas are presented) (Swales, 1990). Here I look at how each of these three features may shape the presence or otherwise of the kinds of metaphor that have the potential to be embodied.

Discourse-Community

An important potential intervening factor in the relationship between discourse community membership and embodied metaphor is *novelty* which, as we have just seen, affects the extent to which metaphors trigger a sensorimotor response. Metaphors which are conventional amongst members of a given discourse community often come across as highly novel to outsiders when they first encounter the discourse community (Deignan, Littlemore and Semino, 2013). We have just seen that novel uses of primary metaphors are more likely to elicit an embodied response than conventional usages, which suggests that new members of a discourse community may be more actively embodying the metaphors that they encounter. In addition to this, it has been shown that many discourse communities, particularly academic ones, use metaphor as a basis for structuring abstract concepts that are specific to their community or discipline. When speaking to someone from outside the discourse community, a speaker may compensate for their interlocutor's lack of shared knowledge by making the metaphorical motivation of these concepts more explicit. We can see examples of this in the gesture studies literature. For example, Mittelberg (2008) reports on how lecturers delivering introductory Linguistics courses at universities in the United States employ a range of gestures corresponding to embodied primary metaphors which underpin grammatical phenomena. By doing so, they 'concretise' theory constitutive metaphors such as LINGUISTIC CATEGORIES ARE OBJECTS, WORDS AND PHRASES ARE OBJECTS/CONTAINERS and SYNTACTIC STRUCTURES ARE HIERARCHICAL SPATIAL STRUCTURES.

Deignan, Littlemore and Semino (2013) investigated the ways in which a lecturer in International Development adjusted her use of metaphor according to whether she was speaking to someone from within her discourse community (a colleague) and to someone from outside her discourse community (a departmental outsider), when explaining aspects of her work. We saw two examples from this study in Chapter 1, one involving a piano-playing metaphor and one involving a Tai Chi metaphor. Both of these examples were taken from the exchange with a departmental outsider and, as we saw in Chapter 1, the metaphorical basis of the ideas was made very explicit by the lecturer in her somewhat exaggerated use of gesture. We observed that when she was talking to the colleague, she was much less likely to signal her use of metaphor, or to repeat her metaphors. Thus it appears that when she was talking to the outsider, she made more effort to draw attention to her use of metaphor, and to make the embodied nature of her metaphors more overt.

Evidence for differences in the way embodied metaphors are *received* by people within and outside the discourse community is provided by Gibbs (2017), who investigated how sports players make use of embodied metaphor to celebrate sporting success. He reports that that many sports players celebrate gesturally by imitating the most activities that are related to fighting and hunting. For example, they might shoot an imaginary arrow into the sky, reel in an imaginary big fish or metaphorically 'machine gun' the opposing team. One of the sportsmen he discusses imitates the act of putting a gun back into its holster, thus enacting an END OF PROCESS FOR PROCESS metonymy, which provides access to the metaphor of him having just 'shot' his opponent. Gibbs found that people who watch sport regularly show greater understanding of these metaphorical gestures and are much less offended by them, as they take them less 'literally' than people who are not regular viewers of sport. For people outside the discourse community, these metaphors appear more novel and are therefore potentially more actively embodied, which may be what makes them more shocking.

Communicative Purpose

One of the key features of a genre that shapes the way in which language is used is the set of communicative goals that it is designed to achieve. In other words, a speaker's use of language will be affected by what it is that they are trying to do with that language. In this section, I would like to tentatively suggest that there may be some types of communicative purpose that attract more potentially embodied metaphors than others.

One such communicative purpose is *persuasion*, which often works through an appeal to the emotions. Indeed, when metaphor is used to persuade, the appeal to the emotions can be very strong. We can see an example of this in Hodder and Houghton's (2014) study (also discussed in Littlemore, 2017), in which they compared the language used on Twitter by the British University and College Union (UCU) (the Trade Union for academic staff working in British universities) during strike periods with the language used during non-strike periods. During non-strike periods, the main communicative purposes of UCU Tweets are to create and develop a feeling of community, to relay news of what is happening in different universities across the United Kingdom and to maintain and increase membership of the union. During strike periods, the

Figure 3.1 Extract from class on the meaning of 'units'

Tweets serve more as a 'call to action', in which members are exhorted to join the strike. Using corpus linguistic techniques, Hodder and Houghton found that during strike periods, there was a significant increase in the number of words that related to the human body, including action words. The majority of the words in this category were used metaphorically or metonymically (or both) and appeared to involve explicit references to the body. For example, one of the Tweets during the strike period contains the question: 'Want to know just how much money our universities are sitting on?' In this Tweet, the universities are metaphorically personified, allowing them to be construed as living organisms that can physically 'sit on' money. In a second example, one of the Tweets contained the words: 'Another big shout out to all our pickets this morning'. Here we have a CAUSE-FOR-EFFECT metonymy combined with a metaphorical use of the word 'shout' to indicate a (written) desire for large numbers of people to hear (i.e., read) and respond to the message being conveyed. These metaphors are all emotive to some extent. What we have here is a possible indication that embodied metaphor is likely to be more prevalent in instances where there is high emotional intensity. The 'physicality' in the text reflects this intensity of feeling.

Another situation where communicative purpose is likely to affect the use of embodied metaphor is teaching, where the need to convey new ideas in easily accessible ways leads to the use of highly foregrounded metaphors that are often novel for the recipients. We can see a good example of this in the following extract, which is taken from a corpus of video-recorded lessons that was put together as part of a project exploring the use of metaphor in mathematics teaching to primary school children (Littlemore, Duffy et al., in prep.).

TEACHER: Units are the same. Get your fingers out
ALL TOGETHER: Units are the same.
TEACHER: And again
ALL TOGETHER: Units are the same.
TEACHER: Show me
ALL TOGETHER: Units are the same.
TEACHER: Good, so units are the same

As we can see in Figure 3.1, the teacher begins by drawing her index fingers closer together as she utters the word 'units are the same', thus enacting the metaphor 'similarity is proximity'. She then encourages the pupils to do the same and, together, they repeat the phrase and its accompanying gesture four times. The fact that this metaphor is accompanied by a clear pedagogical gesture, and that it is repeated five times by the teacher and the pupils, means that it is a candidate for Müller's 'activated metaphoricity', which was referred to in Chapter 1.

Staging

Evidence for the effect of the stage of the genre on the transparency of embodied metaphor can be found in Deignan, Littlemore and Semino's (2013: 128–164) study of an academic exchange, which was discussed earlier. We found that in both the exchanges, dense clusters of metaphor and metonymy were found towards the end of the exchange, and in both cases, these clusters served a summing-up function, drawing together themes that had been covered in the earlier part of the discussion. Similar findings have been made by researchers looking at academic lectures (Corts and Pollio, 1999; Low et al., 2008), reconciliation talk (Cameron, 2007) and religious sermons (Corts and Meyers, 2002). These researchers have all identified dense clusters containing both metaphor and metonymy, which were found at the end of the lecture, sermon or discourse episode, and whose purpose was to combine the various threads that had been proposed earlier into a kind of summing-up paragraph. These clusters are often accompanied by increased levels of gesture use (Corts and Pollio, 1999; Corts and Meyers, 2002), which helps draw attention to the source domain, or in Müller's terms 'awaken' the metaphoricity. Other studies have found that metaphors presented at the beginning of a written or spoken text exert a stronger effect than those presented in the middle or at the end, as they influence the ways in which people interpret subsequent information (Thibodeau et al., 2017). Although the metaphors that they use in their studies are primarily linguistic ('crime is a beast' and 'crime is a virus'), there is a strong embodied underpinning to the idea that crime behaves like a living organism. Taken together, these two sets of findings suggest that there may be primacy and recency effects (Ebbinghaus, 1913) regarding the impact and memorability of embodied metaphor. More research is needed to test this hypothesis.

Register

The three identifying characteristics of a register are its 'field' (what is being talked about), its 'tenor' (the relationship between the interlocutors) and its 'mode' (whether it is written, spoken, visual or gestural, and whether the language is ancillary or constitutive) (Halliday, 1978; Halliday and Hasan, 1985). Here I discuss how each of these may affect the extent to which the metaphors are experienced on an embodied level.

The **field**, i.e., the subject matter of the discourse, is likely to have an important impact on the nature of the metaphors that it contains and will undoubtedly affect the extent to which metaphors are used that will provoke sensorimotor responses. We have already seen that direct references to the human body and things that we do and experience with our bodies are arguably more likely to stimulate sensorimotor parts of the brain. When the human body is referred to in metaphorical terms, these metaphors are likely to evoke a sensorimotor response. This includes metaphors that are used to describe literal physical movement, as well as metaphorical references to movement, including fictive motion. If topics such as these are included in the field of discussion, they are arguably more likely to provoke sensorimotor responses and thus be experienced in a more 'embodied' way.

The **tenor**, i.e., the relationship that one has with one's interlocutor, has been shown to shape the way in which one uses metaphor (Deignan et al., 2013) and intimate relationships between speakers can lead to higher levels of metaphor use (Katz, 2017; Semino et al., 2018) There have to date been no studies investigating whether this applies to embodied metaphor; however, examples can be found suggesting that this is an area worthy of investigation. For example, speakers are more likely to talk more openly about themselves, and to discuss their emotions when they are talking to people with whom they feel at ease. This may lead them to produce more embodied metaphor.

The following extract shows how the speaker makes use of bodily action as a source domain to convey a very personal, emotional response to a negative situation in the following extract, which is taken from a conversation in which two colleagues are discussing their attitudes towards the structure and management of their workplace. They are discussing a model which divides management styles into four types and discussing the advantages and disadvantages of each in terms of their own workplace. The model is represented by a schematic diagram that represents each management style as a quadrant in a square. At one point, one of the interlocutors gets hold of the diagram and points to the different quadrants, saying which he likes and which he does not like. He points to one of the quadrants in particular and says:

I find it very difficult to work in that environment for long. **I retreat there and shut my door**

In this extract, the speaker is talking as if he has metaphorically 'entered' the diagram and become part of it. He conflates the quadrant in the diagram with his office, making use of a creative blend of embodied metaphor and metonymy, within which he exposes his vulnerability. It is unlikely that he would have produced this utterance if he had been speaking to an interlocutor with whom he did not feel at ease. More studies would be required to investigate whether a trusting relationship leads to more creative or ambitious uses of embodied metaphor.

The **mode** of expression, i.e., whether it is spoken, written, pictorial, signed, etc., is also likely to affect the extent to which embodied metaphor is made salient. The embodied nature of a metaphor is much more visible in modes of expression that involve the body, such as gesture (Mittelberg and Waugh, 2009), sign languages (Taub, 2001) and dance (Müller and Ladewig, 2013) than it is in purely linguistic modes of expression, simply because these forms of communication involve the body itself. As we saw in Chapter 2, the use of gesture can foreground, and thus intensify the 'metaphoricity' of an expression or an entire passage by emphasizing the embodied nature of the metaphor that it contains (Müller and Tag, 2010). Müller argues that metaphoricity is by no means an either/or concept, and the intensity of metaphoricity can vary over time and across examples. More 'intense' or 'alive' metaphors are more likely to evoke sensory and motor responses. An important way in which a metaphor can be 'awakened' is through the use of an accompanying gesture, and this effect is even more pronounced when the listener is encouraged to enact the gesture themselves. We saw an example of this in the extract from the mathematics class where the teacher demonstrated the metaphor 'similarity is proximity' and then encouraged the children to perform the metaphor in both language and gesture.

What we have seen in this section is a set of hypotheses regarding the possible impact of genre and register on the uses of embodied metaphor. These are based on the idea that metaphors that are likely to produce sensorimotor responses which are particularly likely to appear in contexts where explication is important, in discussions of subject matter that refers to literal or metaphorical motion, in settings where the interlocutors are familiar with one another, in opening and closing sequences, and in visual and manual modalities. Many of these hypotheses are yet to be fully tested and as such would form the basis of interesting further research.

3.4   Conclusion

In the first part of this chapter, we saw that novelty, emotion, movement, first person perspective and foregrounding can augment the sensorimotor responses triggered by embodied metaphor. These features ought to be considered in accounts of embodied metaphor, and controlled for, or at least considered, in empirical studies of the phenomenon. In the second part of the chapter I proposed some tentative hypotheses concerning ways in which genre and register may affect the salience of embodied metaphor, in relation to these features. I suggested that fertile ground for embodied metaphor may comprise subject matter that involves movement, topics that are characterised by intensity of feeling, subject areas where there are high levels of personal involvement, settings where there is a close relationship between the interlocutors, situations where one needs to explain things clearly, communicative situations that afford the use of gesture and other physical modes of expression, situations that demand persuasive communication and situations where one feels the need to produce a powerful closing sequence. These hypotheses are now in need of further investigation. Such studies would provide insights into the ways in which the embodied nature of metaphor is constrained by intrinsic and environmental features. In the remaining chapters of this book, I focus on individual differences in the experience of embodied metaphor, but it is important to bear in mind throughout these subsequent chapters that one's experience of metaphor will vary according to the nature of the metaphors themselves and the contexts in which they occur.

4 'This One Sounds Like A Bell and This One Sounds Like When You're Dead.'

Age, and the Developmental Nature
of Embodied Metaphor

4.1 Introduction

In order to fully understand how embodied metaphor works, it is important to examine how it develops in infancy and how it changes over the course of a lifetime. Age is therefore a critical factor when looking at variation in the experience of metaphor. The ways in which infants employ embodied metaphors will inevitably be very different from the ways in which adults employ them. Not only does the infant have much less experience from which to draw the metaphors but an infant's brain is much less developed, which means that it may simply not have the capacity to make the connections that an adult might. Whilst there are some embodied metaphors that appear very early on in infancy, almost from birth, others develop over time. By studying the developmental aspect of embodied metaphor, we can gain valuable insights into its nature and origin. It also allows us to distinguish between those metaphors that can be accounted for almost entirely in terms of embodied cognition and those that require a more usage-based explanation. In this chapter, I outline the findings that have been made both with respect to metaphor development in general and embodied metaphor in particular. I suggest new ways in which such developments might usefully be investigated, and report findings from a study that I have conducted, in collaboration with colleagues, into the development in the understanding and use of embodied metaphors relating to quantity, time, valence and music by young children.

4.2 The Development of Embodied Metaphor Comprehension in Infants and Children

Before embarking upon a description of the ways in which the use of embodied metaphor develops with age, it is important to point out that age can only ever be seen as a proxy for some other sort of development. This might be linguistic, conceptual or even the development of one's encyclopaedic knowledge as one spends more time in the world. Age per se should therefore never be viewed as the sole explanatory factor for development but rather as an epiphenomenon. In this discussion, therefore, I focus not just on age but also on other kinds of development that accompany age that are likely to impact upon the way in which people understand and deal with embodied metaphor.

Before focusing specifically on embodied metaphor, I would like to begin with a discussion of the development of metaphor more generally. The development of metaphor comprehension and production in children has received considerable attention in the metaphor literature, and a number of stages of development have been identified. The first stage of development, which occurs in infants of around two to three years, is referred to as 'feature mapping'. During this first stage of metaphor development, children are able to identify feature-based similarities, such as shape, size and colour, and to understand and produce metaphors that are based on these similarities. For example, they might refer to a ball as a bomb because of their comparable shapes. Studies show that these comparisons are deliberate and that children are fully aware of the similarities and the differences between the two entities that they are comparing (Vosniadou, 1987). These apparently 'deliberate' acts all involve mappings that are based on perceptual similarity.

This developmental process then proceeds to a second stage that involves cross-domain mappings that rely more on *relational structure* (Gentner, 1988; Vosniadou, 1987). Gentner (1988) explained the difference between feature mapping and relational structure through two examples. Her first example, 'a snake is like a hose', involves feature mapping, as it is based solely on similarities in appearance between the two entities. Her second example, 'a tyre is like a shoe', involves a relational structure mapping, as the reader needs to think about the purpose of a tyre in order to understand why it is like a shoe. Gentner's studies show that infants and young children have a strong propensity to produce and comprehend metaphors that involve feature mapping, but that a preference for relational metaphors increases steadily with age. In contrast, adults tend to make more use of relational metaphors, and judge them to be more 'apt' than metaphors that involve feature mapping. She refers to this process as a 'relational shift' in metaphorical development. This shift is likely to be due to an increase in encyclopaedic world knowledge; adults are simply more aware than children of the ways in which things relate to one another. They have deeper semantic knowledge, so that, for example, they know what a tyre is for, enabling them to make the sort of relational connection mentioned earlier.

Other researchers (e.g., Winner, 1997) argue that even quite complex metaphorical relationships that involve relational structure are understood from an early age. Evidence for this comes from the fact that children have, quite spontaneously, been found to produce a large quantity of metaphor in the context of language play (Gardner, Kircher, Winner and Perkins, 1975). For example, Deamer (2013) found that children as young as three have the necessary cognitive abilities to help them understand novel metaphoric expressions such as 'the car has a bad foot', which is used to refer to the fact that a car has a broken wheel. These playful metaphors sound odd to adults but only because adults are aware of the real name for the object in question. The processes involved in creating metaphors such as these are just as sophisticated as those employed by adults, as they require an understanding of relational features between different semantic domains as well as in-depth semantic knowledge. Gentner (1988) argues that the capacity to perceive relational similarity between concepts lies at the heart of learning, suggesting that it is likely to be present from birth and that it continues to develop with age. The current consensus is that infants begin to make sense of metaphors during their preschool years but that they only achieve adult-like competence in late childhood years when their linguistic and cognitive behaviour and encyclopaedic knowledge begin to resemble those of adults (Epstein and Gamlin, 1994; Özçalişkan, 2005, 2007; Rundblad and Annaz, 2010; Stites and Özçalişkan, 2012).

So how does all of this relate to *embodied* metaphor? As we saw in Chapter 1, it has been suggested (e.g., Grady, 1997a) that in pre-linguistic infants, the two domains of a primary metaphor are conflated, and that it is only as children grow older that they then start to differentiate between different domains and to associate those domains with one another based on common experience. For example, very young infants may experience affection as warmth and therefore not distinguish between the two sensations, as they always coincide. As they begin to diverge, the two domains become detached and operate as separate domains, but continue to be related via experiential links (Grady, 1997a). Thus, the cross-domain associations between the source and target domains persist and form the basis of the conceptual mappings between the once conflated domains of 'affection' and 'warmth'. The fact that primary metaphors arise from sensorimotor experiences may render them easier to understand than other types of metaphor that are based on cross-domain similarities.

Indeed, the fact that primary metaphors are so closely related to physical experience has led some researchers to suggest that once they have been acquired at an early age, there is little further development (Olofson et al., 2014). Studies have shown that children of pre-school age are capable of understanding primary metaphors that involve cross-domain mapping (e.g., between SPACE and TIME) by the age of four and of explaining this mapping by the age of five (Dryll, 2009; Özçalişkan, 2005, 2007; Stites and Özçalişkan, 2012). Stites and Özçalişkan (2013) found that three-to-six-year-old children were particularly good at understanding metaphors that involve spatial motion, in particular those that involve first-person bodily experience, and argued that this is because children rely more heavily than adults on sensorimotor schemas to make sense of their experiences with the world. Finally, they found working knowledge of the target domain to be the most important factor in determining children's understanding of metaphors of time.

The first study to investigate the development of children's understanding of a range of primary metaphors was Siqueira and Gibbs (2007). They examined children's (aged three to ten) understanding of primary metaphors in two different languages: American English and Brazilian Portuguese. They were interested in investigating the development of primary metaphors and in establishing the extent to which these metaphors are universal or shaped by culture. They predicted that because primary metaphors are universal, the developmental trajectory would be the same across both languages. In order to test these hypotheses, they asked the children to explain a number of linguistic metaphors that corresponded to eight primary metaphors: HAPPINESS IS UP, EMOTIONAL INTENSITY IS HEAT, GOODNESS IT BRIGHTNESS, ACQUIESCING IS SWALLOWING, DIFFICULTY IS WEIGHT, EMOTIONAL INTIMACY IS PROXIMITY, IMPORTANCE IS SIZE and SYMPATHY IS SOFTNESS. They also asked the participants to explain literal sentences corresponding to these target domains and images relating to these metaphors.

Siqueira and Gibbs found that children from both nationalities exhibited almost identical response patterns. Only two of the metaphors (EMOTIONAL INTENSITY IS HEAT and IMPORTANCE IS SIZE) exhibited no significant age-related development in terms of the children's understanding, suggesting that these two metaphors are acquired at a very early age. The children's ability to explain the remaining six metaphors developed with age. A large number of participants experienced problems with the ACQUIESCENCE IS SWALLOWING metaphor, whereas EMOTIONAL INTIMACY IS PROXIMITY was much more easily understood, a finding which led Siqueira and Gibbs to conclude that some metaphors are more primary than others. Understandably, the children's ability to explain the meaning of metaphors with more 'adult' target domains (such as acquiescence) developed at a later stage.

An important question to ask at this point is whether development in children's ability to understand primary metaphors mirrors their ability to understand resemblance metaphors, as the answer to this question will provide insights into the role played by embodied cognition in the development of metaphorical understanding. In order to investigate this question, Almohammadi (2017) conducted a developmental experimental investigation into the ways in which typically developing Arabic-speaking children were able to understand these two theoretically distinct types of metaphor. She focused on four groups of children (aged three, four, five and six) and explored their ability to understand embodied primary metaphors and perceptual resemblance metaphors. The five embodied primary metaphors that she chose to focus on were: PURPOSES ARE DESTINATIONS, AFFECTION IS WARMTH, BAD IS DOWN, TIME IS MOTION and SEEING IS BELIEVING. For each of these primary metaphors, she identified one conventional linguistic expression and one novel linguistic expression, whose comprehension she tested via a reading comprehension task in which the children had to select the right picture to explain the metaphorical ending of a story.

Her hypothesis was that because primary metaphors are embodied they would be more readily understood from the outset, unlike the resemblance metaphors, where comprehension would improve with age. Interestingly, she found that despite her predictions, the children's ability to understand the primary metaphors improved significantly over the four years. However, in line with her predictions, she found that the comprehension of primary metaphors was consistently higher than the comprehension of perceptual resemblance metaphors across all four age groups, and that conventional expressions were more readily understood in both the primary metaphor and the perceptual resemblance conditions. She argues from this that there are qualitative differences in terms of the way young children understand embodied primary metaphors and perceptual metaphors. Most notably, understanding primary metaphor requires the children to draw on bodily experience, rather than engaging in analogical reasoning. These findings are interesting, as they suggest that primary metaphors are more accessible and are therefore more readily evoked than perceptual metaphors.

4.3 Metaphors That Are Particularly Strong in Infancy

In order to better understand the role of the body in the development of metaphor understanding in children, it is useful to look at the types of metaphor that are particularly prevalent in children's language and to assess how these metaphors relate to the human body and children's perceptions of the human body. Three kinds of metaphor have been found to develop in early infancy, all of which relate in one way or another to the human body and/or embodied experiences. These are: personification metaphors, cross-sensory metaphors and metaphors of magnitude. Let us look at each of these in turn.

Personification Metaphor

Personification metaphors, whereby inanimate objects are given 'human' intentions, are present in all forms of communication. For example, we might complain that 'the computer says no' or observe that the sky is looking 'moody'. It has been shown that infants and children have a tendency to over-extend personification metaphors, and are much more likely than adults to attribute goal-seeking intentions to inanimate objects. In other words, for many children, personification metaphors are not metaphor, but literally true. It is only as children get older that they learn to distinguish between the movements of animate and inanimate objects and to attribute agency only to the animate objects (Inagi and Hatano, 1987). We do not really know why it is that children overextend personification metaphors, but Inagi and Hatano hypothesise that they are applying their knowledge of human behaviour to animate and inanimate objects in order to make sense of them. This tendency to attribute intelligence, biology and agency to non-living things has been described as 'animistic intuition' (Okita and Schwartz, 2006). Using animistic intuition, children extrapolate from their knowledge of humans to make reasonable analogical predictions about the ways in which animate or inanimate objects will 'behave'. Okita and Schwartz found that three-year-olds tend to assume that robotic animals resemble humans in biological ways, as well as displaying intelligence and having their own intentions. As they grow older, aspects of these features disappear at different rates in a piecemeal fashion. Interestingly, there is a strong prevalence of personification in child-directed speech (Wills, 1977) and personification metaphors abound in children's literature, where we find talking animals and trees, and cars that interact with one another like humans do. The literature has very little to say about why child-directed speech and media make such extensive use of personification. One possible reason is that adults are subconsciously trying to talk and think like children in order to enter their worlds and increase levels of empathy.

Cross-sensory Metaphor

The second form of metaphor that appears to be particularly strong in infants is cross-sensory metaphor, where, for example, sounds are understood in terms of shapes, tastes are understood in terms of colours and smells are understood in terms of textures. It has been shown that cross-sensory metaphor conforms to a number of cognitive constraints that are determined by the ways in which we experience the environment through our bodies, in particular by the constitution of our sense organs. For instance, there appears to be a degree of systematicity governing which senses are more likely to serve as sources and which are more likely to serve as targets in cross-modal correspondence; the transfer of meaning is significantly more likely to go from the 'lower' sensory modalities of touch, taste and smell to the 'higher' modalities of sound and vision (Popova, 2005; Williams, 1976). This directionality has also been found in a range of languages besides English. For example, in his analysis of 130 instances of cross-sensory mappings in Hebrew poetry, Shen (1997) found that there was a significant tendency for the lower, more 'basic' senses of touch, taste and smell to be mapped onto the higher, more 'complex' senses of sight and sound, and not the other way round. Similar findings were made for

Chinese by Yu (2003), who also added that the domain of space occupies a 'special place' in this hierarchy, as it provides a fundamental basis for abstract thought. He used findings from an empirical study of the use of cross-sensory metaphors in Chinese literature to show that in Chinese, the fields of 'touch' and 'dimension', which are the two categories that correspond most closely to the existence of objects and their locations in space, constitute the most common source domains in cross-sensory metaphor. Finally, Popova (2005) argued that the contribution made by touch to the development of embodied metaphors has been understated in the literature. She demonstrated, through a number of examples, how the sense of touch operates in conjunction with the scale schema to contribute to a number of widely used metaphorical expressions. The findings from this body of work suggest a strong link between the way we use language and the constitution of our sense organs. I discuss cross-sensory metaphor in more depth in Chapter 6, but for now, let us return to the age factor.

The ability to detect cross-sensory mappings develops at an early age, with studies showing that infants who are only a few weeks old are able to identify these relationships. The fact that preschool-aged children can perceive cross-sensory resemblances and comprehend cross-sensory metaphors suggests that these mechanisms play an important role in the development of metaphor comprehension skills (Marks, 2013). Studies that have investigated cross-sensory metaphor awareness in very young infants have employed a cardiac habituation/dishabituation method, which involves taking measurements of changes in heartbeat that occur in response to changes in stimuli. Studies employing this method have shown that infants who are just three weeks old can determine what levels of light intensity correspond to what levels of sound intensity (i.e., the volume of white noise), indicating that there is a cross-modal intensity image schema already present in the early stages of infant development (Lewkowicz and Turkewitz, 1980, 1981). Interestingly, Lewkowicz and Turkewitz did not find such a relationship in the adult population, suggesting that this particular cross-modal correspondence is stronger in infancy and is subsequently reduced as people age.

Other studies have found that cross-sensory associations between texture and taste, brightness and loudness, or size and pitch are amongst the earliest metaphors to occur in infants (Marks, 1982a, b; Marks et al., 1987). For example, at four months, infants are able to collocate high pitch with small shapes (Casasanto, 2014). Mandler (2005) argues that infants combine information from the different senses and simplify it into a more generalised image schema. Similarly, Maurer (1993) suggests that the first month of life is characterised by a kind of 'neonatal synaesthesia' in which babies instinctively integrate all the information that they receive through the different senses and that differentiation of the senses disappears in later life. Both authors argue that the sensitivity that infants display to cross-sensory correspondences suggests that it is a hard-wired property of the human perceptual system.

Dolscheid et al. (2012) investigated four-month old infants' sensitivity to height-pitch and thickness-pitch mappings. They found that, in both cases, the infants looked significantly longer at cross-modally congruent stimuli, indicating that infants are sensitive to height-pitch and thickness-pitch associations prior to language. They suggest that these mappings may only be present in very young infants and get lost in the course of development because of neuronal pruning. They point out that this has been found to be the case for colour–shape associations, which are consistent in two-to-three-month-old infants, but disappear by the age of eight months (Wagner and Dobkins, 2011). They suggest that over time, speakers of languages that describe pitch in terms of height, such as English, strengthen the height-pitch mapping and speakers of languages that describe pitch in terms of thickness (such as Farsi) strengthen the thickness-pitch mapping at the expense of the height-pitch mapping. One interesting observation that Dolscheid et al. make in their review of the literature in this area is that the presence of motion makes it much easier to detect cross-modal mappings. This takes us back to the suggestion made in Chapter 3 that when motion is involved, one's experience of embodied metaphor is more intense.

In a similar study, Walker et al. (2010) investigated whether four-month-old infants were able to perceive a relationship between pitch and height and between musical pitch and pointedness. In order to test this, they displayed two animations, one in which a dot moved up and down a screen and one in which a shape became more and more pointed. In the congruent conditions, the dot moved to the top of the screen and the shape became more pointed when high notes were played and in the 'incongruent' conditions, the dot moved to the bottom of the screen and the shape became more rounded as the pitch of the notes went up. They found that in both parts of the study, three-to-four-month-old preverbal infants fixated on the congruent condition significantly longer than the incongruent condition. In other words, these very young infants were able to associate pitch with both height and thickness.

Other studies have focused on slightly older infants who have been exposed to some language input but who are not yet able to speak themselves. These studies, like some of those mentioned earlier, have tended to involve a 'preferential looking paradigm' in which infants are expected to stare longer at congruent prompts than at incongruent ones. Again cross-modal correspondences have been found, and it has been proposed that relationships such as these are innate, or at least pre-linguistic. Many of these studies have focused on the way in which musical pitch is conceptualised using cross-modal mappings. Dolscheid et al. (2012) report a number of studies showing that speakers of different languages conceptualise pitch differently. For example, in Liberia, it is described as light and heavy, the Suya people of the Amazon basin describe it as young and old, and the Bashi people of central Africa talk of weak and strong. For the Manza people of Central Africa, high pitches are small and low pitches are large, and for speakers of Farsi, high pitches are thin and low pitches are thick. All of these relationships are formed in early infancy.

Studies of older children have focused on their use of cross-sensory mappings in their understanding of emotions and abstract concepts. In relation to emotion, three-to four–year-olds have been found to detect consistent relationships between colours and facial expressions of emotions (Zentner, 2001). In relation to abstract concepts, Bakker et al. (2009) found that young children are able to enact movements that reveal embodied metaphors underlying the way in which they structure their understanding of abstract concepts for sound. They conducted a study designed to identify the embodied metaphors employed by seven-to-nine-year-old children (n = 65) when enacting abstract concepts related to musical sound. They found evidence of a wide variety of embodied metaphors in their data, observing that the children were able to express the concepts through movement well before they could express them in words.

Little is known about why cross-sensory mappings are so strong in childhood. One explanation could be that young children need to engage intensively with a large number of concepts for the first time, many of which are quite abstract, and they need to make sense of these concepts in some way. The easiest way for them to do this is to associate them with things they are already experiencing. This would explain why some of the most common forms of cross-sensory metaphor involve grapheme-colour, spatial sequence and number-form relationships. These are usually the first abstract concepts that educational systems require children to learn. Another possible explanation is that the probabalistic learning processes, which help people form frequency-based associations between stimuli, are particularly strong in infancy, as they are being employed much more intensively due to the large amount of new stimuli that need to be understood and categorised.

Generalised Magnitude Representation

Some of the findings concerning cross-sensory mappings that have just been described can be explained in terms of a more encompassing theory of magnitude representation. It has been proposed that the links between space, time and number are linked in a single system which involves a basic 'more or less' structure, and that this system is present from early infancy. This is sometimes referred to as 'The Theory of Generalised Magnitude Representation' (Lourenco and Longo, 2011). According to this theory, the link between space, number and time is not merely a surface-level epiphenomenon but a fundamental implicit phenomenon that underpins human cognition. There is neurological support for this theory as the processing of all three dimensions (i.e. space, number and time) has been found to be located in a single part of the brain: the inferior parietal lobe (Walsh, 2003).

In Western cultures, generalised magnitude representation involves both the vertical (bottom to top) and the transversal (left to right) axes. It has been shown that cognitive representations of number and time can both be represented spatially along one of these two axes. This has been found to influence the speed of people's manual responses. Lower numbers and earlier time periods tend to be responded to more quickly by the left hand, whereas higher numbers and later time periods tend to be responded to more quickly by the right hand. These are referred to, respectively, as the *spatial-numerical* association of response codes (the 'SNARC effect') (Dehaene et al., 1993) and the *spatial-temporal* association of response codes (the 'STEARC effect') (Ishihara et al., 2008). Both the vertical and horizontal representation could be described as embodied, with the former originating in the experience of 'more' being 'up' and the latter originating in the physical acts of reading and writing.

In addition to linking the 'big three' dimensions of space, number and time, the horizontal and vertical axes have also been found to provide a framework for thinking about other areas of experience, such as sound, light, music, touch and valence. For example, a relation between high musical notes and high positions in space has been found, which is referred to as the *spatial-musical* association of response codes (the 'SMARC effect') (Rusconi et al., 2006).

These effects have been investigated through three different methods: attentional studies, oculomotor studies and studies involving the use of motor bias. Attentional studies have found that people are faster to detect left probes after having been shown smaller numbers, and to detect lower notes and earlier time periods and right probes after having been shown larger numbers, higher notes and later time periods. Oculomotor studies have shown that participants look more quickly to the left after having been asked to detect small numbers, lower notes and earlier time periods and look more quickly to the right after having been asked to detect larger numbers, higher notes and later time periods. Motor bias studies have shown that people respond more quickly with the left hand to smaller numbers, lower notes and earlier time periods, and more quickly with the right hand to larger numbers, higher notes and later time periods. Also, stroke patients who are suffering from left hemispatial neglect have been found to experience difficulties representing events that are associated with the past and which thus fall to the left of the mental time line (Saj et al., 2014).

In order to gain a better understanding of the ways in which these experiments work, it is useful to look at one in more detail. Let us therefore examine a study by Ishihara et al. (2008), which employed a motor bias approach to test the STAERC effect. They conducted a study in which they played participants a series of seven beeps, each 500 milliseconds apart. An eighth, different-sounding, beat was played, sometimes after a time interval that was shorter than 500 milliseconds and sometimes after an interval that was longer than 500 milliseconds. In the congruent condition, participants were asked to indicate if the time interval was shorter (i.e., the beep was earlier than expected) by pressing a button with their left hand and indicate if it was longer (i.e., if the beep was later than expected) by pressing a button with their right hand. In the incongruent condition, the buttons were reversed so that participants had to use their left hand for the 'late' response and their right hand for the 'early' response. All participants in the study took part in four trials (two in the congruent condition and two in the incongruent condition). Ishihara et al. found that participants were faster to respond with their left hand to the early beeps and with their right hand to the late beeps, thus providing support for the STAERC effect.

There is substantial evidence to suggest that generalised magnitude representation appears in very early infancy, with studies detecting a single system linking space, number and time from the age of around eight months (Lourenco and Longo, 2010; Srinivasan et al., 2010). As we saw previously, early associations have also been found between space and luminosity, but interestingly, the relationships that infants perceive between the two are the opposite of those that are normally perceived by adults. Three-to-four-month-old infants are more likely to associate larger objects with darker stimuli, whereas adults are more likely to associate larger objects with lighter stimuli (Smith and Sera, 1992). Correspondences between space and music that are preferred by infants appear to resemble those that are favoured by adults; as we saw previously, three-to-four-month-old infants have been found to make connections between pitch and visuospatial height and between pitch and pointedness, preferring to look at stimuli which combine higher pitch with greater height and greater pointedness (Walker et al., 2010).

There are some culture-specific extensions of the generalised magnitude representation, and these tend to be acquired at a later stage. For example, in many Western cultures, an increase in magnitude is perceived of as sitting along a horizontal left-to-right axis. There is some controversy over whether this is a 'natural' orientation or whether it is influenced by Western reading and writing conventions. There are some studies which suggest that children's acquisition of this form of spatial organization only develops in certain cultures, when they learn to read and write, whereas others suggest that it emerges, at least in part, before children are able to read. In order to investigate this phenomenon, Tversky et al. (1991) conducted an extensive developmental, cross-cultural investigation into the development and use of the horizontal and vertical schemas to represent time, number and valence. Approximately 1200 participants comprising children (in four different age groups: five to six, six to seven, eight to nine and nine to ten), teenagers (in two different age groups: twelve to thirteen and fourteen to fifteen) and adults, from three language cultures, English, Hebrew and Arabic, participated in the study. They were asked to place stickers on square pieces of paper to represent a number of concepts, such as numerical progression, temporal progression (for example, morning, afternoon and evening) and valence (for example, a disliked food, a liked food and a favourite food). Two types of analysis were conducted on these data: a directionality analysis and an interval analysis.

Their analysis of directionality showed that for concepts related to time, the left-to-right orientation was dominant for speakers of English and the right-to-left orientation was dominant for speakers of Arabic, with Hebrew speakers making use of both orientations. For quantity and preference, participants were found to employ both forms of horizontal orientation (left to right and right to left) but only one form of vertical orientation (bottom to top). These findings suggest that left-to-right or right-to-left directionality are to some extent dependent on language and culture, but that there is a more universal association of *more* or *better* relations with upwards movement. Their analysis of the interval data revealed that older children and adults were more likely to provide interval information in their diagrams. The children were most likely to include interval information for time, followed by quantity, then valence. The Arabic and Hebrew-speaking children displayed gradual improvements on all four tasks across the four year groups. No such finding was made for the English-speaking children but this may have been a side effect of the testing conditions. The English children were tested in one large group, whereas the Arabic and Hebrew-speaking children were tested individually.

Taken together, the findings discussed in this section suggest that the ways in which children work with embodied metaphor differ from those favoured by adults. Children are more comfortable mapping space onto time than onto quantity or valence, whereas adults are comfortable with all three. In addition, children are more likely to make use of metaphors based on animacy and personification, and they are more likely to make use of sensory metaphor. By investigating how these characteristics interact, we may obtain useful insights into the ways in which children engage in metaphorical thinking, the nature of the mappings that they create and the ways in which these mappings develop. It would be good to see more qualitative investigations into the use of embodied metaphor by children, as these investigations would tell us more about the ways in which the metaphors develop in the minds of children and about how they use them to make sense of the world around them.

4.4   Maths, Music and Metaphor: A Comparison of Young Children's Representations of Number, Valence, Music and Time with Those of Adults

In the previous section, we saw that children engage with embodied metaphors in slightly different ways from adults and I suggested that it would be interesting to explore this issue in a more qualitative way. By doing so, we would gain more insights into the nature of the metaphorical connections that children make, and their reasons for making them. A more qualitative study would also allow us to identify whether personification and cross-sensory metaphor interact with generalised magnitude representation, and if so, how.

In order to explore these issues, we (Littlemore et al., in prep.) conducted a mixed-methods investigation into the nature of embodied metaphorical mappings in children and compared them to those of adults. We focused on number, valence, music and time, as this combination allowed us to look at the relationship between generalised magnitude representation, personification and cross-sensory metaphor, and therefore to build on some of the findings discussed previously. Although number, valence, music and time are very different phenomena, there are strong conceptual links between them. In particular, there have been extensive discussions of the role played by embodied metaphor in both mathematics (Lakoff and Núñez, 2000) and music (Zbikowski, 2002), and the two subjects have been found to share a number of metaphors. For example, both notes and numbers can be described as 'high' or 'low', both involve 'motion along a path', both notes and numbers can be viewed as 'sets of objects', both musical and mathematic recurrence are conceived as 'circular', and so forth. There are clearly strong links between music and valence, and the understanding of time requires mathematical reasoning abilities.

Our overall aim was to identify similarities and differences in the ways in which children (aged five to eight) and adults use primary metaphor to conceptualise number, valence, music and time, and how the children's understandings of these embodied metaphors change over these three years. We chose to focus on five-to-eight-year-olds as children in this age group are in the first three years of full time education in the United Kingdom. They are starting to learn about number, music and time, and metaphors involving the horizontal and vertical axes are frequently employed in the teaching of these subjects. We looked for evidence of progression across different age groups and sought to identify ways in which such progression could be described. Crucially, we included a qualitative element in which we interviewed all the participants in our study, asking them to explain the reasons for their answers. This allowed us to investigate not only the mappings employed but the different motivations for these mappings.

For number, time, valence and pitch, we based our methodology loosely on Tversky et al.'s (1991) study, as we were interested in exploring whether and to what extent the children employed the horizontal and vertical axes. We followed a procedure similar to Tversky et al. in that we gave the participants stickers and asked them to place them on a piece of paper to show how they related to one another. Unlike Tversky et al., who placed the middle sticker on the page in advance, we simply asked the participants to place the stickers in a way that they thought made sense, as we did not want to influence their responses in any way. We chose to employ no actual axes in the study and presented the children with a blank piece of paper, which was mounted on a vertical stand. Organising the study in this way allowed us to establish whether the participants used the axes at all. Participants were asked to explain their choice after each of the questions and their answers were recorded.

In order to explore the metaphors used to understand other musical features, we employed a somewhat freer task, in which participants were asked both to draw and to explain the differences between two pairs of prompts: a series of notes played in staccato and legato style, and two chords (a major and a minor chord). We then analysed the drawings and the transcripts of the interviews in order to identify types of metaphorical mappings and the motivations for these mappings.

By interviewing the participants after each task about the reasons for their choices, we were able to obtain qualitative data that shed light not only on the ways in which the mappings developed but also the extent to which they 'worked' in the same way in children and adults. The participants in the study (N = 119) were thirty-one year-1 pupils (aged five to six), thirty-two year-2 pupils (aged six to seven), thirty-six year-3 pupils (aged seven to eight) and twenty adults (aged eighteen to forty). All participants were tested individually. The testing of the children took place in a UK primary school and the testing of the adults took place in a variety of quiet locations. In all six tasks we were interested in exploring the development in the children's performance and in comparing it to that of the adults. Details of the six tasks are as follows:

Task 1: Numbers (Paper on Vertical Frame)

The participants were given stickers for numbers 1, 3, 5, 6 and 7. They were also given a blank piece of paper. The instructions were as follows: 'Please stick the numbers on the page in a way which shows how they relate to each other. Then tell me why you have chosen to arrange them like that. There is no right or wrong way to do this.'

Task 2: Time (Paper on Vertical Frame)

The participants were given stickers depicting different ages (baby, toddler, teenager, adult, elderly person). They were also given a blank piece of paper. The instructions were as follows: 'Please stick the people on the page in a way which shows how they relate to each other. Then tell me why you have chosen to arrange them like that. There is no right or wrong way to do this.'

Task 3: Valence (Paper on Vertical Frame)

The participants were given stickers for a happy face, a neutral face, a very happy face, a quite sad face and a very sad face. They were also given a blank piece of paper. The instructions were as follows: 'Please stick the faces on the page in a way which shows how they relate to each other. Then tell me why you have chosen to arrange them like that. There is no right or wrong way to do this.'

Task 4: Pitch (Paper on Vertical Frame)

The participants were played three notes (the 'base' note, Middle C; a fifth above the base note (G); and a third below the base note (A). They were given three stickers, (spots, stripes and diagonals). The instructions were as follows: 'Please put the stickers representing the notes on the page in a way which shows how they relate to each other. Then tell me why you have chosen to arrange them like that. There is no right or wrong way to do this.'

Task 5: Staccato and Legato (Paper on Table)

Five notes (same pitch, repeated) were played one after the other. One set of notes was played in a smooth fashion and one in staccato fashion. The instructions were as follows: 'Please draw each extract in a way that shows how they are different. Then tell me why you have chosen to draw what you have drawn. There is no right or wrong way to do this.'

Task 6: Major and Minor Chords (Paper on Table)

The participants were played two different chords (C major and C minor). They were then asked to draw each chord in a way that shows how they are different.

At the end of the experiment, the participants were asked to say whether they had learned to read music because we hypothesised that an ability to read music would affect their use of metaphors, such as the vertical orientation of pitch. By asking the participants to explain why they had answered each question in the way they had and recording and transcribing their responses, we were able to obtain important data on the reasons for their choices, which allowed us to gain some insights into the ways in which these metaphors were developing in their minds. This qualitative approach also allowed us to explore the roles played by narrative and personal experience in shaping the ways in which they employed metaphor as a thinking tool.

In tasks 1–3, we were interested in exploring whether there were any differences between the children and the adults in terms of their tendency to use the vertical and/or horizontal axes to map number time and valence, and to investigate whether there were any developmental patterns across the three year groups in this respect. Our hypothesis was that the adults would be more likely than the children to place the stickers horizontally across the paper, moving from low numbers to high numbers, young age to old age and sad to happy, respectively, for tasks 1–3. We hypothesised that the children would either favour the vertical axis, as this relates to a more fundamental embodied experience, or that they would simply place the stickers in a random manner across the page. In task 1, we deliberately left uneven differences between the numbers, as we were interested to see whether the children or the adults would place the numbers on the page in a way that reflected these differences (i.e., whether they would leave a larger gap between the numbers 1 and 3 than between the numbers 6 and 7).

In tasks 4–6, we were interested in exploring the participants' metaphorical understanding of music. In task 4, we hypothesised that the adults would be more likely than the children to place the stickers on the page so that they corresponded to the idea of 'high notes' and 'low notes', and that they would be more likely to place the stickers across the page from right to left in line with the order in which they heard them. In task 5, we hypothesised that the adults would be more likely than the children to draw longer or more rounded shapes for the legato notes than for the staccato notes, and in task 6, we hypothesised that the adults would be more likely than the children to draw a happy face for the major chord and a sad face for the minor chord or to draw pictures at the top and bottom of the page, respectively.

Findings

As expected, the performance of the adults differed significantly from that of the children on all six tasks, both in terms of what they drew and what they said about their drawings. The adults were significantly more likely than the children to produce responses that were in line with the conventional meta-phors on all six tasks. The children's responses were a lot more random and in some cases highly 'creative', but not uniformly so. Let us look in more detail at the findings for each of the tasks.

Findings with Respect to Number

The findings from task 1 were not as expected. The children were significantly more likely than the adults to place the numbers in order horizontally across the page ($p < 0.001$). The adults were more likely than the children to arrange the numbers vertically, either from bottom to top or from top to bottom. One reason for this may be that the children were encountering the horizontal number on a regular basis at school, whilst the adults, who were no longer in school, resorted to a more basic MORE IS UP metaphor, or thought in terms of a list and therefore ordered them from top to bottom. These findings suggest that the left-to-right number line is more or less in place by the age of five and that it is a by-product of the school environment. When people move out of this environment they may make use of more basic or embodied metaphors (MORE IS UP or progression goes down the page). The educational context can therefore have a strong but non-lasting effect on the way in which people metaphorically construe abstract concepts, though more research is necessary to test the generalisability of this finding. The adults were significantly more likely than the children to show an awareness of the size of the gaps between the numbers and to leave spaces accordingly on the page ($p < 0.01$). Those children who chose not to place the numbers horizontally across the page tended to arrange them in ways that they found aesthetically pleasing, for example, in the shape of a diamond, with the highest number in the centre.

Findings with Respect to Time

Our findings with respect to time revealed a significant difference between the children and the adults ($p < 0.001$) in terms of whether they placed the different-aged faces along a horizontal axis, with adults doing this in nearly every case and children not. There was also a significant difference ($p < 0.05$) between the five-to-six-year-old children and the older children in terms of this behaviour with the five-to-six-year olds being significantly less likely to use the horizontal orientation. The majority of the children arranged the faces in a pattern that had nothing to do with the vertical or horizontal orientation, or they arranged them randomly on the page. In the few cases where the children did use a horizontal orientation, their answers were highly personalised, with comments such as 'that's Dad' being used to explain why they were arranging the stickers in certain ways (Figure 4.1).

A small number of both adults and children made use of the vertical axis but neither group made used of this axis in a systematic way. Our analysis of the

Figure 4.1 Arrangement of stickers used by a five-to-six-year-old child to represent time horizontally

qualitative data showed that from years one to two (i.e., between the five-to-six-year-olds and the six-to-seven-year olds), there was a marked increase in the verbalisation of order; in year 1 there was no explicit mention of putting things in order at all. Also, with age there was a decreasing tendency amongst the children to relate the task to their own everyday personal experiences (e.g., by referring to members of their own family). As the children got older, their answers became more schematic or abstract. This finding suggests an age-related development from specific experiences to more abstract generalisations as the 'timeline' metaphor falls into place and becomes conventional.

Findings with Respect to Valence

Our findings with respect to valence showed that there was a significant difference between the children and the adults ($p < 0.001$) and between the five-to-six-year-old children and the older children ($p < 0.05$) in terms of their tendency to place the pictures along the horizontal axis. These findings suggest that the horizontal conceptions of valence are not strongly in place by age five to six but that they start to establish themselves around the age of six to seven. These findings are similar to those made with respect to time.

Our qualitative data for valence showed that again the children made considerable use of narrative in their explanations of this task, grounding their answers in real life, producing explanations such as: 'first you start off as sad then your friend comes over to make you happy'. The qualitative data also revealed that, unlike the time data, the use of narrative showed a marked increase from year 1 to year 2. Here are two extracts from interviews with year 2 children:

Extract a:

INTERVIEWER: d'you wanna explain what you've got there then? </interviewer>
CHILD: I put (this) it was happy and
INTERVIEWER: yeah

CHILD: then something happened
INTERVIEWER: yeah
CHILD: and got upset and then he got angry
INTERVIEWER: ah yeah
CHILD: and then he talked to a teacher but he still upset (.) and the teacher told him to
    understand and then he was happy again

Extract b:

CHILD: because you know (.) if you're sad or not
INTERVIEWER: yeah (.) if you're sad or not (.) <1> yeah </1>
CHILD: <1> yeah </1> one day you're happy
INTERVIEWER: yeah
CHILD: one day (.) you're confused or one day you sad one day you're sad
INTERVIEWER: yeah
CHILD: and one day you happy

These examples are indicative of a general trend for the children to personalise
their responses and to add a narrative in a way that the adults did not.
Personalisation and narrative thus appear to have played a role in the development of these metaphors.

Findings with Respect to Pitch

We found a highly significant difference between the children and the adults in
terms of their responses to the 'pitch' task. Only one of the children placed the
stickers in the expected pattern with the low notes lower down the page than
the high notes. The rest of the children arranged the stickers in a random
pattern or simply placed them across the page to show progression but without
making any use of the PITCH IS HEIGHT metaphor, as in Figure 4.2.

This contrasted with the performance of the adults ($p < 0.001$), who all
positioned the notes in such a way as to reflect temporal progression from left
to right and at different heights corresponding to their relative pitch, as shown
in Figure 4.3.

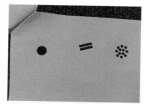

Figure 4.2 Sticker configuration produced by a five-to-six-year-old child to
represent pitch without making use of the vertical axis

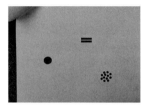

Figure 4.3 Sticker configuration produced by an adult to represent pitch, making use of the vertical axis

As stated previously, most of the children simply positioned the three stickers horizontally to show their chronological order, and only one child displayed an awareness of the relationship between pitch and height. They performed slightly better in the interviews, with three children expressing knowledge of this relationship. All three of these children were in the oldest year group (year 3). The fact that so few children showed an awareness of the relationship between height and pitch is interesting, as it appears to contradict the findings mentioned in Section 4.3, which showed that even very young infants can make this connection. Taken together, these findings suggest that the metaphorical relationship between height and pitch develops at a subconscious level well before people are able to articulate it either verbally or graphically. It may take people years to become aware of some embodied metaphors even though they may use them to understand and reason about their environment on a regular basis. This discrepancy in findings also highlights the fact that different research methods will often produce very different results. Activities which elicit specific actions on the part of participants, such as actively placing stickers along imaginary continua, will inevitably elicit different results from more implicit reaction time studies. This is an important consideration which needs to be taken into account when evaluating the findings from studies such as those discussed in Chapter 2, which provide different kinds of evidence for embodied metaphor. Embodied metaphors reveal themselves in different ways and to different extents, depending on how they are investigated.

Findings with Respect to Legato and Staccato

Our findings with respect to the legato/staccato task suggest that an ability to draw a 'motivated' picture develops gradually across the year groups towards adulthood. Although the numbers are too small to be statistically significant, they are indicative of a general progression across the year groups, though the drawings produced by the children were significantly less likely to be motived

Figure 4.4 Drawing produced by a six-to-seven-year-old child to represent staccato notes as 'an angry girl'

than those produced by the adults (p < 0.001). Our qualitative analyses of the drawings produced by the children and the explanations that they offered for these drawings revealed striking differences between the children and the adults.

The children's answers were less clearly based on conventional metaphoric mappings than those produced by the adults, although there were some exceptions. Many of the children said that the notes were played by different instruments (most commonly the piano and the guitar) and drew pictures to reflect this, even though they were in fact played on the same instrument. It is difficult to ascertain from the interviews whether the children *actually* thought that they were played by different instruments or whether they simply thought these instruments represented the sounds that they had heard. One possible explanation for the high preponderance of musical instruments may relate to the educational setting. The children were learning about different musical instruments in their music lessons and were used to being asked to draw them. They may therefore have inferred that this was required of them in our study.

Interestingly, when the children did use conventional metaphorical mappings, they often extended them in creative ways or personalised them. For example, one of the six-to-seven-year-olds commented that the staccato notes sounded like someone stamping and drew a picture of a girl stamping her foot to illustrate this (see Figure 4.4). Here the 'angry/impatient' sound of staccato is given a human form.

One of the eight-to-nine-year-olds drew bigger piano keys for the legato than for the staccato notes, which is indicative of a cross-sensory mapping from sound to sight or of a generalised magnitude representation. Some of the answers were very difficult to explain in terms of conventional mappings. For example, one seven-to-eight-year-old drew a square and some flowers for the staccato sound and a sun for the legato sound, and one five-to-six-year-old commented that the legato sound was a girl walking with a boy and the staccato sound was a volcano (Figure 4.5).

It is possible to find a motivation for representations such as this if one argues, for example, that the legato represents harmony and therefore

Figure 4.5 Drawing produced by a five-to-six-year-old child to represent legato and staccato notes as 'a girl walking with a boy' and 'a volcano', respectively

Figure 4.6 Drawing produced by a seven-to-eight-year-old child to represent legato and staccato notes as 'a house' and 'somebody creeping up', respectively

friendship and the staccato disharmony, and therefore the volcano. However, these explanations are post-hoc and need to be treated with caution, as one might easily have found an explanation for the opposite pattern had one been presented with such a pattern.

A similar issue can be seen in the following example in which one of the seven-to-eight-year-olds commented that: 'the first song [legato] I feel like it was (the same as) a … house and the other one [staccato] I felt like somebody was like (creeping up)'. Figure 4.6 shows his drawing.

Again, one could possibly find an explanation for these drawings but there is a strong risk of researcher bias. Therefore, in cases such as these, we chose to mark the responses as unmotivated. These examples are illustrative of the fact that many of the children's responses were very personal and involved people, movement and physical or emotional reactions. In contrast, the answers provided by the adults were considerably more abstract and schematic, with many involving long lines and short lines or lines and dots, as seen in Figure 4.7.

Figure 4.7 Drawing produced by an adult to represent legato and staccato notes as a series of lines and a series of dots, respectively

The adult participants often used the terms 'legato' and 'staccato', suggesting that they were clearly familiar with these conventional terms and the concepts they represent.

Findings with Respect to Tonality (Major and Minor Chords)

The children appeared to find discriminating between the major and minor chords the hardest of all the tasks and were significantly less likely than the adults to provide motivated responses ($p < 0.01$). There seemed to be very little development across the year groups. Only two of the thirteen five-to-six-year-olds provided 'motivated' responses to this task, compared with three of the sixteen six-to-seven-year-olds, three of the fifteen seven-to-eight-year-olds and all ten of the adults. Again, some children stated that two different instruments played the clips, most commonly piano and guitar, and drew pictures to represent this, even though this was not the case. Again, this tendency to draw musical instruments may simply have been a reflection of the sorts of tasks that they were being asked to complete during music lessons. Some of the answers produced by the children corresponded to conventional metaphorical ways of describing major and minor chords. For example, one of the seven-to-eight-year-olds drew a 'sunny meadow' for the major chord and some jagged shapes for the minor chord (Figure 4.8).

She offered the following explanation for the minor chord:

> and then on this one (.) it changed the sound a little bit it changed my
>   feelings so
> It's a bit (.) of (.) good but then (.) a sad because like
> I felt (.) 'cause like (.) it was in a movie like something's evil

Other answers appeared to be based on conventional metaphoric mappings but were much more creative. One seven-to-eight-year-old drew a piano and some bears and commented that the minor chord sounded like 'bears', which are aggressive. Figure 4.9 shows her drawing.

Figure 4.8 Drawing produced by a seven-to-eight-year-old child to represent major and minor chords as a 'sunny meadow' and 'jagged shapes', respectively

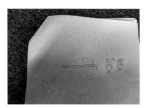

Figure 4.9 Drawing produced by a seven-to-eight-year-old child to represent major and minor chords as 'a piano' and 'bears', respectively

As we saw at the beginning of this chapter, one of the five-to-six-year-olds commented that 'this one sounds like a bell and this one sounds like when you're dead'. Another child drew a happy child with a sun and a scared child with a moon, and commented that the two sounds corresponded to 'a good day and a scary day in the night' (Figure 4.10).

All of these answers are motivate, in that the minor chord sounds like something more negative than the major chord. Like the answers provided for the legato and staccato activity, the children's answers to this task involved references to emotions, personal experiences and narratives.

Again, as with the legato and staccato task, some of the children's drawings were difficult to relate objectively to the sounds. For example, one seven-to-eight-year-old drew a picture of a fire and a jungle with a monkey. Interestingly, this was the same participant who had drawn the square and the flowers in the legato/staccato task.

The adult drawings were much more schematic, abstract and conventional. Many of the adult participants drew a line high on the page with a rising incline for the major chord and a horizontal line low on the page for the minor chord, perhaps reflecting the GOOD IS UP, BAD IS DOWN metaphor (Figure 4.11).

Two of the adult participants drew a wavy line for the minor chord and a straight line for the straight major chord, perhaps reflecting ideas of stability.

Figure 4.10 Drawing produced by a five-to-six-year-old child to represent major and minor chords as 'a good day' and 'a scary day in the night', respectively

Figure 4.11 Drawing produced by an adult to represent major and minor chords as a high line with a rising incline and a low horizontal line, respectively

Three of the adults related the chords to happiness and sadness and drew schematic faces to illustrate this. These findings are very much in line with those made for the legato and staccato task.

To conclude, many of the findings from this study relate to the discussion of children's development of embodied metaphor in the preceding section. Personification, or at least a stronger sense of animacy, appeared to play a role in some of the children's interpretations, as many of their responses involved people (either in the abstract or known to them), animals and nature. The responses provided by the children were more likely than those of the adults to be based around human activities, such as stamping, climbing stairs or walking. They were also more likely to involve personal experiences, relationships, movement, detailed depictions of scenes and narratives. The children also referred to a wider variety of emotions than the adults, suggesting that they are more likely to employ their emotions overtly in the processing of these primary metaphors. In contrast, the responses produced by the adults were highly conventional and none involved references to personal experiences, relationships or narratives. These findings suggest that the development of metaphorical reasoning in children involves the creative use of personal experiences, emotions, relationships and narrative. In other words, it is grounded in everyday experiences. In addition to this, the educational context appears to have shaped some of their responses, particularly with respect to the use of a horizontal trajectory to explain number and the relation of different sounds to different instruments.

4.5   Embodied Metaphor and Older Adults

In contrast to the developmental work on infants and children, there is very little research into the ways in which older adults experience and use embodied metaphor. Even though research in this area is sparse, it is worth reporting its findings, as they shed light on some features of embodied metaphor. Findings from the little research that has been conducted on older adults suggest that, in general, they tend to employ the same primary metaphors as younger adults. Hurtienne et al. (2010) asked sixty-five participants from two age groups (younger and older adults) to produce two-dimensional touch and three-dimensional free-form gestures in response to given abstract keywords and spatial dimensions of movements. The results showed that in 92 per cent of all cases, the participants employed gestures that corresponded to primary metaphors, and that there were no differences between the older and younger participants. However, there is evidence to suggest that those metaphors that are culturally mediated are used differently by older adults if the culture has changed during their lifetime. In other words, the embodied metaphors employed by older adults are sometimes different from those employed by younger individuals because of the experiences that those individuals have had in life. De Sousa (2012) found significant generational differences in the orientation of time: older Cantonese speakers who write in the traditional vertical right-left style were found to be more likely to conceptualise time as moving from right to left, whereas younger Cantonese speakers, who employ the more Western left-to-right style of writing, were found to conceptualise time as moving from left to right.

Older adults have also been found to employ embodied metaphors differently in their interactions with technology. Support for this comes from research that has been conducted by Hurtienne (2011, 2014) into user interfaces, such as heating controls, remote controls and computer screens, which compares the efficacy of traditional interfaces with that of interfaces based on primary metaphors. The latter might include, for example, interfaces where different timeslots are portrayed as containers on a 24-hour timeline (path), or where the user can request 'more' or less heat by enlarging or reducing a shape that corresponds to that heat. Hurtienne found that people interacted significantly better with interfaces that were based on primary metaphor than those that were not, and found them significantly more intuitive. Interestingly, he found that in older adults the difference was significantly more marked than in younger adults. In other words, older adults appear to be more reliant on the intuitive interfaces that are motivated by embodied metaphors. This might be because they are less used to using such devices, and they therefore need them to be designed in as transparent a way as possible.

In both studies discussed in this section, it is interesting to note that both familiarity with and experience in using cultural artefacts that are associated with particular embodied metaphors appear to play an important role in the ways in which people employ those metaphors. These findings show how cognition can be shaped by interactions with the physical and cultural environment, and how this relationship is mediated by metaphorical thinking.

4.6 Conclusion

In this chapter, we have seen how people's understanding of primary metaphor develops over time, and have focused specifically on how children develop in terms of how they interact with these metaphors. We have seen that children understand primary metaphors in ways that are quite different from adults, and that they are much more closely bound up with personal experience, relationships and narrative structure. In other words, children are in many ways 'closer' to the metaphors and are more likely to experience them in the context of their own worlds, whereas for adults the metaphors are more abstract and schematic and in some ways 'removed' from their everyday experiences. The main reason for this is familiarity; adults, who already have the conventional primary metaphors in place, do not appear to 'experience' them in such a vivid and explicit way as children. They feel less compulsion to actively 'experience' the metaphorical mappings or to relate them to their everyday experiences. We saw towards the end of the chapter that Hurtienne's research on older adults has shown that when people are unfamiliar with the way things work (in this case, central heating systems), they find it beneficial to resort to primary metaphors in order to aid their understanding. Both of these findings resonate with the work presented in Chapter 3, which showed that unfamiliar or novel metaphors are more likely than conventional metaphors to evoke embodied experiences. Here we see that finding extending beyond language; when people are faced with an unfamiliar situation which requires metaphorical thinking, the required metaphors come to the surface, are played with, personalised and ultimately internalised, so that eventually we can take them for granted.

Returning to the work on the development of metaphorical thinking in children, another interesting finding from our study was that the educational context appears to play an important role in shaping the way in which children interact with metaphor, but that this effect disappears in adulthood, where more fundamental, embodied motivations resurface. There is, however, a need for more work in this area. For example, it would be interesting to examine a wider range of age groups and metaphors in order to better understand how children develop these metaphors over time. More extensive studies are also needed of children's ability to understand novel metaphors that are based on embodied primary metaphors. It would be interesting to look at the development of these metaphors in unschooled children in order to single out the effects of explicit education. Finally, more work is needed to investigate the development of children's ability to produce language that relates to embodied primary metaphor, as opposed to other kinds of metaphor.

A final interesting finding to come from this chapter is that the 'presence' or otherwise of embodied metaphors appears to vary, depending on how they are elicited and the research paradigm that is employed. We saw in Chapter 2 that evidence can be found in spoken and written data, gesture studies, brain scans and tests involving bodily and environmental manipulations. In this chapter, we have introduced studies that look at infant heart rate and gaze, as well as more active approaches involving sticker placement. These different approaches involve different levels of consciousness, which may explain some of their contradictory findings. More triangulated studies could usefully be conducted in future to investigate the ways in which different levels of consciousness interact in people's experiences of embodied metaphor.

5 'I Did Not Know Where I Started and Where I Ended.'*

Different Bodies: Different Minds? How Handedness, Body Shape and Gender Affect the Way We Experience the World through Metaphor

5.1   Introduction

When Lakoff and Johnson (1999) claimed that 'our conceptual systems draw largely upon the commonalities of our bodies and the environments we live in' (4) and that 'our common embodiment allows for common stable truths' (5), they made no reference to physical diversity. However, if the way in which we experience metaphor is shaped by our bodies and by the ways we interact with those bodies with the physical and social worlds, then this raises the question as to whether people who inhabit different kinds of bodies experience the world differently through metaphor. In order to deepen our understanding of embodied metaphor, it is important for us to consider the impact of physical diversity on metaphorical thinking.

   In this chapter I explore a number of ways in which the bodies that we occupy and our perceptions of those bodies shape the way in which we use embodied metaphor to form our world view. In some cases, as we will see in this chapter, this is mediated by the ways in which our body image is socially constructed and the impact this has on our identity (see Cuccio, 2017). My focus is on groups of people whose bodily interactions with the physical and the social world diverge from what might be described as the 'norm'. In some cases, because these people are members of minority groups or are less powerful members of society, they are forced to see the world through the eyes of others and to borrow metaphors from the dominant group, and these metaphors may not necessarily reflect their own experience.

   In her ground-breaking 1949 book, *The Second Sex*, Simone de Beauvoir argues that humanity is male. Man is the default, while woman is the 'Other'. From this, it follows that:

Representation of the world, like the world itself, is the work of men; they describe it from their own point of view, which they confuse with absolute truth.

If it is the case that 'human' reality is in fact 'male' reality then it might well be the case that many of the so-called primary metaphors through which 'all normal humans' (see Chapter 2) reason about the world are in fact 'male' metaphors. If male and female world views were equally represented in the public sphere, people might be less inclined to talk about politics in terms of sport, and less inclined to discuss argument in terms of strength and war. Equally, if left-handed individuals were as well represented statistically across the human population as right-handed individuals, Jesus might sit at both the right and the left hand of God, untrustworthy people might not be described as 'sinister' and socially awkward people might not be described as 'gauche'. 'Right' may not always be 'right'.

I begin by looking at handedness, which has been shown to have a direct impact on one's use of metaphors associated with the concepts of 'right' and 'left'. I then move on to body size and shape and show how the way we *perceive* our own body size and shape and the shapes of other people's bodies exerts a powerful effect on our use of embodied metaphor. In the final part of the chapter I look at gender, and focus on the ways in which male and female interactions with embodied metaphor are shaped by the social roles that men and women are expected to fulfil. Throughout the chapter, I move between considerations of actual body shape and perceived body shape that are more tightly bound to identity, in particular, socially constructed identity, and where one's learned behaviour is closely tied to socialised feelings of personal value and self-worth.

5.2   How Does Handedness Affect One's Embodied Experience of Metaphor?

It is well established that the majority of humans (approximately 90 per cent) favour their right hand when performing manual tasks because they have better fine motor skills in their right hand. The remaining 10 per cent are either left-handed, ambidextrous or perform different tasks with different hands, although these figures are highly approximate as handedness sits along a cline rather than in discrete categories.

Right-handedness has been shown to be incorporated into metaphorical thinking. In western cultures there is a long-standing metaphor, likely motivated by people's experience of right-handedness, whereby 'RIGHT IS GOOD' and 'LEFT IS BAD'. This metaphor is reflected in language, where words associated with the right hand (such as 'right' or 'dextrous') are positive, whilst words associated with the left hand (such as 'sinister' or 'gauche') have negative connotations. It has been argued that this metaphor has an embodied origin, as greater motor fluency is associated with positive feelings and evaluations (e.g., Ping et al., 2009). In other words, because, for the majority of people, interactions with the environment are more fluent on the right than the left, people have come to implicitly associate positive as being on the right and negative on the left.

There is empirical evidence to suggest that the extent to which one engages with this embodied metaphor is affected by handedness, in that right-handed individuals are more likely than left-handed individuals to associate positive experiences with the right field. Casasanto (2009) conducted five unusual but compelling experiments designed to investigate whether handedness affects decision-making processes involving emotional valence associated with the left and right visual fields. In the first study, participants were shown a cartoon character and told that the character was planning a visit to the zoo, and that he liked zebras but hated pandas. They were then shown two boxes, each representing an animal cage and asked to write or draw the zebra in one cage and the panda in the other. He found that right-handed participants were significantly more likely to write or draw the zebra in the right cage than left-handed participants. This finding provides support for what he refers to as the 'body specificity hypothesis', according to which right-handed individuals are more likely than left-handed individuals to favour the right field. The four subsequent studies in his paper showed that participants were completely unaware of any handedness bias, and that the findings also obtained when the participants were asked to say which animal went where (as opposed to writing). Right-handed participants tended to evaluate characters, items and descriptions appearing on the right-hand side of the page significantly more positively than characters, items and descriptions appearing on the left-hand side of the page, whereas this was not the case for the left-handed participants. It should be noted that, although there were significant differences between the left and right handers, it was not the case that all left handers favoured the left field. There was a general bias in the data towards the 'right-handed' way of responding to the stimuli, which probably reflects that even left handers have been socialised into viewing the right-hand side as positive.

In order to assess the malleability of this metaphor, Casasanto and Chrysikou (2011) investigated whether training participants to use the hand that they are unaccustomed to using changed the way in which they processed valency. In order to do this, they measured the space-valence associations in participants who had or had not undergone a recent reversal of hand dominance. Right handers were asked to wear a glove on their right hand, which impeded their actions, forcing them to use their left hand. They were then asked to complete the panda and zebra task outlined in this section. Following a period of acting more fluently with the left hand than the right, natural right-handers became relatively more likely to associate good with the left field, in line with natural left-handers, suggesting that body-specific patterns of motor action play a causal role in shaping abstract thought.

In an endeavour to establish whether this phenomenon manifests in naturally occurring data, Casasanto and Jasmin (2010) investigated the hands that were used by left-handed and right-handed politicians when they were discussing topics to which they had positive and negative attitudes. They analysed politicians' use of speech and gesture (3,012 spoken clauses, 1,747 gestures) during the final debates of the 2004 and 2008 US presidential elections, which involved two right-handers (John Kerry and George Bush) and two left-handers (Barack Obama and John McCain). The speech clauses were coded for positive or negative valence, and the gestures were coded according to handedness. Their results showed that in both of the left-handed candidates, left-hand gestures were associated more strongly with positive-valence clauses and right-hand gestures with negative-valence clauses; the opposite pattern was found in both right-handed candidates. These findings not only provide evidence for the embodied nature of the metaphor GOOD IS TO THE RIGHT; they also show how embodied metaphor can be affected by the way in which one's body works or is forced to work.

5.3   How Do Body Size and Shape Affect One's Embodied Experience of Metaphor?

If our use of embodied metaphor originates in physical bodily experiences, then it is possible that the size shape of our bodies will affect our use of embodied metaphor. Two key ways in which bodies vary are in terms of height and weight, and both of these have been found to relate to social status and importance. The HIERARCHY IS VERTICALITY and IMPORTANCE IS SIZE metaphors are highly prevalent in the workplace and in society more generally. A number of studies have shown that the prestige of a person's occupation affects judgements about his or her height, and that presidential candidates who win are seen as being taller than their opponents who lose (Hensley and Angoli, 1980). Because height is a metaphor for importance and power, taller people are held in higher esteem than shorter people and are thought to be more convincing and persuasive (Judge and Cable, 2004). Language also provides evidence of the social power of height, as we talk about those we look up to and those we look down on (Frieze et al., 1990). As well as influencing how other people perceive us, height also affects how we see ourselves; tall people have been shown to develop greater feelings of self-worth and self-confidence because they are treated with respect by others and this becomes internalised (Roberts and Herman, 1986). Martel and Biller (1987) found that short males are significantly more likely than tall males to report feelings of inferiority and depression. Clearly, social mediation has a huge part to play in these relationships. The fact that tall people are held in higher esteem is something that children learn as they grow up, and they start to behave accordingly. As they develop confidence, this gives them more respect from their peers. Thus, self-esteem and social esteem are mutually influential. Judge and Cable (2004) argue that this then goes on to affect people's performance in the workplace in both objective and subjective terms, and that ultimately this has a bearing on people's career success, as indexed by both ascendency to leadership roles and their level of earnings. They conducted several studies using data from a number of governmental surveys in the United States and the UK, and found that height correlated significantly and consistently with social esteem, performance, the occupation of leadership positions and salary. The correlations were slightly stronger for males than for females but not significantly so, and the findings held across a wide range of white-collar and blue-collar occupations.

Thus metaphorical associations of height with importance and success appear to have a detrimental effect on the lives of short people. However, there is one attested setting where being short has been shown to be advantageous in terms of the way one is perceived. Van Quaquebeke and Giessner (2010) found a relationship between the height of football (soccer) players and the likelihood with which they would be accused of fouling by the referee. They note that many fouls committed in football are difficult to attribute, and there is no objective way of determining who is the 'true' perpetrator or the 'true' victim. In their study, they found that in seven UEFA Champions League and German Bundesliga seasons, and three FIFA World Cup Championships, referees were significantly more likely to attribute the foul to the taller of the two players. They also found these results to be replicated in two subsequent experimental studies. They attribute these findings to the fact that through embodied metaphor, people relate height to the concepts of strength, power and aggression.

Before leaving the vertical orientation and moving onto a different set of metaphors, it is important to note the way that it impacts upon disabled people. In her 1996 book *Waist High in the World* Nancy Mairs comments that, as a wheelchair user, she finds metaphorical expressions such as 'look down on' offensive, as they artificially position her, and other wheelchair users, as 'perpetually sad'.

As well as height, a person's weight has also been found to affect the ways in which they are perceived. Studies have shown, for example, that fat people are consistently perceived to be friendlier, lazier and less intelligent than thin people (Bessenoff and Sherman, 2000; Cogan et al., 1996; Schwarz et al., 2003) and weight has a significant negative effect on people's promotional prospects, with evidence suggesting that discrimination against overweight individuals can be found at every stage of the employment cycle (Roehling, 1999). Here, the role of embodied metaphor is not quite as straightforward as it was in the height relationships discussed earlier in this section. The most relevant primary metaphor here would be IMPORTANCE IS SIZE, but this metaphor would predict a relationship in the opposite direction. What is most likely to be at play here is metonymic thinking, whereby people associate weight with over-eating and lack of exercise, an over-simplified EFFECT FOR CAUSE metonymy, and do not consider other possible factors that may lead to weight issues (such as underactive thyroid glands). This use of metonymy is embodied insofar as it involves the projection of one's own bodily experiences on to other people, who may in fact be experiencing something very different.

As these studies show, although our actual body shape may not necessarily affect our use of embodied metaphor directly, other people's views of our body shape, if expressed sufficiently frequently and forcefully, may well affect the way we see ourselves and this in turn may impact upon the way we experience metaphor (Cuccio, 2017). In other words, because of the social nature of cognition, our own self-image is likely to be influenced by the views of others, and this may lead to a heightened awareness of our bodies, which may in turn affect the way we experience embodied metaphor. This sense of heightened awareness of one's own body is sometimes referred to as 'dys-appearance' (Leder, 1990). When functioning normally, the human body has a tendency towards self-concealment, which means that we do not tend to think much about our bodies on a day-to-day basis. In other words, as our conscious attention is normally directed towards the world, our body tends to 'disappear' from our conscious thought. However, under some circumstances, such as illness, puberty, anorexia and the effects of ageing, our body demands our attention; it thus 'dys-appears' (Leder, 1990: 91). In some cases, dys-appearance can be brought on by the internalisation of attitudes of other people who may regard us as objectified 'others', for instance because of our skin colour, gender, physical appearance or disability. Bodily dys-appearance is likely to increase the salience of embodied metaphor in the mind of the user (El Refaie, 2014).

The most marked examples of the way in which dys-appearance affects the way in which people process embodied metaphor can be found in the literature on anorexia nervosa, an emotional disorder characterised by an obsessive desire to lose weight by refusing to eat. In anorexia, we see clear cases of how one's image of one's own body shape can radically affect the way in which one experiences metaphor, and how this altered experience of metaphor can impact upon one's everyday life (Knapton, 2013). A key characteristic of anorectics is a tendency to conflate the source and target domains of embodied metaphors. This means that they no longer view metaphor as something that mediates between abstract and concrete experience; for them, everything is 'concrete'. Enkell (2002) refers to these as 'concretised metaphors'. In three linked papers, Skårderud (2007) provided a number of clear examples of these so-called concretised metaphors in data that he obtained from interviews with ten anorectics talking about their experiences with anorexia (2007). He then goes on to propose a theoretical framework for the analysis of these data

(2007) and makes a number of recommendations for therapists working with anorectics (2007).

Let us begin by looking at his examples of concretised metaphors that are used by the anorectics to talk about their experiences. He divides these examples into 'specific body metaphors' which refer mainly to one domain of experience, and 'compound body metaphors', which are based on two or more of these specific metaphors (2007: 167). As Skårderud (2007: 15) points out, in all of these cases, the metaphorical 'as if' is turned into a literal 'is'.

He identifies a number of metaphors that he labels 'specific body metaphors'. These all relate to the body in terms of its emptiness/fullness, purity, spatiality, heaviness/lightness, solidity and removal. These metaphors involve a conflation of literal and metaphorical experiences of the body. Here is an example of one such metaphor in which the anorectic conflates the metaphorical sense of being 'burdened' with the physical experience of being literally 'weighed down':

> I feel sad. And when I am sad, I feel burdened and heavy . . . and then comes the urge to lose weight. (ibid.: 168)

Here is an example where the anorectic conflates the metaphorical idea that purity is cleanliness the literal concept of purity through isolation:

> I became so pure, I hadn't sullied myself with food, conversation with others, or dirt on my body. (ibid.: 168)

He also identifies a number of metaphors that he terms 'complex body metaphors'. These tend to involve more multifaceted domains related to control, vulnerability/protection and self-worth. Here is an example of an anorectic using one of these metaphors to discuss control:

> The questions that haunted me, the fluxes of life, and the inexplicable desires were harnesses when my anorexia and I were working together in our lofty pursuit of some unabashed true me. It was guidance or faint whispers of it, as an alternative to the unfamiliar course I was travelling along without brakes, road signs, and power steering. (ibid.: 170)

In this extract, she is referring to those parts of her life that she is able to control thanks to her anorexia and extends this to control over other parts of her life where she feels more adrift. She does not appear to acknowledge independence between the two domains of experience (literal control over her eating and abstract control over life's events). Interestingly here, as in many of the examples in his data, the anorexia is personified and given an almost human form, displaying another way in which metaphorical thinking is skewed by anorexia.

Metaphors involving vulnerability/protection in Skårderud's study tend to involve physical and abstract boundaries, such as the following:

> I was not able to limit myself; I did not know where I started and where I ended. That is why I did like this: (She describes with her whole body how she diminished herself). Like from a grape to a raisin. (ibid.: 171)

In this example, the anorectic's metaphorical way of thinking is clearly tied to her identity; the patient is striving to achieve a more distinct and 'carved out' experience in life and she aims to do this by having a clearer, well-sculpted bodily silhouette. If the patient has a more clearly defined shape, then she also has a more clearly defined identity and a clearer sense of 'who she is'.

In all of these examples, we see what Skårderud (2007) describes as 'reduced metaphorical capacity', or a disruption to the metaphorical thinking process. As mentioned previously, there is a tendency among these patients to concretise the metaphors that they live by, giving them an increased corporeality and a sense that this is how things 'really are'. Similar examples of this phenomenon can be found in Figueras Bates's (2015) investigation into the metaphorical constructions that are used by members of pro-anorexia websites to describe their condition and how they feel about it. In one of these, the 'self as weight' metaphor, the anorectics personify their own bodies, often setting up a battle ground between the 'good' skeleton and the 'evil' flesh, as can be seen in the following quote:

> I feel savagely surrounded by myself on all sides. I feel the substance sticking to my alabaster bones in contempt; you can rid of me so easily says the flesh, holding and sticking every bite to the pure frame that truly is the heart of me. (ibid.: 195)

These kinds of disruptions to the metaphorical thinking process have been observed elsewhere in the psychoanalysis literature. For example, Enkell (2002) observes that patients suffering from borderline psychiatric conditions sometimes display a tendency to experience life through metaphors but they do not acknowledge these experiences as metaphors. Instead, they are seen by the patients as concrete, literal experiences, which leads Enkell to describe them as 'concretised' metaphors. These 'concretised' metaphors have traditionally been viewed as evidence of an insufficient development of 'symbolic capacity'. However, in recent years they have come to be viewed more as a way of dealing with inner fragmentation; people attempt to bolster their sense of self by strengthening the experience of being grounded in their own bodies. By employing concretised metaphors, anorectics seek to maintain cohesion and stability in the face of 'a very tenuous sense of self' (Skårderud, 2007). What we have here is a situation where people conflate their body schema and their body image (Cuccio, 2017). Their negative perceptions of their bodies impact not only on the types of embodied metaphors that they employ but also on the ways in which they interact with these metaphors. The metaphors become more 'literal' and more 'real'.

5.4   How Does Gender Affect One's Embodied Experience of Metaphor?

In Section 5.1, I referred briefly to the idea that some sections of society find themselves in a position where they are forced to adopt the mainstream metaphors that reflect the world view of the most powerful groups within society, even though these metaphors may not resonate quite so strongly with them. One salient example of this phenomenon is gender. The relationship between metaphor and gender is a complex one. Even the concept of gender itself is difficult to define. On the one hand, gender is a relatively stable bodily feature, so whether one occupies a male or a female body is likely to impact upon the way in which metaphor is embodied. On the other hand, much of the recent work in gender studies has focused on the socially constructed nature of gender, which suggests that the interaction between gender and embodied metaphor is likely to be complex.

As we saw previously, the fact that both the society we live in and the language that we use to describe it are male-dominated means that even so-called primary metaphors may be more likely to reflect a male perspective on the world. It is therefore interesting to investigate whether men and women experience these metaphors in quite the same way. If they are generated from a male perspective then one would expect them to resonate more strongly with male participants than with female participants. It might also be the case that there are different embodied metaphors that appeal more to women than to men.

In this section, I look at gender differences in terms of the production of embodied metaphor and in terms of the way people respond to it. As well as analysing the literature in this area, I report preliminary findings from two studies that I have conducted with colleagues in this area.

Gender Differences in the Production of Metaphor

Interesting gender differences have been found in the production of linguistic metaphor. For example, Hussey and Katz (2006) found that in conversation, men use significantly more metaphor than women and that this includes both conventional and unconventional metaphor. Women are more likely to vary their metaphor use according to their interlocutor, using more metaphor when communicating with close friends. Moreover, when people read a text containing a large amount of overt metaphor, they are more likely to attribute authorship to a male writer than to a female writer, whilst literal texts are more likely to be attributed to female writers (Hussey and Katz, 2009). The idea that males tend to produce more metaphor than women is also supported by the finding that in the British Parliament, men employ more metaphor than women (Charteris-Black, 2009).

In their study of the use of metaphor by male and female German politicians, Stefanowitsch and Goschler (2009) found a small but significant preference for spatial metaphor in the language of the male politicians. They attribute their finding to the greater facility that men have been found to have with spatial reasoning. However, they urge caution in interpreting this finding, as the effect was small and the male advantage that has been found for spatial reasoning is also very small and only emerges under tightly controlled laboratory conditions. They also suggest that the difference they found may be explained by just one or two metaphors. For example, the most significant difference between men and women occurred for the term 'unter' (under), with men employing this term significantly more frequently than women. The fact that this term is frequently used to refer to hierarchical relationships leads Stefanowitsch and Goschler to hypothesise that their finding may simply reflect a stronger obsession with hierarchy amongst the male politicians and may have nothing to do with spatial reasoning ability.

Other studies have identified subtle differences in the ways in which metaphors are used by men and women, and their use has been found to interact with other features of the discourse, such as genre, register and audience design. For example, Semino and Koller (2009) conducted an in-depth investigation of the metaphors used by two Italian politicians, Silvio Berlusconi and Emma Bonino, focusing in particular on their use of sports metaphors. They found that Berlusconi used sports metaphors primarily to represent national and international politics as a match or a race. His aim was to exploit his audience's affinity with their local sports teams and the positive emotions that they associated with them, and he often placed himself as a participant in the metaphorical competitions and races. In contrast, Bonino made use of sports metaphors to criticise the Italian political context and to draw attention to its lack of rules. They concluded that in addition to gender, the ways in which these politicians employed metaphors were also shaped by their political orientation, political goals, the topic under discussion, their institutional roles and the nature of their respective audiences.

Charteris-Black (2012) found interesting gender differences (as well as similarities) in the ways in which men and women make use of embodied primary metaphors when describing their experiences of depression. He conducted thirty-eight interviews with men and women who had experienced depression, and compared the metaphors they produced in order to determine whether or not the expression of depression is gendered. He found the types of metaphor used by women and men to be generally similar. Both genders talked about depression using embodied metaphors that related to 'descent', 'weight and pressure', 'darkness and light' and 'containment and constraint'.

However, there were striking differences between the ways in which the different genders used metaphor. Women were more likely than men to employ mixed metaphors:

> Let it out because if it doesn't come out, it gets stuck, I think. And it builds up and it builds up and it builds up and you get full and you get full of all these feelings that have never been expressed. And [um] for me at the moment in therapy they are pouring out of me, all sorts of feelings, thoughts and feelings and are coming out through all sorts of different means as well. They are coming out through poetry, and through music. (DP39 female, 37) (ibid.: 210)

There was also a tendency in the women's data for one metaphor to 'prime' another related metaphor, as we can see in this example:

> I think that was the other one they put me on instead of the Librium and I just went down and down and down. They weren't doing me any good at all. They got me really low again. To the stage where I was going and sitting in the park ... I was talking to the down-and-outs, and not even knowing I was doing it. I, I did not know I was doing it. (DP25 female, 30) (ibid.: 210)

These findings suggest that, although men and women use similar embodied metaphors to conceptualise and communicate their feelings of depression, they appear to use them differently, with women making more flexible use of metaphor, moving between several different embodied metaphors within a single turn.

Male and Female Use of the Social/Psychological Distance Is Physical Distance Metaphor

Another embodied conceptual metaphor that may be susceptible to gender variation is the SOCIAL/PSYCHOLOGICAL DISTANCE IS PHYSICAL DISTANCE metaphor. A number of studies have found evidence for the psychological reality of this metaphor. For example, Matthews and Matlock (2011) employed a series of drawing and estimation tasks to explore the conceptual structure of social distance. They asked participants to draw a person's route through a map as they passed a series of people who were described as either friends or strangers. They found that people drew the line closer to the people when they had been described as friends than they did when they were described as strangers, which they argued reflects the underlying embodied metaphor whereby social distance is physical distance, or at least that psychological distance and physical distance draw on similar processes (Bar-Anan et al., 2007). However, the ways in which men and women experience social, psychological and physical distance differ; women have been found to form closer emotional bonds than men, and relationships between people of the same gender are often different from relationships across genders. These differences are likely to have an impact on the ways in which men and women employ the SOCIAL DISTANCE IS PHYSICAL DISTANCE metaphor.

In order to test this, we (Littlemore, Turner and Alexander, in prep.) extended Matthews and Matlock's study, to incorporate a gender element. Following Mathews and Matlock, participants (thirty-five females; fourteen males; all adults aged eighteen to thirty-five) were given a map containing a number of obstacles and some people dotted around. The participants were told that the people were either friends or strangers, and that they were either the same sex as them or a different sex from them. Our hypothesis was that female participants would draw the line closer to the people in the picture, as women have been found to former tighter friendship bonds than men (Wright and Scanlon, 1991) and that they may exhibit stronger sensitivity to the fact that the people were either friends or strangers. We also investigated whether individuals would draw the line closer to people who were the same sex as them. In line with Matthews and Matlock, we found a significant effect for the friend/stranger variable overall, with participants drawing the line further away from the strangers than from the friends.

When we split the group into male and female participants we found that this difference was significant for the female participants but not for the male participants. In other words, the gender of the participants in the study appeared to affect their responses, with females being more likely than males to draw the line nearer to friends than to strangers. When we broke the figures down still further, we found that female participants were significantly more likely to walk nearer to friends than to strangers if they were told that they were the opposite sex ($p < 0.05$). When they were told that the people were the same sex as them, there was no difference in behaviour. One could take these findings to suggest that the SOCIAL/PSYCHOLOGICAL DISTANCE IS PHYSICAL DISTANCE metaphor is stronger in women than in men, particularly when they are thinking about members of the opposite sex. However, these findings need to be treated with caution. First, they may have been skewed by the low number of male participants in the study, and secondly they may simply reflect the reality of many women's lives: that in general, it is a good idea to avoid strange men. This is a very literal explanation and doesn't involve metaphor at all. What these findings show, however, is how primary metaphors might build on, and relate to everyday practical experiences that are different for men and women.

Gender Differences in Response to Embodied Metaphors

We saw previously that some of the so-called universal embodied primary metaphors may reflect a somewhat masculine view of the world. As such, one might not expect men and women to respond to them in the same way. There is indeed evidence from behavioural studies to suggest that men and women do not always experience so-called universal embodied metaphors to the same extent or in the same way. Ackerman et al. (2010) investigated how the metaphorical associations that people make with weight affect their decision-making processes. Forty-three passers-by were given either light (453.6 g) or heavy (1,559.2 g) clipboards, featuring a 'social action survey' asking whether particular public issues should receive more or less government funding. The issues included some that could be considered socially important and serious (such as air pollution standards) and some that could be considered more idiosyncratic and less important (such as the regulation of public toilets). They found that male participants allocated significantly more money to social issues in the 'heavy' condition than in the 'light' condition. In contrast, female participants chose to fund nearly all of the social issues in both the 'heavy' and 'light' conditions.

Compared to men, women typically describe themselves as less dominant (Feingold, 1994). Men and women are also likely to view coercion differently, with men being more likely to associate bodily force with exerting influence and gaining power than women, for whom bodily force is more likely to be associated with a breakdown of self-control and a loss of power (Campbell et al., 1992). These differences reflect the different experiences that men and women have of their own bodies and the different societal norms determining appropriate behaviour for males and females. In line with this, Schubert and Koole (2009) found that actions associated with power (such as making a fist) could lead male participants (but not female ones) to perceive themselves as being more assertive, esteemed and powerful. In a similar study, Stepper and Strack (1993) found that when men were in an upright position, they were more likely to feel pride in response to positive feedback than when they were in a slumped position.

Interesting (and somewhat depressing) interactions have been found between gender and the vertical hierarchy metaphor which was discussed in Chapter 2. Meier and Dionne (2009) found that men perceived images of women to be more physically attractive when they appeared in a low position (i.e., at the bottom of the screen) than when they appeared in a high position (i.e., at the top of the screen). Meier and Dionne argue that this is because men are more likely to desire powerless women. Remaining with the vertical hierarchy orientation, Gkiouzepas (2015) found that men with a high 'need for power' orientation were significantly more likely to be persuaded by advertisements where the product is placed higher than the caption, than ones where it is placed below the caption, whereas in women there is no relationship. This finding is discussed in more detail in Chapter 7.

Another interesting investigation into the different ways in which men and women interact with primary metaphors was conducted by Hutchinson and Louwerse (2013). They compared the ways in which male and female participants process primary metaphors in which the vertical schema is associated with valence (e.g., good and bad), authority (e.g., doctor–patient), temperature (e.g., hot–cold) or gender (e.g., male–female). They showed their participants pairs of words displayed one above the other and asked them to say whether or not the words were from the same semantic domain. Their hypothesis was that when the words were displayed in the congruent direction (e.g., with 'good' at the top and 'bad' at the bottom), participants would respond more quickly than when the words were displayed in the non-congruent direction.

In additional to this, they hypothesised that the response patterns of female participants would reflect patterns that have been observed in linguistic data more closely than those of the male participants. The justification for this hypothesis was that females tend to exhibit greater general and spoken language ability than males. They have been found to outperform males on verbal fluency tasks, semantic categorisation tasks and verbal memory tasks (e.g., Andreano and Cahill, 2009). They may therefore be more sensitive to frequencies in linguistic data, which would reflect their more context-sensitive, usage-based approach to concept acquisition. Hutchinson and Louwerse focused in particular on order effects. For example, it is more usual to talk about things being 'up and down' than 'down and up', and we talk more about 'men and women' more often than we do about 'women and men'. In order to obtain data on the most likely levels of linguistic exposure that people will have had to these orderings, for each pair of items, they identified the linguistic frequencies with which these words occur in their canonical and non-canonical orderings in the Web 1T 5-gram corpus (Brants and Franz, 2006). They then compared the log frequency of a-b (e.g., happy-sad) and the b-a (e.g., sad-happy) order of the word pairs. Finally, they correlated these distributions with the results obtained in their study for both male and female participants.

In line with their hypotheses, they found that participants in the study responded significantly more quickly to canonical condition (e.g., when 'happy' was at the top of the screen and 'sad' was at the bottom of the screen). Also in line with their hypotheses, they found that the responses of female participants were significantly more closely aligned with the frequency distributions identified in the corpus data, for all four tests that involved the vertical axis. Therefore, it appears to be the case that, although both genders operate with the same set of primary metaphors, women are more attuned than men to statistical distributions in the linguistic environment when internalising primary metaphors.

Male and Female Perceptions of the Vertical Hierarchy Metaphor: A Reaction Time Study

An area that has been under-investigated to date is the extent to which men's and women's dealings with embodied metaphor are shaped by the social roles that they are brought up to conform to. The beliefs that people hold about gender are underpinned by observations about the social roles that men and women fulfil (Eagly, Wood and Diekman, 2000). Expectations that people have about women and men reflect and are reflected in the sexual division of labour and the gender hierarchy of the society in general: women across the world are expected to perform more domestic work than men, earn lower wages and are less likely to occupy higher status positions (ibid.). In addition, women are frequently expected to display communal traits, such as affection, sensitivity, sympathy and concern for the welfare of others, whereas men are expected to display agentic traits, such as dominance, ambition, aggression and concern for one's own welfare. These expectations account for much of the prejudice that exists in society towards females in positions of power.

These social stereotypes about women and men have been found to be easily and automatically activated in behavioural studies. For instance, in their reaction time study, Banaji and Hardin (1996) found that, when presented with a series of primes relating to gender (e.g., the words 'mother', 'father', 'nurse', 'doctor', 'secretary', 'mechanic'), or neutral with respect to gender (e.g., parent, student, person), followed by a series of target pronouns that were gendered (e.g., she, he), or neutral (it, me), participants were faster at identifying the gender of target pronouns that followed gender-congruent primes, compared to those that followed gender-incongruent primes. In other words, participants were faster at identifying the gender of the pronoun 'she' after having seen prompts such as 'nurse' and 'secretary', and they were faster at identifying the gender of the pronoun 'he' after having seen prompts such as 'doctor' and 'mechanic'. These findings indicate that people who are engaging in gender-based classifications find it difficult to disregard stereotypic associations, even when they are irrelevant to the task.

In order to test the impact of perceived social roles on people's perceptions of gender and hierarchy, we (Duffy et al., in prep.) conducted a reaction time study, building on a previous study by Schubert (2005), which was discussed in Chapter 2. Schubert found that people judge a group's social power to be greater when the group is presented at the top of a computer screen than when it is presented in the lower part of the screen. Participants in Schubert's study were asked to make rapid judgements about pairs of relatively powerful and powerless groups (e.g., employer–employee, king–servant, coach–athlete, teacher–pupil) that were presented on a computer screen, where one of the labels was presented on the top and the other at the bottom of the screen. Schubert found that participants responded more quickly when powerful and powerless groups were presented in the congruent condition with respect to the vertical power axis; that is, when powerful groups appeared at the top of the screen and when the non-powerful groups appeared at the bottom of the screen. This suggests that power is mentally represented by vertical positioning. The study provides evidence for the psychological reality of the vertical image schema of power: conceptual thinking about power involves mental representations of vertical space.

In our study, we factored gender into the original power/hierarchy paradigm by using matched pairs of gendered prompts (e.g., male/female doctor–male/female nurse). The overall aim of the study was to investigate whether preconceived beliefs concerning gender, power and hierarchy interact with one another when judgements are being made about power. In other words, we sought to establish whether people's perceptions of the relative power held by people in certain professions would be affected by both the gender of the prompt and its position on a vertical axis. We hypothesised that participants would respond more rapidly when powerful and powerless groups (in terms of both their professional role and their gender) were presented congruently with respect to the vertical axis. We expected the fastest reaction times to occur when powerful, male prompts appeared at the top of the screen and when less powerful, female prompts appeared at the bottom of the screen. Such a finding would provide empirical evidence for a subconscious gender bias in our participants. Our specific research questions were:

1. Do people respond more quickly when people in more powerful roles are presented at the top of the screen?
2. Does the gender of the prompt affect reaction times?
3. Does the gender of the participant affect reaction times?

Our study involved sixty participants (eleven male and forty-nine female), all of whom were undergraduate students studying at universities in Birmingham. We also interviewed our participants after the reaction time test in order to examine the potential relationship between what the participants perceive their attitudes to be towards the imbrication of gender and power, and the ways in which they responded to the reaction time test. Ultimately, we were interested in testing out the idea that gender plays a role in how people conceptualise power metaphorically.

We found that participants did indeed respond fastest when the male in the powerful profession was at the top, and the female in the less powerful profession was at the bottom. This interaction was modulated by the gender of the participants in that it was significantly stronger in the male participants than in the female participants, which suggests that men are even more biased than women in terms of the way they view the respective roles of men and women within the vertical hierarchy.

These findings, together with the findings mentioned previously regarding male and female attitudes to the SOCIETAL DIFFERENCE IS PHYSICAL DISTANCE metaphor, suggest that gender does have an impact on the way people engage with embodied primary metaphors, and that these differences are largely shaped by societal expectations. These metaphors in turn shape the world views of those who experience them, which means that women adopt men's metaphors (and hence men's world views), but they do so to a lesser extent and through different means.

5.5   Conclusion

We have seen in this chapter that bodily variation affects the way in which people interact with embodied metaphors on a phenomenological level. This variation provides evidence both for the experiential basis of primary metaphors and for the idea that they are socially constructed. Variation can be found not only in the types of primary metaphor that are used but also in the *ways* in which they are used. The findings with respect to handedness clearly indicate that people's interactions with bodily-based metaphors can be affected by the nature of bodies that they inhabit, with right-handed individuals being significantly more likely than left-handed individuals to employ the GOOD IS RIGHT metaphor at a subconscious level. The findings regarding height and weight suggest that embodied metaphors tend to be projected onto others and this affects the ways in which people with different statures and weights are treated by society. The findings with respect to anorexia show how once an embodied metaphor has been internalised it can become an essential, or even all-consuming, part of a person's identity, as people lose sight of the fact that the relationship is in fact metaphorical and start to behave as if it were literal, which can have a detrimental effect on their mental and physical wellbeing. The findings regarding gender show how women internalise dominant (male) metaphorical world views and that these are reinforced through exposure to language. Embodied metaphors that are based on height and strength are experienced at a deeper level by men than by women.

On a more general level, the findings presented throughout this chapter suggest that metaphors whose embodiment resonates with the most dominant members of society tend to become 'mainstream'. They are then taken up and internalised by other, less dominant members of society, who acquire them through more usage-based routes that are based on sensitivity to patterns in language and human behaviour. When they are acquired in this way, they appear to be experienced somewhat less intensely. This does not detract from the fact that large parts of society are living by other people's metaphors.

6 'Those Cookies Tasted of Regret and Rotting Flesh.'

Sensory Metaphor and Associated Impairments and Conditions

6.1   Introduction

The main way through which we interact with the world is through our senses. Because the senses play such a fundamental part in our physical experience of the world, we also use them as a basis for our understanding of more abstract experiences through metaphor. All five senses are used in this way. For example, we talk about understanding and heeding in terms of seeing and listening ('Aha, I see'; 'yes I hear you, and now you hear me' – BNC), we talk about emotion in terms of physical warmth, thus activating the sense of touch ('Charles is a cold fish and Diana needs someone warm' – BNC), and we talk about disgust and trust in olfactory and gustatory terms, thus activating the senses of smell and taste ('[it] leaves a bad taste in their mouths'' 'it has left a bad smell of abuse of power' – BNC). As we saw in Chapter 2, these metaphorical relationships often operate not just on a linguistic level but also on a physical level, and can thus be described as embodied.

People who, for one reason or another, suffer from sensory impairments, or whose senses work in different ways, experience the world in very different ways from people whose senses function 'normally'. In some cases, such individuals compensate by making use of their other working senses, but in other cases, as we will see in this chapter, their sensory impairments or conditions allow them to experience the world in ways that are not available to the mainstream population and they thus consider their lives to be enriched by their condition. A question that therefore arises is whether and how this variation extends to embodied sensory metaphor. Do people who experience sensory impairments use the same sensory metaphors to make sense of the abstract world, and if so, do they use them in the same way? For example, does the fact that a person is blind make it more difficult for them to experience understanding in terms of seeing? Exploring questions such as these not only provides insight into the ways in which people with sensory impairments and conditions experience the world through metaphor but it also deepens our understanding of the link between the linguistic and physical aspects of embodied metaphor. In this chapter, I therefore explore how embodied sensory metaphors are processed by people who experience sensory impairments and/ or unusual sensory conditions. By doing so, I hope to extend our understanding of embodied metaphor beyond the experiences of people who Lakoff and Johnson (1980) describe as 'normal' (115) or 'prototypical' (132).

In the first part of the chapter, I examine the ways in which people with sensory impairments respond to so-called universal primary metaphors that involve the senses, and explore how this impacts on their own metaphorical thinking processes. I look at how their experiences with metaphor differ from those of people who do not have these impairments. Although there is some literature on the role of metaphor in representations of disability (see, for example, Mitchell and Snyder, 2006), there have been very few investigations to date into the impact of disabilities involving the senses on one's use of embodied metaphor. One notable exception is research in deaf studies, where there is a large and growing literature on the role played by embodied metaphor in sign languages (see, for example, Taub, 2001). I discuss this literature in depth and examine the hypothesis that deaf individuals experience embodied metaphor in a more direct way than hearing individuals. During this part of the chapter I explore how various sensory impairments might impact upon a person's experience of metaphor.

In the second part of the chapter, I look at how metaphors involving the senses are experienced by people with synaesthesia, a condition in which one sensory experience automatically triggers another. People who have this condition might experience sounds as visual patterns, numbers as colours, smells as physical sensations and so on. In contrast to people with sensory impairments, people with synaesthesia might be said to have a sensory 'surplus' in that they experience their senses in a more vivid and more inter-related way than people who do not have this condition. I report findings from a small-scale study that I conducted into the different ways in which synaesthetes and non-synaesthetes use metaphor to describe positive and negative sensory experiences.

6.2   Sensory Language and Impairments

Our use of the senses is central to our understanding of the world, and relationships between language and sensory perception are well established. For example, it has been shown that when people read odour-related words (such as 'garlic'), they experience increased activation in the olfactory areas of the brain (González et al., 2006). It has also been demonstrated that when people are asked to verify colour properties of objects (e.g., when they are asked to say whether a banana is yellow), they experience activation in the same part of the visual cortex as they would if they were completing a perceptual task that involves judging colour sequences. Goldberg et al.

(2006) found that the verification of colour, sound, touch and taste properties leads to activation in the cortical regions that are associated with the encoding of visual, auditory, tactile and gustatory experiences. Thus, when we hear property words such as 'loud' and 'sour' we simulate or re-enact sensory experiences of loudness and sourness. They found for example that when participants were asked to make judgements concerning fruit terms, taste and smell areas of the brain show increased blood flow. They also found that when participants were asked to make judgements involving body part and clothing terms, they experienced increased blood flow in brain areas associated with body perception. Finally, it has been found that the processing of sensory words such as 'fragrant', 'smooth' and 'blue' involves the recruitment of the brain areas that are involved in perceiving the corresponding percepts (Pecher et al., 2003). These findings suggest that when we are exposed to sensory concepts via the medium of language, our understanding of them is embodied.

According to Winter (2019), further evidence for a strong link between sensory activation and linguistic processing is provided by two phenomena: the so-called tactile disadvantage and the 'modality switching cost'. The 'tactile disadvantage' (Connell and Lynott, 2010) refers to the fact that the sense of touch is less easy to define and explain than the other four senses, and it takes people longer to detect tactile stimuli than visual and auditory stimuli (Turatto et al., 2004; Karns & Knight, 2009). The disadvantage for tactile processing has been shown to carry over into linguistic processing of sensory words, which suggests that there is a parallel 'tactile disadvantage' in both linguistic and conceptual processing (Connell and Lynott, 2010). The 'modality switching cost' refers to the fact that people are faster at perceiving stimuli when they appear in the same modality as preceding stimuli. It has been observed in both non-linguistic data (Spence et al., 2001; Turatto et al., 2004) and linguistic data (Pecher et al., 2003). Pecher et al. asked participants a series of questions about the properties of objects. For example, participants were asked to say whether a blender can be loud (true) or an oven can be baked (false). They found that when participants had been asked to verify a property in one modality, such as the auditory one (blender-loud), they were subsequently slower when performing a judgement in a different modality (cranberries-tart) as opposed to performing a judgement in the same modality (leaves-rustling). Together with the findings discussed in this section, the tactile disadvantage and the modality switching cost in the processing of sensory words provide evidence that comprehension of these words involves mentally accessing the corresponding perceptual modalities. Language and the senses appear to be intimately connected in that exposure to sensory-related language triggers the activation of sensory brain areas. The comprehension of sensory-related language can thus be said to involve embodied cognition.

As we saw previously, sensory language is often used metaphorically, so people can 'sniff' corruption, things that we hear or say can leave a 'bad taste' in one's mouth, we can talk about 'sharp' cheeses, 'loud' colours and 'smooth' music. There is evidence to suggest that sensory metaphors such as these are embodied. When people hear taste metaphors, such as 'the break up was bitter for him', these metaphors activate the primary and secondary gustatory cortex (Citron and Goldberg, 2014a). Moreover, many of the primary metaphors that have been discussed in the literature involve underlying systematic cross-sensory mappings, where a stimulus that is perceived by one sense correlates systematically with an experience in another sense. For example, in market research studies, the expectations that consumers have regarding the size of the product have been shown to be affected by the pitch of the voice-over, with higher pitched voiceovers leading consumers to expect smaller-sized products (Lowe, 2017). One of the earliest, and most famous, studies of cross-sensory metaphor is Köhler's (1929) identification of the so-called Bouba and Kiki effect, wherein, given the choice of two names ('Bouba' and 'Kiki') for two shapes (a rounded shape and an angular shape), partici-pants almost always label the rounded shapes 'Bouba' and the angular shape 'Kiki', which is indicative of a cross-sensory mapping process between sight and sound. Systematic cross-modal correspondences have also been found between odour and musical pitch. For example, the odour of vanilla is consist-ently more likely to be associated with a higher pitch. These relationships do not correspond to statistical regularities in the environment and cannot there-fore be explained in terms of associative learning, but they do appear to be consistent (Deroy, Crisinel and Spence, 2013). It has also been found that people systematically associate specific colours with particular tastes, and that these widely shared bidirectional cross-modal correspondences generalise across cultures (Spence et al., 2015). The greatest consistencies appear to be between the colour red and sweetness, the colour yellow and sourness, the colour white and saltiness, and the colour black and bitterness. Whereas, in some cases, these correspondences may have been triggered by the colours of the actual foods themselves (for example, sour lemons are yellow and salt is white), there is no association between red foods and sweetness, although there may be an evolutionary explanation in that some fruits and vegetables turn from green to red as they ripen (and thus become sweeter). Interestingly, participants in studies designed to elicit these sorts of correspondences do not report high levels of confidence in their associations, despite exhibiting strong consistency in terms of choice both between and within participants (Wan et al., 2014).

Spence and his colleagues are wary of metaphor-based explanations for this phenomenon as there are no clear mappings from concrete to abstract phenom-ena. They emphasise the complex nature of cross-modal correspondences and the role played by mediating factors. One such mediating factor in these relationships is emotion, and in their most recent work, they have found that emotion appears to play a role in the identification of cross-sensory correspondences. For example, in their study of cross-modal correspondences between classical music and red wine, Wang and Spence (2017) found that the emotional dimensions of dominance (i.e., the cline from weak to powerful) and arousal (the cline between calm and exciting) mediated the matchings. Participants were more likely to match a particular wine with a particular music selection if both were associated with a similar level of dominance and a *contrasting* level of arousal. However, the understanding of metaphors has also been shown to involve mediating factors, such as intensity (Barnden et al., 2003). Moreover, as we saw in Chapter 1, embodied metaphors are best described not in terms of 'mappings' from the source domain to the target domain but in terms of the target domain being 'experienced as' the source domain through a dynamic 'lived' experience that often involves emotion. We also saw that embodied metaphor does not always have to involve a concrete source domain and an abstract target domain; both domains can be concrete if they relate to bodily or sensory experiences. Under this broader and more nuanced definition, the intriguing findings made by Wang and Spence could indeed be seen as involving a form of embodied metaphor.

A key question that is of relevance to this volume is whether variation in people's sensory experiences is reflected in their experiences of sensory metaphors, and how metaphor processing is affected when people lose a particular sense, or experience different senses to different degrees. There is a large body of evidence to suggest that when one of the senses is diminished for whatever reason, other senses become stronger in order to compensate. Merabet and Pascuale-Leone (2010) report that blindness can confer advantages in other sensory modalities. Blind individuals (particularly, when blind from birth or very early in life) demonstrate comparable, and in some cases even superior, behavioural skills compared with sighted subjects. This includes finer tactile discrimination thresholds, superior performance in auditory pitch discrimination and spatial sound localisation. Superior performance has also been shown in various other behavioural and cognitive tasks including spatial navigation skills, speech discrimination and verbal memory recall. Merabet and Pascuale-Leone also report that deaf individuals exhibit enhanced tactile sensitivity and perform better than hearing individuals in distinguishing emotional expression and local facial features. They are also better than hearing individuals at performing peripheral visual tasks and distributing attention to the visual periphery. This augmentation of attentional resources towards the periphery may reflect the fact that they are compensating for an inability to hear references to activity that is taking place outside their direct field of vision.

In contrast, other studies have suggested that when infants suffer a sensory loss this can sometimes have a *negative* impact on the other senses. Gori (2015) and her research team have found that children only begin to integrate multi-sensory information at around the age of 8–10 and that before this the more 'accurate' sense calibrates all the others. When one of the calibrating senses is missing, other senses can be impaired. This is why children with visual impairments sometimes experience difficulties with the haptic or auditory perception of space, and children who have motor impairments sometimes experience difficulties in perceiving the visual dimension of objects. The impact that this is likely to have on embodied metaphor is unknown at this stage, and more empirical studies would be needed to identify such an effect.

Thus sensory impairments may lead to either gains or losses in other senses, depending on the context. In the following sections, I consider each of the five senses, and explore the ways in which sensory impairments or indeed sensory enhancements have been shown to affect, or might be hypothesised to affect, one's use of embodied sensory metaphor.

The Sense of Sight and Blindness

There is strong empirical support for the idea that because vision is the dominant human sense, visual words are more frequent in language (Viberg, 1983; 1993; San Roque et al., 2014), there is a greater variety of visual words, at least in English (Winter et al., 2018), and language is more attuned to visual discriminations than it is to other types of discrimination (Levinson and Majid, 2014: 416). In many languages, including English, the order of frequency with which people use sensory words is as follows, with sight being by far the most frequent: see > hear > touch > taste > smell (Viberg, 1983: 136). This leads to the question of whether embodied metaphors that involve vision, such as KNOWING IS SEEING, are as inherently meaningful to blind individuals, for whom vision is not the dominant sense.

A number of researchers have expressed concern about the inherent bias in language towards able-bodied people. For example, Vidali (2010) observes that if a person is born blind, they will be unlikely to experience an intimate connection between seeing and knowing and may thus experience the well-established metaphorical links between these two domains in a different way from sighted people. She notes that expressions in which disability serves as a metaphor for 'things gone awry with bodily and social disorders' (35), such as 'the blind leading the blind' or 'she was blind to the critique', are offensive to blind people. Such metaphors, Vidali argues, devalue the complex ways in which we 'know'. In order to partially resolve this issue and to combat the normative nature of sensory embodied metaphors, she proposes a 'disability approach to metaphor' that makes a virtue of the diversity offered by disability and encourages able bodied people to see the world from the perspective of disabled people both in literal and metaphorical terms, thus leading to the creative reinterpretation of 'conventional' metaphor. She goes on to argue that researchers should take their cue from artists and work 'critically, ethically and transgressively, and creatively at the edges of disability metaphor' (51) in order to challenge the beliefs that such metaphors are 'naturally' acquired. The main thrust of her argument is that more attention should be given to the creative products of blind or partially sighted individuals, and that following the example of such individuals would allow for the use of a fuller range of sensory experiences through which people experience the world. As an example of one such multi-sensory writer, she cites Nick Flynn's poetic interpretation of the ways in which the blind beekeeper Francois Huber (1750–1831) uses touch and taste to describe his relationship with the bees:

> Sometimes bees, the glittering
> Curtain they form, cling to me face,
> & the moment before knowing
> I can imagine them a leaf, able to be
> Brushed away, but they
> Hold on, their tongues
> Seek each pore,
> As if my cheek offered nectar, they move
> Delicately, caress & shade, as if not threatening
> To flood my eyes.
>
> *Nick Flynn. Blind Huber (2015)*

This poem moves our attention away from our eyes as the main sensory receptor and illustrates how a swarm of bees can be experienced through a variety of sensory modalities.

We can see from Vidali's writing that blindness affects the *salience* of embodied metaphors that draw on the source domain of sight. Blind and partially sighted individuals are arguably more aware of such metaphors and more likely to have an ambivalent attitude towards them. However, it must be noted that the salience of the condition, and of its relationship to language, is unlikely to remain stable and is itself subject to variation. We can see this in a quote from Kleege's (1991) autobiography, *Sight Unseen*:

My blindness is as intrinsically part of me as the shape of my hands or my predeliction for salty snacks. Some days, and in some contexts, my blindness is at the forefront of my consciousness. Other days it is not. When I am trying on gloves, or eating potato chips, my blindness hardly matters at all. It all depends on where I focus my attention. (Georgina Kleege, *Sight Unseen*, Yale University Press (1991), p. 4)

Furthermore, it is important to recognise that the experience of blindness does not preclude visual experiences. As Kleege goes on to note:

Though I see less than 10% of what a normal person does, I would describe myself as intensely visual. Given the choice, I would rather go to an art gallery or movie theatre rather than a concert hall. This is due in part to the fact that both my parents were visual artists. I grew up surrounded by their art and an awareness that vision involves more than aiming one's eyes at a particular object ... The pleasure I derive from visual media, and from the visible world in general, suggests that although my eyes are blind, my brain is still sighted. Through nature or nurture, I know how to make the most of what I see. (Georgina Kleege, *Sight Unseen*, Yale University Press (1991), pp. 1–2)

As for the tendency of blind and partially sighted individuals to make use of primary metaphors involving sight on a day-to-day basis, findings from behavioural studies present a mixed picture. Lossifova and Marmolejo-Ramos (2012) asked three groups of children (typically developing children, children with visual-motor impairments and blind children) to point at space and time locations in relation to their body. In other words, in the spatial deixis situation they were asked to use their hand or forefinger to point 'behind' or 'in front' and in the temporal deixis situation they were asked to use their hand or forefinger to point to 'yesterday' and 'tomorrow'. They found that typically developing children were almost twice as accurate in their performances of spatial deixis than in their performances of temporal deixis, and that the proportion of correct spatial deixis performances to correct temporal deixis performances increased with disability. In other words, blind children found it harder than typically developing children to relate space to time. Interestingly, the blind children were more likely than the sighted to children to point to their bodies and to the space immediately surrounding their bodies.

In a similar vein, Rinaldi et al. (2017) found that, unlike sighted adults, adults who have been blind from birth or from a very early age do not have an embodied conceptualisation of time as sitting along a sagittal spatial axis, with the past as behind and the future in front. They employed a space–time motor congruity task which required participants to classify a series of words as referring to the past or the future by moving their hand backwards or forwards. Sighted participants responded significantly faster in the congruent condition (i.e., when they were asked to move their hand forwards to indicate events occurring in the future and to move their hand backwards to indicate events occurring in the past) than in the incongruent condition. In contrast, blind participants did not show any such preferential time–space mapping. In a second part of the study, they had participants complete a questionnaire to ascertain how near or far they perceived events in the future and the past to be. For example, they were told about events occurring one day, three days, three weeks, one month etc. in the past and in the future, and for each event they were asked to state (on a scale from 1 to 10) how 'close' they felt the event to be, ranging from 0 (really close) to 10 (really far from now). Previous studies have shown that in sighted individuals future events are consistently scored as being closer in space than past events, which may relate to the fact that people can see what is in front of them but not what is behind them. Rinaldi et al. found that this was true for the sighted participants in their study (in line with previous findings) but not for the blind participants. Taken together, the findings from this two-part study suggest that normal visual development is crucial in conceptualisations of time involving the sagittal axis. Interestingly, in the second part of the study, the conceptualisations of the past and the future that were produced by the blind participants were significantly closer to the present than those produced by the sighted participants. Research has shown that blind people's experience of space is qualitatively different from that of sighted individuals, as it relies on haptic exploration and auditory input (Schinazi et al., 2016). Rinaldi et al. put these two facts together and proposed the intriguing hypothesis that the reduced amount of space that can be explored by the tactile and auditory modality (in comparison with the visual modality) may result in a collapse of time for blind individuals. This hypothesis also fits Lossifova and Marmolejo-Ramos's findings, which were mentioned earlier in this section, where blind children were more likely to point to their bodies and to the space immediately surrounding their bodies than the sighted children, who tended to point further away when indicating temporal deixis. The idea that blind individuals experience time in a more collapsed manner than sighted individuals is a hypothesis that is worthy of further investigation.

In contrast to these findings, an embodied metaphor which does not appear to be affected by the presence or absence of sightedness is the vertical representation of positive and negative emotions. Even congenitally blind people have been found to express pride and shame with upwards and downwards postures and gestures, respectively, even though they have never seen these behaviours modelled by other people (Tracy and Matsumoto, 2008). One reason for this finding could be that the representation of emotions along a vertical axis is a more embodied, experiential phenomenon than the representation of time along the sagittal axis. As such, it is experienced through senses other than sight. The link between body posture and emotional experience is an innate one, whilst time is a learned construct. These contrasting findings are interesting, as they show how a focus on the use of metaphor by people with sensory impairments can help us distinguish between different levels of embodiment. More work in this area would help to nuance our understanding of the role played by embodied cognition in the origin of primary metaphors involving the sense of sight.

The Sense of Hearing and Deafness

In the 1970s, many researchers believed that deaf people could not understand metaphor (e.g., Blackwell et al., 1978). However, during the 1980s, this assumption started to be questioned, with findings showing that deaf children and adults were just as able to comprehend metaphor as their hearing counterparts (Rittenhouse et al., 1981). In an attempt to explain these apparently conflicting findings, Siqueira (2016) investigated the ability of hearing-impaired individuals to comprehend different kinds of metaphor. She was interested in testing the hypothesis that hearing-impaired children comprehend primary metaphors but do not comprehend idioms as well as hearing children. She administered a verbal and non-verbal metaphor comprehension task, as well as an idiom comprehension task to seventeen Brazilian Portuguese hearing-impaired monolingual children and thirty-three Brazilian Portuguese monolingual children whose hearing was not impaired. All of these tasks were paper-based and none involved a listening component. She found a significant between-group difference in performance on the verbal metaphor task ($p < 0.001$) and on the idiom task ($p < 0.001$) but not in the non-verbal metaphor task. These findings suggest that although hearing-impaired children are able to form metaphorical mappings, they experience difficulty understanding linguistic metaphors. This may be due to the fact that, even though the comprehension of primary metaphors occurs primarily through embodiment, comprehension skills are reinforced through hearing input. Siqueira's findings support the idea that people who experience hearing impairments are able to form metaphorical connections between ideas, and it is only the linguistic manifestations of these connections that present difficulties. This is unsurprising, as it is difficult to think of a reason why hearing-impaired individuals would experience difficulties in identifying metaphorical links between concepts.

Further evidence to dispel the idea that hearing-impaired individuals experience difficulties with metaphor can be found in analyses of sign languages, which have been shown to be replete with metaphor. These languages contain both conventional and novel metaphors, many of which have a strong embodied basis. Indeed, Taub (2001) provides a book-length survey of the role played by metaphor, particularly embodied primary metaphor, in American Sign Language (ASL). She provides numerous examples of conventional metaphor use based on embodied primary metaphors and of creative extension of these metaphors, which sometimes involve complex combinations of several different metaphors all within the same sign.

A potential source of variation in the way deaf and hearing people experience embodied metaphor can be found in the physical characteristics of sign languages and the affordances that they offer. As Kaneko and Sutton-Spence (2016) point out, the fact that sign languages employ the body and space as their main articulators means that they are more iconic than spoken languages, and this makes the embodied metaphors that are used to express abstract concepts much more salient. The ASL sign THINK-PENETRATE ('to get one's point across') provides an example of this salience. This sign involves the use of the index finger on the dominant hand to represent a long thin object such as a drill bit (representing the idea or thought) 'drilling through' the flat non-dominant hand, which represents a flat wall. Here we can see an example of what Taub (2001) describes as a 'double mapping', where the sign is motivated by both iconicity (where the index finger represents the drill) and metaphor (where the drill represents the penetration of the idea into the brain). Similarly, in Spanish sign language, to say that one understands something, one extends the hand as if one were grasping something in front of one and draws it towards oneself, so the metaphorical idea of 'taking an idea in' is the default way of expressing understanding.

Another feature of sign languages that, according to Kaneko and Sutton-Spence, shapes the way in which deaf people use embodied metaphors is the fact that in sign languages a single sign often encapsulates information that would require a whole phrase or sentence in a spoken language. In addition to the movement of the hand, the hand shape, location, the nature of the movement and the orientation of the palm all add important information to the sign. Because sign languages have this feature, some metaphors that exist in spoken languages are not found in sign languages (Taub, 2001). For instance, the metaphor CONSUMING IS EATING, (e.g., where time can be 'eaten up') is not found in sign languages, as it is impossible to employ this sign without inadvertently providing information, through the hand shape and orientation etc., about the nature of the eating and what is being eaten, which triggers a literal reading of the sign. This information automatically triggers a literal reading of the sign. The underlying issue here is that any information contained in the original iconic mapping needs to be retained in the metaphorical mapping, regardless of its relevance, and metaphors such as eating require a more generic structure, which is simply not possible. There is therefore too much information in the sign to allow it to be used metaphorically. For this reason, this phenomenon is referred to as the 'double-mapping constraint' (Meir, 2010). As Kaneko and Sutton-Spence point out, the fact that a single sign can contain such a large amount of information provides potential for a type of creativity in signed metaphor that is harder to find in spoken languages; signers are able to play with the hand shape, orientation and/or positioning to add nuance and perspective to the metaphorical message that they are conveying.

There is also evidence to suggest that sign languages exploit the affordances offered by having one's whole body at one's disposal as a communicative resource in ways that spoken languages cannot, and that this leads to differences in the way one uses embodied metaphor. For example, Wilcox (2000) reports that in American Sign Language, a signer will normally point to the front of their forehead to indicate 'thinking'. However, he or she can distinguish between conscious and subconscious thought by pointing to the front or the back of the head. The back of the head is the seat of subconscious thought, as it contains information that is hidden from the signer. Wilcox (107) cites an occasion where a signer joked that he had told an interlocutor to remember consciously and to remember subconsciously by pointing to both the front and the back of his head, thus 'covering all bases'. Wilcox also talks about how classifiers involving hand shapes can be used to add entailments to metaphors. For example, when signing IDEAS ARE OBJECTS, the signer can manipulate his or her handshape to indicate the nature of the idea/object. He or she might, for instance, use a hand shape that reflects fine and deliberate motor control to indicate that the idea is a delicate one that needs to be handled carefully. More recently, it has been shown that ASL signers are able to make more nuanced use of event structure metaphors than speakers of American English, as they are able to use the spatial logic of the body as a container during signing (Roush, 2018).

There is also variation in the ways in which sign languages make use of sensory metaphor. Understandably, less use is made of metaphors based on sound and there is a corresponding increase in metaphors based on sight, touch, taste and smell. Some of the metaphorical signs that appear in sign languages reflect the physical experience of being deaf. For example, the metaphor SOUND INTENSITY IS VIBRATION (Peñalba et al., 2015) can be observed in Spanish sign language in words such as roncar (snore). There is also a vibration component in ASL, although the sign is different in terms of handshape configuration, location and orientation. As a second example, in Spanish sign language, to say that something 'sounds interesting' one puts the index finger and the middle finger together and then places the tips of these two fingers on the tip of the nose, so the phenomenon under consideration 'smells interesting'.[1]

Finally, some differences in the ways in which embodied metaphor is employed in sign languages and in spoken languages are more easily explained by a signer's world view. In her study of Brazilian sign language, Siqueira and Marques (2016) found that signers used their left hand to refer to hearing people and their right hand to refer to non-hearing people, thus reversing the normal order. This corresponds to Casasanto's (2009) work, which, as we saw in Chapter 5, shows that people use their dominant hand to refer to more positively valenced concepts.

The Senses of Taste and Smell

The senses of taste and smell are particularly interesting because, of all the senses, these are the two that are most closely tied to memory, particularly emotional memory (Krishna, 2012). The relationship between taste and emotional memory is famously illustrated by Marcel Proust in his (1908) novel *A la Recherche du Temps Perdu*, where the taste of a madeleine (a small cake) takes the protagonist immediately back to his childhood and all that was associated with it. One possible reason for the fact that taste and smell evoke such strong emotional memories is that all three functions (taste/smell, memory and emotion) sit within close proximity in the brain. All are located within the limbic system, which contains the olfactory bulb (taste/smell), the amygdala (emotion) and the hippocampus (memory). In advertising research, it has been shown that when an ambient smell is used, it can lead people to form emotion-based semantic connections with memories and lead to more favourable attitudes towards the product (Bosmans, 2006). Moreover, it has been found that memories that are triggered by scent-retrieval cues tend to be rated as more emotional than those that are triggered by other kinds of cues (Herz, 2004). Winter (2016) found that taste and smell words occur significantly more frequently in emotionally valenced phrases than words related to any of the other senses. He also found that taste- and smell-related words are more emotionally flexible in that they can be used to refer to both positive and negative phenomena. He argues from this that taste and smell words form an 'affectively loaded part of the English lexicon' (1). This may explain why many taboo words involve metaphors that are based on taste and smell (Allan and Burridge, 2006). The use of these two senses renders the words more visceral and more likely to shock.

To the best of my knowledge there has been no research into the impact of taste and smell deficits on people's understanding of taste and smell-related metaphors. The main reason for this is likely to be that taste and smell ability are hard to measure objectively, and the effect of these abilities on metaphor perception would be even harder to measure. The only available findings concerning variation in relation to smell are in the field of cross-cultural variation. In English, smell has been dubbed a 'muted sense' (Olofsson and Gottfried, 2015) because of the relatively limited number of smell terms in Indo-European languages. However, cross-linguistic studies have revealed that some languages have much larger smell vocabularies (Majid and Burenhult, 2014). The fact that the sense of smell is more difficult to describe in English than other senses means that more use needs to be made of metaphors that involve cross-sensory mappings (Williams, 1976; Yu, 2003), e.g., by borrowing taste-related vocabulary as in 'sweet fragrance', whereas in other languages that have more smell-related vocabulary, less use is made of cross-sensory metaphor. I will not describe these findings in detail here because I discuss this variation in more depth in Chapter 8 when I explore cross-linguistic and cross-cultural sources of variation in embodied metaphor.

The Sense of Touch and Apraxia

The sense of touch is the first sense to develop in the womb and the last sense that we lose with age (Krishna, 2012) and perhaps because of this, it forms the basis of a number of embodied metaphors, particularly those used to describe and relate emotional experiences. It has been pointed out that auditory concepts are more likely to be expressed through sound-symbolism, and that when this happens, the sound concepts are frequently described using touch terminology, as in 'rough sound', 'smooth sound' and 'harsh sound' (Winter, 2016). It is difficult to form and test hypotheses about the ways in which these associations might be affected by one's loss of the sense of touch, because there are few reported incidents of people losing their sense of touch. However, a condition that involves the sense of touch that may be interesting to explore in relation to metaphor production is *apraxia*. Apraxia is a cognitive disorder in which the patient loses the ability to accurately perform learned, skilled actions. As well as experiencing difficulties in the production of learned motor activities, apraxic individuals also exhibit impairments in the comprehension of action words. For example, Buxbaum and Saffran (2002) found that, in comparison with other patients who also had left hemisphere (LH) lesions, those patients who had left hemisphere lesions and were also apraxic exhibited difficulties in naming manmade objects, such as tools, but not animals. In addition, they found that apraxics exhibited impairments in body-part knowledge, which they attributed to the fact that body parts are intimately involved in the utilisation of tools. They also found that apraxic patients exhibited deficits in their knowledge of how objects are used (manner of manipulation), but not in their knowledge of what they are used for (their functions). It would be interesting to explore whether apraxic individuals experience difficulties comprehending or producing metaphors that involve tools and actions. To date there are no studies investigating the ways in which apraxics make use of metaphors involving action, touch and tool manipulation but such studies if they were to be carried out would shed interesting light on embodied metaphors and the ways in which they relate to real-world experience.

Although there has been no research on the impact of an impaired sense of touch on the ways in which people interact with embodied metaphor, there has been interesting research on the ways in which the experience of intense pain affects metaphorical thinking. Research has shown that people who experience intense physical pain that is literally 'beyond words' often resort to creative extensions of embodied metaphor when describing this pain to others, including healthcare professionals. Semino (2010) cites examples of patients who describe having tight metal coils wound around their bodies or drowning in piles of rubbish. Images such as these have as their source highly conventional primary metaphors but they are highly creative due to the intensity of the pain that is being described. In a similar study, Charteris-Black (2016) found that patients describing intense pain made extensive use of mixed metaphor when describing their pain. He argued that the use of mixed metaphor in descriptions of pain by such patients emphasises the fact that the pain is 'out of control' and therefore more intense.

So far in this chapter, I have discussed a number of ways in which people's use of embodied sensory metaphor is affected by sensory impairments. I have shown how sensory impairments affect people's choices of embodied metaphor, the ways in which people interact with them and the relative salience of the metaphors. Not all of these impairments should be framed solely in terms of a deficit, as we have seen that some offer opportunities for the use of different embodied metaphors, or facilitate creative manipulation of existing ones. These findings provide evidence for the embodied nature of sensory metaphor both at the physical level and at the phenomenological level. In the final part of the chapter, I discuss a condition that has been found to expand the number and types of sensory connections that are made: the condition is called 'synaesthesia'.

6.3   Synaesthesia

Synaesthesia is an extreme form of cross-sensory association which appears in just over 4 per cent of the total population, who are referred to as 'synaesthetes' (Simner, 2007). For people with this condition, the stimulation of one sense provokes involuntary stimulation of a different sense, leading people to make frequent associations between different senses. A good account of a synaesthesic experience can be found in Claire Morrall's (2003) novel *Astonishing Splashes of Colour*, whose protagonist, Kitty, has synaesthesia. Kitty's synaesthesia leads her to experience strong emotions as colours:

There are only certain times, when I feel right and he feels right. Then his white slows down so that all the yellows and blues and reds in his spectrum meet mine and merge, complementing the frenetic whirls of colour inside me. We look at each other and we match. Things can only work if we can share the colours out properly, evenly, between us. (*Astonishing Splashes of Colour*, Claire Morrall, Tindall Street Press, Birmingham, p. 102)

There are many different kinds of synaesthesia. For some synaesthetes, certain sounds might be associated with particular colours, and for others, certain textures might be associated with particular smells, or certain tastes might be associated with particular sounds, and so on. Thus 'Wednesday' might be perceived as 'orange', the number 4 might be perceived as 'happy', or the smell of diesel might be perceived as being 'blue' (Cytowic, 1989, 1994).

The condition can be broken down into two types: 'associator synaesthesia' (where associations, such as colours that may be triggered by days of the week are experienced in the mind's eye) and 'projected synaesthesia', where they are projected into space or onto the page, and actually 'seen' (Simner, 2007).

Synaesthesia has a neurological root. It is thought to be caused by unusually strong connections between the sensory cortex, which is responsible for receiving and integrating sensory information, and the amygdala, which is responsible for the processing of emotions (Ramachandran and Hubbard, 2001). Thus, synaesthetes experience unusually strong emotional reactions to sensory stimuli. Synaesthetes with auditory-visual synaesthesia have been found to show significantly more brain activation in the inferior parietal cortex during sound perception than non-synaesthetes (Neufeld, 2012). This area is involved in multi-modal integration, the perception of emotions in facial stimuli and the interpretation of sensory information.

Some of the associations that synaesthetes make appear to be motivated and non-arbitrary (Marks 1975). For instance, Simner et al. (2004) found that when asked to associate graphemes with colours, synaesthetes tended to associate higher frequency graphemes with higher frequency colour terms, whereas the choices made by non-synaesthetes were influenced by order of elicitation, and by exemplar typicality from the semantic class of colours. There is also evidence to suggest that synaesthetes experience time, number and space correlations more strongly than non-synaesthetes (Cohen Kadosh and Gertner, 2011), and as we saw in Chapter 4, according to the theory of Generalized Magnitude Representation, the association of time, number or space is a motivated phenomenon (Lourenco and Longo, 2011). However, some of the associations that are made by synaesthetes are motivated in different ways from those made by non-synaesthetes. For example, Cohen Kadosh et al. (2007) found that synaesthetes are likely to associate larger objects with darker stimuli and smaller objects with lighter stimuli. This pattern is in line with behaviour exhibited by infants but not adults. This finding suggests that association patterns favoured by synaesthetes are perhaps more biologically embodied, whereas those favoured by non-synaesthetic adults are more likely to be acquired through socialisation processes.

Other work on synaesthesia (e.g., Ramachandran and Hubbard, 2001) has emphasised the creative nature of the associations that are made by synaesthetes. There is evidence to suggest that synaesthesic individuals are better at creative thinking than non-synaesthesic individuals (Dailey et al., 2010) and that this manifests itself in a range of activities including art, language and music (Mulvenna, 2013). One explanation for this may be the higher levels of neural connectivity that are a significant common denominator to synaesthesia and creativity. This neural connectivity facilitates associative thinking, which is a central component of creative thinking tasks. Synaesthetes also experience strong emotional reactions to some pairings, especially when they are 'incorrect' (e.g., when numbers are printed in the 'wrong' colour). According to Ramachandran and Hubbard, this is likely to be due to the hyperconnectivity that synaesthetes experience between the sensory cortex and amygdala.

This idea has been challenged by Ward et al. (2008), who see creativity as a more intentional, conscious and deliberate process. They point to the role played by the prefrontal cortex in developing retrieval strategies, holding options in mind and verifying whether novel associations have validity. They argue that these deliberate, goal-driven processes are very different from the more automatic connections that are made by synaesthetes. However, the fact that many of the creative connections made by synaesthetes appear to be metaphorically motivated and the fact that synaesthetes experience strong emotional reactions in response to some stimuli, which appear to drive the production of cross-sensory metaphor production, means that their responses are worthy of investigation. They may provide insights into the relationship between the body, the emotions and metaphorical creativity. To date, we know very little about the kinds of cross-sensory metaphoric connections that synaesthetes make and how these differ from those made by non-synaesthetes. We also know very little about the role played by emotion and other affective factors.

How Do Synesthetic Individuals Employ Metaphor When Talking about Sensory Experiences?

In order to investigate some of these issues, we (Littlemore and Turner, in prep.) conducted a study designed to investigate how synaesthetes employ cross-sensory metaphors when asked to write about objects that stimulate the senses. We were interested in finding out what kinds of metaphor they employed when doing so, to what extent and in which ways these metaphors were motivated and/or novel, which cross-sensory mappings were favoured and what role was played by emotion in the creation of synaesthesic associations. We were also interested in finding out whether associations that involve embodied metaphor are experienced more viscerally by synaesthetes than by non synaesthetes. Finally, we were interested in investigating whether individuals with associator synaesthesia differ in any way from individuals with projector synaesthesia in these respects.

In order to answer these questions, we administered an online survey to twenty synaesthetes (recruited via the UK Synaesthesia Association and through online synaesthesia fora) and twenty non-synaesthetes (recruited through social media). We began by asking them to write about something they like to see and something they don't like to see. We then repeated the question for the remaining four senses (taste, hearing, smell and touch). Next we showed them the names of the six basic emotions (happiness, sadness, fear, anger, surprise and disgust) and asked them to write what came to mind when they read these words. In the third part of the study, we asked them to read the following sentences:

- 'Seeing those people again made my skin crawl'
- 'It made me feel sick to see such meaningless cruelty'
- 'The sound of fingernails of a chalkboard set my teeth on edge'
- 'Their constant excuses left a bad taste in my mouth'.

They were asked to imagine that they had just said each of these sentences to a friend and then to indicate on a scale from 1 to 5 how literal they thought they were. Here our hypothesis was that the synaesthesic participants would understand the sentences as being more literal than the non-synaesthesic participants. Finally, we asked the synaesthesic participants what kind of synaesthesia they had (e.g., whether they associated letters/words with colours, sounds with colours, numerical sequences with points in space, ordered sequences, such as days of the week or months of the year, with personalities or genders, words with tastes or whether they experienced other types of associations.

As predicted, the synaesthetes were significantly more likely to understand the above sentences as literal than were the non-synaesthetes ($p < 0.01$), which suggests that embodied metaphor is understood more 'literally' in synaesthesia. When responding to the question about things they liked and didn't like to see, taste, hear, smell and touch, there were differences between the two groups in terms of the number of cross-sensory mappings made, with the synaesthetes making far more cross-sensory mappings than the non-synaesthetes. There were also differences in terms of the source domains that were used by the two groups in their cross-sensory mappings. Across the data, by far the most common sense that participants referred to in their answers was touch (92), followed by sight (53), then sound (10), then taste (6), then smell (3). Interestingly, all the sound, taste and smell responses were produced by the synaesthetes. The non-synaesthetes only made use of touch and sight in their responses.

The majority of the associations made by the synaesthetes were motivated by and corresponded to existing conceptual metaphors. The most common metaphorical correspondences motivating their responses were warmth and coldness, light and dark, order versus chaos, sharpness and bluntness, level of intensity, duration, differentiation and movement. These associations were often extended in novel ways, as we can see in the following examples:

> I hate hearing pure bright high singing because *it sounds like jagged white walls and they become overwhelming and bright.*

> I hate the sound of metal that squeals. When I hear it I see *silver lightning bolts coming from the source.*

A number of the metaphorical explanations produced by the synaesthetes involved personification:

> Ocean air feels like it's calling, *"let me love you!!!"*

> The bass is my favourite instrument. I love its warmth and the way *the sound just holds you in a way.*

The synaesthetes responded on a much more emotional level and on a much more physical level than the non-synaesthetes and were much more likely to report that the stimulus affected their thinking patterns:

> Drips falling from the roof into a pail outside my window. They wear *a hole in your mind*

In addition to cross-sensory correspondences and metaphor, the responses produced by the synaesthetes contained more empathy than those produced by the non-synaesthetes, possibly because of the strong and involuntary tendency to link other senses to the sense of touch:

> I do not like to see pain or things that are painful or disgusting. When viewing someone get a cut or other bodily damage, it is very difficult not to imagine the feeling. *If someone's having their hand or arm cut, I often shake my arm to get the feeling out.* It is very unpleasant.

Interestingly, some synaesthetes even reported feeling empathy with inanimate objects, as we can see in the following example:

> The reason this is enjoyable is that it helps to 'empathize' with things that most people probably wouldn't even know you could empathize with; *yellow street-lines, beehives, computer monitors, etc.*. (I use empathize in a way similar to, but not exactly like it's actual definition. Rather, it is closer to a feeling of 'complete understanding' of that one object).

The fact that the synaesthetes appeared to feel closer to the objects and experiences being described meant that at times they appeared to conflate literal and metaphorical experiences:

> I don't like to see a cluttered room, it clutters my mind.

This conflation of literal and metaphorical meaning is similar to that experienced by individuals with anorexia, which was discussed in Chapter 5.

The synaesthetes were much less likely than the non-synaesthetes to produce literal explanations for their responses or explanations that were based on associations. Here are some examples typical of those produced by the non-synaesthetes:

> Strong body odour/perspiration. *Suggests lack of cleanliness and hygiene.*

> Petunias. *It reminds me of a place where we used to go on holiday*, where there were lots growing by the main footpath.

> I love the smell of a dog after the vet *because it reminds me of my childhood*

The fact that synaesthetes reported enhanced empathy, made stronger metaphorical connections across the senses, displayed stronger personal emotional reactions to stimuli and experienced metaphor in a more physical way than the non-synaesthetes resonates with the findings discussed in Chapter 3, which showed that these factors are strongly related to one another. It therefore appears to be the case that embodied metaphor, empathy, emotion and physical experience are intrinsically linked through a symbiotic relationship, and that this link is particularly prominent in synaesthetes. Here are some specific examples illustrating the differences provided by the synaesthetes and non-synaesthetes in response to the different sensory prompts:

Sight

When describing things they liked and didn't like to see, the synaesthetes reported far more cross-sensory responses than the non-synaesthetes. They described sight predominantly in terms of touch, as we can see in the following examples:

> I like to see words and to read them, *because in my head I "feel" them quite strongly. Not a physical texture, but the meanings, the shapes, and the colors.*

> I like the color purple. *It's like silk fabric that caresses and folds over my mind.*

> Chain-link fence with either very small holes, or a "barbed-wire"-style top. In the first case, *it feels gritty, rough, screechy to look at;* in the latter, the pattern is broken too harshly and in a way that feels very much like running one's hands down slightly rusty metal.

In this last example, we can see a metaphorical link between the idea of small holes which look like barbed wire and which therefore feel rough and 'screechy'. Some of their responses involved sound, such as the following:

> Peacocks. I hate the patterning. *It's like somebody playing the piano out of tune.* It's awful.

The synaesthetes also made more use than the non-synaesthetes of personification:

> The waves seem *angry* and I do not trust them

In many cases, the synaesthetes reported a strong physical response to the stimuli:

> I don't like the colour yellow. *It's too startling and hurts my brain.* It's sudden.

The *synaesthetes* also made some use of resemblance metaphor, again reporting strong emotional reactions to the stimuli:

> *I don't like to look at baby carrots for too long. They remind me of obesity. They're too smooth, and I do not like the little ridges.* I'm not joking, *sometimes the images of carrots keep me up at night. It's been this way since I was little. I was always afraid of becoming fat, and I guess it manifested itself in the texture of baby carrots.*

On the one occasion where taste was used as a source domain to describe a sight stimulus, it appeared to be motivated by a resemblance metaphor in which a sunset was compared to sherbet:

> *It makes me think of rainbow sherbet, even though those colors are not right – too orange and dark mulberry, and not mixed together. However, if sunsets had a flavor, they would be sweet and tangy like rainbow sherbet.*

Sound

Unlike the non-synaesthetes, the synaesthetes reported experiencing physical responses to sounds that they did and did not like, as we can see in the following example:

> The sounds – *I can feel them in my head. Like a little massage.*

The two senses most commonly evoked by sound in the synaesthetes were sight and touch, and these senses were sometimes combined in a single answer, as in the following:

> His voice *melts my mind and makes me warm* ... *[it] looks like deep dark colours* and it is my favourite sound.

Many of the responses produced by the synaesthetes involved metaphorical mappings, such as the following, which relates metaphorical heaviness and thickness to an embodied sinking sensation:

> An example of a voice I don't want to hear (not that it's not a nice voice, it's just uncomfortable to listen to), is the song "Royals" by Lorde. *Her voice is very heavy and thick and makes me feel like I'm sinking down slowly under dark water.*

There were many examples of novel resemblance metaphors in the synaesthetes' data, for example:

> His voice was brown, woody, and prickly like a pine cone.

The reactions reported by the synaesthetes to different sounds were much more physical, emotional and intense than those reported by the non-synaesthetes, as we can see in the following example:

> [very] high-pitched noises. *These terrify me.* If any of my skin is left uncovered when I hear these sounds, I NEED them to be covered immediately, or at the least I need to get off of the ground. *They feel like thousands of red hot needles stabbing in to every inch of my body over and over, and they look like seeing a fire from INSIDE the fire* ...

This reflects findings from neurolinguistics, where it has been shown that during sound perception, synaesthetes show significantly more brain activation in the inferior parietal cortex than non-synaesthetes (Neufeld, 2012). This area is involved in multi-modal integration, the perception of emotions in facial stimuli and the interpretation of sensory information.

In addition to providing further evidence for the already well-established link between sound and vision, our data also revealed associations between sound stimuli and other senses. For example, many synaesthetes reported that sounds made them see colours:

> *Vacuums make me see so much red* it's actually a little uncomfortable.

> I hate the flute. So much. I don't like how airy it is. I get lightheaded thinking about it. *The color of the sound is a terribly obnoxious baby blue.*

The non-synaesthetes did occasionally report physical responses to sounds but these were not motivated by metaphorical correspondences in the same way as those experienced by the synaesthetes. Here is an example:

> Arguments or bickering amongst adults - makes me feel anxious and want to remove myself from the area I'm in. Dogs barking over prolonged periods – very stressful. Whistling – a phobia I have. The noise of a whistle just grates and makes me literally shiver. People clicking their fingers or hands to release whatever it is they have to My arms become riddled in goose bumps!

Smell

As with the other senses, the responses reported by the synaesthetes to various smells involved more cross-sensory mappings than those produced by the non-synaesthetes, and many of these mappings involved metaphor. Some of the responses of the synaesthetes to the bad smells involved a range of senses, such as the following, which involves sound, touch and taste:

Candles that supposedly smell like coffee are disgusting. *They smell like the loud static sound a TV makes when it's turned to a channel you don't have.* It feels like breathing in pepper-spray but without all the coughing and choking. Fake peach scent in candy or candles makes me gag. My stomach doesn't get upset, but it sets off my gag reflex. I don't think there are words to describe how awful that scent is, but it gets in your mouth so that you taste the nasty fake peach flavor when you smell it.

Here the smell of the candles is described in terms of sound ('like the loud static sound a TV makes'), touch ('It feels like breathing in pepper-spray') and taste ('so that you taste the nasty fake peach flavor when you smell it'). Running through the whole response is a metaphorical reference to roughness versus smoothness, though this is not stated explicitly.

The synaesthetes also expressed much more 'personal' relationships with the stimuli, and as a result sometimes expressed annoyance when the cross-sensory mappings were somehow 'wrong', suggesting that they had strong feelings about what they 'should' and 'should not' be:

I don't like to smell gasoline because the color of the smell is bright orange but gasoline isn't and that annoys me. Bleach smells light blue but it is actually clear; that annoys me too.

The responses provided by the synaesthetes to smells also involved more hyperbole than those produced by the non-synaesthetes, as we can see here:

The last time someone bought this and was about to use it, *I quite literally ripped it from their hands and emptied and entire bottle outside.* If you can't tell, I loathe smells, since they almost always taste awful.

Not all of the cross-sensory mappings produced by the synaesthetes were metaphorical, as we can see in the following example:

I don't like to smell cooked green or red peppers because *it reminds me of their texture.*

The synaesthetes sometimes provided literal responses to some of the questions that did not involve cross-sensory mappings, but when they did so, their answers tended to be more novel than those produced by the non-synaesthetes, as we can see in the following example:

Laundry washed without detergent. *A bit of sweat cooked in warm water is quite a musky and unfortunate aroma* and it tends to infect the area for a while.

The synaesthetes were more likely than the non-synaesthetes to describe concrete entities metaphorically in terms of abstract entities:

My favorite scents are citrus or vanilla. Citrus smells fun. Vanilla smells like *refined confidence.*

In contrast, the non-synaesthetes' responses to smells were all either literal or were based on personal associations:

> I do not like the smell of hospitals/disinfectant. The smell is often too strong / overwhelming and *I associate it with illness.*

Taste

Whereas the non-synaesthetes described tastes in very literal terms, the synaesthetes made use of a range of sensory modalities including sound:

> The taste is like a 'burn', but not quite. Take the searing feeling out of a burn and discard the pain and discomfort. If all you have is the searing feeling, that is bell peppers and celery. *Much like the sound of a Harley,* tasting either of these makes me angry, instantly.

And sight:

> I don't like some types of Hershey's chocolate because *they taste like how ripped up tires look.*

And in some cases, a particular flavour or combination of flavours could evoke several different senses at once:

> On their own, bananas and honey are already miraculous. They're so delicious and they invoke so many different senses and thoughts and ideas all at once that it's impossible to describe. But, combined? It is an entirely new level of bliss. Think 'ambrosia' from Greek mythology. It is something so far beyond comprehension. One of very few things that triggers literally every sense at once. I take a bite, and … *It smells like rain. It sounds like a deep pink/ blue noise. It looks like a beautiful, opalescent fractal. It feels like velvet all over my body.*

The synaesthetes' explanations for not liking certain flavours were more likely than those produced by the non-synaesthetes to involve personification:

> Lemons. *Lemons need to chill out.* Eggs and cheese. Feels fake. Anything too bitter, for obvious reasons.

> Water which is flavored, but only slightly. *What are you? Are you water or are you flavored water? Pick something!*

The synaesthetes were also more likely to refer to the texture of the food that they were describing, and many of their responses involved resemblance metaphor, such as the following:

> Pickled beets taste like death. Raw mushrooms *are like eating sliced sponges,* and cooked mushrooms *are like slimy slugs.*

Synaesthetes reported particularly strong emotional reactions to certain stimuli, and these associations were occasionally somewhat idiosyncratic:

Caraway seeds have *an intensely disturbing taste* but I can't exactly describe why.

They also produced some metaphors where a concrete target domain was described in terms of both an abstract and a concrete source domain:

Those cookies tasted of *regret and rotting flesh.*

In this respect, the responses provided by the synaesthetes when describing tastes were similar to those that they provided when describing smells, in that they involved abstract ideas (e.g., regret and confidence) that were closely tied to emotional experiences.

Touch

When talking about touch, again the synaesthetes made more use of cross-sensory mappings than the non-synaesthetes and many of these were metaphorically motivated. Here, for example, a participant associates a soft texture with a 'soft' colour (pink):

Velvet is quite enjoyable. I find that most 'feelings' don't invoke any other senses. *Velvet is always pink, however, (regardless of its actual, physical color).*

And here a participant describes a rough texture in terms of a 'rough' sound:

Rough linen, it feels pretty like thunder.

Here a participant describes a sharp sensation in terms of a sharp sound:

Paper. Feels like the sharp edge of a knife and *sounds like nails on a chalkboard.*

And here a participant describes a sharp sensation in terms of a sharp image:

I hate scratching my nails through paper onto a table. The paper sticks to my nails and *the feeling is very green and has jagged squares all around it.* I can never see it completely though.

The synaesthetes were also more likely than the non-synaesthetes to make use of novel resemblance metaphors in their responses:

I stepped on a pile of wood grubs that were under a piece of wood. *They poured like tiny balloons filled with mashed potatoes.* I only felt the sensation of them popping through my shoe, but it almost made me throw up. I rarely get nauseous from something like that.

When describing things they did not like to touch, both synaesthetes and non-synaesthetes described physical responses to pain (understandably) but, in addition to this, the synaesthetes described physical responses to non–pain-related phenomena, such as the following:

> Many coats and some sweatpants have a lining inside them that's supposedly very soft and very warm, *but to me it's just suffocating. It makes me feel that if I pressed my face in it, the texture would clog my respiratory system.* I don't like how being loved feels like. *It creeps the hell out of me, the involuntary warmth somewhere deep in my chest area and the way my skin crawls along my neck and shoulders.*

As we can see from these examples, not only did the responses produced by the synaesthetes involve more cross-sensory mappings than those produced by the non-synaesthetes but they also involved a great deal of metaphor, and were more novel, empathetic, emotional, physical and 'embodied' than those produced by the non-synaesthetes. Taken together, these findings suggest that embodied metaphor is more active and salient within the synaesthesic population than in the non-synaesthesic population, and that this is a result of increased levels of neural connectivity, particularly in the inferior parietal cortex, which is responsible for the recognition of sensory stimuli, multi-modal integration and the perception of emotion. Thus we can conclude that people with synaesthesia experience metaphor in a very different way from people who do not have this condition and that there is a neurological explanation for this difference.

The most interesting findings here are that the metaphorical cross-sensory associations that synaesthetes form evoke strong, personal and emotional responses and can trigger feelings of empathy even with inanimate objects. The metaphors that they produce are decidedly novel and come across as being highly creative. Although we cannot say for sure whether this creativity was intentional, the metaphors that they produce would be certainly marked as 'creative' according to any objective criteria for creativity, as they involve new correspondences between entities or highly novel twists on existing correspondences. These findings suggest that there may be a symbiotic relationship between cross-sensory metaphor, emotion, empathy and creativity. This resonates with the research findings discussed in Chapter 2, which highlight the key roles played by novelty and emotion in the embodiment of metaphor.

6.4   Conclusion

In this chapter, we have seen yet more evidence for the non-universal nature of embodied metaphor. We have seen that some physical conditions, such as blindness, lead people to resist conventional uses of primary metaphors that have an embodied basis, and even if they cannot stop using the metaphors altogether, they can reclaim them and use them in ironic and creative ways. We have also seen that people with other types of disabilities such as deafness, which lead them to communicate using other modalities, are able to exploit the affordances offered by these modes of expression in order to do new and creative things with conventional metaphors, and to even form new embodied metaphorical associations. Finally, individuals with synaesthesia have been shown to generate highly creative metaphorically motivated cross-sensory connections that trigger strong emotions and physical responses. At times, these associations entail a degree of empathy with the inanimate objects, which suggests an element of personification. These characteristics constitute yet another way of engaging with embodied metaphor that has not been discussed in mainstream accounts of the phenomenon. They bear a striking resemblance to those characteristics that were discussed in Chapter 4 when we looked at the ways in which children relate to embodied metaphors. Like children, people with synaesthesia appear to engage with embodied metaphor on a highly personal and emotional level. They experience a heightened degree of animacy and use their own real-life experiences to generate new mappings. This lends further support to the idea that emotion, creativity and personalisation are strongly implicated in, and can be facilitated by, embodied metaphor.

7 'Things Come Out of My Mouth That Shouldn't Be There.'

'Altered Minds': The Impact of Depression and Psychological Disorders on the Way People Experience the World through Metaphor

7.1 Introduction

In the opening words of an article on depression for the *The Big Issue* magazine,[1] Beth Rowland, who runs a support network for young people who have experienced bereavement, talks about the feelings that she experienced immediately after her mother's death:

> Have you ever wondered what it would be like to be *pulled into a black hole*? The inevitability of the *darkness*, the *struggle against the force*, the *crushing pain*, the emptiness of everything? (*The Big Issue*, 21 May 2018 (p.15))

In this extract, she describes her negative emotional experiences in terms of a series of imagined physical experiences. Although none of us have ever entered a black hole, we all know what it is like to be pulled, to struggle and to experience darkness and pain. We can therefore relate to these metaphors on a physical level, which means that they are to some extent embodied. Metaphors such as these have been shown to be particularly prevalent in the language used when people are communicating about emotionally charged, life-changing experiences (Semino, 2011). As we saw in Chapter 3, studies have shown that the experience of intense emotions leads to the production of metaphor (Fainsilber and Ortony, 1987), and that people generate more *novel* metaphors when writing about their own feelings than when writing about the feelings of others (MacCormac, 1986; Williams-Whitney, Mio and Whitney, 1992). In his study of narratives produced by women suffering from cancer, Gibbs (2002) found a particularly high density of powerful embodied metaphors. He argued that these embodied metaphors helped them to understand and come to terms with their disease. This is perhaps unsurprising: when an experience is not widely shared with the rest of society, metaphor is often the only tool that people have to communicate with (Gibbs, 1994).

As we will see in this chapter, when people have experienced extreme forms of grief, they often report that they have become a 'different person' as a result of the experience, that their minds are somehow 'altered' and that there is 'no going back' to who they were. This idea of 'altered minds', and the impact that these altered minds have on the way people experience the world through metaphor, forms the focus of this chapter. Again, the findings will provide further evidence of diversity in the experience of embodied metaphor, but, perhaps more importantly, they have a real-world application: by understanding the ways in which the experience of grief alters people's metaphorical perceptions of the world, we may find better ways to support them.

I begin the chapter by looking at depression, focusing on grief following bereavement, and explore how this shapes people's metaphorical world view. I discuss findings from work that I am currently conducting, in collaboration with colleagues, on the role played by embodied metaphor in the experience of grief by people affected by pregnancy loss. This is a particularly intense form of bereavement, as the parents are mourning the loss of a child who they never had the opportunity to get to know.

I then go on to discuss two other, very different, *literally* 'mind-altering' psychological/neurological conditions that also appear to affect the ways in which people interact with metaphor: schizophrenia and autistic spectrum disorders (ASD). People with both these conditions have been found to experience difficulties with metaphor, but for different reasons. It has been suggested that the successful comprehension of novel metaphors in neuro-typical individuals requires the well-balanced integration of rigid semantic processing, which is normally conducted by the left hemisphere, and flexible semantic processing, which is normally conducted by the right hemisphere (Faust and Kenett, 2014). This is because, whilst the interpretation needs to be creative, it also needs to make sense. Faust and Kenett argue that the interaction between these two systems sits on a 'rigidity-chaos' semantic continuum with hyper-rigid, rule-based semantic processing at one extreme and chaotic, over-flexible semantic processing at the other extreme. They suggest that individuals with ASD tend to sit at the 'rigid' end of this continuum, whilst individuals with schizophrenia tend to sit at the 'flexible' end of the continuum. For this reason, both sets of individuals experience difficulties with novel metaphor comprehension, although the difficulties that they experience are very different. When making and interpreting metaphorical mappings, people with ASD are thought to conduct searches that are too narrow and focussed, whereas people with schizophrenia are thought to conduct searches that are too broad and all-encompassing.

The focus to date has been on the ways in which people with these conditions understand and produce linguistic metaphor, and there has been no work to date on the ways in which they work with embodied metaphor. Moreover, in both cases, there appear to be contradictory findings, with some studies showing that people suffering from these conditions experience difficulties in understanding and using metaphor, and others showing that they are at times they are able to produce highly creative metaphors. In this chapter, I identify reasons for these apparently contradictory findings and bring in the idea of embodied metaphor. I suggest that a focus on embodied metaphor might help to reconcile these apparently contradictory findings. I then analyse a number of interviews with individuals who have schizophrenia in order to examine how they make use of embodied metaphor to reflect on their illness.

To sum up, in this chapter, I look at how different states of mind and disorders affect the way people experience and use embodied metaphor. By doing so, I hope to reveal yet another way in which this supposedly universal phenomenon is experienced in different ways by different people. More importantly, by examining the different metaphors that are employed by people whose states of mind have been altered either through a traumatic experience or through a psychological or neurological disorder, I hope to provide insights into these unusual states of mind, which will help us to better understand them and ultimately to help those who experience them. I will focus on their use of embodied metaphors, as these go right to the core of people's experiences, and within this subset, I will focus on their creative uses of embodied metaphor, as these show how their psychological experiences and states of mind differ from those of people who are not suffering from these conditions. By understanding the different, and often novel, ways in which people suffering from these conditions employ embodied metaphor to frame their experiences, we can gain insights into their thinking processes and ultimately open up additional lines of communication.

7.2   Depression

There is a large body of literature exploring the ways in which people who have experienced crisis and loss use metaphor to frame the experience (Papp, 1982; Christi and McGrath, 1987; Rosenblatt, 1994, 2000, 2007). Depression itself is often described in very embodied terms, with people referring to notions of darkness, descent, confinement, weight and lack of control (see, for example, McMullen and Conway, 2002). Depression is also frequently given agency (Körner et al., 2011). The concept of depression as agent involves animacy, and depression is even sometimes embodied in animal form, as in the former British Prime Minister Winston Churchill's famous description of his depression as the 'black dog'.

People who are experiencing depression following bereavement are particularly likely to make use of creative metaphors to make sense of their new reality, and their use of such metaphors helps them to express and explore emotions that might otherwise be difficult to express (Nadeau, 2006). We can see this in the aforementioned study by Körner et al., who report one of the participants in their study as saying: 'The black dog just came and sat on my face and built a kennel.' Many of the creative metaphors that depressed individuals produce involve novel extensions of embodied primary metaphors, though they are not usually discussed in these terms. We can see examples of this in Nadeau's analysis of four metaphorical scenarios that people in grief counselling sessions following bereavement used to describe their experience of loss. Although Nadeau does not mention embodied metaphor, we can see that each of these four scenarios involves a creative elaboration of a complex mix of several embodied metaphors.

The first scenario was that of a man who had experienced the loss of several members of his family. He described his experience in the following way:

I'm coming back to where I was. It's like a geodesic sphere coming apart, where you can see spaces between that are dark. The parts reorganize themselves and come back to the whole. You are not really different. You just know that you can come apart and go back together. (Nadeau, 2006: 207)

Although highly creative, this metaphor draws on a number of recognisable embodied primary metaphors. The metaphor as a whole is embodied in that he actually is the geodesic sphere, and within this over-arching embodied metaphor, a number of references are made to other metaphors, such as, THE NATURE OF AN ENTITY IS ITS SHAPE, NEGATIVE AFFECT IS DARKNESS and INTER-RELATEDNESS IS PHYSICAL CONNECTEDNESS.

The second scenario, which was described by a woman who was undergoing a painful divorce, involved embodied metaphor in a slightly different way. She talked about the pleasure she derived from driving long distances away from her home town to smaller towns where she attended events organised for single people, educational seminars and dancing classes. She did all of this in her luxury car, and emphasised the fact that she enjoyed being at the wheel and therefore 'in control of her destiny'. This idea of being 'in the driving seat' dominated much of her self-talk as she went through divorce proceedings. This is an interesting example, as the idea of 'being in the driving seat' works both metaphorically and literally, with real physical enactment of the source domain taking place. By enacting the metaphor, she re-enforces its meaning. As with the previous example, the protagonist placed herself at the centre of a metaphorical scenario, putting herself in the leading role. Within this over-arching enacted and embodied metaphorical scenario, one can see evidence of a number of embodied primary metaphors that are based on the SOURCE-PATH-GOAL schema. These include CHANGE IS MOTION, ACTION IS SELF-PROPELLED MOTION and ACHIEVING A PURPOSE IS ARRIVING AT A DESTINATION.

The third scenario was described by a woman whose daughter had been missing for a year before the remains of her body were found. Her embodied metaphorical scenario first took the form of a recurring nightmare in which she was being buried alive as part of a sacrificial ritual. She then went on to report that this dream expressed how she saw her current situation:

> There had to be a sacrifice made and it had to come from within the family. Dad said 'No!', Mum said 'No!' All said 'No!' It got all the way to me and then there was no choice. I wasn't asked. I didn't resist. In the dream I crawled into a hole in the ground and my family threw dirt on me. It's kinda what they wanted. They seemed pleased as if they could go on living if I wasn't there; if I didn't exist. My presence kept something from them. That's how it always felt to me. (Nadeau, 2006: 212)

Again, the bereaved individual placed herself at the centre of an embodied metaphorical scenario, which draws on a number of embodied primary metaphors, including SAD IS DOWN, PSYCHOLOGICAL HARM IS PHYSICAL INJURY, BAD IS DARK, IMPERFECTION IS DIRT and BEING IN CONTROL IS BEING ABOVE.

The fourth scenario was described by a woman whose father had committed suicide, leaving a wife and four adult children. Her father had been abused in childhood, and as a result, in order to protect his current family, had cut himself off from his parents and siblings. She reported her metaphor in the following way:

> The image I have is of our family clinging to a life raft . . . the raft is the sum of us, the sense of unity. Peggy, my brother's friend, is swimming away and taking my brother, Jake, with her. There are sharks in the water and they are the same for me as they were for Dad. What are the sharks? The sharks are Dad's parents. If sharks ate their young, my father would become the bait. He blocked the abuse by not passing it on to use but he never got over it, being abused himself. The sharks are also the brothers from whom my father was cut off. (Nadeau, 2006: 214)

In this fourth and final scenario, the bereaved individual also placed herself at the centre of a complex, creative embodied metaphorical scenario where she and her family were drifting on a raft. The raft had the advantage of being safe, but the disadvantages of being difficult to steer and forcing them all into close proximity with one another. Again, the scenario appears to be underpinned by several different embodied metaphors, including: ORGANIZATION IS PHYSICAL STRUCTURE, ASSISTANCE IS SUPPORT, EMOTIONAL DISTANCE IS PHYSICAL DISTANCE and CIRCUMSTANCES ARE SURROUNDINGS. This scenario was a little more fluid than the others, as the sharks served two different roles, allowing her to comment in a straightforward way about her attitude towards her grandparents and in a more ambiguous way about her attitude towards her uncles.

We can see that in each of these scenarios, there are strong underlying embodied primary metaphors that are extended and combined in new and creative ways. The bereaved experience their grief through these shared embodied primary metaphors but because each experience is unique the metaphors are combined and developed in different ways. In addition to deepening our theoretical knowledge of the ways in which people think using metaphor, looking at the ways in which these experiences are framed in terms of embodied metaphor has potential practical applications. By attending to, and discussing, both the shared and the novel features of the embodied metaphors within scenarios such as these, those who support bereaved individuals may develop better ways of understanding their experiences, and these can be used to help them.

In addition to testimonies such as these, there are several behavioural studies whose findings indicate that one's emotional state affects the way one interacts with embodied metaphor. For example, in their examination of the effect of emotional stress on embodied perceptions of difficulty, Slepian et al. (2012) explored the embodied metaphor whereby secrets are experienced as physical burdens, which influence the way people perceive and interact with their environment. They conducted four studies which involved the examination of the behaviour of people who harboured important secrets, such as secrets concerning infidelity and sexual orientation. They found that individuals who recalled, were preoccupied with or were trying to suppress an important secret, estimated hills to be steeper, perceived distances to be farther, indicated that physical tasks would require more effort and were less likely to help others with physical tasks. The more burdensome the secret and the more thought devoted to it, the more perception and action were influenced in a manner similar to carrying physical weight. Thus, they concluded that, as with physical burdens, secrets almost literally 'weigh people down'. Interestingly, other studies have shown that this effect can be mitigated by the presence of social support. Schnall, Harber et al. (2008) found that people who were accompanied by a friend estimated a hill to be less steep compared to participants who were alone, and in a related imagery task, participants who were asked to think about a supportive friend whilst completing the task saw a hill as less steep than participants who either thought of a neutral person or a disliked person. These effects were further strengthened when the friend in question was a particularly close friend, or when the friendship had lasted a long time.

There is also some evidence from behavioural studies to suggest that clinical and subclinical depression affects the ways in which people engage with embodied primary metaphor. There is a particularly strong relationship between the vertical hierarchy and the experience of positive or negative affect. For example, Meier and Robinson (2006) found that depressive symptoms affect one's vertical selective attention. Participants who were prone to experiencing higher levels of neuroticism or depressive symptoms responded significantly more quickly to lower (versus higher) spatial attention targets than participants who were less prone to negative affect. We saw in Chapter 2 that Meier et al. (2007) found a strong and automatic relationship between positive affect and brightness. Although they did not carry out their test on depressive individuals per se, they do point out the effectiveness of light therapy in treating certain kinds of depression (Terman et al., 1998).

It has been shown that the adoption of certain body postures or facial expressions can influence the ways in which people process affective information (Strack et al., 1988). People who have been asked to adopt a 'happy' walking style find it harder to recall negative words than people who have been asked to adopt a 'depressed' walking style (Michalak et al., 2015). Similarly, Casasanto and Dijkstra (2010) showed that even the basic, abstract motor action of moving marbles either up-down or down-up affects people's ability to retrieve positive or negative memories, as well as influencing what they choose to remember. They explain these results with reference to the embodied primary metaphor HAPPY IS UP/SAD IS DOWN. They argue that this interaction arises from the fact that throughout life we need to expend physical effort to resist gravity and stay upright, and this leads us to associate 'up' with success, physical wellbeing and happiness, and to associate 'down' with their opposites. El Refaie (2009) showed that the vertical orientation plays a key role in the self-representations of authors of such comics who are experiencing depression.

A slightly different account of the way in which one's use of embodied metaphor is shaped by anxiety and depression is provided by Coker (2004) in her account of the bodily-based metaphors that Southern Sudanese refugees based in Cairo used to describe their suffering. She focuses on the metaphorical role played by both body and illness in the stories that the refugees told, in order to articulate their feelings of social, economic, physical and psychological loss. Her study arose from conversations with a British medical director, who had at first identified a great deal of 'somatisation', a condition in which people conflate physical symptoms with psychological symptoms (Lipowski, 1988). However, after having analysed his patients in more depth, he had come to realise that it was not in fact somatisation per se but rather a metaphorical projection of the mental state onto their bodies. She comments that most refugees preferred to discuss their illnesses in social or existential terms rather than in physical terms. Following Becker (1997), Coker argues that the term 'somatisation' is a reflection of the dualistic nature of western medical thought and of the western cultural tendency to intellectualise stress. It is therefore an inappropriate term for describing the experiences of these refugees.

One particularly prominent metaphor in her data was the idea that pain travelling around one's body corresponds to the experience of moving from place to place. There is an underlying idea here of loss of control and of not knowing where one (or one's pain) is going to be next. Whilst this metaphor conveys a feeling of lack of control, it also carries an underlying message of enduring strength, as it suggests that the body is ultimately able to withstand the constant onslaught of the different types of pain.

Some of the participants in her study also reported an inability to move, which was at once physical and metaphorical, as we can see in this extract from an interview with a twenty-four-year-old Pojulu woman:

My body stiffens and my head and legs and hands are forced to turn backwards. It started suddenly when I was preparing supper. I had a severe pain after the incident and I found a wound on my hand. (Coker, 2004: 31)

The conflation of metaphorical and physical experiences reported by Coker resonates with Low's (1994) study of 'nerves', a phenomenon whereby emotional anguish is experienced as physical pain. For example, people who are suffering from anxiety or depression might report symptoms such as trembling and dizziness, which are combined with feelings of loss of control. Cases of 'nerves' have been reported in many Western cultures as well as in Costa Rica, Guatemala and Newfoundland. The condition 'nerves' gives perceptual prominence to the types of embodied metaphors that have been described in this section. For cultural reasons, they are described in more visceral terms, but they reflect a fundamental human experience, which is to merge source and target domains when under stress. It is thus a culturally mediated, metaphorical embodiment of distress.

In light of these findings, it is encouraging to note that recent work in psychotherapy has paid more attention to the role of the body in shaping and expressing people's experiences with depression and other types of mental illness, with some therapists acknowledging that bodily sensations can provide insights into mental states (Leijsen, 2006). Tay (2017) expresses these ideas in terms of embodied metaphor, citing a number of examples where therapists listen out for the use of embodied metaphors by their clients, then, through discussion, make the embodied nature of these metaphors more salient, thus providing the clients with opportunities to think about more bodily based ways of dealing with their illnesses. For example, he cites one client who talked about his abdomen feeling bloated and another who complained that he felt like a plant that had out-grown its pot. In both cases, the therapists and clients were able to work collaboratively with these metaphors, making use of their literal and metaphorical meanings.

7.3   Pregnancy Loss

A particularly intense source of depression that may give rise to different metaphorical conceptualisations of the world is pregnancy loss. Because the parents of a stillborn baby are mourning a person who they will never really know, the feelings of loss that they experience are especially poignant.

Moreover, in many societies pregnancy loss is not widely discussed, and people who have not experienced often feel awkward talking about it to those who have. This means that it can be a very isolating experience. This sense of isolation is often expressed in metaphorical terms, as we can see in this short extract from a speech by a British MP, Byron Davies, who was speaking in a parliamentary debate on the grief he experienced following the loss of his baby:

> In an instant, the whole world, your family and your life *spiral out of your control*. You are a *bystander* to your fate and future.[2]

To date, there has been no research in the metaphor literature into the ways in which people who have experienced the loss of a baby through miscarriage, termination and stillbirth use metaphor to frame the experience and to come to terms with it. Such research is likely to prove useful because by identifying the metaphors used by the bereaved when talking about this emotionally complex, potentially isolating experience, it may be possible to gain insights into their thinking processes and open up additional lines of communication. In doing so, we might go some way towards breaking the silence around the subject of pregnancy loss.

For these reasons, in a research project entitled 'Death before Birth: Understanding, Informing and Supporting Choices Made by People Who Have Experienced Miscarriage, Termination and Stillbirth' (https://deathbeforebirthproject.org/), we (Fuller et al., 2016–2018) explored the ways in which people who have been affected by stillbirth or pregnancy loss use metaphor to come to terms with and communicate their grief. One of the things that we focused on was the role played by embodied metaphor in these experiences, and the ways in which people produce creative extensions of embodied metaphors, in an attempt to make sense of, come to terms with and express their experiences. We identified thirty-five individuals who had experienced pregnancy loss and asked them to talk about their experiences. We also interviewed twelve individuals who work with people who have experienced pregnancy loss in a professional supporting role.

Our findings to date are reported in Littlemore and Turner (in press) and Turner, Littlemore, Fuller et al. (in press). Here, I report on some of the headline findings that are reported in these two publications. One of our main findings was that individuals who have experienced pregnancy loss use a great deal of embodied metaphor and that in many cases, these metaphors resemble those used by people experiencing other kinds of bereavement. For example, like others who have been bereaved, they employed embodied metaphors that were very spatial, as we can see in these examples from Littlemore and Turner (in press):

when you're grieving *you can sort of enter sort of a grief world* where y- you start to push people away. (Bereaved parent)

the all thoughts get all jumbled and you get claustrophobic and it all just keeps going round and round so *you need I need somewhere else to try and put it*. (Bereaved parent)

Like others who have experienced bereavement, the participants in our study described their grief in very physical terms, and talked about being 'completely broken', experiencing the 'crushing weight' of grief and feeling that they were 'drowning' in self-pity.

However, other uses of embodied metaphor were more peculiar to this group. One way in which the embodied metaphors that they used differed from those associated with grief more generally is that they often involved a conflation of metaphorical and literal experiences, particularly around the idea of loss. This is understandable, as the women involved were experiencing a physical loss at the same time as a metaphorical loss. They often talked of losing part of themselves in both literal and metaphorical terms, as we can see in the following examples, also from Littlemore and Turner (ibid.):

Yes for instance erm I feel a lot stronger cos not many people go through this and it err it like it's not like losing a parent or erm a it's not like I've lost grandparents and even friends that have died but *it's NOT like that because it's part of you and he's a part of me it's like I lost myself for a long long time* and then you have to try and rebuild yourself and your confidence and everything. (Bereaved parent)

we're all sort of left like with *this emptiness inside of us* which is very physical as well as emotional. (Bereaved parent)

In order to compensate for this loss, some of the women we interviewed had had their baby's name tattooed on their body, which we (ibid.) argue may serve as a means to help them re-establish some kind of physical contact by enacting a kind of 'reunification' metaphor.

As we point out in Turner, Littlemore, Fuller et al. (in press), another form of altered metaphorical thinking that they experienced, which again can be found in people experiencing bereavement more generally, was that their metaphorical conceptions of time were altered, with many people in our study reporting that they felt as if they were somehow 'outside' of time:

it's so hard because you come out of hospital and *the world is still carrying on but your world has stopped*. (Bereaved parent)

The bereavement midwives who we interviewed appeared to be used to this phenomenon, and one reported that she often warns newly bereaved parents that this is how they may feel:

> this is what I describe to parents *if the world is going round that's the world you know* and then when you have a baby that's died *you get off*; you know *the world is still going around* and then as time goes on you know *you might go round a couple of times and then get off again and get on again* do you know what I mean and then gradually you'll get back on but you have to do it at your own pace *so it's kind of dipping in and out you know.* (Midwife)

However, we go on to argue in that paper that their metaphorical experiences of time also differed in some ways from those experienced by people who have been through more 'conventional' forms of bereavement. These differences appear to be partly due to the fact that they were experiencing the loss of a person they would never meet, and a life that would never be lived. As a result, their metaphorical experiences of time were sometimes compressed. Consider, for example, this extract from an interview with two hospital workers who work with bereaved parents:

A: Before the funeral, it's your time to do the things that you wanted to do, so I understand that many dreams you had aren't achievable, but if there are some, our job is to help you dream the dream basically, and lots of them are to do with dad, but we've had dad who always wanted beer, and he said *I want a can of beer, dad and lad*, we've facilitated that. (Bereavement midwife)

B: Yeah he wanted a can of beer with his da- his son and sadly his son was stillborn, *so we let him have some beer in the family room with his baby.* (Bereavement midwife)

In this extract, which is discussed in detail in Turner, Littlemore, Fuller et al. (in press), the father metaphorically 'shared a beer' with his son, an activity that he might normally have engaged in on his son's eighteenth birthday. Because of the circumstances, he had to compress those eighteen years into a single moment. This allows the father to reconcile two incompatible realities. This metaphorical compression of time can be explained in terms of Blending Theory (Fauconnier and Turner, 2008): there has been a temporal compression of a real and an imagined world, which makes sense in the eyes of the father and the hospital workers, but which might appear paradoxical to an outsider. Again, midwives who work with bereaved parents acknowledge the importance of this and try to find ways of facilitating these enacted metaphors:

A: He dreamt the dream . . . and that's his memory so I think from then we learned that this is the time to capture the memories, so now when I do speak to the families and say to them, *is there a dream that you're dreaming, let's do it.* (Bereavement midwife)

As we point out in Littlemore and Turner (in press), this kind of metaphorical thinking also extended to the women's attitudes towards their stillborn babies. In the majority of cases, the lost babies were, on some level, still very much 'alive'. One parent commented that 'I wanted to bury him with other babies to keep him company' and one of the healthcare professionals observed that it was important for the parents to be allowed to cuddle, wash the stillborn baby, change nappies and keep the baby close. This view was expressed by one of the parents, who was concerned about her baby attending the post mortem on his own:

> I went back the following day actually on my own cause I wanted to see him again and I wanted to give him the soft toy and the photo of us because those are the things that he was going to go to the post-mortem with. *Didn't want him to be on his own when he went.* (Bereaved parent)

These cases of metaphorical thinking perhaps reflect the fact that when people find themselves in a situation where what was real has become unreal and what is unreal has become real, they blend the two different realities. Many of the people interviewed in our study expressed the need to continue engaging in parenting behaviour, despite the loss of their baby. They would then direct that behaviour towards other targets, with one couple commenting for example that their charity work constituted the only way in which they could 'parent' their lost baby.

In Littlemore and Turner (in press), we show how the experience of pregnancy loss shaped our participants' relationships with their own minds and bodies, with many employing the metaphor of becoming a 'different person', who is taking a different 'journey' and or living in a different 'world':

> But I go through it and I *came out the other side* and you know you can *look back* and erm you know think about it *almost sort of looking at it as if you're another person* but you know I I you know went through it got through it don't know how cos it was yeah dreadfully horrible. (Bereaved parent)

> You can't have a break from grief. It's with you all the time. In varying degrees and it's how you deal with it. So just be prepared for it to be all consuming and life changing ... *and just don't try to be who you were before* cause you can't be I don't see how you could be. It changes everything. (Bereaved parent)

We also argue that there were many references to a 'divided self', as we can see in these examples, where the participants are seeing their minds and brains (or parts of their minds and brains) as being separate from their main identities:

> So if I go there and think about them and cry maybe I can go home and cry a bit less because I can *siphon off my crying into that part.* (Bereaved parent)

> I think *the sensible part of my head KNEW* (that it wasn't going to happen). (Bereaved parent)

> I think you just put up a barrier of being normal to protect yourself but your brain isn't really functioning the same way *your brain is just getting you*

through the motions rather than . . . disconnect from what's happening in your life EMOTIONALLY to get you through the day. (Bereaved parent)

Many of our participants also distanced themselves from their bodies, sometimes going so far as to personify their bodies and to give them agency:

I knew my body could do what it had to do. (Bereaved parent)

Mine stopped growing at six weeks but I was twelve to thirteen weeks pregnant cause *my body hadn't realised that nothing was happening.* (Bereaved parent)

it'd been several weeks already and that *my body hadn't caught on* that I'd probably need to have some kind of induction. (Bereaved parent)

And in some cases, once the body had been personified and distanced from the 'self', it could then be 'blamed' for the pregnancy loss:

My primary feeling, the first feeling was that *my body had failed me totally.* (Bereaved parent)

There is a whole range of emotions from *feeling really angry with my body* and myself not knowing that it was happening and for *my body for letting me down.* (Bereaved parent)

To sum up, the experience of pregnancy loss appears to shape the ways in which people view the world through metaphor. Some of the ways in which it does this resemble those that can be seen in the reactions that people have to bereavement more generally, but in other cases, the metaphorical thinking that takes place appears to be unique to this experience. The embodied metaphorical experiences that appear to be a more distinctive feature of pregnancy loss involve: the co-occurrence of physical and metaphorical loss (and attempts to redress this in a physical way, using tattoos), the compression and heightened awareness of time, the use of the 'divided self' metaphor, which allows a woman to 'blame' her body for what has happened, the metaphorical idea that on one level, the baby is still alive and needing to be protected, and the metaphorical enactment of parenting which is re-directed towards other targets.

As we point out in both papers, the implications of these findings are that it is important for those who care for people who have experienced pregnancy loss (including healthcare professionals, support workers, family and friends) to be sensitive to, and tolerant of, metaphorical responses to the situation which at first sight may seem 'irrational' but which are in fact powerful ways of dealing with and coming to terms with the situation. They should listen to the language that is being used and respond to this language in non-judgemental ways, taking the lead from the bereaved.

7.4   Schizophrenia

We saw in the opening section to this chapter that schizophrenics are thought to experience difficulties with metaphor, perhaps because the connections they make between the source and target domain are too loose and unconstrained. Indeed, for many years it has been thought that schizophrenics experience difficulties with metaphor comprehension (Searles, 1962; Mo et al., 2008). Langdon et al. (2002) found that schizophrenic patients' understanding of metaphor was impaired in comparison with healthy controls. Their metaphor test involved asking participants to read a short story and to decide whether or not a metaphorical ending made sense. Schizophrenic patients were significantly less likely than healthy controls to recognise metaphors as meaningful. They argued that the metaphor deficit experienced by the schizophrenic patients could be explained by 'degraded' semantic representations. By this they meant that they were unable to access relevant characteristics of the prompt words. For example, their inability to understand the metaphor 'my lawyer is a shark' may have been due, in part, to their difficulties in activating the 'predator' features of the word 'shark'. This account of the metaphor comprehension difficulties experienced by schizophrenics is somewhat incompatible with the idea that the connections they make are too loosely constrained, as one might expect that a tendency to form loose connections may make them *more* likely to find meaning in metaphor. It is indicative of the fact that findings from studies concerning the metaphor comprehension difficulties experienced by schizophrenics, and the possible reasons for these difficulties, are somewhat inconclusive.

Schizophrenics have also been found to experience difficulties with metaphoric gestures. Straube et al. (2014) conducted an in-depth investigation into the processing of metaphoric gesture by schizophrenics, focusing on brain activation while they were doing so. They were particularly interested in two parts of the brain: the left superior temporal sulcus (STS) and the inferior frontal gyrus (IFG). The STS has been associated with the processing of iconic and metaphoric gestures in healthy subjects (Holle, Gunter et al., 2008; Holle, Obleser et al., 2010). Furthermore, the successful processing of metaphorical gesture comprehension has been associated with intact connectivity between the left STS and the left IFG (Kircher et al., 2009). Straube et al. found that, unlike the controls, schizophrenic patients experienced difficulties in processing metaphoric gestures. Moreover, unlike the controls, they exhibited no functional connectivity between the left STS and the IFG during the processing of such gestures. They argue that this disconnectivity might be the basis of dysfunctional integration of the gestural information and the abstract meaning of the sentence. The successful integration of metaphoric gestures requires the perceiver to build an abstract relationship between concrete visual and abstract verbal information.

There are, however, some studies whose findings suggest that, in certain cases, schizophrenics are able to understand and use metaphor. It has, for example, been reported that the purposeful use of metaphor in psychotherapy significantly improves the curing of schizophrenia (Hains, 2014), which suggests that schizophrenics can understand metaphor when it is contextualised and relevant to them. Shaw (1996) found that the use of metaphors involving 'energy flow' in psychotherapy can in fact help schizophrenics develop a stronger awareness of their illness. Schizophrenia patients must retain some metaphor comprehension capacity if they are to make use of psychotherapeutic metaphors such as these. It may be the case that the difficulties that schizophrenic individuals experience with metaphor depend on the type of metaphor involved. Energy flow metaphors, for example, are much more embodied than the resemblance metaphors commonly used in laboratory-based tests of metaphor comprehension. Another factor might be that the widely used metaphor comprehension tests are highly artificial and have limited contextual information. It may also be the case that metaphor comprehension is more strongly impaired than metaphor production.

The focus of most studies to date has been on metaphor comprehension, and it may not necessarily be the case that the findings from these studies extend to metaphor production. In her study of language produced by Croatian-speaking schizophrenics, Despot (2017) used the Pragglejaz Group (2007) Metaphor Identification Procedure (MIP) to measure the amount of linguistic metaphor produced by schizophrenics. She found that they produced quantities of metaphor that were comparable to those produced by people in the non-schizophrenic control group and therefore questions the idea that schizophrenics are unable to use metaphor.

Indeed, there have been a number of studies whose findings have shown that schizophrenic patients are able to use metaphor to describe their experiences of the illness, though some of the authors of these studies have argued that, in many cases, their cognitive difficulties lead them to employ metaphor literally, instead of using it as a bridge between their experiences and the 'real' world (Kitayana, 1987). More recently, Demjen at al. (2019) observed that when schizophrenic patients were asked to talk about the voices that they heard, those who used metaphors related to disempowerment were more likely to report high levels of distress. Mould et al. (2010) conducted an extensive review of twenty-eight studies in which the use of metaphor was examined in first person accounts by patients with schizophrenia and other psychotic disorders. All of these studies took place within a therapeutic setting and explored the potential benefits of using metaphor as a way of understanding the illness and promoting its recovery. They found that two types of metaphor dominated this work. The first was the use of ontological metaphors to describe experiences such as the loss of a sense of self. Examples included: 'I am losing contact with myself' (284) and 'I am no longer in my body, it is someone else' (285). The second was the use of orientational metaphors to describe the recovery process. They argue that therapists could usefully explore both types of metaphor with their patients to aid recovery. They argue that ontological metaphors are particularly useful, as they help make the patients' subjective realities more concrete. They might therefore be used to help consolidate the patients' sense of self.

These findings suggest that schizophrenia has the potential to alter a person's thinking patterns and their relationship with the world, and that schizophrenics are able to express these altered experiences through the use of embodied metaphor. It would be interesting to explore this phenomenon further, focusing not only on the metaphorical language used but also on the metaphorical gestures that are employed. Researchers investigating schizophrenia have argued that it would be beneficial to focus on the general use of gesture by people who have the condition (Walther and Mittal, 2016), but no mention has been made of the benefits of focusing on *metaphorical* gesture. Such a focus would be worthwhile, as it would provide insights into the way in which people with schizophrenia conceptualise their experience, and these insights would be useful for people who work with schizophrenic patients, as they may help them to better understand the illness. As we saw in Chapter 1, studying the gestures that accompany spoken metaphors, or indeed metaphorical gestures that are unaccompanied by speech, often leads to a richer understanding of the ways in which people are using embodied metaphor to make sense of their reality.

Such a study could usefully investigate (a) whether schizophrenics make use of embodied metaphor, in language and gesture, (b) if so, whether the embodied metaphors that they use differ from those that are employed by people who do not have schizophrenia and (c) whether any of these metaphors provide insights into the ways in which their illness shapes their world view. Having access to this information may open up new lines of communication and help others to support their recovery. In preparation for such a study, we (Littlemore and Turner, in prep.) conducted a small pilot study[3] whose aim was to explore how people with schizophrenia experience the world through embodied metaphor. In order to do this, we analysed the language used by schizophrenics when describing their symptoms, focusing in particular in the embodied metaphors they used. We defined a metaphor as 'embodied' when it was strongly related to a primary metaphor or when it had the patient's body as its source domain. We aimed to establish the extent to which schizophrenics are able to use embodied metaphor to frame their ideas when describing their illness, to examine the types of metaphors produced and to identify and analyse any creative uses of embodied meta-phor that appeared in the dataset.

Our dataset consisted of one video transcript and ten audio transcripts of individuals with schizophrenia in consultations with their doctors.[4] All of the recordings were made in the United States and involved adult patients who were on medication and who had agreed to have their consult-ations recorded and used for research purposes. Our initial findings suggest that schizophrenic individuals are able to make use of embodied metaphor when describing the symptoms of the illness, and that in a small number of cases they use embodied metaphor creatively. This becomes par-ticularly apparent when we look beyond purely linguistic communication and consider their use of illustrations and gesture. Let us look, for example, at the following extract, taken from a video-recorded interview with one of the schizophrenics:

INTERVIEWER: Where do you see how schizophrenia impacts you? So kind of like, if you can draw yourself, just a very simplistic [sic], you don't have to be an artist.

PATIENT: Yeah

INTERVIEWER: And then just to point out to us . . . how this thing, schizophrenia, what do you think of it as?

PATIENT: *[Draws a picture of the front of train approaching a man on a track]* I guess that sort of describes it, like almost like getting run over by a train

INTERVIEWER: Wow. Was it always a train? Was it something different years ago? Was it a different feeling?

PATIENT: Well at one time it might have seemed like bird poop coming from the sky

INTERVIEWER: *[Laughs]*

PATIENT: You know . . . That was I guess in the early stages when I still thought I had the bipolar disorder but when it came on with the schizophrenia, wham it was . . .

INTERVIEWER: So the bipolar years were more of an annoyance?

PATIENT: Yeah

INTERVIEWER: You could kind of deal with that?

PATIENT: You could kind of deal with that. But the schizophrenia, no. It seems there was always that train moving there, just on the other side of the great divide and er . . . no matter what cargo it may be carrying, it represents more and more . . . pressure from without *[cupped hands moving towards head from either side three times]*, to have to deal with *[cupped hands coming together in front of stomach]* the schizophrenia . . . er, since I've been on the Latuda and the Seroquel together, I don't notice that train so much.

INTERVIEWER: So you say you don't notice it but it's still there?

PATIENT: It's still there

INTERVIEWER: OK, it doesn't go away? It's just

PATIENT: No

INTERVIEWER: You pay attention to it less?

PATIENT: Less, yeah

INTERVIEWER: OK

PATIENT: Well, usually I try to deal with it on my own. I try to tell myself, look, the damn train isn't there right now, it's not out to get you so, what are you feeling hyper or nervous about? I try to reason it out myself ... to try to reach the point where the train isn't coming at me, it's just parked standing still, as it were, somewhere in the distance ... and that I've got plenty of time to get off that railroad track before it does come.

Male patient, aged 19–34 years, Medication: Abilify

In this extract, the patient makes use of embodied metaphor, both in his language and in his gesture. He begins by representing himself as a person on a train track, about to be run over by an oncoming train. He has no control over this train because it is approaching from the other side of 'the great divide'. However, he closes by saying that when he is on the medication, he tries to 'reach the point where the train isn't coming at [him]' and tells himself and that he has 'plenty of time to get off the track before it [the train] does come'. He thus positions himself 'inside' the metaphorical scenario throughout the exchange. He expresses more agency towards the end of the interview, when he comments that he will try to 'get off the tracks'. The metaphorical content of the exchange increases dramatically and becomes much richer at the point where he begins to use gesture, as predicted by Müller and Tag (2010), and the metaphors become mixed at this point, combining the idea of a 'heavy cargo' with that of 'pressure'. It is interesting to note that his hands come together at the point where he talks about 'dealing' with the schizophrenia, almost as if the schizophrenia is a physical entity that he can get hold of and control. Again, both in his verbal and gestural use of metaphor, he shifts from being a passive agent at the mercy of the schizophrenia to being someone who has the illness under control.

There was also a substantial amount of embodied metaphor in the audio transcripts, although here we do not have the video data that would have allowed us to study the gestures that accompanied them. As with the pregnancy loss dataset, a particularly common metaphor in this dataset was the 'divided self' metaphor (Lakoff, 1996), an example of which can be seen in the following extract:

> And so I, I find myself, you know, just finding a corner and, you know, *just trying to talk it out with myself.* (Male patient, 35–54 years old, on medication (Risperdal and Prozac))

This example is conventional, but other examples of the 'divided self' metaphor were more marked, possibly reflecting the experience of personal fragmentation, which is a well-documented symptom of Schizophrenia (see Davidson et al., 2004). In many of the patients, these metaphors revealed a certain lack of control over their own behaviour. Here is an example in which the patient feels as if he is sharing his body with another living being, in this case, the Devil:

I'm, *I'm just a holy ghost*. So, you know, *sometimes things come out of my mouth that shouldn't be there* and I've explained to my parents on many occasions that it has nothing to do with how I feel about them, it's just the devil at work. So, if, I apologize to them and I tell them many times over that if you would bear with it and considering that I have bipolar then I would apologize and make it a daily issue avoiding because it's not me, it's just the devil.

> Male patient, 35–54 years old, on medication (Haldol decanoate and Depakote)

Here is another example in which the patient discusses the relationship that he has with the voice in his head (which for him is real, not metaphorical), which he embodies as a person who he can, at times, control:

DR: He, he's not intruding himself on you?
PT: Right.
DR: Because you talked about splitting your mind before, and, um –
PT: *Theoretically he could maybe take it over, but that's if I put way too much thought into him.*
DR: [PATIENT NAME], take your, take over your mind?
PT: *Uh, it's really just another person my brain has to keep up with.*
DR: Right.
PT: So I could beat him theoretically, but it, as of right now, my personality is the dominant one.

> Male patient, aged 19–34 years, Medication: Abilify

This same patient also appears to have an unusual relationship with his body in which he attributes more agency to the body than one would normally, and he talks about parts of his body as if they can operate independently of his mind. Here he is explaining his aversion to eating:

DR: What's gross about it?
PT: *You, your [INAUDIBLE] skeleton crushes it up and then a meat tentacle pushes it into a vat of acid and then you poop it out later.*
DR: That whole process is disgusting?
PT: It's supposed to be painful.
DR: Supposed to be painful?
PT: Like the stomach acid eats through your stomach like four times. Uh –
DR: Well, there are special cells in your stomach so that acid doesn't bother your stomach.

> Male patient, aged 19–34 years, Medication: Abilify

Several patients made explicit use of metaphors involving physical actions and experiences to describe how they were feeling. Some of these were creative, such as the following, which makes use of two contrasting scenarios:

> I guess because, you know, this isn't, you know, *it's not McDonald's and you're on the playground equipment sliding down a slide. You know? It's like going to the dentist and you're getting your teeth drilled. This is not like a,*

not a place for me to be. (Male patient, aged 18–34, on medication (Perphenazine Effexor XR))

Here, in order to understand the referential meaning of the utterance, the addressee has to move their attention momentarily away from the target domain to the source domain that is evoked by the metaphorical expression. When doing so, they are invited to mentally simulate and then contrast the experiences of playing on a slide at McDonalds and paying a painful trip to the dentist. In both of these examples we can see references to metaphorical 'place'. This was common in the data. A further example is as follows:

> I mean, I like, I mean, I like doing construction work, you know, and when I'm doing that, *it's like I'm in, I'm in a whole, another world, like I'm free or something.* (Male patient, 35–54 years old, on medication (Risperdal and Prozac))

As we saw previously, the feeling of having been transported to another place is a common way of expressing both severe depression and the feelings of relief when the depression has subsided.

The findings from this exploratory study suggest that individuals with schizophrenia are able to make use of embodied metaphor and that the ways in which they use it are closely bound to their mental experiences and emotional states. They use metaphor, amongst other things, to take themselves 'somewhere else', to describe the experience of a 'divided self' and to distance themselves from their illness and its symptoms. It would be useful to conduct a more extensive exploration of the different embodied metaphors that schizophrenic patents employ, in both language and gesture, as these metaphors provide a richer understanding of the subjective experience of schizophrenia, which may feed into clinical descriptions of the illness, making these descriptions more nuanced and more reflective of the lived experiences of those who suffer from it.

7.5 Autistic Spectrum Disorders and Asperger Syndrome

We saw in the introduction that people with Autistic Spectrum Disorders (ASD) and Asperger syndrome also experience difficulties with metaphor comprehension. However, as with schizophrenia, the picture is somewhat complex, as people with these conditions do seem to be able to use some types of metaphor. I would like to illustrate this with an example from literature. In Mark Haddon's novel, *The Curious Incident of the Dog in the Night-Time*, we meet Christopher, a boy with Asperger syndrome, who, like any people with this condition, does not understand metaphor and who therefore worries about why people 'keep skeletons in cupboards' and wonders whether it is actually possible for someone to 'laugh their socks off':

People often talk using metaphors. These are examples of metaphors

> **I laughed my socks off.**
> **He was the apple of her eye.**
> **They had a skeleton in the cupboard.**
> **We had a real pig of a day.**
> **The dog was stone dead.**

The word metaphor means carrying something from one place to another, and it comes from the Greek words μετα (which means one place to another) and φέρω (which means to carry and it is when you describe something by using a word for something that it isn't. This means that the word metaphor is a metaphor.

I think it should be called a lie because a pig is not like a day and people do not have skeletons in their cupboards. And when I try and make a picture of the phrase in my head it just confuses me because imagining an apple in someone's eye doesn't have anything to do with liking someone a lot and makes you forget what the person was talking about.

> *The Curious Incident of the Dog in the Night-Time*,
> Mark Haddon, Vintage Press (2004) pp. 19–20

Interestingly, although Christopher professes to experience difficulties with metaphor, at one point in the novel, he comments that getting onto a London Underground train is 'like standing on a cliff in a really strong wind ... like stepping off the cliff on a tightrope'. He uses this metaphor to express not only how he feels about getting onto an Underground train but also how he feels about the unpredictable nature of life. Eventually, he learns to overcome his fear and 'steps off the cliff'. This example suggests that he is able to think in terms of embodied metaphor.

As this fictional example suggests, there is a lack of clarity concerning the ability of individuals with ASD and Asperger syndrome to understand and produce metaphor. Whilst conventional idioms present problems, embodied metaphors appear to be readily used and understood. This discrepancy can also be seen in the research literature. There is a substantial body of research whose findings suggest that people with ASD and Asperger syndrome experience difficulties in metaphor comprehension and production, whilst other studies suggest that they are able to provide plausible explanations for metaphors that they encounter and even produce them in their own speech.

Let us begin by looking at some of the literature whose findings suggest that there is a deficit. In an experimental study, in which participants were asked to find meanings for a series of metaphors, Gold and Faust (2010) found that individuals with Asperger syndrome exhibited difficulties in novel metaphor comprehension. In line with the proposals discussed at the beginning of this chapter, they also found that participants with Asperger syndrome showed no right hemisphere advantage for the processing of novel metaphors, unlike control group participants. Later in this section, we will look at some of the examples of the metaphors that were used in their study. For now, I would like to concentrate on the explanation that they offer for their findings. Gold and Faust argued that the difficulties experienced by the people with Asperger Syndrome were caused by a dysfunctional right hemisphere. There is a body of literature showing that the right hemisphere is involved in the processing of novel metaphor (Mashal et al., 2007). As we saw in the introduction to this chapter, successful novel metaphor comprehension is thought to require the integration of flexible semantic processing (normally carried out by the right hemisphere) and rigid semantic processing (which is normally carried out by the left hemisphere). This line of reasoning is inspired by Jung-Beeman's (2005) theory of 'fine' versus 'coarse' semantic coding, according to which the right hemisphere is recruited in order to activate larger diffuse semantic fields, which are then narrowed down by the left hemisphere.

Three further theories have been advocated to explain the apparent difficulties experienced by individuals with ASD and Asperger Syndrome in understanding and producing metaphor. These are: Theory of Mind deficit, weak coherence theory, and a lack of broad semantic knowledge (Rundblad and Annaz, 2010).

The most widely adhered-to theory in explaining ASD individuals' apparent difficulties with metaphor is *Theory of Mind* deficit (Baron-Cohen et al., 1985). This refers to the problems that ASD individuals experience in attributing mental states (such as beliefs and intentions) to others. It is widely argued that the comprehension of metaphor relies upon an understanding of the communicative intent of the speaker (MacKay and Shaw, 2004). This means that the listener needs to attribute mental states to the speaker in order to arrive at the correct meaning of the metaphoric expression (Winner et al., 1988). In an fMRI study, Gallagher et al. (2000) found indirect support for a link between metaphor comprehension ability and Theory of Mind ability, since the completion of tasks designed to measure these two different abilities both led to activation of the medial frontal cortex. Studies designed to test this relationship in individuals with ASD have produced mixed results. On balance, the evidence seems to fall in favour of a relationship (e.g., Happé, 1993, 1995), though it has been argued that many of these studies have not controlled sufficiently well for age range (Rundblad and Annaz, 2010).

According to the second theory, the *Weak Central Coherence (WCC) theory*, individuals with ASD have a tendency to process information locally rather than globally, which prevents them from making full use of the context when extracting metaphorical meaning. There have to date been no direct tests of this theory; however, studies have shown that autistic individuals experience difficulties integrating information from different senses (Russo et al., 2010), which suggests that they may experience difficulties with cross-sensory metaphor.

Finally, it has been argued that *broad semantic knowledge* is required in order to establish common ground between two referents that belong to the different conceptual domains, as one needs to be able to interpret words on multiple levels in order to select potential relevant properties and similarities. For example, in order to understand the metaphor 'raising children is gardening', one needs to know that raising children involves an element of nurturing, that there is no direct link between the way they are brought up and the way they turn out, that outside forces may exert an influence, and so on. Norbury (2005) found evidence for a link between broad semantic knowledge and successful metaphor comprehension, but did not separate out metaphor from other types of figurative language, such as irony (Rundblad and Annaz, 2010).

Now let us turn to the body of literature whose findings suggest that people with ASD and Asperger Syndrome experience no difficulties with metaphor, and that in some cases may even exhibit an advantage in this area. The underlying characteristic of these studies is that they have focused on embodied metaphor and/or novel metaphor. Olofson et al. (2014) created a number of novel metaphorical expressions related to underlying primary metaphors. Then, by means of a story comprehension task, they compared the understanding of these metaphors by individuals with ASD with that of a typically developing control group. They found no differences between the two groups. They attributed their findings to the fact that these metaphors are related to sensorimotor experiences and are therefore understood earlier than other types of metaphors by individuals with ASD.

It has also been found that individuals with ASD are able to explain novel metaphoric phrases in unique ways that rely on unusual semantic associations (Melogno et al., 2012). In a similar vein, Kasirer and Mashal (2014) found that individuals with ASD were as good as their age-matched typically developing peers at comprehending novel metaphors. Moreover, they were significantly better than them at *producing* novel metaphor, displaying levels of verbal creativity that surpassed those of the control group. Examples of creative metaphors included phrases such as 'Feeling successful is like seeing the view from the mountaintop' and 'feeling worthless is like offering a salad to South Americans'. In contrast, typically developing adults were more likely to produce conventional metaphors, such as 'feeling sad is to get the blues'. Kasirer and Mashal attribute their findings to the fact that the ASD individuals have a superior attention to and memory for details and that they are less constrained by the context. They also suggest that another possible reason why adults with ASD generated more original metaphors involves the difficulties they experience in Theory of Mind. They suggest that an inability to see things from another person's perspective makes people with ASD more likely to focus on their own thoughts, and to ignore the addressee (Happé and Vital,

2009), which may lead them to produce expressions that are less conventional (Liu et al., 2011). This idea is not new. Kanner noted in 1946 that the unique phrases produced by the children he studied could be interpreted as metaphoric language.

Individuals with Asperger Syndrome have also been found to exhibit a capacity for novel metaphor production. Asperger (1941) identified certain expressions in the speech of his patients that resembled the novel linguistic forms produced by young typically developing children. Asperger and others have proposed that characteristics such as concrete intelligence and disregard of social conventions might be prerequisites for certain forms of 'new thinking' and creativity (Gillberg, 2002). It has also been noted that individuals with Asperger syndrome have heightened capacities for persistence and observation, high levels of energy and motivation, distinctive patterns of cross-sensory association, and a strong ability to focus on a single topic (Happé and Frith, 2009). It therefore appears to be the case that some individuals with ASD and Asperger syndrome are highly creative, imaginative and original and that this may extend to their use of metaphor.

One possible explanation for the apparent discrepancies in the findings with respect to the ability of ASD and Asperger patients to comprehend metaphor relates to the prompts that are used to investigate this phenomenon. As we saw earlier, Gold and Faust (2010) found that individuals with Asperger syndrome exhibited difficulties with metaphor comprehension. Let us look in detail at some of the prompts that were used in their study:

> Firm words
> Winding plot
> Fragile pride
> Misty scarf
> Dying star
> Dead words
> Stormy dream
> Leaden rain
> Silent tears

What we see here is a very mixed set of items. The first thing to notice about this list is that some of the items contain abstract concepts (e.g., fragile pride, winding plot, dead words) and therefore have the potential to evoke primary metaphors (in these cases, potential candidates could be CERTAINTY IS FIRMNESS, MOVEMENT THROUGH TIME IS MOVEMENT THROUGH SPACE, INACTIVITY IS LOSS OF LIFE, respectively). Others involve combinations of concrete entities and may be more likely to evoke resemblance metaphors (e.g., leaden rain, misty scarf). These items may involve a very different type of cognitive processing from that required by the more abstract items. As we saw in Chapter 4, primary metaphors and resemblance metaphors are acquired at different stages of development and may in fact be very different entities. Another striking source of variation among these items relates to the level of novelty. Some items (e.g., misty scarf) appear to be very novel in that they bring together two concepts that are not normally combined. Other items, such as 'leaden rain' simply involve modifications of conventional metaphors (heavy rain). The item 'dying star' is also conventional (Google produces 22,000,000 hits for this expression) and there is an added complication here in that it could be interpreted in different ways. It could refer to an actual star that is reaching the end of its life or it might refer, for example, to a person or to a dream. Other items in this list are metonymic or almost literal: the term 'silent tears' could simply refer to the fact that someone is crying without making a sound, or it could refer to the fact that someone's grief is going unnoticed. The level of metaphorical activation triggered by this item might therefore vary between individuals. It is also somewhat conventional, like 'dying star' and 'winding plot'.

This short literature review suggests that individuals with ASD and/or Asperger Syndrome do deal with metaphor in slightly different ways from people who do not have these syndromes but that, in order to investigate this phenomenon more thoroughly, it is important to choose the prompts that one uses very carefully. In particular, attention needs to be paid to whether these prompts are novel or conventional and whether they involve primary metaphors or resemblance metaphors. Embodied primary metaphors appear to present less of a problem than conventional linguistic metaphors and idioms. More studies are needed of the ways in which people with these syndromes produce embodied metaphor, and it would be good if such studies, like those proposed for individuals with schizophrenia, could include a focus on gesture. The findings from both sets of studies would provide valuable insights into the different ways in which people with these syndromes experience the world.

7.6   Conclusion

In this chapter, we have seen that a person's state of mind can radically alter the way in which they experience the world through embodied metaphor. Arguably, the most striking observation from the chapter is that when people are under stress, they tend to merge source and target domains, resulting in a metaphorical embodiment of distress, which is culturally mediated. This merging of the domains takes people back to where the metaphors originate, leading them to engage with them in an almost 'literal' way. This suggests that the primary, physical basis of metaphor is always present at some level, and that, although it might be hidden from view most of the time, it can be called upon and used, either constructively or destructively, in times of stress or when regular, 'conventional' communication patterns are disrupted in some way. It would be useful to conduct more studies into the ways in which embodied metaphor is used by people with depression, schizophrenia, ASD, Asperger Syndrome and other conditions that radically alter a person's state of mind. In order to provide a fuller picture of these people's experiences, such studies would require the careful selection of prompts and a strong focus on the use of gesture. The findings would provide insights into the types of embodied metaphors that are employed by these individuals and the ways in which they are employed. They would thus constitute a rich source of data that could be used to help them.

8 'This Is My Body Which Will Be Given Up for You.'[*]

Individual Differences in Personality, Thinking Style, Political Stance and Religious Beliefs

8.1   Introduction

One of the main doctrinal disputes between the Roman Catholic Church and the Protestant Church involves transubstantiation. For Roman Catholics, when the priest utters the words in the title of this chapter, the bread and wine offered during mass become the body and blood of Christ. For Protestants, the relationship is symbolic. The bread and wine are metaphors for the body and blood of Christ. This difference in literal/metaphorical perspective, in combination with various socio-political factors, has led to bitter conflict and many hundreds of thousands of deaths over the years. Differences in metaphorical perspective can therefore have serious consequences.

As this example shows, religious beliefs are often articulated through embodied metaphor. Religious views can shape and be shaped by the metaphors that we use to understand the world, and people often find it hard to reconcile opposing metaphorical perspectives, possibly because they are so deeply held and embodied. In this chapter, I look at a broad range of individual differences, starting with internally driven individual differences involving personality and cognitive style, and then moving onto more externally driven, socially mediated individual differences that are more likely to be shaped by the external context in which one operates. These are ideology, politics and religion. In each case, I explore how these differences shape the ways in which people experience the world through metaphor, and discuss the implications that these have, both for theories of metaphor and for our understanding of the way people think about the world.

8.2   Internally Driven Individual Differences

In this section, I look at internally driven individual differences, focusing on a range of cognitive styles and personality traits. The dimensions that have been selected for discussion have all been shown, in one way or another, to affect the ways in which individuals experience the world through embodied metaphor. They are the cognitive, analogical reasoning ability, conscientiousness,

176

body consciousness, need for power, need for cognition, creativity and psychopathy.

Cognitive Styles

The metaphor literature is replete with conflicting accounts of how metaphors are understood (see Gibbs, 2001). Two of the most widely accepted accounts are those proposed by Lakoff and Johnson (1980) and Fauconnier and Turner (2008). According to Lakoff and Johnson, metaphor comprehension involves the mapping of correspondences between two separate domains: the source domain and the target domain. So, for example, the source domain of WAR-FARE might be used to structure the target domain of ARGUMENTATION. According to Fauconnier and Turner, metaphor comprehension involves a process of 'blending', which results in a novel 'mental space' with its own 'emergent features', so for example, in the metaphor 'a surgeon is a butcher', notions of ineptitude emerge that are a feature of neither surgery nor butchery. Other theorists have suggested that imagery plays a role in metaphor comprehension with people extrapolating from stereotypical images (McGlone, 1996, 2007). There are likely to be different explanations for these contradictory views. It has been suggested, for example, that conceptual metaphor theory provides a good account of conventional metaphor, whilst blending theory provides a good account of creative metaphor (Kövecses, 2015). A second possibility is that these different intuitions about the workings of metaphor reflect differences in individuals' cognitive styles. Two cognitive style dimensions that are particularly pertinent to this distinction are the holistic-analytic dimension, which refers to an individual's preference for processing information either as chunks or as separate parts (Kirby, 1988) and the verbaliser/imager dimension, which refers to whether people process conceptual information in words or in images (Katz, 1983). 'Holistic' thinkers may be more likely than 'analytic' thinkers to blend their conceptions of the source and target domain and to come up with interpretations that emerge from the blend of the two domains, and 'imagers' may be more likely than 'verbalisers' to refer to stereotypical images to explain the meanings of metaphors.

This is an idea that we (Boers and Littlemore, 2000) put to the test. We conducted a study in which we investigated the ways in which people with different cognitive styles (holistic/analytic and verbaliser/imager) interpreted conceptual metaphors. We began by asking participants to provide explanations for three conceptual metaphors: ECONOMIC COMPETITION IS RACING, AN ECONOMY IS A MACHINE and ECONOMICS IS HEALTH. We measured cognitive style dimensions using Riding's (1991) reaction time and computer-based 'Cognitive Styles Analysis' (CSA). In order to place participants on the holistic/analytic dimension, the program calculates the ratio between their average response speeds on an analytic test, in which they have to identify a smaller shape within a large one, and their average response speeds on a 'holistic' test, in which they have to decide whether two shapes are identical. In order to place participants on the verbaliser/imager continuum, the program calculates the ratio between their average response speeds on a 'verbaliser' test in which they have to decide whether two items are from the same semantic field (e.g., apple and banana) and their average response speeds on an 'imager' test, in which they have to decide whether two items are the same colour (e.g., banana and canary).

We found that 'holistic' thinkers were indeed significantly more likely than 'analytic' thinkers to blend their conceptions of the source and target domain and to come up with interpretations that emerged from the blend of the two domains. These interpretations were often only very tenuously related to the source domain (e.g., one of their explanations of the metaphor ECONOMIC COMPETITION IS RACING was that 'economics is a merciless jungle where only the fittest survive').We also found that 'imagers' were indeed significantly more likely than 'verbalisers' to refer to stereotypical images to explain the metaphors (e.g., for the HEALTH metaphor, they reported the image of a healthy, well-fed population as a reflection of economic prosperity). The relationship between holistic processing and a preference for blending over mapping resonates with an earlier finding in which I observed that individuals with a holistic cognitive style are able to find meaning in creative metaphor significantly more quickly than individuals with an analytic cognitive style (Littlemore, 2001). In that paper, I attributed this finding to their stronger analogical reasoning abilities (see later in this chapter) and to the fact that they were paying less attention to detail. However, an alternative explanation is that they were simply processing the metaphors in a different way from the analytic individuals, and that blending processes take place more rapidly than mapping processes. Further empirical studies would need to be conducted in order to test this hypothesis. Taken together, the findings from the two studies outlined in this section go right to the core of the thesis presented in this book. A person's cognitive style can significantly affect the way in which they process metaphor, which goes some way to explaining why it is that the same metaphor can give rise to very different interpretations, even amongst individuals with the same cultural and linguistic background.

Analogical Reasoning Ability

Another individual difference variable that has been found to affect the way people interact with embodied metaphor is analogical reasoning ability. Analogical reasoning ability refers to the ability to perceive relationships between different entities and to draw inferences from these relationships (Holyoak et al., 1984). It is therefore somewhat similar to holistic processing, which I have just discussed. It has been shown to be related to the ability to find meaning in linguistic metaphors (Kogan et al., 1980). It has also been shown to affect the way in which people interact with embodied metaphors. Marin et al. (2014) investigated the impact of bodily based visual metaphors on the creative process. They found that when people were exposed to positive metaphors, such as 'thinking outside the box', they displayed an improved performance in subsequent tests of creativity, whereas when they were exposed to negative metaphors such as 'burnt out', they displayed a worsened performance in creativity. This effect was significantly stronger in people who exhibited higher levels of analogical reasoning ability, suggesting that these individuals are particularly susceptible to the effects of persuasive embodied metaphors. Thus one's cognitive style not only shapes the way in which they process metaphor, and the speed with which they do so, but also exerts an influence on the extent to which their behaviour is likely to be influenced by embodied metaphor. These findings have important implications for all those who use metaphor to persuade and to influence, as they go some way towards explaining why some people are easier to influence than others; some people are affected by, and 'get more out of', metaphor than others, and this is a relatively stable individual difference variable.

Conscientiousness

Conscientiousness is a personality dimension which contrasts people who are efficient and/or organised with those who are more easy-going and/or careless (Goldberg, 1992). Conscientious individuals tend to show self-discipline, act dutifully, aim for achievement and prefer planned rather than spontaneous behaviour. People with low levels of conscientiousness tend to be more flexible and spontaneous. This personality dimension has been found to interact with the way in which people experience embodied metaphors of time. We saw in Chapter 2 that in English, there are two contrasting ways in which a person's spatial relationship with time can be expressed: the *moving time* metaphor conceptualises time as moving forwards towards the person and the *moving ego* metaphor conceptualises the person as moving forwards towards the future. When people are asked 'Next Wednesday's meeting has been moved forwards two days; when is the meeting now that it has been rescheduled?', individuals employing a 'moving time' metaphor will report that it has been moved to Monday, whereas individuals employing a 'moving ego' metaphor will report that it has been moved to Friday. Research by Duffy and Feist (2014a) has shown that people who have higher conscientiousness scores are more likely to conceptualise time as moving forwards towards them than people with low conscientiousness scores, who are more likely to conceptualise the ego as moving forwards towards the future. In other words, they are more likely to adopt a 'moving ego' perspective when thinking about time metaphorically in terms of movement through space. They also found, in a follow-up study, that participants who adopted the 'moving time' perspective were more likely to exhibit conscientious behaviours, while those who adopted the 'moving ego' perspective were more likely to procrastinate, suggesting that the earlier effects reach beyond the laboratory (Duffy et al., 2014b). One possible reason for these findings might be that conscientious individuals feel the pressure of future events and deadlines approaching and that this is what motivates them to get things done on time. Again we have a clear example of an internally driven individual difference shaping people's behaviour through embodied metaphorical thinking.

Body Consciousness and Predisposition towards Cleanliness

Another individual difference variable that has been found to affect people's experience of metaphor is body conscientiousness. We saw in Chapter 3 that the presence of an unpleasant smell in the room can increase the harshness of the moral judgements that a person is likely to make (Schnall, Haight et al., 2008). In a follow-up study that is also reported in the same paper, Schnall et al. went on to include an individual differences variable: 'body consciousness'. It has been observed that some individuals are more sensitive than others to their own physical sensations, and this individual difference variable can be measured using the Body Consciousness Questionnaire (Miller et al., 1981). This questionnaire comprises five items that are rated on a scale from 1 (disagree strongly) to 6 (agree strongly). The items are: 'I am sensitive to internal bodily tensions'; 'I know immediately when my mouth or throat gets dry'; 'I can often feel my heart beating'; 'I am quick to sense the hunger contractions of my stomach'; and 'I am very aware of changes in my body temperature.' Schnall, Haidt et al. found that participants who scored highly on this scale were significantly more likely than those who had low scores to be affected by an unpleasant smell when making morality judgements.

Staying with the theme of morality, it has been found that another individual differences variable, 'predisposition towards cleanliness', can also affect the extent to which moral judgements are embodied. Sherman and Clore (2009) found that people were faster to name the colour black when it was used to present an immoral word (such as 'greed') and faster to name the colour white when it was used to present a moral word (such as 'honesty'). Interestingly, when they introduced the 'predisposition towards cleanliness' variable into their study, they found that the effect was significantly stronger among participants who attached a greater importance to cleanliness. Taken together, these findings show that individual differences in the way in which people experience their own bodies and the environment in which they operate can have a profound effect on the ways in which they engage in abstract thinking through metaphor.

Need for Power

As its name suggests, 'need for power' refers to an individual's need to be in charge of a situation and to have power over others (McClelland and Burnham, 2008). We saw in Chapter 2 that people's perceptions of the weight of objects can be affected by the perceived importance of those objects. Research has also shown that people's perceptions of weight are affected by their own sense of power. Lee and Schnall (2014) found that people who have a strong sense of their own personal power are more likely to judge objects as being lighter than people with a lower sense of personal power. They also found that manipulating people's sense of power led to the same result. In a similar vein, Gkiouzepas (2015) found that 'need for power' as a personality trait affected people's responses to the HAVING CONTROL IS UP metaphor as it appeared in advertisements. In an earlier study, Gkiouzepas (2013) found that adverts where the image of the product is placed above the caption were easier to understand than adverts where the image of the product is placed below the caption. He then extended this study (Gkiouzepas, 2015) to incorporate the individual difference variable 'need for power' and extended the research questions to include a wider range of responses to the advert. He found that male participants with a strong need for power found the metaphor-consistent layout (where the product is placed above the caption) to be more positive and more persuasive than the metaphor-inconsistent layout (where the product was placed below the caption). Interestingly, this result did not obtain for the female participants in the study, which resonates with the gender-related findings discussed in Chapter 5. Taken together, these findings suggest that men may be more likely than women to internalise the metaphor of the vertical hierarchy. This difference has interesting implications for models of management structure and for organisational power relations, as they appear to encapsulate a gender bias.

Need for Cognition

Another individual differences variable which appears to affect the way in which people engage with embodied metaphor is 'need for cognition', which refers to an individual's tendency to engage in effortful endeavours (Cacioppo and Petty, 1982). People with a high need for cognition are more likely to be inclined towards a high level of elaboration in terms of appreciation of debate, idea evaluation and problem solving. In the context of metaphor, Chang and

Yen (2013) showed that people with a high need for cognition are more likely to succeed in the interpretation of visual metaphors compared with participants with a low need for cognition. Chang and Yen's study focused on visual metaphors in advertising, as the use of such metaphors has been shown to trigger positive responses in potential consumers (McQuarrie and Mick, 2003). However, they did not focus on embodied metaphors per se.

Indirect evidence for a link between need for cognition and use of *embodied* metaphor comes from a small study in which we (Pérez-Sobrino, Littlemore and Houghton, 2018) investigated responses to metaphor and metonymy in advertisements. Some advertisements make use of simple metaphors or metonyms, either in the pictures or in the words that accompany them, whereas others make use of complex combinations of metaphor and metonymy, which combine pictorial and verbal information. Prior to our study, there had been no research investigating whether this complexity has any bearing on the extent to which advertisements are understood or appreciated. Nor had there been any research into the ways in which individual differences, such as need for cognition, affect the ways in which people respond to these differing levels of complexity. In order to explore some of these issues, we conducted a study to investigate whether individuals with a high need for cognition would prefer greater figurative complexity in advertisements than those with a low need for cognition. We hypothesised that individuals with a greater need for cognition would (a) comprehend adverts more quickly, (b) have greater appreciation for adverts and (c) perceive the advert as more effective, if the advert contained greater figurative complexity.

In order to test these hypotheses, we had ninety participants from the United Kingdom, Spain and China view thirty advertisements that contained either simple or complex figurative operations. Simple operations involved either metaphor or metonymy and complex figurative operations involved metonymic chains (where one metonymy leads to another), metaphorical complexes (where several metaphors work together to convey a single message) and metaphtonymies (where metaphor and metonymy combine) (Ruiz de Mendoza and Galera, 2014). Participants were shown the advertisements on a computer screen and asked to indicate as soon as they had understood the message the advertisement was trying to convey. They were then asked to complete the Need for Cognition Scale, which is an assessment instrument that measures quantitatively 'the tendency for an individual to engage in and enjoy thinking' (Cacioppo and Petty, 1982: 116).

We found that individuals' levels of need for cognition significantly influenced the ways in which they reacted and responded to the advertisements. Individuals with a high need for cognition understood the adverts that contained complex figurative operations significantly more quickly than adverts that contained simple operations. This finding did not hold for individuals with low levels of need for cognition. However, need for cognition was not found to relate to levels of appreciation or perceived effectiveness; other variables, such as the use of colour in the advertisement or the participants' attitude towards the project being advertised, are likely to have affected participants' levels of appreciation.

Our findings have interesting implications for embodied metaphor. Although many of the metaphors in our study were resemblance metaphors, in nearly all cases, there were references to physical experiences, and, as we saw in Chapter 1, the distinction between correlational embodied metaphor and resemblance metaphor is often very blurred in practice, as resemblance metaphors can often provoke visual, kinaesthetic, somaesthetic or haptic imagery (Ureña and Faber, 2010).

An example of a resemblance metaphor that has the potential to evoke an embodied metaphor can be found in an advertisement produced by Audi which features two of the white lines that are often painted along the middle of the road, accompanied by the caption 'Audi Fatigue Detector: Wake up!' This advertisement involves the visual equivalent of word play where the two lines can have different meanings. Under one interpretation, they represent closed eyes, and thus refer to the physical act of sleeping. Under a second interpretation, they can be seen to represent the lines in the middle of the road, which can become hypnotic as one drives through the dark, thus sending the driver to sleep. In both cases, the driver will find it useful to be awoken by the fatigue detector that is built into the car. Both interpretations have the potential to involve sensorimotor responses, as they evoke (a) sleeping and (b) driving. However, such responses are more likely to be triggered via a process of metonymy rather than metaphor, as the physical experiences are only hinted at indirectly via the picture. Our findings showed that individuals with a higher need for cognition were able to find meaning in complex advertisements such as this more rapidly than individuals with a lower need for cognition.

Creativity

We saw in Chapter 2 that creative instantiations of primary metaphors are more likely to evoke an embodied response in the hearer than conventional ones. Creativity as an individual differences variable has also been found to affect the ways in which people produce metaphors that have an embodied basis (Birdsell, 2017). Birdsell administered a series of creative metaphor production and comprehension tasks to a large number of Japanese students of English in their first and second language. He also administered a series of established tests of creativity. He found significant correlations across the two sets of tests in both the first and second language, which led him to conclude that creative metaphoric competence is a stable individual difference involving an inherent disposition towards uniqueness or novelty. He argues that 'some individuals are more inclined and prone to seek out semantic relations between distant concepts and this combinatorial ability is an important part of the creative process' (309). The metaphor tests used in his study did not explicitly request embodied metaphorical responses per se, but the responses produced by the participants, particularly those that were scored as creative, nearly all involved bodily based experiences. For example, in the task where participants were asked to complete the sentence 'memories are . . . ', responses that were scored as 'creative' included 'memories are handcuffs', 'memories are stairs' and 'memories are wings'. These responses suggest that the participants were thinking of memories in a very embodied way and that this helped them produce these creative responses. The responses produced by the less creative individuals were much less likely to make reference to bodily based experiences. They included 'memories are moments', 'memories are pictures' and 'memories are the most valuable treasure'. Thus, creative individuals appear to be more likely to exploit the creative potential of embodied metaphor. These findings are, however, only indicative, as they did not arise from studies that focused specifically on embodied metaphor. It would be interesting to conduct further research, focussing only on those metaphors that have a bodily basis.

Psychopathy

A final internal source of variation that has been found to affect the ways in which people interact with embodied metaphor is the presence of psychopathic tendencies, sometimes referred to as 'psychopathy'. Psychopathy involves a cluster of personality characteristics that include grandiosity, manipulativeness, impulsivity, a lack of empathy or remorse and an inclination towards immoral behaviour (Hare, 1996; Meier et al., 2007). These psychopathic traits lie on a continuum and can be found in the 'normal' population as well as amongst institutionalised individuals. We saw in Chapter 2 a number of studies whose findings indicate that morality is embodied as cleanliness. Another possibility, proposed by Meier, Selbom and Wygant (2007), is that it is also represented on a vertical hierarchy, with morality positioned at the top of the hierarchy and immorality at the bottom. This follows the embodied metaphor GOOD IS UP, BAD IS DOWN, which was also documented in Chapter 2. They hypothesised that because individuals with psychopathic disorders rarely activate the concept of morality, they may make less use of the MORAL IS UP, IMMORAL IS DOWN axis than individuals without psychopathic disorders.

In order to test this hypothesis, they conducted two experiments. In the first experiment they sought to establish whether people tend to associate morality (or lack thereof) with vertical space. In order to do this, they employed an Implicit Association Test (Greenwald, McGhee and Schwartz, 1998) in which participants were asked to categorise words according to whether they had a moral or immoral meaning and to categorise a series of asterisks according to whether they appeared either above or below the centre of the screen. In some trials, the same response button was used for both the 'moral' and the 'high' responses, whereas in others, the same response button was used for both the 'moral' and the 'low' responses. They were interested in assessing whether there was a facilitating effect in the former condition and an interference effect in the latter condition. They found that participants were faster at categorising the words as moral when they were paired with the asterisks that appeared above the centre of the screen, and faster at categorising the words as immoral when they were paired with the asterisks that appeared lower down the screen. These findings suggest that people do indeed associate morality with vertical space.

In the second experiment, they simply asked participants to rate words as having high or low morality, with the words appearing randomly at the top and the bottom of the screen. They then asked participants to complete Levenson et al.'s (1995) Self-Reported Psychopathy Scale (LSRP). They found the interaction between morality and verticality to be significantly stronger in those participants who had received low scores on the LSRP than those who had received high scores on the LSRP. These findings suggest that the vertical representation of morality is indeed less well developed in people with psychopathic traits than in people without these traits.

To sum up, these studies show that internally driven individual differences appear to shape the ways in which people respond to embodied metaphors, the types of embodied metaphorical relationships that they favour, the meanings that they will extract from embodied metaphor, their tendency to adopt one metaphor over another, the strength of the relationship that they form with the metaphors and the extent to which certain embodied metaphors influence their world view. We thus have further evidence of the non-universal nature of embodied metaphor, and a better appreciation of the ways in which a person's understanding of the world can vary, depending on the relationship that they have with embodied metaphor.

8.3 Externally Driven (Social) Sources of Variation

So far in this chapter the emphasis has been on internal, individual sources of variation. In this second part of the chapter I turn to sources of variation, which despite being deeply personal and internal on one level, are more clearly shaped by societal forces. These are ideology, political persuasion and religion. I look at how these influence the ways in which people experience and use embodied metaphor. Although ideology, political persuasion and religion are, on one level, internal, they both draw on external, social constructs.

Ideology and Political Persuasion

It has been observed that ideological and political positioning can both shape and be shaped by the metaphorical lens through which people see the world. For example, bodily based metaphors involving health, racing and fitness have been found to underlie much of the rhetoric employed by right-wing advocates of the free market economy (Boers, 1997a). Furthermore, a move to the right in the political atmosphere in the United Kingdom during the 1980s led people to conceptualise the welfare state as a 'safety net' rather than as a 'shelter', thus de-emphasising the vulnerability of its users (Boers, 1997b). In his analysis of the use of metaphor in *The Economist* (a right-wing magazine) and *The Guardian* (a left-wing newspaper) during the Thatcherite era in the United Kingdom (an era that was characterised by a strong push towards the free market and a concomitant reduction of union power), Caers (2006) found that *The Economist* made more salient use of metaphors associated with health, conflict and mobility (in particular forwards movement), whereas *The Guardian* made more salient use of metaphors related to crime and living organisms. He identified a correlation in *The Guardian* between the use of living organism metaphors and positive evaluations regarding the welfare state, which was talked about in terms of its 'health', and negative ones concerning privatisation, which was portrayed as a 'disease'.

The majority of the research in this area has focused on metaphors employed by journalists and the political elite (e.g., Musolff, 2004; Charteris-Black, 2005), but in recent years there have been a small number of studies that have focused on the metaphors employed by people outside these professional spheres. Within this area, one of the most widely investigated metaphors is the NATION AS A BODY metaphor. This metaphor is often shaped by the political system within which one lives and can also be used to prime political views. Landau, Sullivan and Greenberg (2009) found that when American individuals were exposed to the nation-as-body metaphor, they were more likely to display harsher attitudes towards immigrants entering the United States. This metaphor is discussed in more depth in Chapter 9, when I discuss cross-cultural variation in the experience of metaphor.

The idea that metaphor can prime political views has been explored in depth by Thibodeau and Boroditsky (2011), who investigated how the use of metaphor can influence the ways in which people reason about the causes of and solutions to complex social issues. They presented participants with a fictional scenario about crime rates in the fictitious city of 'Addison', and asked them to propose a solution. For half of the participants, crime was metaphorically described as a 'beast' that was 'preying on' Addison, and for the other half as a 'virus' that was 'infecting' Addison. The rest of the report contained crime statistics that were identical for the two metaphor conditions. Participants who had read the text in which crime was framed metaphorically as a beast were more likely to recommend catching and jailing criminals and enacting harsher enforcement laws. Participants who had read the text in which crime was framed metaphorically as a virus were more likely to recommend investigating the root causes and treating the problem by enacting social reform to inoculate the community, with emphasis on eradicating poverty and improving education. Interestingly, when questioned, very few participants thought that the metaphor played an important part in their decision. Finally, participants who had no explicit memory of the metaphor were just as likely to be affected by the metaphor as participants who were able to remember the metaphorical frame. These findings suggest that metaphors can act covertly in reasoning. Boroditsky et al. also examined the role of political affiliation on reasoning about crime, and their results showed that Republicans are more likely to generate enforcement and punishment solutions for dealing with crime, and are less swayed by metaphor than are Democrats or Independents. Furthermore, Democrats and Independents were significantly more likely to be influenced by the frame than Republicans.

Political attitudes and behaviour have also been found to be embodied as physical experiences. We saw in Chapter 3 that there is a close link between feelings of disgust and attitudes towards immoral behaviour. The embodied nature of this relationship is illustrated by Cannon et al.'s (2011) finding that judging moral disgust induces 'disgusted' facial expressions. People of a conservative political persuasion are often thought to be more concerned with morality and purity, which has led some to suggest that they are more likely to experience disgust in both the literal and metaphorical sense (Landau et al., 2009). Support for this contention comes from a study by Inbar et al. (2009), who administered both a 'sensitivity to disgust' questionnaire and a political orientation questionnaire to a group of US individuals and found significant correlations between the two variables. They found that conservatives were significantly more likely to be sensitive to disgust than liberals and thus concluded that conservatives are more likely to have 'morally queasy brains'. Thus political viewpoint appears to affect both the types of embodied metaphors that are favoured and the intensity with which they are experienced.

Religious and Spiritual Beliefs

It is a well-established fact that religious language is highly metaphorical (Ptzemyslaw et al., 1998) and there is increasing recognition of the impact that religious beliefs can have on embodied metaphor. Strong religious beliefs have been found to strengthen people's experience of the embodied metaphor through which MORALITY is perceived as 'UP' and IMMORALITY is 'DOWN'. Li and Cao (2016) hypothesised that if moral concern affects the spatial representation of morality, then its effects will be stronger in religious individuals or in people who have been primed with religious concepts. In order to test this hypothesis, they extended Meier and Robinson's (2004) aforementioned study and asked participants to evaluate words with moral meanings (e.g., righteousness) and with immoral meanings (e.g., sinfulness) displaying them randomly at the top or the bottom of the screen. The participants were asked to indicate on a scale from 1 to 7 how 'moral' they felt the meaning of the word to be. The participants (all of whom were from China) were divided into those who held strong religious beliefs (Buddhism and/or Taoism) and those who did not. They found that participants who held religious beliefs were significantly more likely to display the kinds of effects found by Meier and Robinson (i.e., they responded more quickly to moral words when displayed at the top of the screen and to immoral words when they were displayed at the bottom of the screen). These findings suggest that religious belief strengthens the relationship between notions of morality and the vertical image schema. Buddhists and Taoists do not belief in Heaven and Hell, so these findings cannot be explained by the teaching that one 'ascends' to Heaven or 'descends' into Hell. In order to test the relationship further, Li and Cao repeated the study with two groups of non-religious participants; one group was primed with religious concepts by being asked to complete a sentence-scrambling activity involving sentences that contained religious concepts, while the other group was given non-religious sentences to unscramble. They found that those who had been primed with religious concepts were more likely to exhibit evidence of a vertical schema for morality. These findings are interesting, as they suggest that although religion can affect the strength of the vertical morality schema, the relationship is highly fluid and can be easily manipulated by the preceding activity. This change is testimony to the contextual, dynamic nature of embodied metaphor.

People with different religious beliefs have been found to make differential use of embodied metaphors involving a SOURCE-PATH-GOAL schema. Richardson (2012) analysed the use of metaphors of movement and proximity, which carry a strong embodied motivation, in testimonials produced by Muslim and Christian converts, and found that they exhibited varying patterns of emphasis. These included a focus on a relationship with God derived from the language of intimate human relationships in the Christian testimonials, which contrasted with a focus on a personal journey of research and reflection in the Muslim testimonials. In other words, the Christians are more likely to be travelling *with* God, whilst the Muslims are more likely to be travelling *towards* God.

Further evidence for the impact of religious beliefs on embodied metaphor can be found in the material objects associated with those religions. A good example of this is the architecture that different religions employ. In their descriptions of two religious buildings, Chartres cathedral in France and the ninth-century Buddhist monument of Borobudur in Indonesia, Stec and Sweetser (2013) show how the buildings are designed so that visitors experience different embodied metaphors as they progress through them. In Chartres cathedral, visitors are immediately faced with a lofty building in which the eye is drawn up towards the ceiling. The altar is on a raised platform and the cross is suspended from the ceiling, thus we have the physical enactment of a power is up metaphor. In Borobudur, visitors gradually circle up through a lotus flower, starting in its roots, progressing up through its stem and finally ascending into its flower to reach nirvana. These different architectural designs evoke POWER IS UP and CHANGE OF STATE IS PHYSICAL MOTION metaphors. However, when we look more closely at each of the buildings we see a number of differences in the way these metaphors are developed. In Chartres Cathedral, there is a strong emphasis on hierarchy and the need for the visitor to know his or her place in relation to the deity: a deity who is both physically and metaphorically unreachable. In contrast to this, in Borobudur, there is a clear assumption that one can reach enlightenment through one's own effort, and this belief system is built into the architecture of the building.

Finally, evidence of the dynamic nature of embodied metaphor in religion can be found in Winchester's (2016) paper 'Hunger for God', in which he describes an ethnographic study of fasting among converts to Eastern Orthodox Christianity in the United States. Winchester found that the act of fasting reshaped converts' subjective thinking and subsequent actions through a series of metaphorical associations between concrete bodily experiences related to appetite, food and hunger and more abstract religious discourses involving the soul, sin and religious virtue. He concludes that for these converts, embodied metaphor constitutes a cognitive process which accounts for the 'dynamic, mutually informing interactions between these two cognitive registers' (585).

We can see two contrasting perspectives in the work discussed in this section. While Richardson's study exemplifies the potential for linguistic analyses to reveal differences in religious experience, Li and Cao's shows how a purely cognitive approach tends to emphasise commonality. In order to further investigate the ways in which the presence or otherwise of religious beliefs affects the way in which people perceive the world through embodied metaphor, we (Turner and Littlemore, in prep.) are currently investigating the role of an individual's religious and spiritual beliefs in the metaphors they use to describe these beliefs. We are focusing in particular on embodied metaphor as manifested through language and gesture.

In our study, participants with a range of religious affiliations or none are being video recorded whilst speaking about their beliefs. We are investigating the use of embodied metaphor and metaphorical gesture in the participants' testimonials, with a particular focus on the extent to which there are commonalities and variations in the metaphors (both linguistic and gestural) used by members of different faith groups or traditions. We are interested in establishing how bodily based metaphor is used when talking about religious or spiritual beliefs, or lack thereof; how metaphorical gesture is used when talking about religious or spiritual beliefs, or lack thereof; the extent to which there are commonalities in the metaphors (both linguistic and gestural) used by members of different faiths or none when describing religious or spiritual beliefs, or lack thereof; and the nature of the relationship (if any) between religious/spiritual belief, or lack thereof; the metaphorical language/gestures used when describing religious/spiritual beliefs, or lack thereof; and personality type as measured by the Big Five Personality Test. Our initial findings show that both religious and non-religious participants place abstract concepts (both spiritual and religious) and goodness in higher gestural space than concrete concepts and 'human' behaviour and they use width to indicate vagueness and openness. Further analysis is needed, however, to discover how people with different belief systems or indeed people who have no belief systems make use of embodied primary metaphors, such as those involving the vertical hierarchy, and the use of proximity and distance, and openness and closedness, in natural language.

8.4   Conclusion

In this chapter, we have seen that both internally driven and more socially driven individual differences can lead people to construct very different metaphorical construals of the world. Internally driven differences in personality and cognitive style affect not only the types of metaphors that people use, but also the ways in which they process these metaphors and the speed with which they do so. They also affect the extent to which their behaviour is susceptible to manipulation by metaphorical framing. These differences can be very deep, affecting, for example, the way in which people experience time, and the way they feel about ethical and moral issues. We have also seen that more socially driven individual differences such as religion and political viewpoint shape, or are shaped by, different kinds of embodied metaphorical thinking. Evidence of these different metaphorical construals can be found both in religious discourse and in religious architecture. These differences go some way towards explaining why it is that people so often misunderstand each other, interpret the same information in different ways and ultimately find it difficult to resolve conflict. Embodied metaphors reify abstract concepts in ways that lead people down different paths, and once they are reified they can become somewhat less malleable. This lack of malleability has the potential to become problematic where ideology, political persuasion and religion are concerned, as it can lead to conflict and misunderstanding. On the other hand, looking at these differences through the lens of metaphor gives grounds for some degree of optimism, as in some cases, it is only the entailments that are different; the underlying metaphors are often very similar. Moreover, as some of the studies discussed in this chapter have shown, by making the metaphorical nature of the reasoning process more overt and by presenting people with alternative metaphorical models, it is possible to induce more flexible thinking.

9 'Malodorous Blacksmiths and Lazy Livers.'
Cross-Linguistic and Cross-Cultural Variation in Embodied Metaphor

9.1 Introduction

'Whether you like it or not, history is on our side. We will bury you.'
Nikita Khrushchev, 1956

This statement was an impromptu utterance made by Khrushchev in addressing Western ambassadors at a reception at the Polish embassy in Moscow, simply intended to express conviction in the ultimate triumph of communism. Western politicians, unfamiliar with the Russian meaning of this expression, misinterpreted it as an annihilation threat, with serious consequences for international relations. The source of the misunderstanding in this example was Khrushchev's metaphorical use of the word 'bury', which was interpreted literally by western politicians. Research has shown that misunderstandings of metaphorical language such as these are common, particularly across linguistic and cultural barriers (Musolff, 2014), and more worryingly, people are often unaware of them: they think they have understood when they have not, and act accordingly. As the example shows, differences in the ways in which people from different linguistic backgrounds understand and use metaphor can have serious consequences.

There is increasing recognition of the fact that embodied metaphor does not arise in the body alone, but that it 'emerges from bodily interactions that are to a large extent defined in the cultural world' (Gibbs, 1999: 155). The aim of this chapter is to explore the impact of linguistic and cultural variation on the way in which people experience and engage with metaphor. I focus on the ways in which our linguistic and cultural experiences interact with the ways in which we experience our physicality in order to shape the way we use metaphor to reason and communicate our thoughts. In doing so, I explore the dynamic relationship between language, culture, the body and metaphor. I begin by focusing on the ways in which languages and cultures have been found to shape people's experiences of embodied metaphor. I then look at what happens when people are exposed to more than one language and culture, and consider how embodied metaphor operates in a first and second language. I report findings from two studies that I have conducted in this area, one looking at how the use of embodied metaphor shapes one's use of gesture cross-linguistically, and one looking at how it shapes the associations that people form between abstract concepts and colours in their first and second language. As we develop a more nuanced understanding of the ways in which people with different linguistic and cultural backgrounds make use of embodied metaphor to understand the world, we should hopefully see fewer examples of the type of misunderstanding that I have just described.

9.2 Different Language, Different Embodied Metaphor?

There are important differences in the way in which different cultures conceptualise both the body and bodily experiences, and in the levels and types of significance and emotional meanings that they attach to different body parts (Yu, 2002, 2003). The role of cultural conceptions of the body in shaping embodied language and thought is encapsulated in Sharifian's (2017) notion of 'embodied cultural metaphor', which places culture at the heart of embodied metaphor.

Traditional accounts of cross-cultural variation in metaphor view embodied metaphor as a universal phenomenon, with culture-specific variation taking place only in terms of the ways in which these metaphors are elaborated. Musolff (2017) questions this assumption, and provides evidence (which we will see in this chapter) to show that even some of the so-called universal embodied primary metaphors can vary cross-culturally, at a fundamental level. This variation can affect the way in which people think about both abstract and concrete concepts (Schröder, 2009). For example, Schröder (2009) found that Brazilian and German speech communities make very different use of embodied metaphors for a fundamental human emotion: love. She found that in the Brazilian data, metaphors involving conquest, eating and plants were frequently employed, whereas in the German data, metaphors involving journeys and systems were more prominent.

In this section, I explore three areas where cross-linguistic and cross-cultural variation has been found in the ways in which people employ embodied metaphor. My focus is on: metaphorical relationships between time, number and space, metaphors that use parts of the body as a source domain, and metaphors that involve the senses.

Linguistic and Cultural Variation in the Embodied Metaphorical Relationship between Time and Space

Within the area of cross-linguistic and cross-cultural variation in metaphor, one of the most widely researched topics is the relationship between time and space. Many of the world's languages conceptualise time as sitting along a straight trajectory in space. In English, this trajectory follows the egocentrically grounded anterior/posterior (back-front) axis, so we talk about putting the past 'behind' us or 'looking forward' to the future. English speakers also use the left-to-right trajectory for time, as we saw in Chapter 4 (Tversky et al., 1991). However, these trajectories are by no means universal. Chinese uses the vertical axis with earlier time-points located above and later time-points located below (Fuhrman et al., 2011). Boroditsky et al. (2011) investigated whether these differences lead English and Mandarin speakers to think about time differently. In order to test this hypothesis, they showed both native Mandarin and native English speakers a sequence of images depicting simple temporal progressions – of, for instance, a person at different ages, or of a banana being eaten. Participants were then asked to identify the chronological order of these sequences by using the directional pad on a keyboard, a task which was conducted under two different conditions, each of which had a canonical and a non-canonical ordering. In the first condition, the 'left' directional key corresponded to 'earlier' and 'right' directional key corresponded to 'later' in the canonical version, whereas in the non-canonical version, the 'right' directional key corresponded to 'earlier' and the 'left' directional key corresponded to 'later'. In the second condition, the 'up' directional key corresponded to 'earlier' and the 'down' key to 'later' in the canonical version, whereas in the non-canonical version, the 'down' directional key corresponded to 'earlier' and the 'up' directional key corresponded to 'later'. The results from this study showed that the reaction times for the Mandarin speakers were significantly affected by the canonical nature of the relationship in the vertical condition (and not the horizontal condition), whereas the reaction times for the English speakers were significantly affected by the canonical/non-canonical nature of the relationships in the horizontal condition (and not the vertical condition). These findings suggest that Mandarin speakers are more likely than English speakers to conceptualise time vertically, in accordance with vertical spatio-temporal metaphors in their native language. Evidence for cross-linguistic and cross-cultural variation in meta-phorical conceptualisations of time is also provided by Fedden and Boroditsky's (2012) study, which found that speakers of Mian, a Papua New Guinea language that conceptualises time as flowing towards the body or from east to west, arranged cards corresponding to different times according to these paths. Variation has been found even amongst cultures that employ a horizontal axis in their conceptualisation of time. As we saw in Chapter 4, Tversky et al. (1991) found that metaphorical conceptualisations of time are also shaped by the direction in which people write, with English speakers favouring a left-to-right pattern, speakers of Arabic favouring a right-to-left pattern and Hebrew speakers showing mixed results.

Evidence for cross-linguistic and cross-cultural variation in embodied meta-phorical conceptions of time can also be found in gesture. Núñez and Sweetser

(2006) report that speakers of the Aymara language refer to the past as being in front and the future as being behind. These relationships are also manifested in the gestures that speakers of this language employ when talking about time; they gesture in front when they are talking about the past and behind when they are talking about the future.

People's perceptions of the *way* in which time moves through space also appear to be susceptible to cross-linguistic and cross-cultural variation. The world's languages have been found to divide into two types with respect to how they describe manner of movement. In so-called satellite-framed languages (such as English), the path of movement is encoded in the particle, whilst the manner of movement is encoded in the verb, leading to expressions such as 'jump out', 'slide into' 'crawl along' etc. (Talmy, 1991; Slobin, 2005). So-called verb-framed languages, such as Spanish, for example, directly encode motion path, and may leave out the manner of motion or express it in a complement of manner (typically a participle): entró corriendo 'he ran in', literally 'he entered running'; 'salió flotando', 'it floated out', literally 'it exited floating'. Özçalişkan (2004) found that this difference extends into the ways in which space is used to refer metaphorically to the abstract notion of time, when it is described as an object moving through space. In a story-retelling task that she administered to English- and Turkish-speaking children, she found that English-speaking children used a wider variety of motion verbs than Turkish speakers and that they paid greater linguistic attention to the manner of motion even when talking about time. She argues that this cross-linguistic difference in the lexicalisation of the source domain reflects different ways of conceptualising the target domain of time.

Thus we have seen that there is substantial variation in the ways in which people from different linguistic and cultural backgrounds use embodied metaphor to construe time in terms of space. There are significant differences both in terms of directionality, and in terms of the manner of movement that time can make. Evidence for this variation comes from experimental data as well as from gesture studies.

Linguistic and Cultural Variation in Metaphors That Use the Body as a Source Domain

There is evidence to suggest that languages and cultures vary in terms of the way they employ metaphors that have the parts of body as a source domain. The edited volume by Sharifian et al. (2008) contains a wide variety of studies showing how the heart, the liver and the stomach embody the mind and the emotions in different ways in different cultures. In one of the papers in that volume, Ibarretze-Antuñano (2008) shows how in Basque, the word 'gibel', which translates as 'liver', is used metonymically to refer to a wide range of meanings related to the back and behind. These include: 'gibeldu' (delay, be late), 'gibelarat hartu' (push back, withdraw) and 'gibelondo' (neglect). These meanings are then extended metaphorically to refer to a range of negative emotions, including laziness, disdain, disgust, aversion and rancour. In the same volume, Sharifian (2008) talks about how, in Persian, people often refer to the 'del', which roughly translates as the 'heart-stomach'. This is the seat of the emotions, desires, patience, courage and compassion as well as thoughts and memories. The 'del' is often personified, made responsible for people's desires, and evoked in descriptions of character and personality traits. Cross-cultural variation in the way we use our bodies to denote source domains can also be found in non-verbal communication. For example, in Japanese manga, bodies shrink to show embarrassment. In the west, such shrinkage would be more likely to be associated with a lessening of importance.

The human body is often employed as a source domain in metaphors of nationhood and collective identity. This particular source domain has been shown to be susceptible to a substantial amount of cross-linguistic and cross-cultural variation. Musolff (2017) conducted an extensive survey into the ways in which the NATION-AS-A-BODY metaphor is understood by people of different nationalities. He asked people from thirty different countries to think about how his metaphor applied to their home country and to produce a visual representation of the metaphor. He found that in many non-Chinese responses, the nation state tended to be conceptualised through functionally and hierarchically motivated analogies to the human body. For example, one UK participant wrote that the head of the body represents the Queen and that the features of the head represent politicians, the Prime Minister and the government. In contrast, many Chinese participants tended to map the geographical shape of a nation onto the shape of a human body. One Chinese participant, for example, wrote that Beijing is the heart and brain of China, Shanghai is the face (as it is the economic centre), Tianjin is the hands (as it houses the army) and Shenzen is the eyes (as it was the first place to be open to the world). Here the respondent is using cities in China to refer metonymically to the main 'functions' that those cities serve. Musolff argues that for these Chinese respondents, the basic geopolitical metonymy serves as a foundation upon which they construct the metaphor. He also notes that many of the participants in the study talked in terms of the nation as a person, and that the Chinese participants showed a marked preference for mother-personifications. The Chinese respondents appear to be using this metaphor in an entirely different way from the non-Chinese respondents. In both cases, the responses are likely to have been shaped by their political conceptions of the role of the state, and political/historical developments that have affected the relationship between the state and its people.

These findings show that the role played by the human body in shaping our understanding of the world is not a direct one; it is mediated by cultural constructions of the human body. In other words, people from different nationalities use the human body to reason about abstract concepts in different ways, but this variation exists at the phenomenological level rather than at the neural level (see Gibbs, 2005).

Linguistic and Cultural Variation in Cross-Sensory Metaphor

A third kind of embodied metaphor that has been found to be affected by linguistic and cultural variation is cross-sensory metaphor. We saw in Chapter 6 that people's experiences of cross-sensory metaphor have been found to be affected by sensory deficits, and conditions that involve a sensory 'surplus', such as synaesthesia. There is some evidence to suggest that cross-sensory metaphors exhibit both universality and variation across different languages and cultures. For example, in their study of the Himba people of Northern Namibia, Bremner et al. (2013) found evidence in support of Köhler's (1929) 'Bouba' and 'Kiki' effect, whereby round shapes are more likely to be labelled 'Bouba' and hard angular shapes are more likely to be labelled 'Kiki'. However, when they explored shape-taste matches, they found a pattern of behaviour that was very different from that of Westerners. The Himba people matched spark-ling water and non-bitter tastes to rounded shapes, rather than to angular ones, which is the opposite of the behaviour exhibited by Westerners.

Evidence of linguistic and cultural variation has also been found in the role played by cross-sensory metaphor in descriptions of music. For example, it has been shown that speakers of different languages employ different metaphors to conceptualise pitch. In English, pitch is described in terms of high and low notes, in Liberia, it is described as 'light' and 'heavy', the Suya people of the Amazon basin describe it as 'young' and 'old', and the Bashi people of central Africa talk of 'weak' and 'strong'. For the Manza people of Central Africa, high pitches are 'small' and low pitches are 'large'. For other languages, such as Farsi (as we saw in Chapter 4), high pitches are 'thin' and low pitches are 'thick'. In order to establish whether this linguistic variation affects cognitive processing, Dolscheid et al. (2013) conducted a 'double-dissociation' study, in which they played both Dutch and Farsi speakers a number of notes of different pitches whilst asking them to look at a computer screen on which were displayed lines of varying heights and thicknesses. They then asked the participants to watch the lines and to sing the notes immediately after they had heard them. For the Dutch speakers, the accuracy of the notes that they produced was affected by the height of the lines (with higher lines leading them to pitch the notes higher and lower lines leading them to pitch the notes lower), whilst with the Farsi speakers, the accuracy of the notes produced was affected by the thickness of the lines, with thinner lines pushing the pitch up and thicker lines pushing the notes down. Thus Dutch speakers, who talk about musical notes as being 'high' (hoog) and 'low' (lag), incorporated irrelevant height information into their pitch estimates, whilst Farsi speakers, who talk about pitch as being thin (nazok) and thick (koloft), incorporated irrelevant thickness information into their estimates of pitch. They thus conclude that these linguistic differences shape the ways in which Dutch and Farsi speakers 'experience' pitch.

Another area of linguistic and cultural variation involves the so-called hierarchy of the senses, which was discussed in Chapter 6. According to this hierarchy, which has been proposed largely as a result of studies of English, vision is thought to be the 'dominant sense', followed by hearing, smell, taste and touch (Jütte, 2005). Support for this hierarchy comes from corpus linguistic studies which show that metaphorical meanings associated with these senses appear in decreasing order of frequency along the continuum (Viberg, 1983). Sweetser (1990) identifies the following key metaphorical mappings that are employed by western cultures:

> Vision > knowledge (e.g., 'I can see what you're driving at', BNC)
> Hearing > Heeding (e.g., 'I hear all the arguments about injuries', BNC)
> Taste > Likes/dislikes (e.g., 'I must say it is not to my taste', BNC)
> Touch > Feelings (e.g., 'We were deeply touched to receive your gift', BNC)
> Smell > Disliked feelings (e.g., 'I can smell disruption', BNC).

The universality of this hierarchy has been questioned by Aikhenvald and Storch (2013), who argue that the language samples used by both Viberg and Sweetser are highly Eurocentric and are thus not representative of the world's languages. They note that although in many of the world's languages cognition is indeed expressed in terms of seeing, in others it is associated with verbs of auditory perception, touch or smell.

This contention is supported by experimental findings. For example, San Roque et al. (2014) investigated the use of sensory metaphors in spontaneous conversations from thirteen different languages. They found that although references to sight were, in general, significantly more frequent than references to the other senses, the relative frequency of the other senses varied cross-linguistically, with some languages favouring senses other than vision. These included Semai, a Malaysian language, which ranks the sense of smell particularly highly. They concluded that because sensory perception is as much a cultural as a physical phenomenon, cultures make use of different sensory domains in different ways, and there is therefore substantial variation in the processes and values that are associated with them.

An interesting example of the way in which cultural perceptions shape the metaphorical exploitation of sensory perception can be found amongst the

Kapsiki people of Cameroon and Nigeria. When talking metaphorically about cognition, they prioritise the sense of smell and distinguish between fourteen different kinds of smell (van Beek, 1992). Interestingly, from the point of view of embodied metaphor, they express complex social relations metonymically through reference to odours. An important odour-based distinction is drawn between blacksmiths (rerhe) and 'normal' Kapsiki people (melu, pl. melimu) with the 'good'-smelling melu having distinctly higher status than the 'malodorous' blacksmiths. These (presumably metonymic) references to smell serve as an important symbol of social status, as blacksmiths are seen as 'dirty and dangerous people' (40). In addition to forging iron, blacksmiths are also responsible for leatherworking, pottery, medicine, divination, magic, music and, rather importantly, funeral rituals. As part of the funeral ritual, blacksmiths dress the corpse, dance with it for two consecutive days, provide musical accompaniment with their drums and flutes, prepare the corpse for burial, direct the digging of the grave and bury the dead after three days of intense ritual. The main motivation for the blacksmiths being described as 'smelly' appears to come from the fact that they deal with the dead and eat meat that is taboo for the non-blacksmiths. Van Beek concludes that 'the strong emotional content of smell, its persistence over time and its sensitiveness to minute differences render it well suited to symbolic representation of enduring divisions of society into a higher and a lower stratum ... in this way, the nose is man's finest instrument of social discrimination' (52).

Another researcher to question the universality of sight as the most prominent source domain in cross-sensory metaphor is Classen (1990), who details the varied and complex ways in which the indigenous peoples of South America attach literal and metaphorical meanings to different sensory perceptions. She compares the sensory models of indigenous cultures from two contrasting South American regions: the central Andean highlands and the Amazonian lowlands. In order to compensate for the fact that Andean culture is now heavily influenced by Western culture, she supplements contemporary data with data taken from a corpus of Inca traditions recorded after the Spanish Conquest in the sixteenth century.

Her data show that in both groups of indigenous people, hearing is the sense with the highest cultural value and, as such, gives rise to the widest variety of metaphorical meanings. The fact that in the Inca traditions the sense of hearing is relatively more dominant than the sense of sight is reflected in practices such as the ears of males being 'opened' during male puberty rites, so that they can receive oral communications from the deities, and holy objects, such as mummies and rocks, which are able to 'speak' to their worshippers'. Desana Indians, who inhabit the North of Brazil, employ the term 'pe mahsiri yiri', which literally means 'to hear-to know-to act', and which roughly translates into 'free will'. The opposite term to this is 'inya mahsibiri', which literally translates as 'to see-to know not'. Odour is also an important sense in both groups. For Desana Indians, odour is thought to be the result of a combination of colour and temperature, and people, animals and plants are all classified according to their 'odours'. These multi-sensory experiences resonate with some of the experiences reported by the synaesthetes in Chapter 7.

Like the Kapsiki people of Cameroon and Nigeria, a common feature of the Amazonians, which distinguishes them from the Andeans, is the importance that they attach to the sense of smell. Smell-related words have acquired a range of literal and metaphorical meanings. For example, the Aymara-speaking residents of the Chilean Andes use the term 'kisa' to refer to the concentrated sweetness of dried fruit, pleasant speech, soft tactile sensations and a rainbow effect in weaving. Although its original meaning relates to smell, its metaphorical meanings move freely between the senses of smell, sound, touch and sight.

Linguistic and cultural variation in sensory preferences means that some languages have far more elaborate sets of verbs for some senses than others. Howes and Classen (1991: 263) interpret the presence of an elaborate set of smell verbs in Quechua as proof of smell's importance in that speech community, and Ritchie (1991) draws attention to the basic perception verb inventory in Hausa, which includes one verb for seeing (gani) and one for all other sensory perception (ji), including hearing, touching, smelling and tasting. This means that the range of metaphorical meanings that speakers of English and other Indo-European languages associate with hearing, touching, smelling and tasting are more restricted in Quechua.

Researchers have also found linguistic and cultural variation in the ways in which metaphors involving the senses are interpreted. For example, Wang and Dowker (2010) administered a survey to English and Chinese participants in which they provided a number of metaphors and asked them to select the 'best' interpretation from a set of four. In each case, one response was deemed to be 'perceptual', one was 'psychological', one was 'both perceptual and psychological' and one was 'evaluative'. They found that Chinese adults were significantly more likely to produce interpretations that related to the mind and the emotions, whilst British adults were significantly more likely to provide more physically grounded perceptual interpretations. It is difficult to identify a reason for these differences beyond cultural convention.

Thus we can see that even in an area of human experience as fundamental as the senses there is extensive cross-linguistic and cross-cultural variation, with some languages and cultures prioritising one sense over the others, others using different cross-sensory mappings to describe experiences and others attaching deeper cultural metaphorical meanings to certain senses and not others. These differences are shaped both by the physical environment and by cultural conventions. We can conclude from this that it is impossible to disentangle the impact of language from the impact of culture, as they are mutually enforcing. Our experience of our own bodies serves as a starting point for the development of embodied metaphor, but cultural perceptions of what our bodies do and what they are for play a key role in shaping our metaphorical thinking processes.

9.3 Does Speaking a Second Language Affect the Way in Which We Understand and Use Embodied Metaphors?

We saw in Chapter 2 that subtle manipulations of language can affect the ways in which we think metaphorically. This leads to the question of what happens to one's embodied metaphors when one learns a second language. Do people who learn another language that employs embodied metaphors in a different way from their own start to 'think' using these new metaphors and do they use them in the same way as native speakers of a language?

As we saw in the previous section, there is substantial cross-linguistic variation in embodied metaphors used to conceptualise time, with Chinese speakers viewing time along a vertical axis and speakers of English conceptualising it along a horizontal axis. Fuhrman et al. (2011) looked at how these metaphors work in English-speaking learners of Mandarin. They found that more proficient native English speakers of Mandarin were more likely to arrange time vertically and that bilinguals were more likely to arrange time vertically when they were tested in Mandarin than in English. They therefore concluded that both previous language experience and the immediate linguistic context affect the way people conceptualise time metaphorically. Thus learning another language appears to affect the way people think about time.

These findings can be explained by Casasanto's (2014) Hierarchical Mental Metaphors Theory (HMMT), which, as we saw in Chapter 1, accounts for the co-existence of universality and variation in embodied metaphor. He suggests that primary metaphors develop universally through co-occurring childhood experiences. However, due to the influence of language, culture and bodily dispositions (e.g., right- or left-handedness), only a number of these universal mappings emerge and become strengthened, and the development of these metaphors weakens the strength of other mappings as a consequence. The dormant metaphors may still manifest in behavioural, social and physical experiences even though they may not be present in the language spoken. The linguistic metaphors that end up being used in adulthood are only a minority of a larger family of mappings that a person experiences during childhood. The result is a relative universality in which some primary metaphors are language-specific, culture-specific and/or body-specific.

Casasanto (2014) arrived at the HMMT after having investigated the cross-linguistic differences in metaphors for time that are employed by English and

Greek speakers (see Casasanto et al., 2004; Casasanto, 2008). English speakers tend to express time in terms of spatial extent (e.g., a long time), whereas Greek speakers tend to express it in terms of volume or amount (e.g., a lot of time). In the Casasanto (2008) study, participants were given a series of non-linguistic psychophysical tests of their ability to estimate duration. They were invited to reproduce the durations of stimuli that they had seen on a computer screen, which consisted of lines gradually extending across the screen or containers gradually filling up. They were asked to focus either on the spatial extent of the lines or on the fullness of the containers and ignore other things that were happening on the screen. The English speakers had difficulties screening out interference from spatial distance, while the Greek speakers had difficulty screening out interference from volume. These results suggest that the embodied metaphors that people employ when conceptualising time are strongly influenced by the language they speak. In order to investigate the impact of language over a shorter time period, Casasanto then trained the English speakers to use Greek-like metaphors for time. He found that after around twenty minutes of exposure to these new metaphors, the performance of the English speakers on the test became indistinguishable from that of the Greek speakers. In a similar study, Dolscheid et al. (2013), who I referred to earlier, trained Dutch speakers to talk about musical pitch using Farsi-like metaphors, where pitch is described in terms of thickness rather than height. They found that after having received training their performance on an interference task, similar to the one just described for time, became indistinguishable from that of native Farsi speakers.

These findings suggest that linguistic experience plays a causal role in shaping metaphorical representations of time, and that these effects can develop even over very short timeframes. They are important, as they suggest that learning another language actually does have the potential to open up new ways of seeing and understanding the world through metaphor, which makes learning new languages a valuable endeavour.

Embodied Metaphor in Gestures Employed By Native and Non-Native Speakers of English

We saw in Chapter 2 that gesture can provide strong evidence for the subconscious activation of embodied metaphor and that it is very much involved in the formulation and expressions of abstract ideas. We saw in Chapter 1 that, according to Kita et al.'s (2017) *Gesture-for-Conceptualization Hypothesis*, we use gesture to work out, both conceptually and linguistically, what information needs to be conveyed and how it can best be conveyed. We also saw that, according to Hostetter and Alibali's (2008) *Gestures as Simulated Action Framework*, the use of gesture reflects simulated action in the premotor cortex, the cerebellum and other subcortical areas, which spreads to other motor areas under certain circumstances, thus resulting in the production of gesture.

According to these authors, information that is perceived to be important or that contains difficult conceptual content is likely to trigger the use of gesture. I would argue that another potential source of gestural activation is communicative stress, and that one situation where the level of communicative stress is particularly high is when one is speaking a second language (McCafferty, 2004). It is clearly more difficult for second language speakers to put their ideas into words than it is for native speakers of the language, and one might expect this extra cognitive effort to engender the production of gesture. It follows from this that the increased effort required by learners when expressing abstract concepts in a second language may give rise to a more overt spatio-motoric mode of thinking (see Gullberg and McCafferty, 2008; Kita, 2000). One might therefore expect speakers of a second language to make more use of gesture when they employ metaphorical language to express abstract concepts.

Although no studies to date have compared the amount of metaphorical gesture employed by second language learners with that employed by native speakers of a language, Gullberg (1999) found that many of the gestures employed by lower level learners of English to help them produce the target language were indeed metaphorical. For example, when they faced grammatical problems related to the use of tense, they used gestures to refer to certain time axes, thus metaphorically mapping the time they wanted to express onto space. They did this even when their speech did not include any references to temporality (Gullberg, 1999, 2006). She also found that they employed metaphorical gestures to help with the cohesion of their output, in particular, with respect to anaphoric reference. For example, they placed events, objects or people in their speech through gestures along sagittal and transversal axes in the space around them, and referred back to using deictic gestures to point to the location they had just established, whenever they mentioned these points again (Gullberg, 1998, 2006; McCafferty, 2004). They thus employed gesture metaphorically to anchor abstract concepts in imagined temporal space. Interestingly, they employed these types of gestures even when their interlocutors could see them. This means that these gestures were not necessarily motivated by interaction but that they served a cognitive function, in that they helped the speakers structure their ideas and put them into words. What we do not yet know is whether speakers of a second language employ more metaphorical gestures than native speakers of the language when talking about the same sorts of subjects, and whether they employ these metaphorical gestures in a similar way.

In order to investigate these questions, we (Littlemore and Kwong, in prep.) conducted a small exploratory study in which we investigated the ways in which native and non-native (Chinese-speaking) speakers of English made use of primary metaphors in language and in gesture to talk about a similar set of topics. We analysed the use of gesture by a group of four advanced Chinese learners of English and four native speakers of English when talking about the following issues:

1. How do you manage your time for your study, work, family and personal interest?
2. What do you think the global economy will be like in the coming five years?
3. What makes you really angry?
4. In what ways do you think men and women should take control of finances in a relationship?

These issues were chosen to elicit discussions of abstract concepts related to 'balance', 'time', 'emotions' and 'control', as it was believed that these would stand a good chance of eliciting conceptual metaphors and their corresponding gestures.

The discussions were video recorded and the recordings of the gestures were examined for evidence of the influence of native/first language (L1) construals and for the role of embodied cognition in the production of English. We were aware of the inevitable fact that the two groups would diverge in terms of the actual detail of the topics discussed. This reflects a trade-off inherent in all studies of this kind between authenticity and controllability. Rather than carrying out the somewhat artificial tasks that are normally employed in gesture studies we wanted to look at how participants performed when carrying out a fairly authentic type of discussion task, a task which they might typically be asked to carry out in a language classroom.

We studied both the metaphors used (in both language and gesture) and the ways in which they were used. Here I report on some of the findings from this study regarding the ways in which metaphorical gestures were used by the two groups of participants.

Differences in the Way the Metaphorical Gestures Were Used

The main finding from our study was that, whereas the native speakers used metaphoric gestures instead of the actual words, the non-native speakers appeared to use gesture to help them formulate their messages. Here I present some examples of this phenomenon, as illustrated by two of the speakers in the study.

The first two examples are produced by native speakers of English in the study. In Figure 9.1, the speaker appears to be using a metaphorical gesture to represent the 'rigidity' of his housemate, although he does not actually put this idea into words. In all the examples given in this chapter, the speech segment

Figure 9.1 'Rigidity'

Figure 9.2 'Knitting together'

that was accompanied by the gesture is highlighted in bold. It is indicated by ** if no actual words accompanied the gesture.

Here, the gesture that he is using appears to imply that his housemate was rigid, orderly and somewhat fixed in his way of doing things. He liked to have things 'just so'. The words and the gesture work well together in the example to provide a clear picture of the personality of the housemate. The speaker does not need to accompany the gesture with any words. We know what meaning is intended. This appears to be a good example of 'metaphorical thinking' in action; the visual metaphor is so strong and so efficient that no further words are needed.

In the second example, which is shown in Figure 9.2, the speaker uses a gesture to convey the idea that in a relationship there needs to be someone who takes a more conciliatory role, who is involved in compromising, ironing out differences, making sure that people get on and ensuring that things knit

Figure 9.3 'Cross-disciplinary approach'

together. There is a certain amount of ambiguity in this gesture that the speaker does not attempt to resolve, but is relatively clear from the context that the gesture refers to people or viewpoints meshing together:

Again, this example confirms Cienki's (2008) assertion that metaphoric gestures need not always be accompanied by corresponding linguistic expressions. The gestures in both of these examples are, however, co-expressive with the concepts that are expressed by the words, suggesting common underlying conceptual content.

None of the non-native speakers in the study made use of metaphorical gestures in this way to replace the actual words. In contrast, they often appeared to use metaphorical gestures to help them formulate their ideas and put them into words. We can see an example of this in Figure 9.3, where the Chinese speaker of English crossed his hands repeatedly over each other in the seconds before he produces the phrase 'cross-disciplinary approach'.

Here, the speaker starts to use the gesture before he produces the actual corresponding words. The metaphorical nature of the term 'cross-disciplinary' is first made apparent in this gesture. In line with Kita et al.'s (2017) *Gesture-for-Conceptualization Hypothesis*, the speaker appears to be using this gesture to help him both form his idea and to put this idea into words. This use of gesture may have been provoked by the communicative stress of the situation in which he is attempting to discuss complex abstract concepts in a second language whilst being video recorded.

A similar situation can be seen in Figure 9.4, in this same speaker's attempt to convey the metaphorical idea of 'growth'.

In this excerpt, we can see how the speaker moves his right hand upwards, thus conveying the idea of growth well before expressing this idea verbally. Again, we appear to have evidence of the embodied metaphor appearing in the

Figure 9.4 'Growth'

*We **don't**..., we just, we **don't need, we don't** um, **we mustn't** focus on study only*
Both hands moving towards one another resulting in the tips of the fingers touching

Figure 9.5 'Focusing'

gesture before the metaphorical phrase is actually uttered, thus increasing the metaphorical 'thickness' of the utterance (see Chapter 1).

In Figure 9.5, we see this phenomenon again, where the metaphorical nature of the word 'focusing' is conveyed through gesture well before it appears in the verbal code.

Here the gesture seems to be highlighting a slightly different aspect of the metaphor, that of 'narrowing'. As well as apparently helping the learner to produce the word 'focusing', this use of gesture enriches the message that he manages to convey. This is in line with Cienki's (2008a) observation that different aspects of the metaphorical construal can be highlighted simultaneously by speech and gesture. It emphasises the complexity of source domain knowledge in the use of metaphor.

As I said previously in this section, this is only a small exploratory study, but the examples discussed appear to support Kita et al.'s (2017) ideas on the use of gesture to support conceptualisation (see Chapter 1). The increased cognitive effort and communicative stress caused by speaking a second language may lead speakers to employ more metaphorical gestures to scaffold their thinking and to help them articulate abstract concepts. In order to do this, they may need to access the underlying embodied nature of the metaphors that they employ to express abstract concepts. More controlled empirical studies would be needed to investigate these ideas further. Such studies could also be used to establish whether these findings hold for larger data sets and for people from different linguistic backgrounds.

So far, I have dealt only with language production. For language comprehension, the picture is somewhat different. Here it seems to be the case that higher-level learners are more sensitive than lower-level learners to the use of metaphorical gestures by their interlocutors. Ibáñez et al. (2010) conducted an EEG study (see Chapter 2 for details of how these studies work) to investigate whether lower-level and advanced-level learners of German were sensitive to incongruences in gesture and figurative language production. They found evidence of sensitivity in the higher-level learners but not the lower-level learners, which suggests that one needs to reach a certain level before one pays attention to gestures involving simulated metaphorical action. So here we have another source of variation in the way people employ embodied metaphor: variation according to whether or not one is producing the metaphor or witnessing it. The former appears to be affected by the amount of effort involved in producing the metaphor, whereas the latter is more related to ability. Again, more work is needed in this area.

9.4   Are Bodily Based Word–Colour Associations More Likely to Be Universal Than Less Bodily Based Associations?

Throughout this chapter, and indeed throughout this book, we have seen that embodied metaphors vary in terms of their universality. One explanation for this variability may relate to the *extent* to which the relationship is embodied. One might hypothesise that the more strongly embodied the relationship, or at least the greater the potential that it has to be embodied, the more likely it is to be universal. A good way to test this hypothesis is to look at the relationships between words and colours. Abstract concepts and emotions are often associated with particular colours. For example, for many speakers of English, anger is red, jealousy is green and purity is white. A number of studies have investigated similarities and differences in the associations that people from different cultures and linguistic backgrounds form with colours. Some associations, such as the association between the colour red and anger, have been found to be widespread across a number of languages and cultures (Waggoner and Palermo, 1989; Matsuki, 1995; Mikolajczuk, 1998; Kövecses, 2005; Chen et al., 2014), whereas other associations, such as the colour red and good luck, are limited to just a few languages and cultures (Zhiqun Xing, 2008).

One possible explanation for the fact that some word–colour associations are more universal than others involves the degree to which the association is bodily based or 'experiential'. Some word–colour associations appear to have a stronger experiential basis than others. For example, the association between anger and the colour red may be explained by the fact that when we are angry our faces may turn red because more blood flows to the surface. In other cases, it is difficult to identify an experiential motivation for the association, as in the case of jealousy being 'green'.

In order to test whether there is a relationship between the 'perceived embodiment' of a particular word–colour association and its level of universality, we (Littlemore, Pérez-Sobrino, Julich and Leung, forthcoming) investigated word–colour associations using English and Cantonese as our test languages. Using online word–colour association questionnaires in these two languages, we sought to identify the kinds of word–colour associations that are most likely to exhibit intra-cultural and cross-cultural variation in English and Cantonese, and the extent to which intra-cultural and cross-cultural variation (or lack thereof) correlates with the perceived experiential nature of the association.

In the first part of our study, participants (99 native English speakers responding in English and 195 native Cantonese responding in Cantonese) were shown 41 words. The sequence of words was randomised in order to avoid any learning effects. For each word, they were asked to select from ten different colours (yellow, orange, red, blue, green, purple, brown, black, white and grey) the one which they felt it was most strongly associated with. Our findings showed that some colour–word pairs appeared to be universal across the groups, but there was also a degree of cross-cultural variation across the two languages. Universal associations included associations between the words 'angry', 'dangerous' and 'furious' and the colour red, which might be related to the physical reactions that people have to these emotions or experiences, in that they cause blood to rush to the surface of the skin. Some cases of divergence could be explained in terms of culture. For example, the word 'erotic' was associated with the word 'yellow' in Cantonese but not in English, which probably relates to the fact that pornographic magazines are referred to as 'yellow magazines'.

In the second part of our study, in which we aimed to identify the extent to which the word–colour associations were thought to have a physical basis, we selected the most frequently associated colour for each of the concepts from Part 1 in both languages and asked English and Cantonese participants to rate the associations according to their perceived degree of physical motivation. They were asked to rate on a sliding scale ranging from 0 ('very weak') to 100 ('very strong') the extent to which they perceived the colour–word pair to have a physical origin. We labelled this variable 'perceived embodiment', using a very general definition of the term 'embodiment' (see Chapter 1). We then correlated the 'perceived embodiment' ratings for word–colour associations with their relative frequency of selection in the first study to see whether degree of 'perceived embodiment' was related to the popularity of the responses.

The 'perceived embodiment' ratings and the 'strength of association' ratings (operationalised by how frequently a colour was selected for a given word in the first study) were found to be highly correlated for both English ($p < 0.001$) and Cantonese ($p < 0.001$). This finding suggests that there is a tight correlation between the most prominent word–colour choices and their perceived level of embodiment. Moreover, there was a significant correlation between 'perceived embodiment' ratings and the likelihood that the association would be shared across the two languages ($p < 0.01$), which indicates that more universally shared word–colour associations also tend to have a more bodily based motivation. Thus, we concluded that the degree of 'perceived embodiment' of a word–colour association appears to play a key role in explaining its level of universality.

9.5   Are Bodily Based Word–Colour Associations More Likely to Be Adopted by Second Language Learners?

Given the previous discussion of the use of embodied metaphor by speakers of a second language, a second question that is of interest is whether these metaphorical associations carry over to a second language. There is evidence to suggest that the second language, including its metaphors, is as embodied as the first language. For example, De Grauwe et al. (2014) examined the processing of literal motor verbs by Dutch advanced learners of German and native speakers of German. When the participants were exposed to German verbs, both the learners and native speakers showed similar activations in their motor and somatosensory regions. This finding suggests that the motor-related semantic representations were rich enough in second language (L2) processing to activate the motor and somatosensory brain areas.

There is also evidence to suggest that at least some of the embodied metaphors that operate in one's first language also operate in one's second language. Dudschig et al. (2014) found evidence among non-native speakers for the embodied association of positive and negative emotions with the up-down orientation which, as we saw in Chapter 2, has been identified in native speakers (Meier and Robinson, 2004). Meier and Robinson found that positive words appearing at the top of a computer screen were more quickly recognised than positive words appearing at the bottom of a computer screen, and that for negative words the situation was reversed. They argued that the reason for this is that the association of the up-down orientation with positive and negative feelings is embodied. Dudschig et al. took twenty non-native speakers of English, all of whom had German as their native language and administered a test in which participants were shown a number of positive and negative emotional words in English. They were asked to press a high button on a vertical keyboard if the word was in one colour and press a low button on a vertical keyboard if the word was in the other colour. The prediction was that the valency of the word would interfere with the response time for the test so that it would take longer to press a low button for a positive word than for a positive word, and vice versa. Their hypothesis was confirmed: words referring to positive emotions facilitated upwards, and words referring to negative emotions facilitated downwards responses. This suggests that positive and negative emotions correspond to the same vertical orientation in the foreign language as they do in one's native tongue. Dudschig et al. concluded that the reactivation of the experiential traces of embodied metaphor is not limited to first language processing, and that L2 words are associated with the sensory motor system in the same way as L1 words are.

Returning to word–colour associations, we do not know whether when people learn a second language they transfer the word–colour associations from their first language, whether they adopt the associations that are common in the second language or whether they form associations that are a mixture of L1 and L2 associations. Furthermore, we do not know what it is that drives language learners to adopt L2 word colour associations rather than retaining their L1 associations, even when speaking the L2. It could be the case that this relates to embodiment, with more bodily based associations being more likely to be adopted than culturally based associations.

In order to test this hypothesis, we (Littlemore, Pérez-Sobrino, Juhlich and Leung, in press) extended the study mentioned previously to include Cantonese speakers of English as a second language (N = 126). They were invited to complete the word–colour association questionnaire, and we examined their responses in order to establish the extent to which they adopted second language-type associations and whether their tendency to adopt these associations was related in any way to the level of 'perceived embodiment' that the associations had been found to have in the first part of our study. We compared the distribution of colours selected for each word across the three groups in order to find out whether this new group of participants was more likely to respond in a similar way to the Cantonese L1 group, thus retaining the associations present in their native language, or converge with the English L1 group, thereby revealing a move towards the L2 associations in their responses. We then correlated the 'perceived embodiment' ratings for word–colour associations with their relative frequency of selection in the first study to see whether degree of 'perceived embodiment' was related to the popularity of the responses. For those items where the associations in Cantonese and English were different, we were interested in establishing whether Cantonese speakers of English as an L2 would be more likely to adopt bodily based L2 associations than non-bodily based ones. In order to do this, we inspected the 'perceived embodiment' ratings in all cases where speakers of the two languages differed in their associations to establish whether the associations used by Cantonese/English L2 speakers converged to the more bodily based association.

We found that, in most cases, the responses given in the second language resembled those that were given in the L1. There were, however, some cases where the associations produced by the L2 speakers clearly diverged from Cantonese. For example, in their L1, Cantonese speakers associated the word 'happiness' with the colour red, whereas when they were answering the questionnaire in their L2 (English), they were more likely to associate the word happiness with the colour yellow, as English speakers do. We therefore concluded that speakers move from typical L1 word–colour associations to those of the L2, but also exhibit interference from the L1. Most importantly, our statistical analyses showed that the more bodily based the association was perceived to be, the more likely it was that the L2 speakers would adopt that association, meaning that associations such as 'erotic is red' were more likely to be adopted than associations such as 'jealousy is green'. Moreover, the less bodily based an association was perceived to be in the L1, the less likely it was that a person would make that association when they were operating in their L2, so associations such as 'erotic is yellow' were less likely to be retained than associations such as 'comfortable is green' (which is motivated by the idea that people are more likely to feel 'comfortable' in natural surroundings). Thus, we concluded that the extent to which a word–colour association is perceived to be bodily based affects the extent to which that association will be formed in the L2. L2 speakers are therefore sensitive to the bodily based motivation of word–colour associations in their L2. Taken together, the findings from our two-part study suggest that more bodily based relationships are more likely to be universal and more likely to be adopted by second language speakers.

9.6   Conclusion

We have seen in this chapter that, although many embodied metaphors may have a universal component, the ways in which they are experienced are not universal. People from different cultures think about their bodies in different ways, attach different levels of importance to different parts of the body and form different metaphorical sensory connections, which are then extended metaphorically in different ways. We have also seen that the embodied metaphors that people use to think about abstract concepts such as time and number vary widely across languages and cultures. Language and culture therefore appear to play a key role in shaping our use of embodied metaphor.

Crucially, we also saw that, at least in the case of word–colour associations, there is a relationship between the extent to which an association is perceived to be embodied and the extent to which it is likely to be universal. Studies could usefully be conducted to establish whether the relationship between 'perceived embodiment' and universality also applies to other types of metaphor. We also saw that more strongly bodily based word–colour relationships are more likely to be adopted by second language learners. However, we do not know how such associations are acquired and how their acquisition relates to other more attested features that are known to shape acquisition, such as frequency and salience. Studies could therefore usefully be conducted to investigate the role of 'perceived embodiment', alongside other factors, in shaping the acquisition of word–colour combinations and other metaphorical relationships that exist in the second language but not in the first. It would also be useful to investigate the impact of the learning context and the style of teaching on the acquisition of bodily based metaphorical relationships in a second language. Taken together, the findings from such studies would tell us more about the ways in which embodied metaphorical associations are acquired, as well as identifying key sources of shared understanding across languages and cultures.

10   Conclusion

10.1   Introduction

The aim of this book has been to challenge the idea that embodied metaphor is homogeneous, and to move beyond the perspective of the 'normal' human being proposed by Lakoff and Johnson (1999). I am by no means calling into question the notion of embodied metaphor itself. Throughout the book, we have seen that there is strong support for the premise that the mind and the body do not operate as separate entities and that this extends to metaphor. Our bodily experiences shape the ways in which we use metaphor to understand abstract concepts, and our use of embodied metaphor does indeed shape our understanding of the world. However, we have seen that there is considerable variation in the way this happens and that this variation is shaped not only by the bodies that we occupy but also by the physical, socio-cultural and discourse contexts in which we operate, our age, gender, personality, cognitive style, state of mind, political and religious beliefs, and linguistic background. These factors do not only influence the kinds of metaphor we employ but also the ways in which and the extent to which we experience and use embodied metaphor. In Chapter 1, we saw that metaphors that are referred to as 'embodied' can be viewed as sitting along a cline. At one end of this cline we have metaphors that are embodied in the 'purest' sense in that they evoke sensorimotor responses that can be taken as direct evidence of perceptual simulation of the movements and senses to which they correspond. At the other end of the cline we have metaphors that refer to the human body and its interactions with the environment, but that do not necessarily trigger sensorimotor responses. We *may* use our understanding of our bodies to access the meanings of these metaphors, but it is by no means always necessary to do so, at least not on a conscious level. In this book, I have explored a number of factors that determine where on this cline a metaphor is likely to sit, and the extent to which it is likely to move along the cline. Some of these factors relate to the metaphor themselves, others refer to the different contexts in which they are used and the people who are using them. In this chapter, I present what I believe to be the key findings from studies of these different sources of variation and discuss the implications that these findings have for our

214

understanding of embodied metaphor and the way we use it to experience the world. I close with a discussion of what remains to be explored in order to better understand how humans use metaphor to reason and communicate, of how variation in our physical and social contexts translates into variation in metaphorical thinking and of the different ways in which metaphorical thinking can shape our world views.

10.2   Sources of Variation in the Experience of Metaphor

In this volume I have identified a number of factors that affect the types of embodied metaphor that people experience and the intensity with which they experience them. The findings from this body of work tell us quite a lot about embodied metaphor itself. Let us now consider each of these factors in turn.

What Is Being Communicated: Novelty and Emotion

The first source of variation to shape our experience of embodied metaphor relates to the content of the message and the person who is communicating it. There is a wealth of evidence suggesting that novel metaphors are significantly more likely to evoke a sensorimotor response in the listener than conventional metaphors, and that this is particularly likely to be the case when the listener has to access a primary metaphor in order to understand the meaning of a novel entailment or linguistic metaphor. Novel metaphors, which as we have seen are more likely to provoke a physical embodied response, are more likely to be produced when people are describing their emotions, and they are more likely to be produced when people are communicating their own personal feelings rather than the feelings of others. High levels of emotional engagement lead to more creative metaphor use, which in turn is experienced on a more physical level. There is also evidence to suggest that simply being exposed to metaphor can provoke an emotional response, and that emotional arousal during metaphor comprehension is affected by the novelty of the metaphor.

We have also seen that there is a strong neurological link between motion and emotion, which is reflected in their shared etymology; emotion leads to bodily movement and bodily movement can lead to emotion. There is a corresponding relationship between the presence of movement and embodied responses to metaphor. We have also seen that emotive 'calls to action' are particularly likely to involve the use of metaphors that have a bodily basis.

The Context and the Co-Text

A second source of variation in the extent to which a metaphor is experienced as embodied relates to the context and the co-text in which it appears. The perspective of the speaker or listener is also important in that metaphors are more likely to be experienced as embodied when they are presented from the perspective of the reader or listener. This is unsurprising given that when people are talking and thinking about their own experiences, they are arguably more vivid and more 'lived'.

A person's experience of embodied metaphor can also be affected by the relationship they have with their interlocutor. When speaking to someone from outside the discourse community who is not familiar with the material being discussed, for example in a teaching context, speakers have been shown to compensate for their interlocutor's lack of shared knowledge by making the metaphorical motivation of the concepts under discussion more explicit. This may be done verbally or through gesture.

The *physical* context also shapes the way in which we use metaphor to structure our thinking. For example, we have seen that the cleanliness of our environment, the quality of the lighting, the temperature, the season and even the position in which we are sitting have all been found to influence the way in which we employ metaphor to reason about subjects that are completely unrelated to our environment.

Finally, the linguistic co-text also affects the extent to which a metaphor is experienced as embodied. This idea is encapsulated in Müller's (2008) notion of 'activated metaphoricity', which applies to both linguistic and gestural metaphor. Under this view, metaphors that are emphasised within the context, for example through the exaggerated use of gesture, the use of metaphor signalling devices or exaggerated intonation are more likely to be experienced on a physical level by both the speaker and the interlocutor.

Age and Development

Another factor that shapes one's experience of embodied metaphor is age. We have seen that pre–school-aged children are capable of understanding primary metaphors that involve cross-domain mappings (e.g., between SPACE and TIME) by the age of four, and of explaining these mappings by the age of five. We have also seen that metaphors involving spatial motion, in particular those that involve first-person bodily experience, are easier for young children to understand, as children rely more heavily on sensorimotor schemas to make sense of their experiences with the world. Our study of the ways in which children develop an understanding of embodied metaphors related to mathematics and music showed that children are more likely than adults to produce explanations that are based on human activities, personal experiences, relationships, emotions, movement, detailed depictions of scenes and narratives. These explanations contrast sharply with those provided by adults, which are more schematic, conventional and detached. These findings suggest that for children primary metaphors are much more of a vivid 'lived experience' than they are for adults. This may be due to the novelty of the metaphors, or it may be due to the way in which children process information about the world around them more generally. Findings from comparative developmental studies of children's acquisition of primary metaphors indicate that as some ways of understanding the world open up, others close down, as children adopt the prominent metaphorical world view of the culture into which they are born.

Physical Differences

Physical differences and the way in which we perceive our own bodies affect how we experience the world through embodied metaphor. We have seen that left-handed individuals experience the GOOD IS TO THE RIGHT metaphor much less intensely than right-handed individuals, but that right handers start to behave like left handers if they are forced to use their left hand for a certain period of time. This finding is interesting, as it emphasises the malleability of some types of embodied metaphor.

Unlike the relationship between handedness and the GOOD IS TO THE RIGHT metaphor, which appears to sit at the sensorimotor end of the embodied metaphor continuum, the metaphorical relationship between height and importance sits more towards the non-physical end of the continuum, as it involves the internalisation of societal norms. However, this metaphorical relationship is likely to have had physical origins in a world where stature was related to survival. The relationship between weight and importance is more complex. Although it appears in non-human contexts (e.g., heavy books are deemed to be more important), the relationship does not appear to hold for humans, as it comes into conflict with the more widely held belief (at least in western cultures) that being thin is desirable. In the case of anorectics, the metaphorical mappings are even more complex. People with anorexia, who have developed a heightened (negative) awareness of their bodies, are inclined to employ concretised metaphors, where the line between the literal and the metaphorical is blurred. These conflations of source and target domain are often very difficult to disentangle. This form of metaphorical thinking has its roots in societal norms, but these are then internalised and twisted and taken to extremes, often with severe physical consequences.

Gender

The ways in which gender affects the way people experience embodied metaphors are interesting. Some embodied metaphors appear to be more strongly established in men than in women. These include the use of the vertical axis to represent hierarchy, power and status, the positioning of women at the bottom of this hierarchy and the metaphorical use of physical force to represent abstract power and strength. It is interesting to note that these metaphors relate directly to height and strength, which are two of the main ways in which men differ from women in physical terms. Moreover, societal norms means that men are more likely than women to be defined (and in some cases, to define themselves) in terms of height and strength. These characteristics are more important for boys, when they are growing up and interacting with one another, than they are for girls, who are more likely to be concerned with physical attractiveness and likability. One might tentatively conclude from this that these metaphors are acquired and experienced more directly by men and boys, and that women and girls acquire and experience them more vicariously. Indeed, there is evidence to indicate that women are more likely than men to respond to these metaphors in ways that reflect their linguistic patternings, which suggests that women may acquire the metaphors through a more usage-based process. It would be interesting to explore this issue further and to look at gender differences across a wider variety of embodied metaphors, including both those that involve physical differences between men and women and those that do not. It would also be useful to conduct more developmental studies in order to identify the ages at which these different embodied metaphors start to appear in each sex. The combined findings from such studies would tell us more about the origins of different embodied metaphors and the reasons why they develop. They would also provide information on the extent to which women are living by men's metaphors. The findings relating to gender and embodied metaphor also have implications for interactions between the sexes and for women's position in society more generally. If it is the case that in professional contexts, women are living by men's metaphors then this needs to be acknowledged, and if we are to achieve gender equality, we may need to find less 'masculine' ways of viewing both power and a person's position within the workplace.

Sensory Deficits and Conditions

We have seen that sensory deficits and conditions can affect the ways in which people engage with embodied metaphor both in terms of their physical ability to do so and their attitudes towards the metaphors. A key finding is that sensory deficits and conditions are in many cases just as likely to open up new ways of experiencing sensory metaphor, which at times are richer, more personal and more involved than those experienced by others. Many of the cross-sensory associations experienced by synaesthetes, for example, are based on conventional metaphorical mappings, but these mappings are extended in novel ways, and often involve higher levels of empathy and strong emotional responses. Synaesthetes appear to experience a heightened sense of cross-sensory metaphor which radically shapes the way in which they interact with the physical world.

Depression and Psychological Disorders

One's psychological state has a profound effect on the way one experiences the world through embodied metaphor. The experience of depression, particularly following bereavement, appears to affect both the types of metaphors that people employ and the ways in which people engage with them. In the case of bereavement following pregnancy loss, the source and target domains of embodied metaphors can become conflated, and metaphorical conceptions of time can be altered, with some people experiencing time in a more compressed manner and others developing a heightened awareness of the metaphorical passing of time. For some, the metaphor of the 'divided self' becomes more marked and the body is given agency, which allows for it to be blamed for what has happened. Metaphorical ways of thinking that are associated with depression can have an impact on physical experiences, with depressed people assessing hills as being much steeper than their non-depressed counterparts. Metaphorical thinking that is associated with depressive states can also take the form of physical symptoms, via a process which, although resembling somatisation, is in fact a culturally mediated, metaphorical embodiment of distress.

People with psychological and neurological disorders such as schizophrenia, Autistic Spectrum Disorders (ASD) and Asperger Syndrome also experience metaphor in ways that differ from the mainstream population. The schizophrenic individuals whose interviews we looked at made extensive use of creative extensions of embodied metaphor to describe their symptoms. Like the anorectics, they sometimes appeared to merge metaphorical and literal understandings of the world, and like the individuals who had experienced pregnancy loss, they made extensive use of metaphors of the divided self, personifying parts of their bodies and attributing external agency to their thinking processes. People with ASD and Asperger syndrome have also been shown to exhibit a greater ability to produce creative extensions of embodied metaphors, though traditional studies have suggested that they experience difficulties with metaphor. We saw that one reason for these conflicting findings in this area may be the types of prompts that are used in studies of metaphor comprehension, as these prompts contain different types of metaphors as well as metonymy, idioms and similes. More work could usefully be conducted to investigate how people with these disorders engage in metaphorical thinking, as this would allow others to enter their mental worlds and provide them with support.

Personality and Cognitive Style

Individual differences in personality and cognitive style show that there is no 'one size fits all' explanation when it comes to the way we process incoming stimuli, and that a single piece of information can be interpreted in different ways by different people, which may lead to misunderstandings. We have seen in this book that cognitive style differences also affect the ways in which people engage with metaphor. We saw that people with holistic, analytic, verbaliser and imager cognitive styles process conceptual metaphors in very different ways, that these differences map on to longstanding arguments that have existed in the metaphor literature concerning the nature of metaphor itself and that they may even go some way towards explaining these arguments.

Other, less widely studied personality and cognitive style differences have also been shown to affect the ways in which people react to embodied metaphor. Analogical reasoning ability increases the extent to which people are susceptible to the effects of persuasive embodied metaphors, and need for cognition affects the extent to which people benefit from, or enjoy working with, complex metaphors. People with psychopathic tendencies do not appear to employ a vertical schema when reasoning about morality, which suggests that this schema may play a fundamental role in this type of reasoning. In terms of the embodied metaphorical relationship between time and space, conscientious individuals are more likely to adopt a moving time perspective, whereas less conscientious people favour a moving ego perspective. People who experience high levels of body consciousness are more likely to associate the colour black with immoral deeds and to associate cleanliness with morality. A highly developed 'need for power' is likely to make a person more responsive to the CONTROL IS UP metaphor, and need for cognition has been found to relate to a preference for more complex and more creative metaphors. Thus the intensity to which one experiences an embodied metaphor is shaped to a large extent by one's personality or cognitive style.

One of the main contributions that the work on individual differences has made to society is that it has helped people, both within the workplace and in more social settings, to better understand one another, which allows them to work better together and to create more effective teams. Understanding how individual differences shape *metaphorical* thinking allows us to take this work a stage further by showing how these individual differences explain why it is that different people can take very different meanings away from the same piece of information, and how this can lead to conflict and misunderstanding. It provides us with a deeper, more embodied, understanding of these varying perspectives.

Political and Religious Beliefs

Nowhere is the societal impact of differing world views more noticeable and more consequential than in politics and religion. Both fields involve a significant amount of abstract thought which is framed by metaphor, and both fields are, in many respects, defined by conflict, which can have a significant and lasting effect on people's lives. In this book, we have seen that both political and religious beliefs affect, and are affected by, the ways in which people think about the world through metaphor.

In politics, empirical studies have shown that right-wing individuals are more likely than left-wing individuals to link moral disgust to physical disgust, and the welfare state is more likely to be described as a safety net in the right-wing press, whereas it is more likely to be viewed as a shelter in the left-wing press. The use of embodied metaphors can also influence political beliefs, and vice versa, with the use of the crime-as-a-body metaphor engendering more hostile attitudes towards immigration, and the metaphorical framing of crime as a 'beast' is more likely to lead to recommendations that criminals need to be caught and jailed, whereas the framing of crime as a 'virus' is more likely to lead to recommendations for social reform.

In religion, people with strong religious beliefs are more likely than atheists or agnostics to exhibit evidence of a vertical schema for morality and this behaviour can be trained through exposure to religious concepts. People with different religious backgrounds have been found to interact in different ways with the same underlying embodied metaphor. For example, the source-path-goal metaphor is prominent in the discourse of both Christians and Muslims; however, Christians talk more about travelling *with* God, whereas Muslims tend to focus on a personal journey *towards* God.

If we could develop a stronger understanding of the ways in which these abstract concepts are embodied and reified through metaphor, and a more widespread appreciation of the role of metaphor in the thinking processes that shape these beliefs, then it would be easier to find common ground, paying more attention to the underlying metaphors that unite different political and religious views than to the entailments that separate them.

Linguistic and Cultural Background

Finally, we have seen that our linguistic and cultural background shapes the way in which we experience the world through metaphor by affecting both the metaphors that we employ and the ways in which we employ them. In particular, our linguistic background has been found to affect the way in which we construe fundamental concepts such as time, number and emotion. Different metaphorical construals of time are important, as they affect the tense systems of different languages, leading us to divide up the different periods of our lives in different ways. Bodily based and sensory metaphors are also susceptible to cross-linguistic variation in ways which suggest that people think about their bodies differently in both literal and metaphorical ways. We have also seen that new embodied metaphors can be learned or unlearned through brief exposure to other languages. This suggests that by learning other languages, it is possible to acquire other world views and that metaphorical thinking plays an important role in this process.

We also saw that people appear to engage with embodied metaphor in slightly different ways when communicating in a second language, and that the novelty and communicative stress that one encounters when speaking a second language appear to activate embodied metaphors that may be relatively 'dead' for native speakers. Finally, we saw that the extent to which a given metaphor has an embodied motivation goes some way towards explaining its universality. This last finding is particularly important, as it shows that shared physical experiences do translate, at least at one level, into shared linguistic experiences.

10.3   What Does This Variation Tell Us about Embodied Metaphor?

In the opening sections of this book, I argued that by looking at variation in people's experiences of the supposedly universal phenomenon of embodied metaphor, we would learn more about embodied metaphor itself. We are now in a position to reflect on what has been learned.

The first observation is that embodied metaphorical associations develop at different times and at different rates. For understandable reasons, the metaphorical embodiment of emotions appears earlier than the metaphorical embodiment of more abstract concepts, such as time and number. Children's early interactions with embodied metaphor are more likely than those of adults to be characterised by emotion, empathy and personal involvement. Interestingly, in adulthood, these same experiences reactivate otherwise dormant embodied metaphors, allowing them to be used more creatively.

Second, even so-called universal embodied metaphors are shaped not only by the bodies that we inhabit and the immediate physical environment in which we find ourselves but also by the socio-cultural settings in which we use and think about our bodies. Although our bodies play an important role in underpinning our use of embodied metaphor, our perceptions of those bodies play an equally important role in shaping metaphorical thinking processes. These perceptions are shaped by culture at both a local and a global level.

Third, things that we consciously notice about our bodies play a key role in shaping our self-identities through acts of conscious introspection. We have seen that embodied metaphors are made more salient for people who for one reason or another are 'outside' mainstream society. These include disabled people, people with body dysmorphic disorders and people who have experienced unusually traumatic events. We have seen that under extreme stress the source and target domains of embodied metaphors become conflated and embodied metaphors are experienced in a much more 'literal' way.

Fourth, lack of familiarity, a heightened sense of awareness, new surroundings, heightened emotion and novelty all lead to stronger embodied metaphorical experiences. Under these conditions, we develop a heightened awareness of the fundamentally embodied and metaphorical nature of abstract thought.

Fifth, culturally sanctioned embodied metaphors tend to be those that most closely reflect the physical experiences of the dominant group. The data available to date suggest that these metaphors are experienced more strongly by the dominant group. For example, there are significant interactions between gender and embodied metaphors that involve height and power, with men being more likely to think in terms of these metaphors than women. Those who are not members of the dominant group do think in terms of the dominant group's metaphors, but the relationship is less entrenched, as it is less physically motivated. There is no evidence of metaphors reflecting the physical experiences of the non-dominant group being shared across a culture, a fact which reinforces inequality at the very deepest level.

Finally, different embodied metaphors exhibit differing degrees of malleability. Types of embodied metaphor that are less susceptible to variation include the most basic and arguably important human experiences, such as EMOTION IS WARMTH. Types of embodied metaphor that are more susceptible to variation include more abstract concepts that develop later in life and in human evolution; things that need to be measured, such as time and number. Early-acquired concepts are universal, but variation starts to appear when these concepts start to be understood in a more nuanced way.

Taken together, these findings suggest that embodied metaphors, even those that underlie the most conventional uses of language and that many people would describe as 'dead' metaphors, are always available, at one level, for reinvigoration. Situations that trigger this reinvigoration include intense emotional experiences, communicative stress and finding oneself in new situations with novel stimuli. It is perhaps no coincidence that these same situations have been found to act as strong catalysts for human creativity. Successful creativity involves a combination of the new and the old, the familiar and the unfamiliar. Embodied metaphors provide access to the oldest, most fundamental areas of human experience, and by exploring the entailments of these metaphors we can find new ways of expressing ourselves that are grounded in universal human experiences. For this reason, creative extensions of embodied metaphors resonate across different times and different cultures.

10.4   What Remains to Be Explored?

In this book, I have identified a number of sources of variation in people's experiences of embodied metaphor and by extension, the ways in which they experience the world through metaphor. I have drawn some tentative conclusions, but much remains to be done. For example, it would be useful to conduct more work on the ways in which embodied metaphors are experienced by people with different physical, emotional and cultural experiences of life, as these studies would provide richer information on the nature and origin of different embodied metaphors and help us to reach a better understanding of where and how they originate. We have seen in this book that some embodied metaphors operate at the phenomenological level, while others operate at the neurological level. We still know very little about how these levels of engagement interact and the extent to which they influence one another.

A second area that is still in need of investigation is the possibility that learning a second or third language leads to increased flexibility in one's ability to switch between different metaphors. There is a large body of work showing that as people learn a second language they acquire more cognitive flexibility, but no work to date has looked at the ways in which bilinguals engage flexibly with embodied metaphor. One might hypothesise, based on extrapolations from existing studies, that bilingual individuals will find it easier than monolinguals to switch between different metaphors and thus different ways of construing the world. If it does turn out to be the case that people who speak more than one language exhibit this deep form of cognitive flexibility, then this would provide a stronger justification for the teaching of languages in cultures where second language learning is not seen as a priority. Related to this, more research could usefully be conducted to build on the finding presented in Chapter 9 that the extent to which a metaphorical relationship is embodied predicts the likelihood of it being universal.

A third area that merits further study is the relationship between embodied metaphor, emotion and creativity. We have seen indications that in some circumstances, intense emotional experiences lead people to extend embodied metaphors in creative ways. Emotional engagement, creativity and sensorimotor activation appear to be related to one another in mutually enforcing ways. More work could usefully be conducted to unpack and explain this relationship, as this would shed more light on the creative thinking process and its relationship to metaphorical thinking.

A fourth area of development relates to methodology. More work is needed to investigate the extent to which metaphor is experienced as embodied when it is encountered in authentic communicative contexts rather than in the laboratory. As we saw in Chapter 2, the ways in which people respond to metaphor are likely to be heavily skewed by the artificial settings in which the studies have been conducted. More work is needed, for example, to investigate the impact of the relationship between the speakers on their use of metaphor. Such work could also usefully investigate the differences between the ways in which people employ embodied metaphor in language production and in language comprehension. More attention also needs to be paid to the types of prompts that are employed. As well as being more authentic, the prompts should be screened for other types of figurative language, such as metonymy, idioms and similes, which may be processed differently from metaphor. In addition to this, resemblance metaphors need to be disentangled from primary metaphors, to the extent that this is possible. Finally, the impact of mode of expression on the degree of embodiment also needs to be explored further. It is to be expected that metaphors that are expressed through gesture will evoke a stronger embodied response than metaphors that are expressed linguistically, as the sight of the gesture will evoke a motoric response in the perceiver. However, we do not know about the relative impact of metaphors that are expressed through music, art or other modes of expression.

A final area that would be worthy of further investigation is the effect of embodied metaphor on long-term memory. Embodied metaphors are important in the laying down of memories for two reasons: first, they provide a kind of over-arching structure to the information that we receive, and second, they are likely to be susceptible to muscle memory. Abstract concepts and emotions that are metaphorically grounded in bodily actions are more likely to be remembered than those that are less grounded; higher levels of sensorimotor simulation are likely to lead to longer retention times. We have seen that those metaphors that evoke sensorimotor simulation are most likely to be novel, presented from the perspective of the viewer, emotional, involve motion and convey negative evaluation. Other factors, such as age, gender, personality, state of mind, belief system, ideology and language background are likely to interact with the factors to shape a person's experiences of embodied metaphor. Future studies could usefully explore interactions between all the variables discussed in this book.

10.5   Conclusion

It has long been argued that different people experience different realities. Our physical, emotional and social experiences shape our world views, and these can change considerably over the course of a lifetime. Less is known about the mechanisms through which our world views are shaped by these experiences. In this book, we have seen that embodied metaphor constitutes a key mechanism through which the nature of our bodies, our position in society, our linguistic and cultural background and our state of mind affect the way in which we understand the world around us. We have also seen how people use embodied metaphor to generate their own world views as well as to internalise other people's world views. The examples discussed in this book show that

this variation has social, political, medical, practical and interpersonal implications. By endeavouring to understand the different metaphors through which
other people experience the world, and the forces that have brought these
metaphors into being, we will gain a deeper understanding of how others think
and develop a stronger appreciation of the rich variety in human experience,
and all that this affords.

Notes

Preface

1 All of the examples in this book are taken from authentic data, including language corpora. These examples are taken from the British National Corpus (BNC).

Chapter 1

1 These examples are taken from the British National Corpus (BNC).
2 It is the convention within cognitive linguistics to represent overarching metaphorical mappings, such as primary metaphors and conceptual metaphors, using small capitals.
3 In this example and the one that follows, metaphorically used words are italicised and words that were accompanied by gestures are shown in bold.
4 Kövecses' notion of image schema is similar to what Grady (1997) refers to as a primary metaphor. Grady, in contrast, uses the term 'image schema' to refer only to the source and not to the target of his primary metaphors.

Chapter 2

1 I would like to thank my research associate, Dr Sarah Turner, who conducted this corpus analysis.

Chapter 3

1 This dataset was gathered by Penelope Tuck at the Birmingham Business School at the University of Birmingham, as part of an investigation into perceptions of talent in the UK Civil Service.

Chapter 5

* Skårderud, F. (2007). Eating one's words, Part 1: 'Concretised metaphors' and reflective function in anorexia nervosa – An interview study, *European Eating Disorders Review*, 15: 163–174, p. 171.

Chapter 6

1 Thanks to Ana Laura Rodríguez Redondo, Universidad Complutense de Madrid for the Spanish sign language examples.

Chapter 7

1 www.bigissue.com/about/
2 UK House of Commons Debate on Pregnancy Loss, 13 October 2016 (Hansard).
3 This study will form the basis of a proposal for a much larger study investigating the use of embodied metaphor by schizophrenic individuals in both language and gesture.
4 I would like to thank Verilogue, Inc., 100 Penn Square East, 11 FL S, Philadelphia, PA 19107, USA, for providing access to this data for the development of a proposal for an externally funded research project.

Chapter 8

* A central part of the Roman Catholic liturgy in which the bread and wine are allegedly transubstantiated into the flesh and blood of Christ.

References

Ackerman, J., Nocera, C. and Bargh, J. (2010). Incidental haptic sensations influence social judgments and decisions. *Science, 328*, 1712–1715.

Adolphs, R. (2003). Cognitive neuroscience of human social behaviour. *Nature Reviews Neuroscience, 4*, 165–178.

Aikhenvald, A. and Storch, A. (2013). Linguistic perception of perception and cognition. In A. Aikenvald and A. Storch (eds.) *Perception and Cognition in Language and Culture*, Leiden: Brill, pp. 1–46.

Akpinar, E. and Berger, J. (2015). Drivers of cultural success: The case of sensory metaphors. *Journal of Personality and Social Psychology, 109* (1), 20–34.

Alan, K. and Burridge, K. (2006). *Forbidden Words: Taboo and the Censoring of Language*, Cambridge: Cambridge University Press.

Alibali, M. W. and DiRusso, A. A. (1999). The function of gesture in learning to count: More than keeping track. *Cognitive Development, 14*, 37–56.

Alibali, M. W. and Nathan, M. J. (2007). Teachers' gestures as a means of scaffolding students' understanding: Evidence from an early algebra lesson. In R. Goldman, R. Pea, B. Barron and S. J. Derry (eds.) *Video Research in the Learning Sciences*, Mahwah, NJ: Erlbaum, pp. 349–365.

(2012). Embodiment in mathematics teaching and learning: Evidence from learners' and teachers' gestures. *Journal of the Learning Sciences, 21* (2), 247–286.

Almohammadi, A. (2017). The development of metaphor comprehension in Arabic-speaking children. Unpublished PhD Thesis, Kings College London.

Anderson, S., Matlock, T. and Spivey, M. J. (2010). On the path to understanding the on-line processing of grammatical aspect. *Spatial Cognition, 7*, 139–151.

Andreano, J. and Cahill, L. (2009). Sex influences on the neurobiology of learning and memory. *Learning and Memory, 16*, 248–266.

Andric, M. and Small S. L. (2012). Gesture's neural language. *Frontiers in Psychology, 3*, 99.

Antle, A., Corness, G. and Droemeva, M. (2009). What the body knows: Exploring the benefits of embodied metaphors in hybrid physical digital environments. *Interacting with Computers, 21*, 66–75.

Asperger, H. (1941). Education Issues within Children's Week (Vienna 1st to 7th September 1940). *NERVENARZT, 14* (1), 28–31.

Avenanti, A., Candidi, M. and Urgesi, C. (2013). Vicarious motor activation during action perception: Beyond correlational evidence. *Frontiers in Human Neuroscience, 7*, 185.

Avanzini, P., Fabbri-Destro, M., Dalla Volta, R., Daprati, E., Rizzolatti, G. and Cantalupo, G. (2012). The dynamics of sensorimotor cortical oscillations during the observation of hand movements: An EEG study. *PLoS ONE, 7* (5), e37534.

Aziz-Zadeh, L. and Damasio, A. (2008). Embodied semantics for actions: Findings from functional brain imaging. *Journal of Physiology, 102* (1–3), 35–39.

Aziz-Zadeh, L., Wilson, S. M., Rizzolatti, G. and Iacoboni, M. (2006). Congruent embodied representations for visually presented actions and linguistic phrases describing actions. *Current Issues in Biology, 16* (8), 1818–1823.

Bakker, S., Antle, A. N. and Van den Hoven, E. (2009). Identifying embodied metaphors in children's sound-action mappings. *Proceedings of the Eighth International Conference on Interaction Design and Children, ACM, Como, Italy,* 140–149.

Banaji, M. E. and Hardin, C. D. (1996). Automatic stereotyping. *Psychological Science, 7* (3), 186–192.

Bar-Anan, Y., Liberman, N., Trope, Y. and Algom, D. (2007). Automatic processing of psychological distance: Evidence from a Stroop task. *Journal of Experimental Psychology, 136,* 610–622.

Barchard, K. A., Grob, K. and Roe, M. J. (2017). Is sadness blue? The problem of using figurative language for emotions on psychological tests. *Behavior Research Methods, 49* (2), 443–456.

Bardolph, M. and Coulson, S. (2014). How vertical hand movements impact brain activity elicited by literally and metaphorically-used words: An ERP study of embodied metaphor. *Frontiers in Human Neuroscience, 8,* 1031.

Bargh, J., Chen, M. and Burrows, L. (1996). Automaticity of social behaviour: Direct effects of trait construct and stereotype activation on action. *Journal of Personality and Social Psychology, 71* (2), 230–244.

Barnden, J. A., Glasbey, S. R., Lee, M. G. and Wallington, A. M. (2003). Domain-transcending mappings in a system for metaphorical reasoning. In *Conference Companion to the 10th Conference of the European Chapter of the Association for Computational Linguistics* (EACL'03).

Baron-Cohen, S., Leslie, A. M. and Frith, U. (1985). Does the autistic child have a "theory of mind"? *Cognition, 21* (1), 37–46.

Baron-Cohen, S., Wheelwright, S., Hill, J., Raste, Y. and Plumb, I. (2001). The 'Reading the Mind' test revised version: A study with normal adults, adults with Asperger Syndrome or high functioning autism. *Journal of Child Psychology and Psychiatry, 42* (2), 241–251.

Barsalou, L. W. (1999). Perceptual symbol systems. *Behavioural and Brain Sciences, 22,* 577–660.

(2008). Grounded cognition. *Annual Review of Psychology, 59,* 617–645.

(2010). Grounded cognition: Past, present, and future. *Topics in Cognitive Science, 2* (4), 716–724.

Becker, G. (1997). *Disrupted Lives: How People Create Meaning in a Chaotic World,* Berkeley: University of California Press.

Benor, S. B. and Levy, R. (2006). The chicken or the egg? A probabilistic analysis of English binomials. *Language, 82,* 233–278.

Bergen, B. (2012). *Louder Than Words, The New Science of How the Mind Makes Meaning,* New York: Basic Books.

Bergen, B. and Wheeler, K. (2010). Grammatical aspect and mental simulation. *Brain and Language*, *112*, 150–158.

Bessenoff, G. R. and Sherman, J. W. (2000). Automatic and controlled components of prejudice toward fat people: Evaluation versus stereotype activation. *Social Cognition*, *18* (4), 329–353.

Birdsell, B. (2017). Creative metaphor production in a first and second language and the role of creativity. Unpublished PhD Dissertation, University of Birmingham.

Blackwell, P. M., Engen, E., Fischgrund, J. E. and Zarcadoolas, C. (1978). *Sentences and Other Systems: A Language and Learning Curriculum for Hearing-Impaired Children*, Washington, DC: The Alexander Graham Bell Association for the Deaf.

Blomberg, J. and Zlatev, J. (2014). Actual and non-actual motion: Why experientialist semantics needs phenomenology (and vice versa). *Phenomelogical Cognitive Science*, *13* (3), 395–418.

Blomberg, J. and Zlatev, J. (2015). Non-actual motion: Phenomenological analysis and linguistic evidence. *Cognitive Process*, *16*, S153–S157.

Boers, F. (1997a). Health, fitness and mobility in a free-market ideology. In J. P. van Noppen and M. Maufort (eds.) *Voices of Power: Co-operation and Conflict in English Language and Literatures*, Liège University Press, pp. 89–96.

(1997b). No pain, no gain in a free-market rhetoric: A test for cognitive semantics? *Metaphor and Symbol*, *12*, 231–241.

(1999). When a bodily source domain becomes prominent: The joy of counting metaphors in the socio-economic domain. In R. Gibbs and G. Steen (eds.) *Metaphor in Cognitive Linguistics*, Amsterdam: John Benjamins, pp. 47–56.

Boers, F. and Littlemore, J. (2000). Cognitive style variables in participants' explanations of conceptual metaphors. *Metaphor and Symbol*, *15* (3), 177–187.

Bohrn, I. C., Altman, U. and Jacobs, A. M. (2012). Looking at the brains behind figurative language – a quantitative meta-analysis of neuroimaging studies on metaphor, idiom, and irony processing. *Neuropsychologia*, *50*, 2669–2683.

Bohrne, I. C., Altann, U., Lubrich, O., Menninghaus, W. and Jacobs, A. M. (2012). Old proverbs in new skins – an fMRI study on defamialiarization. *Frontiers in Psychology*, *3*, 204.

Bonda, E., Petrides, M., Frey, S. and Evans, A. (1994). Frontal cortex involvement in organized sequences of hand movements: Evidence from a positron emission topography study. *Society for Neurosciences Abstracts*, *20*, 353.

Borghi, A. M., Glenberg, A. M. and Kaschal, M. P. (2004). Putting words in perspective. *Memory and Cognition*, *32*, 863–873.

Boroditsky, L. (2000). Metaphoric structuring: Understanding time through spatial metaphors. *Cognition*, *75*, 1–28.

(2001). Does language shape thought? English and Mandarin speakers' conceptions of time. *Cognitive Psychology*, *43*, 1–22.

Boroditsky, L., Fhurman, O. and McComick, K. (2011). Do English and Mandarin speakers think about time differently? *Cognition*, *118* (1), 123–129.

Boroditsky, L., Ramscar, M. and Frank, M. C. (2002). The roles of body and mind in abstract thought. *Psychological Science*, *13*, 185–189.

Bosmans, A. (2006). Scents and sensibility: When do (in) congruent ambient scents influence product evaluations? *Journal of Marketing*, *70* (3), 32–43.

Bottini, G., Corcoran, R., Sterzi, R. et al. (1994). The role of the right hemisphere in the interpretation of figurative aspects of language: A positron emission tomography activation study. *Brain, 117* (6), 1241–1253.

Boulenger V., Hauk, O., and PulverMüller, F. (2009). Grasping ideas with the motor system: Semantic somatotopy in idiom comprehension. *Cerebral Cortex, 19,* 1905–1914.

Bowdle, B.F. and Gentner, D. (2005). The career of metaphor, *Psychological Review, 112,* 193–216.

Bowes, A. and Katz, A. N. (2015). Metaphor creates intimacy and temporarily enhances theory of mind. *Memory and Cognition, 43,* 953–963.

Bråten, S. (2007). (Ed.) *On Being Moved: From Mirror Neurons to Empathy,* Amsterdam: Benjamins.

Brants, T. and Franz, A. (2006). Web 1T 5-gram version 1.

Brdar, M., Strkalj Despot, K., Tonkovic, M., Brdar-Szabo, R. And Tomic, I. (2015). How heavy are things in Croation and elsewhere? A contrastive experimental study. Paper presented at the Biennial Conference of the International Cognitive Linguistics Association, Newcastle, UK.

Bremner, A., Caparos, S., Davidoff, J., de Fockert, J., Linnell, K. and Spence, C. (2013). Bouba and Kiki in Namibia? A remote culture make similar shape-sound matches but different shape-taste matches to Westerners. *Cognition, 126,* 165–172.

Brown, R. (1973). *A First Language: The Early Stages.* Cambridge, MA: Harvard University Press. In the CHILDES Corpus: https://talkbank.org/share/.

Brunyé, T. T., Ditman, T., Mahoney, C., Augustyn, J. S. and Taylor, H. (2009). When you and I share perspectives: Pronouns modulate perspective raking during narrative comprehension. *Psychological Science, 20* (1), 27–32.

Brunyé, T. T., Ditman, T., Mahoney, C. and Taylor, H. (2011). Better you than I: Perspectives and emotion simulation during narrative comprehension. *Journal of Cognitive Psychology, 23* (5), 659–666.

Buxbaum, L. and Saffran, E. (2002). Knowledge of object manipulation and object function: Dissociations in apraxic and nonapraxic subjects. *Brain and Language, 82,* 179–199.

Caballero, R. et al. (2013). *Sensuous Cognition,* Berlin: Mouton de Gruyter.

Cacciari, C. and Glucksberg, S. (1994). Understanding Figurative Language. In M. A. Gernsbacher (ed.) *Handbook of Psycholinguistics,* San Diego: Academic Press, pp. 447–477.

Cacciari, C., Bolonini, N., Senna, I., Pellicciari, M. C., Miniussi, C. and Papagno, C. (2011). Literal, fictive and metaphorical motion sentences preserve the motion component of the verb: A TMS study. *Brain and Language, 119,* 149–157.

Cacioppo, J. and Petty, R. (1982). The need for cognition. *Journal of Personality and Social Psychology, 42,* 116–131.

Cacioppo, J, Petty, R., Feinstein, J., Jarvis, W. and Blair G. (1996). Dispositional differences in cognitive motivation: The life and times of individuals varying in Need for Cognition. *Psychological Bulletin, 119* (2), 197–253.

Caers, E. (2006). When ministers were digging in for a fight. Metaphors of liberal common sense during the Winter of Discontent, 1978–1979. https://doclib .uhasselt.be/dspace/bitstream/1942/1672/1/whenministers.pdf.

Calbris, G. (2008). From left to right . . . Coverbal gestures and their symbolic use of space. In A. Cienki and C. Müller, (eds.) *Metaphor and Gesture*, Amsterdam: John Benjamins, pp. 27–53.

Cameron, L. (2003). *Metaphor in Educational Discourse*, London: Continuum Press.
   (2007). Patterns of metaphor use in reconciliation talk. *Discourse and Society, 18* (2), 197–222.

Campbell, A., Muncer, S. and Coyle, E. (1992). Social representation of aggression as an explanation of gender differences: A preliminary study. *Aggressive Behavior, 18*, 95–108.

Cannon, R., Schnall, S. and White, M. (2011). Transgressions and expressions: Affective facial muscle activity predicts moral judgments. *Social Psychological and Personality Science, 2* (3), 325–331.

Cardillo, E. R., Watson, C. E., Schmidt, G., Kranjec, A. and Chatterjee, A. (2012). From novel to familiar: Tuning the brain for metaphors. *Neuroimage, 59*, 3212–3221.

Casasanto, D. (2008). Who's afraid of the Big Bad Whorf? Cross-linguistic differences in temporal language and thought. *Language Learning, 58* (1), 63–79.
   (2009). Embodiment of abstract concepts: Good and bad in right- and left-handers. *Journal of Experimental Psychology: General, 138* (3), 351–367.
   (2011). Different bodies, different minds: The body-specificity of language and thought. *Current Directions in Psychological Science, 20* (6), 378–383.
   (2014). Development of metaphorical thinking: The role of language. In M. Borkent, J. Hinnell and B. Dancygier (eds.) *Language and the Creative Mind*, Stanford, CA: CSLI Publications.
   (2016). Linguistic relativity. In N. Riemer (ed.) *Routledge Handbook of Semantics*, New York: Routledge, pp. 158–174.
   (2017). The hierarchical structure of mental metaphors. *Metaphor: Embodied Cognition and Discourse*, 46–61.

Casasanto, D. and Boroditsky, L. (2003). Do we think about time in terms of space? In R. Alterman and D. Kirsch (eds.) *Proceedings of the 25th Annual Meeting of the Cognitive Science Society*, Mahwah, NJ: Lawrence Erlbaum Associates, pp. 216–221.

Casasanto, D. and Bottini, R. (2014). Mirror-reading can reverse the flow of time. *Journal of Experimental Psychology: General, 143*(2), 473–479.

Casasanto, D. and Chrysikou, E. (2011). When left is 'right': motor fluency shapes abstract concepts, *Psychological Science, 22* (4), 419–422.

Casasanto, D. and Dijkstra, K. (2010). Motor action and emotional memory. *Cognition, 115*, 179–185.

Casasanto, D. and Gijssels, T. (2015). What makes a metaphor an embodied metaphor? *Linguistics Vanguard, 1* (1), 327–337.

Casasanto D. and Jasmin, K. (2010). Good and bad in the hands of politicians: Spontaneous gestures during positive and negative speech. *PLoS ONE, 5* (7), e11805. doi:10.1371/journal.pone.0011805.

Casasanto, D., Boroditsky, L., Phillips, W., Greene, J., Goswami, S., Bocanegra-Thiel, T. et al., (2004). How deep are effects of language on thought? Time estimation in speakers of English, Indonesian, Greek, and Spanish. Paper presented at the 26th Annual Conference Cognitive Science Society, Austin, Texas.

Chandler, J., Reinhard, D. and Schwarz, N. (2012). To judge a book by its weight you need to know its content: Knowledge moderates the use of embodied cues. *Journal of Experimental Social Psychology*, *48* (4), 948–952.

Chang, C. T. and Yen, C. T. (2013). Missing ingredients in metaphor advertising: The right formula of metaphor type, product type, and need for cognition. *Journal of Advertising*, *42* (1), 80–94.

Charteris-Black, J. (2004). *Politicians and Rhetoric: The Persuasive Power of Metaphor*, Basingstoke: Palgrave MacMillan.

   (2009). Metaphor and gender in British parliamentary debates. In K. Ahrens (ed.) *Politics, Gender and Conceptual Metaphors*, Basingstoke: Palgrave MacMillan, pp. 139–165.

   (2012). Shattering the Bell jar: Metaphor, gender and depression. *Metaphor and Symbol*, *27* (3), 199–216.

   (2016). The "dull roar" and the "burning barbed wire pantyhose": Complex metaphor in accounts of chronic pain. In R. Gibbs (ed.). *Mixing Metaphor*, Amsterdam: John Benjamins, pp. 155–176.

Chen, J., Kacinik, N. A., Chen, Y. and Wu, N. (2014). Metaphorical color representations of emotional concepts in English and Chinese speakers: Evidence from behavioral data. Poster session presented at the Society for Personality and Social Psychology conference, Long Beach, CA.

Chiou, W. B. and Cheng, Y. Y. (2013). In broad daylight, we trust in God! Brightness, the salience of morality, and ethical behaviour. *Journal of Environmental Psychology*, *36*, 37–42.

Christi, M. and McGrath, M. (1987). Taking up the challenge of grief: Film as therapeutic metaphor and action ritual. *Australian and New Zealand Journal of Family Therapy*, *8* (4), 193–199.

Chu, M. and Kita, S. (2011). The nature of gesture's beneficial role in spatial problem solving. *Journal of Experimental Psychology: General*, *137*, 706–723.

Cienki, A. (1997). Some properties and groupings of image schemas. In M. Verspoor, K. D. Less and E. Sweester (eds.) *Lexical and Syntactical Constructions and the Construction of Meaning*, Amsterdam: John Benjamins.

   (2008). Why study metaphor and gesture. In A. Cienki and C. Müller (eds.) *Metaphor and Gesture*, Amsterdam: John Benjamins, pp. 5–25.

Cienki, A. and Müller, C. (eds.) *Metaphor and Gesture*, Amsterdam/Philadelphia: John Benjamins Publishing Company.

Cienki, A. and Müller, C. (2008a). Introduction. In A. Cienki and C. Müller (eds.) *Metaphor and Gesture*, Amsterdam/Philadelphia: John Benjamins Publishing Company, pp. 1–4.

   (2008b). Metaphor, gesture and thought. In R. W. Gibbs (ed.) *The Cambridge Handbook of Metaphor and Thought*, Cambridge: Cambridge University Press, pp. 483–501.

Cienki, A., Becker, R., Boutet, D., Morgenstern, A. and Iriskhanoval, O. (2016). Grammatical aspect, gesture, and mental simulation in Russian and French International Conference of the Cognitive Linguistics Association.

Citron F. M. and Goldberg A. E. (2014a). Metaphorical sentences are more emotionally engaging than their literal counterparts. *Journal of Cognitive Neuroscience*, *6*, 1–11.

Citron, F. M. and Goldberg, A. E. (2014b). Social context modulates the effect of hot temperature on perceived interpersonal warmth: A study of embodied metaphors. *Language and Cognition*, 6, 1–11.

Citron, F. M., Cacciari, C., Kucharski, M., Beck, L., Conrad, M. and Jacobs, A. (2015). When emotions are expressed figuratively: Psycholinguistic and affective norms of 619 idioms for German (PANIG). *Behavioural Research Methods*, 1–21.

Clark, K. B. and Clark, M. P. (1940). Skin color as a factor in racial identification of Negro preschool children. *Journal of Social Psychology*, S.P.SS.SI. Bulletin, II, 159–169.

Classen, C. (1990) Sweet colors, fragrant songs: Sensory models of the Andes and the Amazon. *American Ethnologist*, 17 (4), 722–735.

Coker, E. M. (2004). "Traveling pains": Embodied metaphors of suffering among southern Sudanese refugees in Cairo. *Culture, Medicine and Psychiatry*, 28 (1), 15-39.

Cogan, J. C., Bhalla, S. K., Sefa-Dedeh, A. and Rothblum, E. D. (1996). A comparative study of United States and African Students on Perceptions of Obesity and Thinness. *Journal of Cross-cultural Psychology*, 27 (1), 98–113.

Cohen Kadosh, R. and Gertner, L. (2011). Synaesthesia: Gluing together time, number and space. In S. Dehaene and E, Brannon (eds.) *Space, Time and Number in the Brain, Searching for the Foundations of Mathematics Thought*, Cambridge, MA: Elsevier, pp. 123–132.

Cohen Kadosh, R., Henik, A. and Walsh, V. (2007). Small is bright and big is dark in synaesthesia. *Current Biology*, 17, 834–835.

Connell, L. and Lynott, D. (2010). Look but don't touch: Tactile disadvantage in processing modality-specific word. *Cognition*, 115, 1–9.

Cook, K. and Alfonso, R. (2015). Erotic metaphors jazz musicians play by, *Paper presented at the International Cognitive Linguistics Conference*, Newcastle, UK.

Cornejo, C., Simonetti, F., Ibáñez, A., Aldunate, N., Ceric, F., López, V. and Núñez, R. E. (2009). Gesture and metaphor comprehension: Electrophysiological evidence of cross-modal coordination by audiovisual stimulation. *Brain and Cognition*, 70 (1), 42–52. doi:http://dx.doi.org/10.1016/j.bandc.2008.12.005.

Corts, D. P. and Pollio, H. R. (1999). Spontaneous production of figurative language and gesture in college lectures. *Metaphor and Symbol*, 14 (2), 81–100.

Corts, D. P. and Meyers, K. (2002). Conceptual clusters in figurative language production. *Journal of Psycholinguistic Research*, 31 (4), 391–408.

Coslett, H. B. (1998). Evidence for disturbance of the body schema in neglect. *Brain and Cognition*, 37, 529–544.

Coslett, H. B., Saffran, E. M. and Schwoebel, J. (2002). Knowledge of the human body: A distinct semantic domain. *Neurology*, 59, 357–363.

Costa, A., Foucart, A., Hayakawa, S., Aparici, M., Apesteguia, J., Heafner, J. et al. (2014). Your morals depend on language. *PLoS ONE*, 9(4), e94842. doi:10.1371/journal.pone.0094842.

Crawford, E. L. (2009). Conceptual metaphors of affect. *Emotion Review*, 1, 129–139.

Crawford, E. L., Margolies, S., Drake, J. and Murphy, M. (2006). Affect biases memory of location: Evidence for the spatial representation of affect. *Cognition and Emotion*, 20, 1153–1169.

Cuccio, V. (2017). Body-schema and body-image: What are they and what is their role in embodied metaphor processing? In B. Hampe and G. Steen (eds.) *Metaphor: From Embodied Cognition to Discourse*, Cambridge: Cambridge University Press, pp. 82–98.

Cytowic, R. E. (1989). *Synaesthesia: A Union of the Senses*, New York: Springer-Verlag.

(1994). *The Man Who Tasted Shapes*, London: Abacus.

Dailey, A., Martindale, C. and Borkum, J. (2010). Creativity, synesthesia, and physiognomic Perception. *Creativity Research Journal, 10* (1), 1–8.

Damasio, A. (2006). *Descartes' Error*, New York: Avon Books.

Daniel, A. C. (2010). Immorality-blackness associations and the moral-purity metaphor in African Americans, *Unpublished PhD Dissertation*, Tennessee State University.

Davidson, L., Sells, D., Sangster, S. and O'Connell, M. (2004). Qualitative studies of recovery: What can we learn from the person? In R. O. Ralph and P. W. Corrigan (eds.) *Recovery in Mental Illness: Broadening our Understanding of Wellness*, Washington, DC: American Psychological Association, pp. 147–170.

Deamer, F. (2013). An investigation into the processes and mechanisms underlying the comprehension of metaphor and hyperbole, *Unpublished PhD Dissertation*, University College London.

De Beauvoir, Simone (1949). *The Second Sex*, trans. (2009), Constance Borde and Sheila Malovany-Chevallier. Random House: Alfred A. Knopf.

De Grauwe, S., Willemsa, R. M., Rueschemeyera, S. A., Lemhöfera, K. and Schriefersa, H. (2014). Embodied language in first- and second-language speakers: Neural correlates of processing motor verbs. *Neuropsychologia, 56*, 334–349.

Dehaene, S. and Brannon, E. (eds.) (2011). *Space, Time and Number in the Brain: Searching for the Foundations of Mathematical Thought*, Amsterdam: Elsevier.

Dehaene, S., Bossini, S. and Giraux, P. (1993). The mental representation of parity and number magnitude. *Journal of Experimental Psychology: General, 122*, 371–396.

Deignan, A., Littlemore, J. and Semino, E. (2013). *Figurative Language, Genre and Register*, Cambridge: Cambridge University Press.

Deroy, O., Crisnel, A-S. and Spence, C. (2013). Crossmodal correspondences between odors and contingent features: Odors, musical notes and geometrical shapes. *Psychonomic Bulletin Review, 20*, 878–896.

Desai, R., Binder, J., Conant, L., Mano, Q. and Seidenberg, M. (2011). The neural career of sensory-motor metaphors. *Journal of Cognitive Neuroscience, 23*, 2376–2386.

De Sousa, H. (2012). Generational differences in the orientation of time in Cantonese speakers as a function of changes in the direction of Chinese writing. *Frontiers in Psychology, 3*, 1–8.

Despot, K. (2017). The production of metaphor by patients with Schizophrenia, Paper presented at the RaAM specialised Seminar, Odense, Denmark.

Dijkstra, K., Kaschak, M. and Zwaan, R. (2007). Body posture facilitates retrieval of autobiographical memories. *Cognition, 102*, 139–149.

Di Paulo, E. (2009). Editorial: The social and enactive mind. *Phenomenology and the Cognitive Sciences, 8* (4), 409–415.

Dolcos, F., LaBar, K. S. and Cabeza, R. (2005). Remembering one year later: Role of the amygdala and the medial temporal lobe memory system in retrieving emotional memories. *Proceedings of the National Academy of Sciences, USA*, 102, 2626–2631.

Dolscheid, S., Hunnius, D., Casasanto, D. and Majid, A. (2012). The sound of thickness: Prelinguistic infants' associations of space and pitch. Cognitive Science, 2012: Proceedings of the 34th Annual Meeting of the Cognitive Science Society, N. Miyake, D. Peeples and R. P. Cooper (eds.) Austin, Tx: Cognitive Science Society, pp. 306–311.

Dolscheid, S., Shayan, S., Majid, A. and Casasanto, D. (2013). The thickness of musical pitch: Psychophysical evidence for linguistic relativity. *Psychological Science*, *24* (5), 613–621.

Domes, G., Heintrichs, M., Michel, A., Berger, C. and Herpertz, S. (2007). Oxytocin improves 'mind reading' in humans. *Biological Psychiatry*, *61*, 731–733.

Droit-Volet, S., Brunot, S. and Niedenthal, P. (2004). Perception of the duration of emotional events. *Cognition and Emotion*, *18*, 849–858.

Dryll, E. (2009). Changes in metaphor comprehension in children. *Polish Psychological Bulletin*, *40*, 204–212.

Dudschig, C., de la Vega, I. and Kaup, B. (2014). Embodiment and second-language: Automatic activation of motor responses during processing spatially associated L2 words and emotion L2 words in a vertical Stroop paradigm. *Brain and Language*, *132*, 14–21.

Duffy, S. E. (2014). The role of cultural artefacts in the interpretation of metaphorical expressions about time. *Metaphor and Symbol*, *29* (2), 94–112.

Duffy, S. E. and Feist, M. I. (2014). Individual differences in the interpretation of ambiguous statements about time. *Cognitive Linguistics*, *25* (1), 29–54.

Duffy, S. E., Feist, M. I. and McCarthy, S. (2014). Moving through time: The role of personality in three real life contexts. *Cognitive Science*, 1662–1674.

Duffy, S., Littlemore, J., Heritage, F. and Winter, B. (in prep.). Gender and the social hierarchy.

Dunn, R. and Dunn, K. (1993). *Teaching Secondary Students through Their Learning Styles*, Boston: Allyn and Bacon.

Eagly, A. H., Wood, W. and Diekman, A. (2000). Social role theory of sex differences and similaritries: A current appraisal. In T. Eckes and M. Trautner (eds.) *The Developmental Social Psychology of Gender*, Mahwah, NJ: Lawrence Erlbaum Associates, pp. 123–173.

Earp, B., Everett, J., Madva, E. and Hamlin, J. (2014). Out, damned spot: Can the 'Macbeth effect' be replicated? *Basic and Applied Social Psychology*, *36* (1), 91.

Ebbinghaus, H. (1913). *On Memory: A Contribution to Experimental Psychology*, New York: Teachers College.

Ekman, P. (1992). An argument for basic emotions. *Cognition and Emotion*, *6* (3/4), 169–200.

Ekman, P., Sorenson, E. and Friesen, W. V. (1969). Pan-cultural elements in facial displays of emotion. *Science*, *164*, 86–88.

El Refaie, E. (2009). Metaphor in political cartoons, exploring audience responses. In C. Forceville (ed.) *Multimodal Metaphor*, Berlin: Mouton de Gruyter, pp. 173–196.

(2014). Appearances and dis/dys-appearances: A dynamic view of embodiment in Conceptual Metaphor Theory. *Metaphor and the Social World*, *4* (1), 109–125.

Enkell, H. (2002). Metaphor and the psychodynamic functions of the mind, *Unpublished PhD Dissertation*, Kuopio, Finland, Kuopion Yliopisto.

Epstein, E. L. and Gamlin, P. J. ((1994). Young children's comprehension of simple and complex metaphors presented in pictures and words. *Metaphor and Symbolic Activity*, *9*, 179–191.

Fainsilber, L. and Ortony, A. (1987). Metaphorical uses of language in the experience of emotions. *Metaphor and Symbolic Activity*, *2*, 239–250.

Fauconnier, G. and Turner, M. (2008). *The Way We Think: Conceptual Blending and the Mind's Hidden Complexities*, New York: Basic Books.

Faust, M. and Kenett, Y. N. (2014). Rigidity, chaos and integration: Hemispheric interaction and individuals differences in metaphor comprehension. *Frontiers in Human Neuroscience*, *8*, 511.

Fedden, S. and Boroditsky, L. (2012). Spatialization of time in Mian. *Frontiers of Psychology*, *3* (485), 1–10.

Feingold, A. (1994). Gender differences in personality: A meta-analysis. *Psychological Bulletin*, *116*, 429–456.

Feist, M. and Duffy, S. (2015). Moving beyond 'Next Wednesday': The interplay of lexical semantics and constructional meaning in an ambiguous metaphoric statement. *Cognitive Linguistics*, *26* (4), 633–656.

Feldman, J. and Narayanan, S. (2004). Embodied meaning in a neural theory of language. *Brain and Language*, *89*, 385–392.

Fetterman, A., Robinson, M. and Meier, B. (2012). Anger as "seeing red": Evidence for a perceptual association. *Cognition & Emotion*, *26* (8), 1445–1458.

Figueras Bates, C. (2015). I am a waste of breath, of space, of time: Metaphors of self in a pro-anorexia group. *Qualitative Health Research*, *25* (2), 189–204.

Foolen, A., Ludtke, U., Racine, T. P. and Zlatev, J. (eds.) (2012). *Moving Ourselves and Moving Others: Motion and Emotion in Intersubjectivity, Consciousness and Language*, Amsterdam: John Benjamins

Forceville, C. and Urios-Aparisi, E. (eds.) (2009). *Multimodal metaphor*, Berlin: Mouton De Gruyter.

Foroni, F. (2015). Do we embody second language? Evidence for 'partial' simulation during processing of a second language. *Brain and Cognition*, *99*, 8–16.

Foroni F. and Semin G. R. (2013). Comprehension of action negation involves inhibitory simulation. *Frontiers in Human Neuroscience*, *7*, 1–7.

Frank, M. C., Everett, D. L., Fedorenko, E. and Gibson, E. (2008). Number as a cognitive technology: Evidence from Pirahã language and cognition. *Cognition*, *108* (3), 819–824.

Frieze, I. H., Olson, J. E. and Good, D. C. (1990). Perceived and actual discrimination in the salaries of male and female managers. *Journal of Applied Social Psychology*, *20*, 46–67.

Fuhrman, O. and Boroditsky, L. (2010). Cross-cultural differences in mental representations of time: Evidence from a non-linguistic task. *Cognitive Science*, *34*, 1430–1451.

Fuhrman, O., McCormick, K., Chen, E., Jiang, H., Shu, D., Mao, S. and Boroditsky, L. (2011). How linguistic and cultural forces shape conceptions of time: English and Mandarin time in 3D. *Cognitive Science*, *35*, 1305–1328.

Fuller, D., Littlemore, J., McGuinness, S., Turner, S., Kuberska, K., and Burgess, M. (2016–2018). 'Death before Birth: Understanding, informing and supporting choices made by people who have experienced miscarriage, termination and stillbirth' *ESRC-funded project: ES/N008359/1*, https://deathbeforebirth project.org/.

Fussell, S. R. and Moss, M. M. (1998). Figurative language in emotional communication. *Human Computer Interaction Institute*, *82*, 113–141.

Gallagher, H. L., Happe, F., Brunswick, N., Fletcher, P. C., Frith, U. and Frith, P. C. D. (2000). Reading the mind in cartons and stories: An fMRI study of 'theory of mind' in verbal and nonverbal tasks. *Neuropsychologia*, *38* (1), 11–21.

Gallagher, S. (2008). Understanding others: Embodied social cognition. In P. Calvo and A. Gomila (eds.) *Handbook of Cognitive Science: An Embodied Approach*, Amsterdam: Elsevier, pp. 439–452.

Gallese, V. (2001). The shard manifold hypothesis: From mirror neurons to empathy. *Journal of Consciousness Studies*, *8*, 33–50.

(2006). Intentional attunement: A neurophysiological perspective on social cognition and its disruption in autism. *Brain Research*, *1079*, 15–24.

Gallese, V. and Goldman, A. (1998). Mirror neurons and the simulation theory of intelligence. *Trends in Cognitive Science*, *2*, 439–450.

Gallese, V. and Lakoff, G. (2005). The Brain's concepts: The role of the sensory-motor system in conceptual knowledge. *Cognitive Neuropsychology*, *22* (3), 455–479.

Gamez, E., Diaz, J. and Marrero, H. (2011). The uncertain universality of the Macbeth effect with a Spanish sample. *The Spanish Journal of Psychology*, *14* (1), 156–162.

Gamez-Djokic, V., Narayanan, S., Wehlong, E., Sheng, T., Bergen, B., Davis, J. and Aziz-Zadeh, L. (under review). *Morally queasy: metaphors implying moral disgust activate specific subregions of the insula and basal ganglia*.

Gardner, H., Kircher, M., Winner, E. and Perkins, D. (1975). Children's metaphoric productions and preferences, *Journal of Child Language*, *2* (1), 125–141.

Gentilucci, M. and Volta, R. D. (2008). Spoken language and arm gestures are controlled by the same motor control system. *The Quarterly Journal of Experimental Psychology*, *61* (6), 944–957.

Gentner, D. (1988). Metaphor as structure mapping: The relational shift. *Child Development*, *59*, 47–59.

Gibbs, R. W. (1994). *The Poetics of Mind: Figurative Thought, Language, and Understanding*, New York: Cambridge University Press.

(1999). Taking metaphor out of our heads and putting it into the cultural world. *Amsterdam Studies in the Theory and History of Linguistic Science Series 4*, 145–166.

(2001). Evaluating contemporary models of figurative language understanding. *Metaphor and Symbol*, *16* (3 & 4), 317–333.

(2002). Embodied metaphor in women's narratives about their experiences with cancer. *Health Communication*, *14* (2), 139–165.

(2005). The psychological status of image schemas. In B. Hampe (ed.) *From Perception to Meaning: Image Schemas in Cognitive Linguistics*, Amsterdam: Mouton de Gruyter, pp. 113–136.

(2006a). *Embodiment and Cognitive Science*, New York: Cambridge University Press.

(2006b). Metaphor interpretation as embodied simulation. *Mind & Language*, *21*, 434–458.

(2008). Metaphor and thought: The state-of-the-art. In R. Gibbs (ed.), *Cambridge Handbook of Metaphor and Thought*, New York: Cambridge University Press.

(2011). Evaluating conceptual metaphor theory. *Discourse Processes*, *48* (8), 529–562.

(2012). Walking the walk while thinking about the talk: Embodied interpretation of metaphorical narratives. *Journal of Psycholinguistic Research*, *42* (4), 363–378.

(2013). Why do some people dislike conceptual metaphor theory? *Journal of Cognitive Semiotics*, *5* (102), 14–36.

(2015). Embodied metaphor. In J. Littlemore and J. Taylor (eds.) *The Bloomsbury Companion to Cognitive Linguistics*, London: Bloomsbury, 167–184.

(2017). *Metaphor Wars, Conceptual Metaphors in Human Life*, Cambridge: Cambridge University Press.

Gibbs, R. W. and Colston, H. (2012). *Interpreting Figurative Meaning*, New York: Cambridge University Press.

Gibbs, R. W. and Franks, H. (2002). Embodied metaphors in womens' narratives about their experiences with cancer. *Health Communication*, *14*, 139–165.

Gibbs, R. W. and Perlman, M. (2010). Language understanding is grounded in experiential simulations: A reply to Weiskopf. *Studies in the History and Philosophy of Science*, *41*, 305–308.

Gibbs, R. W, Costa Lima, P. and Francozo, E. (2004). Metaphor is grounded in embodied experience. *Journal of Pragmatics*, *36*, 1189–1210.

Gibbs, R. W, Gould, J. and Andric, M. (2006). Imagining metaphorical actions: Embodied simulations make the impossible plausible. *Imagination, Cognition, and Personality*, *25*, 221–238.

Gibbs, R. W., Bogdanovich, J. M., Sykes, J. R. and Barr, D. J. (1997). Metaphor in idiom comprehension. *Journal of Memory and Language*, *37*, 141–154.

Gibson, J. J. (1977). The Theory of Affordances. In R. E. Shaw and J. Bransford (eds.) *Perceiving, Acting, and Knowing*, Hillsdale, NJ: Lawrence Erlbaum Associates.

Giessner, S. and Schubert, T. (2007). High in the hierarchy: How vertical location and judgments of leaders' power are interrelated. *Organizational Behaviour and Human Decision Processes*, *104*, 30–44.

Gil, S., Niedenthal, P. M. and Droit-Volet, S. (2007). Anger and time perception in children. *Emotion*, *7*, 219–225.

Gillberg, C. (2002). *A guide to Asperger syndrome*, Cambridge: Cambridge University Press.

Giora, R., Fein, O., Kronrod, A., Elnatan, I., Shuval, N. and Zur, A. (2004). Weapons of mass distraction: Optimal innovation and pleasure ratings. *Metaphor and Symbol*, *19*, 115–141.

Gkiouzepas, L. (2013). Is your ad headline high enough? The influence of orientational metaphors on affect and comprehension for print advertisements. The 12th International Conference on Research in Advertising (ICORIA), Zagreb, Croatia: European Academy of Advertising.

Gkiouzepas, L. (2015). Metaphor-ad layout consistency effects: The moderating role of personality traits. In *Advances in Advertising Research (Vol. V)*, Wiesbaden: Springer.

Glenberg, A. (1999). Why mental models must be embodied. In *Advances in Psychology* (Vol. 128) North-Holland, pp. 77–90.

Glenberg, A. M. and Kaschak, M. P. (2002). Grounding language in action. *Psychonomic Bulletin Review*, *9*, 558–565.

Gold, R. and Faust, M. (2010). Right hemisphere dysfunction and metaphor comprehension in young adults with Asperger syndrome. *Journal of Autistic Developmental Disorders, 40,* 800–811.

Goldberg, L. R. (1992). The development of markers for the Big-Five factor structure. *Psychological Assessment, 4,* 26–42.

Goldberg, R. F., Perfetti, C. A. and Schneider, W. (2006). Perceptual knowledge retrieval activates sensory brain regions. *Journal of Neuroscience, 26,* 4917–4921.

Goldin-Meadow, S. (2003). *Hearing Gesture: How our Hands Help us Think,* Cambridge, MA: Harvard University Press.

Goldin-Meadow, S. and Wagner, S. M. (2005). How our hands help us learn. *Trends in Cognitive Sciences, 9,* 234–241.

Goldinger, S., Papesh, M., Barnhart, A., Hansen, W. and Hout, M. (2016). The poverty of embodied cognition. *Psychonomic Bulletin and Review, 23* (4), 959–978.

González , J., Barros-Loscertales, A., Pulvermueller, F., Meseguer, V., Sanjuan, A., Belloch, V. et al. (2006). Reading cinnamon activates olfactory brain regions. *Neuroimage, 32,* 906–912.

González-Cutre, D., Sicilia, Á., Sierra, A. C., Ferriz, R. and Haggerd, M. S. (2016). Understanding the need for novelty from the perspective of self-determination theory. *Personality and Individual Differences, 102,* 159–169.

Gori, M. (2015). Multisensory integration and calibration in children and adults with and without sensory and motor disabilities. *Multisensory Research, 28,* 71–99.

Goschler, J. (2005). Embodiment and Body Metaphors. *Metaphorik, 9,* 33–52.

Grady, J. E. (1997a). Foundations of meaning: primary metaphors and primary stress, PhD Dissertation, University of Berkeley. Available at: http://escholarship.org/uc/item/3g9427m2#page-1.

(1997b). Theories are buildings revisited. *Cognitive Linguistics, 8* (4), 267–290.

Grady, J. E. (2007). *Metaphor.* In D. Geeraerts and H. Cuyckens (eds.) *Handbook of Cognitive Linguistics,* Oxford University Press, pp. 188–213.

Greenwald, A., McGhee, D. and Schwartz, J. (1998). Measuring individual differences in implicit cognition: The implicit association test. *Journal of Social Psychology, 74,* 1464–1480.

Gullberg, M. (1998). *Gesture as a Communication Strategy in Second Language Discourse: A Study of Learners of French and Swedish,* Lund, Sweden: Lund University Press.

(1999). Communication strategies, gesture and grammar. *Acquisition et Interaction en Langue Etrangère, 2,* 61–71.

(2006). Handling discourse: Gestures, reference tracking, and communication strategies in early L2. *Language Learning, 56,* 155–196.

Gullberg, M. and McCafferty, S. (2008). Introduction to gesture and SLA: Toward an integrated approach. *Studies in Second Language Acquisition, 30,* 133–146.

Haddon, M. (2004). *The Curious Incident of the Dog in the Night-Time,* Vintage Press.

Hains, A. (2014). Metaphor comprehension in the treatment of people with schizophrenia, *Unpublished PhD Thesis,* University of Wollongong.

Halliday, M. A. K. (1978). *Language as Social Semiotic: The Social Interpretation of Language and Meaning.* Hodder Arnold.

Halliday, M. A., Hasan, R. and Hasan, R. (1985). *Language, Text and Context*. Victoria: Derkin University.

Happé, F. (1991). The autobiographical writings of three Asperger syndrome adults: Problems of interpretation and implications for theory. In U. Frith (ed.) *Autism and Asperger syndrome*, Cambridge: Cambridge University Press, pp. 207–242.

(1993). Communicative competence and theory of mind in autism: A test of relevance theory. *Cognition*, *48*, 101–119.

(1995). Understanding minds and metaphors: Insight from the study of figurative language in autism. *Metaphor and Symbolic Activity*, *10*, 275–295.

Happé, F. and Frith, U. (2009). The beautiful otherness of the autistic mind. *Philosophical Transactions of the Royal Society*, https://royalsocietypublishing.org/doi/full/10.1098/rstb.2009.0009.

Happé, F. and Vital, P. (2009). What aspects of autism predispose to talent? *Philosophical Transactions of the Royal Society B: Biological Sciences*, *364* (1522), 1369–1375.

Hardin, C. L. and Maffi, L. (1997). *Color Categories in Thought and Language*, Cambridge: Cambridge University Press.

Hare, R. D. (1996). Psychopathy: A clinical construct whose time has come. *Criminal Justice and Behavior*, *23*, 25–54.

Hartman, J. and Paradis, C. (2018). Emotive and sensory simulation through comparative construal. *Metaphor and Symbol*, *33* (2), 1–21.

Hartmann, M., Martarelli, C., Mast, F. and Stocker, K. (2014). Eye movements during mental time travel follow a diagonal line. *Consciousness and Cognition*, *30*, 201–209.

Hasson, U. and Glucksberg S. (2004). Does understanding negation entail affirmation? An examination of negated metaphors. University of Chicago.

Hauk, O., Johnsrude, I. and PulverMüller, F. (2004). Somatotopic representation of action words in human motor and premotor cortex. *Neuron*, *41*, 301–307.

Havas, D., Glenberg, A. and Rinck, M. (2007). Emotion simulation during language comprehension. *Psychonomic Bulletin, and Review*, *14* (3), 191–201.

Hellmann, J. H., Thoben, D. F. and Echterhoff, G. (2013). The sweet taste of revenge: Gustatory experience induces metaphor-consistent judgments of a harmful act. *Social Cognition*, *31* (5), 531–542.

Hensley, W. E. and Angoli, M., (1980). Message, valence, familiarity, sex and personality effects on the perceptual distortion of height. *Journal of Psychology*, *104*, 149–156.

Herz, R. S. (2004). A naturalistic analysis of autobiographical memories triggered by olfactory visual and auditory stimuli. *Chemical Senses*, *29* (3), 217–224.

Hodder, A. and Houghton, D. (2014). Linguistic markers of Tweets: Giving unions a voice, *Seminar presented at the University of Birmingham English Language Research Seminar Series*, October, 2014.

Holle, H., Obleser, J., Rueschemeyer, S. A. and Gunter, T. C. (2010). Integration of iconic gestures and speech in left superior temporal areas boosts speech comprehension under adverse listening conditions. *Neuroimage*, *49*, 875–884.

Holle, H., Gunter, T. C., Rüschemeyer, S. A., Hennenlotter, A. and Iacoboni, M. (2008). Neural correlates of the processing of co-speech gestures. *Neuroimage*, *39*, 2010–2024.

Holyoak, K. J., Junn, E. N. and Billman, D. (1984). Development of analogical problem-solving skill. *Child Development*, *55*, 2042–2055.

Horstmann, G. and Ansorge, U. (2011). Compatibility between tones, head movements, and facial expressions. *Emotion*, *11*, 975–980.

Horton, W. S. (2007). Metaphor and readers' attributions of intimacy. *Memory and Cognition*, *35* (1), 87–94.

(2013). Character intimacy influences the processing of metaphoric utterances during narrative comprehension. *Metaphor and Symbol*, *28*, 148–166.

Hostetter, A. B. (2011). When do gestures communicate? A meta-analysis. *Psychological Bulletin*, *137* (2), 297–315.

Hostetter, A. B. and Alibali, M. (2007). Raise your hand if you're spatial: Relations between verbal and spatial skills and gesture production. *Gesture*, *7* (1), 73–95.

(2008). Visible embodiment: Gestures as simulated action. *Psychonomic Bulletin and Review*, *15* (3), 495–514.

(2010). Language, gesture, action! A test of the Gesture as Simulated Action framework. *Journal of Memory and Language*, *63* (2), 245–257.

Houghton, D. and Littlemore J. (in prep.). The role played by figurative messaging and emotion in viral videos.

Howe, J. (2007). Argument is argument: An essay on conceptual metaphor and verbal dispute. *Metaphor and Symbol*, *23* (1), 1–23.

Howes, D. and Classen, C. (1991). Sounding sensory profiles. In D. Howes (ed.) *The Varieties of Sensory Experience: A Sourcebook in the Anthropology of the Senses*, Toronto: University of Toronto Press, pp. 257–288.

Huette, S., Winter, B., Matlock, T., Ardell, D. H. and Spivey, M. (2014). Eye movements during listening reveal spontaneous grammatical processing. *Frontiers in Psychology*, *5*, 1–7.

Hupka, R., Zalaski, Z., Otto, J., Reidl, L. and Tarabrina, N. (1997). The colors of anger, envy, fear and jealousy, a cross-cultural study. *Journal of Cross-Cultural Psychology*, *28* (2), 156–171.

Hutchins, E. (1995) *Cognition in the Wild*, Cambridge MA: MIT Press.

(2005). Material anchors for conceptual blends. *Journal of Pragmatics*, *37*, 1555–1577.

Hutchinson, S. and Louwerse, M. (2013). Language statistics and individual differences in processing primary metaphors. *Cognitive Linguistics*, *24* (4), 667–687.

Hurtienne, J. (2011). Image Schemas and Design for Intuitive Use. Exploring New Guidance for User Interface Design. *PhD Dissertation*; http://opus.kobv.de/tuberlin/volltexte/2011/2970/pdf/hurtienne_joern.pdf.

(2014). Non-linguistic applications of cognitive linguistics: On the usefulness of image-schematic metaphors in user interface design. In J. Littlemore and J. Taylor (eds.) *The Bloomsbury Companion to Cognitive Linguistics*, London: Bloomsbury, pp. 301–324.

Hurtienne, J., Stößel, C., Sturm, C., Maus, A., Rötting, M., Longdin, P. and Clarkson, J. (2010). Physical gestures for abstract concepts: Inclusive design with primary metaphors. *Interacting with Computers*, *22* (6), 475–484.

Hussey, K. and Katz, A. N. (2006). Metaphor production in online conversation: Gender and friendship status. *Discourse Processes*, *42* (1), 75–98.

(2009). Perception of the use of metaphor by an interlocutor in discourse. *Metaphor and Symbol, 24,* 203–236.

Ibáñez, A., Manes, F., Escobar, J., Trujillo, N., Andreucci, P. and Hurtado, E. (2010). Gesture influences the processing of figurative language in non-native speakers: ERP evidence. *Neuroscience Letters, 471* (1), 48–52. doi:https://doi.org/10.1016/j.neulet.2010.01.009.

Ibáñez, A., Toro, P., Cornejo, C., Urquina, H., Manes, F., Weisbrod, M. and Schroder, J. (2011). High contextual sensitivity of metaphorical expressions and gesture blending: A video event-related potential design. *Psychiatry Research, 191* (1), 68–75. doi:10.1016/j.pscychresns.2010.08.008.

Ibarretze-Antuñano, I. (2008). Guts, heart and liver: The conceptualization of internal organs in Basque. In F. Sharifian, R. Dirven, Y. Ning and S. Niemeier (eds.) *Culture, Body, and Language: Conceptualizations of Internal Body Organs across Cultures and Languages,* Berlin: Mouton de Gruyter, pp. 103–128.

Inagi, K. and Hatano, G. (1987). Young children's spontaneous personification as analogy. *Child Development, 58,* 1013–1020.

Inbar, Y., Pizarro, D. A., and Bloom, P. (2009). Conservatives are more easily disgusted than liberals. *Cognition and Emotion, 23,* 714–725.

Ishihara, M., Keller, P., Rossetti, Y. and Prinz, W. (2008). Horizontal spatial representations of time: Evidence for the STEARC effect. *Cortex, 44* (4), 454–461.

Iverson, J. M. and Goldin-Meadow, S. (2001). The resilience of gesture in talk: Gesture in blind speakers and listeners. *Developmental Science, 4,* 416–422.

Jacobs, A., Võ, M., Briesemeister, B., Conrad, M., Hofmann, M., Kuchinke, L., Lüdtke, J. and Braun, M. (2015). 10 years of BAWLing into affective and aesthetic processes in reading: What are the echoes? *Frontiers in Psychology, 1* (8).

Jamalian, A. and Tversky, B. (2012). Gestures alter thinking about time. In N. Miyake, D. Peebles and R. Cooper (eds.), *Proceedings of the 34th Annual Conference of the Cognitive Science Society,* Austin, TX: Cognitive Science Society, pp. 503–508.

Jarvis, S. (2003). Probing the effects of the L2 on the L1: A case study. In V. J. Cook (ed.) *Second Language Acquisition, 3: Effects of the Second Language on the First,* Clevedon: Multilingual Matters Limited.

Jensen, T. (2013). New perspectives on language, cognition and values. *Journal of Multicultural Discourses, 9* (1), 71–78.

(2014). Emotion in languaging: An ecological approach to the intertwined nature of language and emotion. *Frontiers in Psychology, 5,* 720.

Jensen, T. and Cuffari, E. (2014). Doubleness in experience: Toward a distributed enactive approach to metaphoricity. *Metaphor and Symbol, 29,* 278–297.

Johansson-Falck, M. (2010). Review of Müller (2008) *Metaphors Dead and Alive, Sleeping and Waking* (University of Chicago Press). *Metaphor and Symbol, 25,* 114–121.

Johansson-Falck, M. and Gibbs, R. (2012). Embodied motivations for metaphorical meanings. *Cognitive Linguistics, 23* (2), 251–272.

John, O. P. and Srivastava, S. (1999). The Big Five trait taxonomy: History, measurement, and theoretical perspectives. *Handbook of personality: Theory and research, 2* (1999), 102–138.

Johnson, C. 1997. Metaphor vs. Conflation in the Acquisition of Polysemy: The Case of See. In M. K. Hiraga, C. Sinha and S. Wilcox (eds.) *Cultural, Typological and Psychological Perspectives in Cognitive Linguistics*, Albuquerque, NM: John Benjamins.

Johnson, M. (1987). *The Body in the Mind*, Chicago: University of Chicago Press.
 (2007). *The Meaning of the Body: Aesthetics of Human Understanding*, Chicago, IL, and London: University of Chicago Press.

Johnson, M. and Larson, S. (2003). "Something in the way she moves" – Metaphors of musical motion. *Metaphor and Symbol, 18* (2), 63–84.

Jostmann, N. B., Lakens, D. and Schubert, T. W. (2009). Weight as embodiment of importance. *Psychological Science, 20* (9), 1169–1174.

Judge, T. A. and Cable, D. M. (2004). The effect of physical height on workplace success and income: Preliminary test of a theoretical model. *Journal of Applied Psychology, 89* (3), 428–441.

Jung-Beeman, M. (2005). Bilateral brain processes for comprehending natural language. *Trends in Cognitive Sciences, 9* (11), 512–518.

Jütte, R. (2005). *A History of the Senses: From Antiquity to Cyberspace*, Cambridge: Polity Press.

Kahneman, D. (1991). Anomalies: The endowment effect, loss aversion, and status quo bias. *The Journal of Economic Perspectives, 5* (1), 193.

Kaneko, M. and Sutton-Spence, R. (2016). In E. Semino and Z. Demjen (eds.) *Metaphor in Sign Language, The Routledge Handbook of Metaphor and Language*, London: Taylor and Francis, pp. 263–279.

Kanner, L. (1946). Irrelevant and metaphorical language in early infantile autism. *The American Journal of Psychiatry, 103* (2): 242–246.

Karns, C. M. and Knight, R. T. (2009). Intermodal auditory, visual, and tactile attention modulates early stages of neural processing. *Journal of Cognitive Neuroscience, 21*, 6690–6683.

Kasirer, A. and Mashal, N. (2014). Verbal creativity in autism: Comprehension and generation of metaphoric language in high-functioning autism spectrum disorder and typical development. *Frontiers in Human Neuroscience, 8*, 615.

Katz, A. N. (1983). What does it mean to be a high imager? In J. C. Yuille (ed.) *Imagery, Memory and Cognition*, New Jersey: Lawrence Erlbaum Associates, pp. 39–63.

Katz, A. N. and Bowes, A. (2015). Embodiment in metaphor and (not?) in bilingual language. In R. R. Heredia and A. B. Cieślicka (eds.) *Bilingual Figurative Language Processing*, Cambridge: Cambridge University Press.

Kaup B. (2001). Negation and its impact on the accessibility of text information. *Memory and Cognition, 29*, 860–967.

Kaup B. and Zwaan R. A. (2003). Effects of negation and situational presence on the accessibility of text information. *Journal of Experimental Psychology: Learning, Memory, and Cognition, 29*, 439–446.

Kaup, B., Yaxley, R. H., Madden, C. J., Zwaan, R. A. and Lüdtke, J. (2007). Experiential simulations of negated text information. *The Quarterly Journal of Experimental Psychology, 60* (7), 976–990.

Kay, A. C., Wheeler, S. C., Bargh, J. A. and Ross, L. (2004). Material priming: The influence of mundane physical objects on situational construal and competitive behavioural choice. *Organizational Behaviour and Human Decision Processes*, *95*, 83–96.

Kendon, A. (2004). *Gesture: Visible Action as Utterance*, Cambridge: Cambridge University Press.

Kensinger, E. and Corkin, S. (2003). Memory enhancement for emotional words: Are emotional words more vividly remembered than neutral words? *Memory and Cognition*, *31*, 1169–1180.

Kirby, J. R. (1988). Style, strategy and skill in reading. In R. Schmeck (ed.) *Learning Strategies and Learning Styles*, New York: Plenum Press, pp. 230–274.

Kircher, T., Straube, B., Leube, D. et al. (2009). Neural interaction of speech and gesture: Differential activations of metaphoric co-verbal gestures. *Neuropsychologia*, *47*, 169–179.

Kita, S. (2000). How representational gestures help speaking. In D. McNeill. (ed.) *Language and Gesture*, Cambridge: Cambridge University Press, pp. 162–185.

Kita, S., Alibali, M. W. and Chu, M. (2017). How do gestures influence thinking and speaking? The gesture-for-conceptualization hypothesis. *Psychological Review*, *124* (3), 245–266.

Kitayana, O. (1987). Metaphorization – Making terms. *International Journal of Psycho-Analysis*, *68* (4), 499–509.

Kleege, G. (1999). *Sight Unseen*, New Haven, CT: Yale University Press.

Knapton, O. (2013). Pro-anorexia: Extensions of ingrained concepts. *Discourse & Society*, *24* (4), 461–477.

Köhler, W. (1929). *Gestalt Psychology*, New York: Liveright.

Kogan, N., Connor, K., Gross, A. and Fava, D. (1980). Understanding visual metaphor: Developmental and individual differences. *Monographs of the Society for Research in Child Development*, 1–78.

Kok, K. and Cienki, A. (2014). Taking simulation semantics out of the laboratory: Towards an interactive and multimodal reappraisal of embodied language comprehension. *Language and Cognition*, *25*, 1–22.

Koller, V. and Semino, E. (2009). Metaphor, politics and gender: A case study from Germany. In K. Ahrens (ed.) *Politics, Gender and Conceptual Metaphors*, Basingstoke: Palgrave Macmillan, pp. 9–35.

Körner, H., Newman, C. and Mao, L. (2011). 'The black dog just came and sat on my face and built a kennel': Gay men making sense of 'depression'. *Health: An Interdisciplinary Journal for the Social Study of Health, Illness and Medicine*, *15* (4), 417–436.

Kouchaki, M., Gino, F. and Jami, A. (2014). The Burden of Guilt: Heavy Backpacks, Light Snacks, and Enhanced Morality. *Journal of Experimental Psychology: General*, *143* (1), 414–420.

Kousta, S.T., Vinson, D. and Vigliocco, G. (2009). Emotion words, regardless of polarity, have a processing advantage over neutral words. *Cognition*, *112*, 473–481.

Kousta, S. T., Vigliocco, G., Vinson, D. P., Andrews, M. and Del Campo, E. (2011). The representation of abstract words: Why emotion matters. *Journal of Experimental Psychology: General*, *140* (1), 14–34.

Kövecses, Z. (2002). *Metaphor: A Practical Introduction*, Oxford: Oxford University Press.

(2005). *Metaphor in Culture: Universality and Variation*. Cambridge: Cambridge University Press.

(2006). *Language, Mind and Culture*, New York: Oxford University Press.

(2015). *Where Metaphors Come From: Reconsidering Context in Metaphor*, Oxford: Oxford University Press.

(2019). Metaphorical creativity – The case of emotion. Paper presented at The Creative Power of Metaphor Conference, Worcester College, University of Oxford, 30–31 March 2019.

Krishna, A. (2012). An integrative review of sensory marketing: Engaging the senses to affect perception, judgement and behavior. *Journal of Consumer Psychology, 22*, 332–351.

Lacey, S., Stilla, R. and Sathian, K. (2012). Metaphorically feeling: Comprehending textural metaphors activates somatosensory cortex. *Brain and Language, 120*, 416–421.

Lakens, D., Semin, G. and Foroni, F. (2011). Why your highness needs the people: Comparing the absolute and relative representation of power in vertical space. *Social Psychology, 42* (3), 205–213.

Lakoff, G. (1996). Sorry, I'm not myself today: The metaphor system for conceptualising the self. In G. Fauconnier and E. Sweetser (eds.) *Spaces, Worlds and Grammar*, Chicago: University of Chicago Press, pp. 91–123.

(2008). The neural theory of metaphor. In R. W. Gibbs (ed.) *The Cambridge Handbook of Metaphor and Thought*, Cambridge: Cambridge University Press, pp. 17–38.

(2012). Explaining embodied cognition results. *Topics in Cognitive Science, 4*, 773–785.

Lakoff, G. and Johnson, M. (1980). *Metaphors we live by*, Chicago, IL: University of Chicago Press.

(1999). *Philosophy in the Flesh: The Embodied Mind and Its Challenge to Western Thought*, New York: Basic Books.

(2002). Why cognitive linguistics requires embodied realism. *Cognitive Linguistics, 13* (3), 245–263.

Lakoff, G. and Núñez, R. (2000). *Where Mathematics Comes From: The Embodied Mind Brings Mathematics into Being*, New York: Basic Books.

Landau, M. J., Robinson, M. and Meier, B. (Eds.) (2015). *The Power of Metaphor: Examining the Influence on Social Life*, Washington, DC: APA Books.

Landau, M. J., Sullivan, D. and Greenberg, J. (2009). Evidence that self-relevant motives and metaphoric framing interact to influence political and social attitudes. *Psychological Science, 20* (11), 1421–1427.

Langdon, R., Coltheart, M., Ward, P. B. and Catts, S. V. (2002). Disturbed communication in schizophrenia: The role of poor pragmatics and poor theory-of-mind. *Psychological Medicine, 32* (7), 1273–1284.

Langston, W. (2002). Violating orientational metaphors slows reading. *Discourse Processes, 34*, 281–310.

Larson, S. (2012). *Musical Forces: Motion, Metaphor and Meaning in Music*, Bloomington: Indiana University Press.

Leder, D. (1990). *The Absent Body*, Chicago, IL: University of Chicago Press.

Lee, E. H. and Schnall, S. (2014). The influence of social power on weight perception. *Journal of Experimental Psychology: General, 143*, 1719–1725.

Lee, W. S. and Schwarz, N. (2010). Washing away post-decisional dissonance. *Science*, *329*, 709.

(2012a). Bidirectionality, mediation, and moderation of metaphorical effects: The embodiment of social suspicion and fishy smells. *Journal of Personality and Social Psychology*, *103* (5), 737–749.

(2012b). Metaphor in judgement and decision making. In M. J. Landau, M. D. Robinson and B. P. Meier (eds.) *Metaphorical Thought in Social Life*, Washington, DC: American Psychological Association.

Leijssen, M. (2006) Verification of the body in psychotherapy. *Journal of Humanistic Psychology*, *46* (2), 126–146.

Lempert, H. and Kinsbourne, M. (1982). Effect of laterality of orientation on verbal memory. *Neurophysiologia*, *20*, 211–214.

Leung, A. et al. (2012). Embodied metaphor and creative acts. *Psychological Science*, *23*, 502–509.

Levenson, M., Kiehl, K. and Fitzpatrick, C. (1995). Assessing psychopathic attributes in a non-institutionalised population. *Journal of Personality and Social Psychology*, *68*, 151–158.

Levinson, S. C. and Majid, A. (2014). Differential ineffability and the senses. *Mind and Language*, *29*, 407–427.

Lewkowicz, D. J. and Turkewitz, G. (1980). Cross-modal equivalence in early infancy: Auditory-visual intensity matching. *Developmental Psychology*, *16*, 597–607.

(1981). Intersensory interaction in newborns: Modification of visual preferences following exposure to sound. *Child Development*, *52*, 827–832.

Li, H. and Cao, Y. (2016). Who's holding the moral high ground: Religiosity and the vertical conception of morality. *Personality and Individual Differences*, *106*, 178–182.

Li, X. (2010). Conceptual Metaphor Theory and Teaching of English and Chinese Idioms. *Journal of Language Teaching And Research*, *1* (3), 206–210.

Liljenquist, K., Zhong, C-B. and Galinsky, A. (2010). The smell of virtue: Clean scents promote reciprocity and charity. *Psychological Science*, *21*, 381–383.

Lindsay, S., Scheepers, C. and Kamide, Y. (2013). Ro dash or dawdle: Verb-associated speed of motion influences eye movements during spoken sentence comprehension. *PLoS ONE*, *8* (6), e67187.

Linell, P. (1998). *Approaching Dialogue: Talk, Interaction and Contexts in Dialogic al Perspectives*, Amsterdam: John Benjamins.

Lipowski, Z. J. (1988). Somatization: The concept and its clinical application. *American Journal of Psychiatry*, *145* (11), 1358–1368.

Littlemore, J. (2001). Metaphoric competence: A possible language learning strength of students with a holistic cognitive style? *TESOL Quarterly*, *35* (3), 459–491.

(2015). *Metonymy: Hidden Shortcuts in Language, Thought and Communication*, Cambridge: Cambridge University Press.

(2017). On the role of embodied cognition in the understanding and use of metonymy. In B. Hampe (ed.) *Metaphor, Embodied Cognition and Discourse*, Cambridge: Cambridge University Press.

Littlemore, J. and Kwong, R. (forthcoming). The use of metaphoric gestures by speakers of English as a first or second language: a comparative case study, In C. Lee (ed.) Language Choice, Use, and Pedagogies in the Bilingual Context, Berlin: Springer.

Littlemore, J. and Turner (in prep.). A comparison of metaphor use by synaesthetes and non-synaesthetes.

Littlemore, J., Turner, S. and Alexander, H. (in prep.). Investigating the Relationship between Metaphor, Gender and Social Distance.

Littlemore, J., Pérez-Sobrino, P., Leung, D. and Julich, N. (forthcoming). What happens to word-colour associations when we speak a foreign language? In A. Piquer-Piriz and R. Alejo-Gonzalez (eds.) Metaphor in Foreign Language Instruction, Berlin: Mouton de Gruyter.

Littlemore, J., Turner, S., Tuck, P. and Cassell, C. (in prep.). Soapy conveyor belts and wet sponges: The role of metaphor in evaluative conversations about the workplace.

Littlemore, J. and Turner, S. (in press). Metaphors in communication about pregnancy loss, Metaphor and the Social World.

Littlemore, J., Duffy, S., Turner, S., Pérez-Sobrino, P., Woodin, G. and Winter, B. (in prep.) Maths, music and metaphor: Conceptual developments in 5–8-year-old children.

Liu, M.-J., Shih, W.-L. and Ma, L.-Y. (2011). Are children with Asperger syndrome creative in divergent thinking and feeling? A brief report. Res. Autism Spectr. Disord. 5, 294–298. doi: 10.1016/j.rasd.2010.04.011.

Lossifova, R. and Marmolejo-Ramos, F. (2012). Spatial and temporal deixis: The role of age and vision in the ontogeny of a child's spatial and temporal cognition. Journal of Speech and Language Pathology, 2 (2), 75–98.

Lourenco, S. F. and Longo, M. R. (2010). General magnitude system in young infants. Psychological Science, 21, 873–881.

  (2011). Origins and the development of generalized magnitude representation. In S. Dehaene and E. Brannon (eds.) Space, Time and Number in the Brain: Searching for the Foundations of Mathematical Thought, Amsterdam: Elsevier, pp. 225–244.

Louwerse, M. (2008). Embodied relations are encoded in language. Psychonomic Bulletin and Review, 15, 838–844.

Low, G., Littlemore, J. and Koester, A. (2008). The use of metaphor in three university lectures. Applied Linguistics, 29 (3), 428–455.

Low, S. M. (1994). Embodied Metaphors: Nerves as lived experience. In T. J. Csordas (ed.) Embodiment and Experience: The Existential Ground of Culture and Self (Cambridge Studies in Medical Anthropology), Cambridge: Cambridge University Press, pp. 139–162.

Lowe, M. (2017). Sounds Big: The Effects of Acoustic Pitch on Product Perceptions. Journal of Marketing Research, 54 (2), 331–347.

Lynott, D. and Connell, L. (2010). Embodied conceptual combination. Frontiers in Psychology, 1, 1–14.

Lynott, D., Corker, K. S., Wortman, J., Connell, L., Donnellan, M. B., Lucas, R. E. and O'Brien, K. (2014). Replication of "Experiencing Physical Warmth Promotes Interpersonal Warmth". Social Psychology, 45, 216–222.

Maalej, Z. (2004) Figurative language in anger expressions in Tunisian Arabic: An extended view of embodiment. *Metaphor and Symbol*, *19* (1), 51–76.

Maalej, Z. A. and Yu, N. (eds.) (2011). *Embodiment Via Body Parts: Studies from Various Languages and Cultures*, Amsterdam and Philadelphia, PA: John Benjamins.

MacCormac, E. R. (1986). Creative metaphors. *Metaphor and Symbolic Activity*, *1*, 171–184.

Macedonia, M. (2014). Bringing back the body into the mind: Gestures enhance word learning in foreign language. *Frontiers in Psychology*, *5*, 1–7.

Macedonia, M. and Klimesch, W. (2014). Long-term effects of gestures on memory for foreign language words trained in the classroom. *Mind, Brain and Education*, *8* (2), 74–88.

Macedonia, M., Müller, K. and Friederici, A. D. (2010). The impact of iconic gestures on language word learning and its neural substrate. *Human Brain Mapping*, *32*, 982–998.

MacKay, G. and Shaw, A. (2004). A comparative study of figurative language in children with autistic spectrum disorders. *Child Language Teaching and Therapy*, *20* (1), 13–32.

Maglio, S. and Trope, Y. (2012). Disembodiment: Abstract construal attenuates the influence of contextual bodily state in judgment. *Journal of Experimental Psychology: General*, *141* (2), 211–216.

Mahon, B. and Carramazza, A. (2008). A critical look at the embodied cognition hypothesis and a new proposal for grounding conceptual content. *Journal of Physiology*, *102* (1–3), 59–70.

Mairs, N. (1996). *Waist High in the World: A Life among the Disabled*, Boston MA: Beacon Press.

Majid, A. and Burenhult, N. (2014). Odors are expressable in language, as long as you speak the right language. *Cognition*, *130* (2), 266–270.

Mandler, J. (2005). How to build a baby: III. Image schemas and the transition to verbal thought. In B. Hampe (ed.) *From Perception to Meaning: Image Schemas in Cognitive Linguistics*, Amsterdam: Mouton de Gruyter, pp. 137–164.

Marin, A., Reimann, M. and Castano, R. (2014). Metaphors and creativity: Direct, moderating and mediating effects. *Journal of Consumer Psychology*, *24* (2), 290–297.

Marks, L. E. (1975). On colored hearing synesthesia: Cross-modal translations of sensory dimensions. *Psychological Bulletin*, *82*, 303–331.

(1982a). Bright sneezes and dark coughs, loud sunlight and soft moonlight. *Journal of Experimental Psychology: Human Perception and Performance*, *8*, 177–193.

(1982b). Synaesthesic perception and poetic metaphor. *Journal of Experimental Psychology: Human Perception and Performance*, *8*, 15–23.

(2013). Weak synesthesia in perception and language. In J. Simner and E. Hubbard (eds.) *The Oxford Handbook of Synesthesia*, Oxford: Oxford University Press.

Marks, L. E., Hammeal, R. J. and Bornstein, M. H. (1987). *Perceiving Similarity and Comprehending Metaphor*, Chicago: Chicago University Press.

Martel, L. F. and Biller, H. B. (1987). *Stature and Stigma: the Biopsychosocial Development of Short Males*, Lexington, MA: Lexington Books.

Martin, J. and White, P. (2005). *The Language of Evaluation: Appraisal in English*, Basingstoke: Palgrave MacMillan.

Mashal, N. and Kasirer, A. (2011). Thinking maps enhance metaphoric competence in children with autism and learning disabilities. *Research in Developmental Disabilities*, *32*, 2045–2054.

Mashal, N., Faust, M., Hendler, T. and Jung-Beeman, M. (2007). An fMRI investigation of the neural correlates underlying the processing of novel metaphoric expressions. *Brain and Language*, *100*, 115–126.

Matlock, T. (2004). Fictive motion as cognitive simulation. *Memory and Cognition*, *32* (8), 1389–1400.

Matsuki, K. (1995). Metaphors of anger in Japanese. In J. R. Taylor and R. E. MacLaury (eds.), *Language and the Cognitive Construal of the World*, Berlin: de Gruyter, pp. 137–151.

Matthews, J. and Matlock, T. (2011). Understanding the link between spatial distance and social distance. *Social Psychology*, *42* (3), 1850192.

Maurer, D. (1993). Neonatal synaesthesia: Implications for processing of speech and faces. In B. de Boysson-Bardies, S. de Schoenen, P. Jusczyk, P. Mc Neilage and J. Morton (eds.) *Developmental Neurocognition: Speech and Face Processing in the First Year of Life*, Dordrecht, The Netherlands: Kluwer, pp. 109–124.

McCafferty, S. (2004). Space for cognition: Gesture and second language learning. *International Journal of Applied Linguistics*, *14* (1), 148–165.

McClelland, D. and Burnham, D. (2008). *Power is the Great Motivator*, Boston, MA: Harvard Business Press.

McGlone, M. (1996). Conceptual metaphors and figurative language interpretation: Food for thought? *Journal of Memory and Language*, *35*, 544–565.

  (2007). What is the explanatory value of a conceptual metaphor? *Language and Communication*, *27*, 109–126.

McGlone, F., Howard, M. and Roberts, N. (2002). Brain activation to passive observation of grasping actions. In M. Stamenov and V. Gallese (eds.) *Mirror Neurons and the Evolution of Brain and Language*, Amsterdam: John Benjamins Publishing Company, 125–134.

McMullen, L. and Conway, J. (2002). Conventional metaphors for depression. In S. R. Fussell (ed.) *The Verbal Communication of Emotions: Interdisciplinary Perspectives*, London: Taylor and Francis., pp. 167–181.

McNeill, D. (2005). *Gesture and Thought*, Chicago: University of Chicago Press.

McQuarrie, E. F. and Mick, D. (2003). The contribution of semiotic and rhetorical perspectives to the explanation of visual persuasion in advertising. In L. Scott and R. Batra (eds.) *Persuasive Imagery: A Consumer Response Perspective*, Mahwah, NJ: Lawrence Erlbaum, pp. 191–221.

McRae, K., Cree, G. S., Seidenberg, M. S. and McNorgan, C. (2005). Semantic feature production norms for a large set of living and nonliving things. *Behavioural Research Methods*, *37*, 547–559.

Meier, B. and Dionne, S. (2009). Downright sexy: Verticality, implicit power, and perceived physical attractiveness. *Social Cognition*, *27*, 883–892.

Meier, B. and Robinson, M. (2004). Why the sunny side is up. *Psychological Science*, *15*, 243–247.

——— (2006). Does 'feeling down' mean seeing down? Depressive symptoms and vertical selective attention. *Journal of Research in Personality*, *41*, 451–461.

Meier, B., Selbom, M. and Wygant, D. B. (2007). Failing to take the moral high ground: Psychopathy and the vertical representation of morality. *Personality and Individual Differences*, *43* (4), 757–767.

Meier, B., Robinson, M., Crawford, L. and Ahlvers, W. (2007). When 'light'and 'dark' thoughts become light and dark responses: Affect biases brightness judgements. *Emotion*, *7*, 366–376.

Meir, I. (2010) Iconicity and metaphor: Constraints on metaphorical extension of iconic forms. *Language*, *86* (4), 865–896.

Melogno, S., Pinto, M. A. and Levi, G. (2012). Metaphor and metonymy in ASD children: A critical review from a developmental perspective. *Research in Autistic Spectrum Disorders*, *6*, 1289–1296.

Merabet, L. and Pascuale-Leone, A. (2010). Neural reorganization following sensory loss: The opportunity of change. *Natural Review of Neurosciences*, *11* (1), 44–52.

Meteyard, L., Rodriguez Cuadrado, S., Bahrami, B. and Vigliocco, G. (2012). Coming of age: A review of embodiment and the neuroscience of semantics. *Cortex*, *48* (7), pp. 788–804.

Miall, D. S. (1987). Metaphor and affect: The problem of creative thought. *Metaphor and Symbolic Activity*, *2*, 81–96.

Michalak, J., Rohde, K. and Troje, N. F. (2015). How we walk affects what we remember: Gait modifications through biofeedback change negative affective memory bias. *Journal of Behavior Therapy and Experimental Psychiatry*, *46*, 121–125.

Mikolajczuk, A. (1998). The metonymic and metaphoric conceptualization of 'anger' in Polish. In A. Athanasjadou and E. Tabakowska (eds.) *Speaking of Emotions: Conceptualization and Expression*, Berlin: Mouton, pp. 153–191.

Miles L. K., Nind L. K. and Macrae C. N. (2010b). Moving through time. *Psychological Science*, *21*, 222–223.

Miles L. K., Betkra, E., Pendry L. and Macrae C. N. (2010a). Rapid communication mapping temporal constructs: Actions reveal that time is a place. *The Quarterly Journal of Experimental Psychology*, *63* (11), 2113–2119.

Miller, L. C., Murphy, R. and Buss, A. H. (1981). Consciousness of body: Private and public. *Journal of Personality and Social Psychology*, *41* (2), 397.

Mitchell, D. and Snyder, S. (2006). Narrative prosthesis and the materiality of metaphor. In L. J. David (ed.) *The Disability Studies Reader*, London: Routledge, pp. 205–220.

Mittal, V. A., Tessner K. D., McMillan A. L., Delawalla Z., Trotman H. D. and Walker E. F. (2006). Gesture behavior in unmedicated schizotypal adolescents. *Journal of Abnormal Psychology*, *115*, 351– 358.

Mittelberg, I. (2008). Peircean semiotics meets conceptual metaphor: Iconic modes in gestural representations of grammar. In A. Cienki and C. Müller (eds.), *Metaphor and Gesture*, Amsterdam/Philadelphia, PA: John Benjamins, pp. 115–154.

——— (2013). The exbodied mind: Cognitive-semiotic principles as motivating forces in gesture. In C. Müller, A. Cienki, E. Fricke, S. H. Ladewig, D. McNeill and S.

Teßendorf (eds.), *Body – Language – Communication. An International Handbook on Multimodality in Human Interaction*, 1, Berlin: De Gruyter, pp. 755–784.

Mittelberg, I. and Waugh, L. (2009). Metonymy first, metaphor second, a cognitive semiotic approach to multimodal figures of thought in co-speech gesture. In C. Forceville and M. Urios-Aparisi (eds.) *Multimodal Metaphor*, Berlin: Mouton de Gruyter, pp. 336–350.

Mo, S., Su, Y., Chan, R. and Liu, J. (2008). Comprehension of metaphor and irony in schizophrenia during remission: The role of theory of mind and IQ. *Psychiatry Research, 157* (1–3), 21–29.

Molnar-Szakacs, I., Wu, A., Robles, F. and Iaconabi, M. (2007). Do you see what I mean? Corticospinal excitability during observation of culture-specific gestures. *PLoS ONE, 2* (7), e626.

Morrall, C. (2003). *Astonishing Splashes of Colour*, Birmingham: Tindal Street Press.

Most, S. B., Verbeck Sorber, A. and Cunningham, J. G. (2005). Auditory Stroop reveals implicit gender associations in adults and children. *Journal of Experimental Social Psychology, 43*, 287–294.

Mould, T., Oades, L. and Crowe, T. (2010). The use of metaphor for understanding and managing psychotic experiences: A systematic review. *Journal of Mental Health, 19* (3), 282–293.

Müller, C. (2008). *Metaphors Dead and Alive, Sleeping and Waking*, Chicago: University of Chicago Press.

Müller, C. and Ladewig, S. H. (2013). Metaphors for sensorimotor experiences: Gestures as embodied and dynamic conceptualizations of balance in dance lessons. In M. Borkent, B. Dancyger and J. Hinnell (eds.) *Language and the Creative Mind*, Stanford, CA: CSLI Publication, pp. 295–324.

Müller, C. and Tag, S. (2010). The dynamics of metaphor: Foregrounding and activating metaphoricity in conversational interaction. *Cognitive Semiotics, 6*, 85–120.

Mulvenna, C. (2013). Synaesthesia and creativity. In J. Simner and C. Hubbard (eds.) *The Oxford Handbook of Synaesthesia*, Oxford: Oxford University Press, pp. 607–631.

Musolff, A. (2004). *Metaphor and Political Discourse: Analogical Reasoning in Debates about Europe*, Basingstoke: Palgrave MacMillan.

(2014). Metaphors: Sources for intercultural misunderstanding? *International Journal of Language and Culture, 1* (1), 242–259.

(2017). Metaphor and Cultural Cognition. In F. Sharifian (ed.) *Advances in Cultural Linguistics*, Springer Singapore, pp. 325–344.

Nadeau, J. W. (2006). Metaphorically speaking: The use of metaphors in grief therapy. *Illness Crisis and Loss, 14* (3), 201–221.

Neufeld, J., Sinke, C., Dillo, W., Emrich, H. M., Szycik, G. R., Dim, D., Bleich, S. and Zedler, M. (2012). The neural correlates of coloured music: A functional MRI investigation of auditory–visual synaesthesia. *Neuropsychologia, 50* (1), 85–89.

Norbury, C. (2005). The relationship between theory of mind and metaphor: Evidence from children with language impairment and Autistic Spectrum Disorder. *British Journal of Developmental Psychology, 23*, 383–399.

Núñez, R. (2005). Do real numbers really move? Language, thought, and gesture: The embodied cognitive foundations of mathematics. In F. Iida, R. Pfeifer, L. Steels and Y. Kuniyoshi (eds.), *Embodied Artificial Intelligence*, Berlin: Springer-Verlag, (pp. 54–73).

Núñez, R. and Sweetser, E. (2006). With the future behind them: Convergent evidence from Aymara language and gesture in the crosslinguistic comparison of spatial construals of time. *Cognitive Science, 30*: 401–450.

Ohala, J. J. (1994). The frequency code underlies the sound-symbolic use of voice pitch. In N. Hinton and J. J. Ohala (eds.) *Sound Symbolism*, Cambridge: Cambridge University Press, pp. 325–347.

Okita, S. and Schwartz, L. (2006). Young children's understanding of animacy and entertainment robots. *International Journal of Humanoid Robotics, 3* (3), 1–20.

Olofson, E. L., Casey, D., Oluyedun, O. A., Van Herwegen, J., Becerra, A. and Rundblad, G. (2014). Youth with autism spectrum disorder comprehend lexicalized and novel primary conceptual metaphors. *Journal of Autism and Developmental Disorders*, 1–16.

Olofsson J. and Gottfried, J. (2015). The muted sense: Neurocognitive limitations of olfactory language. *Trends in Cognitive Sciences, 19* (6), 314–321.

Ooi, R. L., Wu, B. and He, Z. J. (2001). Distance determined by the angular declination below the horizon. *Nature, 414*, 197–200.

Ortony, A., Teynolds, R. E. and Wilson, P. T. (1984). Sources of difficulty in the young child's understanding of metaphorical language. *Child Development, 55*, 1588–1606.

Özçalişkan, Ş. (2002). *Metaphors We Move By: A Crosslinguistic-Developmental Analysis of Metaphorical Motion Events in English and Turkish*, Berkeley: University of California.

(2004). *Time can't fly, but a bird can*: Learning to think and talk about time as spatial motion in English and Turkish. *European Journal of English Studies, 8* (3), 309–336,

Özçalişkan, S. (2005). On learning to draw the distinction between physical and metaphorical motion: Is metaphor an early emerging cognitive and linguistic capacity? *Journal of child language, 32*, 291.

(2007). Metaphors we move by: Children's developing understanding of metaphorical motion in typologically distinct languages. *Metaphor and Symbol, 22*, 147–168.

Ozturk, O., Krehm, M. and Vouloumanos, A. (2013). Sound symbolism in infancy? Evidence for sound-shape: Cross-modal correspondences in 4-month-olds. *Journal of Experimental Child Psychology, 114* (2), 173–186.

Papagno, C. (2001). Comprehension of metaphors and idioms in patients with Alzeimer's disease, A longitudinal study. *Brain, 124*, 1450–1460.

Papagno, C., Cappa, S. F., Forelli, A., Garavaglia, G., Laiscona, M., Capitani, E. and Vallar, G. (1995). La comprehension non letteral del linguaggio: Tartura di un test di comprensione di metafore e di espressioni idiomatche. *Archivo di Psicologia Neurologia e Psichiatroia, 4*, 402–420.

Papesh, A. H. (2015). Just out of reach: On the reliability of the action-sentence compatibility effect. *Journal of Experimental Psychology (General), 144* (6), 116–141.

Papp, P. (1982). Staging reciprocal metaphors in a couples group. *Family Process, 21* (4), 453–467.

Pecher, D., Zeelenberg, R. and Barselou, L. W. (2003). Verifying properties from different modalities for concepts produces switching costs. *Psychological Science, 14*, 119–124.

Peñalba Acitores, A., Moriyón Mojica, C., Luque Perea, S. and Cabezas Clavijo, G. (2015). La metáfora conceptual como recurso pedagógico musical para personas sordas y con discapacidad auditiva, *Actas del Congreso CNLSE de la Lengua de Signos Española*, 87–108.

Pérez-Sobrino, P., Littlemore, J. and Houghton, D. (2018). The role of figurative complexity in the comprehension and appreciation of advertisements. *Applied Linguistics*.

Perlman, M. and Gibbs, R. (2013). Sensorimotor simulation in speaking, gesturing and understanding. In C. Müller, A. Cienki, E. Fricke, S. Ladewig, D. McNeill and S. Tessendorf (eds.) *Body-Language-Communication: An International Handbook on Multimodality in Human Interaction*, (vol. 1). Walter de Gruyter,. pp. 512–532.

Phelps, E. A. (2004). Human emotion and memory: Interactions of the amygdala and hippocampal complex. *Current Opinion in Neurobiology, 14*, 198–202.

Ping, R., Dhillon, S. and Beilock, S. (2009). Reach for what you like: The body's role in shaping preferences, *Emotion Review, 1* (2), 140–150.

Pollick, F., Paterson, H., Bruderlin, A. and Sanford, A. (2001). Perceiving affect from arm movement. *Cognition, 82*, 51–61.

Popova, Y. (2005). Image schemas and verbal synaesthesia, In B. Hampe and J. E. Grady (eds.) *From Perception to Meaning: Image Schemas in Cognitive Linguistics*, Berlin: Mouton de Gruyter, pp. 395–419.

Pragglejaz Group (2007). MIP: A Method for Identifying Metaphorically Used Words in Discourse. *Metaphor and Symbol, 22* (1), 1–39.

Proust, M. (1908). *A La Recherche du Temps Perdu*, New Haven, CT: Yale University Press.

Ptzemyslaw, J., van der Lans, J. and Hermans, C. (1998). Metaphor theories and religious language understanding. *Metaphor and Symbol, 13*, 287–292.

Ramachandran, V., Blakeslee, S. and Shah, N. (1998). *Phantoms in the Brain: Probing the Mysteries of the Human Mind*, New York: William Morrow.

Ramachandran, V. and Hubbard, E. (2001). Synaesthesia: A window into perception, thought and language. *Journal of Consciousness Studies, 8* (12), 3–34.

Richardson, D. and Matlock, T. (2007). The integration of figurative language and static depictions: An eye movement study of fictive motion. *Cognition, 102* (1), 129–138.

Richardson, M. P., Strange, B. A. and Dolan, R. J. (2004). Encoding of emotional memories depends on amygdala and hippocampus and their interactions. *Nature Neuroscience, 7*, 278–285.

Richardson, P. (2012). A closer walk: A study of the interaction between metaphors related to movement and proximity and presuppositions about the reality of belief in Christian and Muslim testimonials. *Metaphor and the Social World, 2* (2), 233–261.

Riding, R. J. (1991). *Cognitive Styles Analysis*, Birmingham: Learning and Training Technology.

Rieser, J. J., Garing, A. E. and Young, M. F. (1994). Imagery, action, and young children's spatial orientation: It's not being there that counts, it's what one has in mind. *Child Development*, *65* (5), 1262–1278.

Rinaldi, L., Vecchi, T., Fantino, M., Merabet, L. and Cattaneo, Z. (2017). The ego-moving metaphor of time relies on visual experience: No representation of time along the sagittal space axis in the blind, *Journal of Experimental Psychology*, http://dx.doi.org/10.1037/xge0000373.

Ritchie, I. (1991). Fusion of the Faculties: A Study of the Language of the Senses in Hausaland. In D. Howes (ed.) *The Varieties of Sensory Experience: A Sourcebook in the Anthropology of the Senses*, Toronto: University of Toronto Press, pp. 193–195.

Rittenhouse, R. K., Morreau, L. E. and Iran-Nejad, A. (1981). Metaphor and conservation in deaf and hard-of-hearing children. *American Annals of the Deaf*, *126* (4), 450–453.

Rizzolatti, G. and Buccino, G. (2005). The mirror-neuron system and its role in imitation and language. In S. Dehaene, J.-R. Duhamel, M. D. Hauser and G. Rizzolatti (eds.) *From Monkey Brain to Human Brain*, Cambridge, MA: MIT Press, pp. 213–234.

Rizzolatti, G., Fadiga, L., Gallese, V. and Fogassi, L. (1996). Premotor cortex and the recognition of motor actions. *Brain Research*, *3*, 131–141.

Roberts, J. V. and Herman, C. P. (1986). The psychology of height: An empirical review. In C. P. Herman, M. P. Zanna and E. T. Higgins (eds.) *Physical Appearance, Stigma and Social Behaviour*, Hillsdale, NJ: Erlbaum, pp. 113–140.

Robinson, M. D., Zabelina, D. L., Ode, S. & Moeller, S. K. (2008). The vertical nature of dominance–submission: Individual differences in vertical attention. *Journal of Research in Personality*, *42*, 933–948.

Robinson, M. D. and Fetterman, A. K. (2015). The embodiment of success and failure as forward versus backward movements. *PLoS ONE*, *10* (2), e0117285. doi:10.1371/journal.pone.0117285.

Roehling, M.V. (1999). Weight-based discrimination in employment: Psychological and legal aspects. *Personnel Psychology*, *52*, 969–1016.

Rohrer, T. (2006). The body in space: Dimensions of embodiment. In J. Zlatev, T. Ziemke, R. Frank and R. Dirven, (eds.) *Body, Language and Mind*, vol. 2. Berlin: Mouton de Gruyter, 339–378.

Rosch, E., Thompson, E. and Varela, F. (1991): *The Embodied Mind: Cognitive Science and Human Experience*, Cambridge, MA: MIT Press.

Rosenblatt, P. C. (1994). *Metaphors of Family Systems Theory*, New York, Guildford.
(2000). *Parent Grief: Narratives of Loss and Relationships*, Philadelphia, PA: Brunner/Mazel.
(2007). Recovery following bereavement: Metaphor, phenomenology, and culture. *Death Studies*, *32* (1), 6–16.

Rozin, P. and Royzman, E. B. (2001). Negativity bias, negativity dominance, and contagion. *Personality and Social Psychology Review*, *5* (4), 296–320.

Ruby, P. and Decety, J. (2001). Effect of subjective perspective taking during simulation of action: A PET investigation of agency. *Nature Neuroscience*, *4*, 546–550.

Rueckert, L., Breckinridge Church, R, Avila A. and Trejo, T. (2017) Gesture enhances learning of a complex statistical concept. *Cognitive Research: Principles and Implications*, 2, 2.

Ruiz de Mendoza, F. and Galera, A. (2014). *Cognitive Modelling: A Linguistic Perspective*, Amsterdam/Philadelphia, PA: John Benjamins.

Rundblad, G. and Annaz, D. (2010). Development of metaphor and metonymy comprehension: Receptive vocabulary and conceptual knowledge. *British Journal of Developmental Psychology*, 28 (3), 547–563.

Rusconi, E., Kwan, B., Giordano, B. L., Umilta, C. and Butterworth, B. (2006). Spatial representation of pitch height: The SMARC effect. *Cognition*, 99 (2), 113–129.

Russo, N., Foxe, J. J., Brandwein, A. B., Altschuler, T., Gomes, H. and Molholm, H. (2010). Multisensory processing in children with autism: High-density electrical mapping of auditory–somatosensory integration. *Autism Research*, 3, 1–15.

Saikaluk, P., Pexman, P., Aguilera, L., Owen, W. and Sears. C. (2008). Evidence for the activation of sensorimotor information during visual word recognition: The body object interaction effect. *Cognition*, 106, 433–443.

Saj, A., Fuhrman, O., Vuileumier, P. and Boroditsky, L. (2014). Patients with left spatial neglect also neglect the 'left side' of time. *Psychological Science*, 25 (1), 207–214.

Samur, D., Lai, V. T., Hagoort, P. and Willems, R. M. (2015). Emotional context modulates embodied metaphor comprehension. *Neuropsychologia*, 78, 108–114.

San Roque, L., Kendrick, K., Norcliffe, E., Brown, P., Defina, R., Dingemanse, M., Dirksmeyer, T., Enfield, N. J., Floyd, S., Hammond, J., Rossi, G., Tufvesson, S., van Putten, S. and Majid, A. (2014). Vision words dominate in conversation across cultures, but the ranking of non-visual words varies. *Cognitive Linguistics*, 26 (1), 31–60.

Sato, M. and Bergen, B. K. (2013). The case of the missing pronouns: Does mentally simulated perspective play a functional role in the comprehension of person. *Cognition*, 127 (3), 361–374

Saygin, A. P., McCullough, S., Alac, M. and Emmorey, K. (2010). Modulation of BOLD response in motion-sensitive lateral temporal cortex by real and fictive motion sentences. *Journal of Cognitive Neurosciences*, 22 (11), 2480–2490.

Schnall, S. (2016). Disgust as embodied loss aversion. *European Review of Social Psychology*, 28, 50–94.

(2017). Social and contextual constraints on embodied perception. *Perspectives on Psychological Science*, 12, 325–340.

Schnall, S., Benton, J. and Harvey, S. (2008). With a clean conscience: Cleanliness reduces the severity of moral judgments. *Psychological Science*, 19, 1219–1222.

Schnall, S., Haidt, J., Clore, G. L. and Jordan, A. H. (2008). Disgust as embodied moral judgment. *Personality and Social Psychology Bulletin*, 34, 1096–1109.

Schnall, S., Harber, K., Stefanucci, J. and Proffit, D. R. (2008). Social support and the perception of geographical slant. *Journal of Experimental Social Psychology*, 44, 1246–1255.

Schneider, I. K., Rutjens, B. T., Jostmann, N. B. and Lakens, D. (2011). Weighty matters: Importance feels heavy. *Social Psychological and Personality Science*, 2 (5), 474–478.

Schneider, W., Eschman, A. and Zuccolotti, A. (2002). *E-Prime Reference Guide*, Pittsburgh, PA: Psychology Software Tools.

Schroder, U. (2009). Preferential metaphorical conceptualizations in everyday discourse about love in Brazilian and German speech communities. *Metaphor and Symbol*, *24*, 105–120.

Schubert, T. (2004). The power in your hand: Gender differences in bodily feedback from making a fist. *Personality and Social Psychology Bulletin*, *30* (6).

—— (2005). Your highness: Vertical positions as perceptual symbols of power. *Journal of Personality and Social Psychology*, *89* (1–21), 757–769.

Schubert, T. W. and Koole, S. L. (2009). The embodied self: Making a fist enhances men's power-related self-conceptions. *Journal of Experimental Social Psychology*, *45*, 828–834.

Schubert, T. W. and Semin, G. R. (2009). Embodiment as a unifying perspective for psychology. *European Journal of Social Psychology*, *39* (7), 1135–1141.

Schwartz, M. B., O'Neill Chambills, H., Brownel, K. D., Blair, S. N. and Billington, C. (2003). Weight bias among health professionals specializing in obesity. *Obesity Research*, *11* (9), 1033–1039.

Searles, H. (1962). The differentiation between concrete and metaphorical thinking in the recovering schizophrenic patient, *Journal of the American Psychoanalytic Association*.

Semin, G. and Cacioppo, J. (2009). From embodied representation to co-regulation. In J. A. Pineda (ed.) *Mirror Neuron Systems*, New York: Humana Press, 107–120.

Semino, E. (2010). Descriptions of pain, metaphor and embodied simulation. *Metaphor and Symbol*, *25*, 205–226.

—— (2011). Metaphor, creativity, and the experience of pain across genres. In J. Swann, R. Carter and R. Pope (eds.) *Creativity, Language, Literature: The State of the Art*, Basingstoke: Palgrave Macmillan, pp. 83–102.

—— et al. (2014). 'Metaphor in end-of-life care' http://gtr.rcuk.ac.uk/project/864ABFAA-A301–42CD-8DA1–1FF5967527AF.

Semino, E. and Koller, V. (2009). Metaphor, politics and gender: A case study from Italy. In K. Ahrens (ed.) *Politics, Gender and Conceptual Metaphors*, Basingstoke: Palgrave Macmillan, pp. 36–61.

Sharifian, F. (2008). Conceptualizations of *del* 'heart-stomah' in Persian. In F. Sharifian, R. Dirven, Y. Ning and S. Niemeier (eds.) *Culture, Body, and Language: Conceptualizations of Internal Body Organs across Cultures and Languages*, Berlin: Mouton de Gruyter, pp. 247–266.

—— (2017). *Cultural Linguistics*, Cognitive Studies in Cultural Contexts, 8, Amsterdam: John Benjamin Publishing Company.

Sharifian, F., Dirven, R., Yu, N. and Niemeier, S. (eds.) (2008). *Culture, Body, and Language: Conceptualizations of Internal Body Organs across Cultures and Languages*, Berlin and New York: Mouton de Gruyter.

Shaw, M. (1996). How metaphoric interpretations effect dynamic insight: Development of a model to represent how metaphoric interpretations effect dynamic insight in psychotherapy patients, *Unpublished PhD Thesis*, University of California, Berkeley.

Shayan, S., Ozturk, O. and Sicoli, M. A. (2011). The thickness of pitch: Cross-modal metaphors in Farsi, Turkish, and Zapotec. *The Senses and Society*, *6* (1), 96–105.

Shen, Y. 1997). Cognitive constraints on poetic figures. *Cognitive Linguistics, 8* (1), 33–71.

Sherman, G. and Clore, G. (2009). The color of sin: White and black are perceptual symbols of moral purity and pollution. *Psychological Science, 20* (8), 1019–1025.

Schinazi, V. R., Thrash, T. and Chebat, D. R. (2016). Spatial navigation by congenitally blind individuals. *WIREs* Cognitive Science, *7*, 37–58.

Shintel, H., Nusbaum, H. C. and Okrent, A. (2006). Analogue acoustic expression in speech communication, *Journal of Memory and Language, 55*, 167–177.

Simner, J. (2007). Beyond perceptuion: Synaesthesia as a psycholinguistic phenomenon. *Trends in Cognitive Science, 11* (1), 23–29.

Simner, J., Ward, J., Lanz, M., Jansaric, A., Noonan, K., Glovera, L and Oakley, D. (2004). Non-random associations of graphemes to colours in synaesthetic and non-synaesthetic populations. *Cognitive Neuropsychology, 22* (8), 1069–1085.

Siqueira, M. and Gibbs, R. W. (2007). Children's acquisition of primary metaphors: A cross linguistic study. *Organon (UFRGS), 21*, 161–179.

Siqueira, M. and Marques, D. F. (2016). Figurative language comprehension by hearing impaired children. *Paper presented at the 11th International Conference of the International Association of Researching and Applying Metaphor*, Freie Universitat, Berlin.

Siqueira, M., Marques, D. F. and Gibbs, R. W. (2016). Metaphor-related figurative language comprehension in clinical populations: A critical review. *Scripta, Belo Horizonte, 20* (40), 36–60.

Skårderud, F. (2007). Eating one's words, Part 1: 'Concretised metaphors' and reflective function in anorexia nervosa – An interview study. *European Eating Disorders Review, 15*, 163–174.

Skipper, J., Goldin-Meadow, S., Nusbaum, H. and Small, S. (2007). Speech-associated gestures, Broca's area and the human mirror system. *Brain and Language, 101* (3), 260–277.

Slepian, M., Weisbuch, M., Rule, N. O. and Ambady, N. (2011). Tough and tender: Embodied categorization of gender. *Psychological Science, 22* (1), 26–28.

Slepian, M. L., Masicampo, E. J., Toosi, Negin R. and Ambady, N. (2012). The physical burdens of secrecy. *Journal of Experimental Psychology: General, 141* (4), 619–624.

Slepian, M. L. and Ambody, N. (2014). Simulating sensorimotor metaphors: Novel metaphors influence sensory judgments. *Cognition, 130*, 309–314.

Slobin, D. (1996). From "thought and language" to "thinking for speaking". In J. Gumperz and S. Levinson (eds.) *Rethinking Linguistic Relativity*, New York: Cambridge University Press, pp. 70–96.

Slobin D. (2005), Linguistic representations of motion events: What is signifier and what is signified? In C. Maeder, O. Fischer and W. Herlofsky (eds.) *Iconicity Inside Out: Iconicity in Language and Literature 4*, Amsterdam/Philadelphia, PA: John Benjamins.

Smith, L. B. and Sera, M. D. (1992). A developmental analysis of the polar structure of dimensions. *Cognitive Psychology, 24*, 99–142.

Speed, L. and Vigliocco, G. (2014). Eye movements reveal the dynamic simulation of speed in language. *Cognitive Science, 38*, 367–382.

Speer, N., Zacks, J. and Reynolds, J. (2007). Human brain activity time-locked to narrative event boundaries. *Psychological Science, 18* (5), 449–455.

Spence, C. (2015). On the psychological impact of food colour. *Flavour, 4* (21).

Spence, C., Nickolls, M. and Driver, J. (2001). The cost of expecting events in the wrong sensory modality. *Perception and Psychophysics, 63* (2), 330–336.

Spence, C., Wan, X., Woods, A., Velasco, C., Deng, J., Youssef, J. and Deroy, O. (2015). On tasty colours and colorful tastes? Assessing, explaining, and utilizing crossmodal correspondences between colours and basic tastes, *Flavour, 4* (23), 1–17.

Srinivasan, M. and Carey, S. (2010). The long and short of it: On the nature and origin of functional overlap between representations of space and time. *Cognition, 16,* 217–241.

Stamenov, M. (2002). Some features that make mirror neurons and the human language faculty unique. In M. Stamenov and V. Gallese (eds.) *Mirror Neurons and the Evolution of Brain and Language,* Amsterdam: John Benjamins Publishing Company, pp. 249–272.

Stanfield, R. A. and Zwaan, R. A. (2001). The effect of implied orientation derived from verbal context on picture recognition. *Psychological Science, 12,* 153–156.

Stayman, D. and Kardes, F. (1992). Spontaneous inference processes in advertizing: Effects of need for cognition and self-monitoring on inference generation and utlization. *Journal of Consumer Psychology, 1* (2), 125–142.

Stec, K. and Sweetser, E. (2013). Borobudur and Chartres: Religious spaces as performative real-space blends. In R. Caballero and J. E. Diaz Vera (eds.) *Sensuous Cognition, Explorations into Human Sentience,: Imagination, Emotion and Perception,* Berlin: Mouton de Gruyter, pp. 265–291.

Steen, G. (2015). Developing, testing and interpreting deliberate metaphor theory. *Journal of Pragmatics, 90,* 67–72.

Steen, G., Reijnierse, G. and Burgers, C. (2014). When do natural language metaphors influence reasoning? A follow-up study to Thibodeau and Boroditsky (2013). *PLoS ONE* DOI: 10. 1371/journal.pone.0113536.

Stefanowitsch, A. and Goschler, J. (2009). Sex differences in the usage of spatial metaphors: A case study of political language. In K. Ahrens (ed.) *Politics, Gender and Conceptual Metaphors,* Basingstoke: Palgrave Macmillan, pp. 166–183.

Stepper, S. and Strack, F. (1993). Proprioceptive determinants of emotional and nonemotional feelings. *Journal of Personality and Social Psychology, 64,* 211–220.

Stites, L. and Özçalışkan, Ş. (2012). Developmental changes in children's comprehension and explanation of spatial metaphors for time. *Journal of child language, 1.*

(2013). Teasing apart the role of cognitive and verbal factors in children's early metaphorical abilities. *Metaphor and Symbol, 28,* 116–129.

Storbeck, J. and Clore, G. (2008). Affective arousal as information: How affective arousal influences judgments, learning, and memory. Social and Personality *Psychology Compass, 2,* 1824–1843.

Strack, F., Martin, L. L. and Stepper, S. (1988). Inhibiting and facilitating conditions of the human smile: A nonobtrusive test of the facial feedback hypothesis. *Journal of Personality and Social Psychology, 54* (5), 768.

Straube, B., Green, A., Sass, K. and Kircher, T. (2014). Superior temporal sulcus disconnectivity during processing of metaphoric gestures in schizophrenia. *Schizophrenia Bulletin, 40* (4), 936–944.

Stroop, J. R. (1935). Studies of interference in serial verbal reactions. *Journal of Experimental Psychology, 18,* 643–662,

Swales, J. (1990). *Genre Analysis, English in Academic and Research Settings,* Cambridge: Cambridge University Press.

Sweetser, E., 1990, *From Etymology to Pragmatics,* Cambridge: Cambridge University Press.

Talmy, L. (1991). Path to realization: A typology of event conflation. Berkeley Working Papers in Linguistics, 480–519.

(1996). Fictive motion in language and "ception". In P. Bloom, M. A. Peterson, L. Nadel and M. F. Garrett (eds.) *Language and Space,* Boston, MA: MIT Press, pp. 211–276.

(2000). *Toward a Cognitive Semantics* (vols. 1–2), Cambridge, MA: Massachusetts Institute of Technology.

Taub, S. (2001). *Language from the Body: Iconicity and Metaphor in American Sign Language,* Cambridge: Cambridge University Press.

Tay, D. (2017). Exploring the metaphor-body-psychotherapy relationship. *Metaphor and Symbol, 32* (3), 178–191.

Taylor, J. (2003). *Linguistic Categorisation,* Cambridge: Cambridge University Press.

(2012). *The Mental Corpus, How Language is Represented in the Mind,* Cambridge: Cambridge University Press.

Terman, M., Terman, J. S. and Ross, D. C. (1998). A controlled trial of timed bright light and negative air ionization for treatment of winter depression. *Archives of General Psychiatry, 55,* 875–882.

Thagard, P. and Shelley, C. (2006). Emotional analogies and analogical inference. In P. Thagard (ed.) *Hot Thought Mechanisms and Applications of Emotional Cognition,* Cambridge MA: MIT Press, pp. 27–50.

Thibault, P. (2011). First-order languaging dynamics and second-order language: The distributed language view. *Ecological Psychology, 23,* 210–245.

Thibodeau P. H. and Boroditsky L. (2011). Metaphors we think with: The role of metaphor in reasoning. *PLoS ONE, 6* (2), e16782. doi:10.1371/journal.pone.0016782.

(2013). Natural language metaphors covertly influence reasoning. *PLoS ONE, 8,* e52961.

Thibodeau, P., Hendricks, R. and Boroditsky, L. (2017). Jow linguistic metaphor scaffolds reasoning. *Trends in Cognitive Sciences.*

Tomasello, M. (2003). *Constructing a Language: A Usage-based Theory of Language Acquisition,* Cambridge, MA: Harvard University Press.

Tracy, J. and Matsumoto, D. (2008). The spontaneous expression of pride and shame: Evidence for biologically innate nonverbal displays. *Proceedings of the National Academy of Sciences, 105* (33), 11655–11660.

Turatto, M., Galfano, G., Bridgeman, B. and Umilta, C. (2004). Space-independent modality-driven attentional capture in audirtory, tactile and visual systems. *Experimental Brain Rsesearch, 155,* 301–310.

Turner, S. and Littlemore, J. (in prep.). Metaphor, Personality and Religiosity.

Turner, S., Littlemore, J., Burgess, M., Fuller, D., Kuberska, K. and McGuinness, S. (forthcoming). The production of time-related metaphors by people who have experienced pregnancy loss. In A. Gargett and J. Barnden (eds.) *The Production of Metaphor*, Amsterdam: John Benjamins.

Tversky, B., Kugelmass, S. and Winter, A. (1991). Cross-cultural and developmental trends in graphic productions. *Cognitive Psychology*, *23*, 515–557.

Ureña, J-M. and Faber, P. (2010). Reviewing imagery in resemblance and non-resemblance metaphors. *Cognitive Linguistics*, *21* (1), 123–149.

Van Beek, W. E. A. (1992). The dirty smith: Smell as a social frontier among the Kapsiki/Higi of north Cameroon and north-eastern Nigeria. *Africa: Journal of the International African Institute*, *62* (1), 38–58.

Van Herwegen, J., Dimitriou, D. and Rundblad, G. (2013). Development of novel metaphor and metonymy comprehension in typically developing children and Williams syndrome. *Research in Developmental Disabilities*, *34*, 1300–1311.

Van Quaquebeke, Niels and Giessner, S. R., How Embodied Cognitions Affect Judgments: Height-Related Attribution Bias in Football Foul Calls (January 2010 2,). ERIM Report Series Reference No. ERS-2010-006-ORG. Available at SSRN: http://ssrn.com/abstract=1542487.

Viberg, Å. (1983). The verbs of perception: A typological study. *Linguistics*, *21*, 123–162.

    (1993). Crosslinguistic perspectives on lexical organization and lexical progression. In K. Hyltenstam and Å. Viberg (eds.) *Progression and Regression in Language: Sociocultural, Neuropsychological and Linguistic Perspectives*, 340–385. Cambridge: Cambridge University Press.

Vidali, A. (2010). Seeing what we know: Disability and theories of metaphor. *Journal of Literary and Cultural Disability Studies*, *4* (1), 33–54.

Vosniadou, S. (1987). Children and metaphors. *Child Development*, *58*, 870–885.

    (1989). Context and the Development of Metaphor Comprehension. *Metaphor and Symbolic Activity*, *4*, 159–171.

Waggoner, J. E. and Palermo, D. S. (1989). Betty is a bouncing bubble: Children's comprehension of emotion-descriptive metaphors. *Developmental Psychology*, *25*, 152–163.

Wagner, K. and Dobkins, K. R. (2011). Synaesthetic associations decrease during infancy. *Psychological Science*, *22* (8), 1067–1072.

Walker, P., Bremner, J. G., Mason, U., Spring, J. Mattock, K. Slater, A. and Johnson, P. (2010). Preverbal infants' sensitivity to synaesthetic cross-modality correspondences. *Psychological Science*, *21*, 21–25.

Wallbott, N. (1998). Bodily expression of emotion. *European Journal of Social Psychology*, *28*, 879–896.

Wallentin, M., Nielsen, A. H., Vuust, P., Dohne, A., Roepstorff, A. and Lund, T. E. (2011). BOLD response to motion verbs in left posterior middle temporal gyrus during short story comprehension. *Brain and Language*, *119* (3), 221–225.

Walsh, V. (2003). A Theory of Magnitude, common cortical metrics of time, space and quantity. *Trends in Cognitive Science*, *7* (11), 483–488.

Walther, S. and Mittal, V. (2016). Why we should take a closer look at gestures. *Schizophrenia Bulletin*, *42* (2): 259–261.

Walther, S., Stegmayer K., Sulzbacher J. et al. (2015). Nonverbal social communication and gesture control in schizophrenia. *Schizophrenia Bulletin, 41,* 338–345.

Wan, X., Woods, A. T., van den Bosch, J., McKenzie, K. J., Velasco, C. and Spence, C. (2014). Cross-cultural differences in cross-modal correspondences between tastes and visual features. *Frontiers of Psychology and Cognition, 5,* 1365.

Wang, C. and Dowker, A. (2010). A cross-cultural study of metaphoric understanding, In G. Low, Z. Todd, A. Deignan and L. Cameron (eds.) *Researching and Applying Metaphor in the Real World,* Amsterdam: John Benjamins, pp. 105–122.

Wang, Q. and Spence, C. (2017). Assessing the role of emotional associations in mediating crossmodal correspondences between classical music and red wine. *Beverages, 3* (1).

Ward, J., Thompson-Lake, D., Ely R. and Kaminski, F. (2008). Synaesthesia, creativity and art: What is the link? *The British Journal of Psychology, 99,* 127–141.

Webb, T. L., Miles, E. and Sheeran, P. (2012). Dealing with feeling: A meta-analysis of the effectiveness of strategies derived from the process model of emotion regulation. *Psychological Bulletin, 138,* 775–808.

Wehling, E., Gamez-Djokic, V. and Aziz-Zadeh, L. (2015). Does the brain grasp politics, even when it doesn't?: Modulation of motor and premotor areas by affirmative and negated hand-action metaphors, *Paper presented at the Biennial Conference of the International Cognitive Linguistics Association, Newcastle, UK.*

Weiss, G. (1999). *Body Images: Embodiment as Intercorporality,* New York: Routledge.

Wilcox, P. (2000). *Metaphor in American Sign Language,* Washington, DC: Gallaudet University Press.

Wilcox, S. (2004). Conceptual spaces and embodied actions: Cognitive iconicity and signed languages. *Cognitive Linguistics, 15* (2), 119–147.

Willems R.M. and Hagoort P. (2007). Neural evidence for the interplay between language, gesture, and action: A review. *Brain and Language, 101,* 278–289.

Williams, J.M. (1976). Synaesthesic adjectives: A possible law of semantic change. *Language, 52,* 461–478.

Williams, L., and Bargh, J. (2008). Experiencing physical warmth influences interpersonal warmth. *Science, 322,* 606–607.

Williams-Whitney, D., Mio, J. S. and Whitney, P. (1992). Metaphor production in creative writing. *Journal of Psycholinguistic Research, 21,* 497–509.

Wills, D. D. (1977). Participant deixis in English and baby talk. In C. E. Snow and C. A. Ferguson, eds. *Talking to Children: Language Input and Acquisition,* Cambridge: Cambridge University Press, pp. 271–298.

Wilson, N. and Gibbs, R. (2007). Real and imagined body movement primes metaphor comprehension. *Cognitive Science, 31,* 721–731.

Winchester, D. (2016). A hunger for God: Embodied metaphor as cultural cognition in action. *Social Forces, 95* (2), 585–606.

Winner, E., Engel, M. and Gardner, H. (1980). Misunderstanding metaphor: What's the problem? *Journal of Experimental Child Psychology, 30* (1), 22–32.

Winner, E., Levy, J., Kaplan, J. and Rosenblatt, E. (1988). Children's understanding of nonliteral language. *The Journal of Aesthetic Education, 22* (1), 51–63.

Winner, E. (1997). *The Point of Words: Children's Understanding of Metaphor and Irony,* Harvard, MA: Harvard University Press.

Winter, B. (2014). Horror movies and the cognitive ecology of primary metaphors. *Metaphor and Symbol, 29* (3), 151–170.

(2016). Taste and smell words form an affectively loaded and emotionally flexible part of the English lexicon, *Language, Cognition and Neuroscience*, DOI: 10.1080/23273798.2016.1193619.

(2019) *Sensory Linguistics: Language, Perception and Metaphor*, Amsterdam: John Benjamins.

Winter, B. and Bergen, B. (2012). Language comprehenders represent object distance both visually and auditorily: Evidence for the immersed experiencer view. *Language and Cognition, 4* (1), 1–16.

Winter, B and Matlock, T (2013) Making Judgments Based on Similarity and Proximity. *Metaphor & Symbol, 28.*

Winter, B., and Matlock, T. (2013). More is up and right: Random number generation along two axes. *Proceedings of the 35th annual meeting of the Cognitive Science Society*. Austin, TX: Cognitive Science Society.

Winter, B., Perlman, M. and Matlock, T. (2014). Using space to talk and gesture about numbers: Evidence from the TV News Archive. *Gesture, 13*, 377–408.

Winter, B. and Matlock, T. (2017). Primary metaphors are both cultural and embodied. *Metaphor: Embodied Cognition and Discourse*, 99–115.

Winter, B., Perlman, M. and Majid, A. (2018). Vision dominates in perceptual language: English sensory vocabulary is optimized for usage. *Cognition, 179.*

Woodin, G., Winter, B., Perlman, M., Littlemore, J. and Matlock, T. (forthcoming) Metaphoric gestures for numerical quantities and emotional valence in the TV News Archive. Submitted to *PLoS ONE.*

Wright, P. H. and Scanlon, M. B. (1991). Gender role orientations and friendship: Some attenuation, but gender differences abound. *Sex Roles, 24* (9019), 551–566.

Yu, N. (1995). Metaphorical expressions of anger and happiness in English and Chinese. *Metaphor and Symbol, 10, 59–92.*

(2002). Body and emotion: Body parts in Chinese expression of emotion. *Pragmatics & Cognition, 10* (1), 341–367.

(2000). Figurative uses of finger and palm in Chinese and English. *Metaphor and Symbol, 15*, 159–175.

(2003). Synesthetic metaphor : A cognitive linguistic perspective. *Journal of Literary Semantics, 32* (1): 19–34.

Zanolie, K. et al., (2012). Mighty metaphors: Behavioural and ERP evidence that power shifts attention on a vertical dimension. *Brain and Cognition, 78, 50–58.*

Zbikowski, L. M. (2002). *Conceptualizing Music: Cognitive Structure, Theory and Analysis*, Oxford: Oxford University Press.

Zentner, M. R. (2001). Preferences for colours and colour-emotion combinations in early childhood. *Developmental Science, 4* (4), 389–398.

Zhiqun Xing, J. (2008). Semantics and Pragmatics of Color Terms in Chinese. *Journal Of Historical Pragmatics, 9* (2), 315–319.

Zhong, C. B. and Leonardelli, G. J. (2008). Cold and lonely. Does social exclusion literally feel cold? *Psychological Science, 19* (9), 838–842.

Zhong, C. B. and Liljenquist, K. (2006). Washing away your sins: Threatened morality and physical cleansing. *Science, 313*, 1451–1452.

Zhong, C. B., Strejcek, B. and Sivanathan, N. (2010). A clean self can render harsh moral judgement. *Journal of Experimental Social Psychology, 46* (5), 859–862.

Zlatev, J. (2012). Prologue: Bodily motion, emotion and mind science. In Foolen, A., Ludtke, U., Racine, T.P. and Zlatev, J. (Eds.) (2012). *Moving Ourselves and Moving Others: Motion and Emotion in Intersubjectivity, Consciousness and Language*, Amsterdam: John Benjamins, pp. 1–28.

Zwaan, R. (2003). The immersed experiencer: Toward an embodied theory of language comprehension. *Psychology of Learning and Motivation, 44*, 35– 62.

(2014). Embodiment and language comprehension: Reframing the discussion. *Trends in Cognitive Sciences, 18* (5), 229–234.

Zwaan, R., Stanfield, R., and Yaxley, R. (2002). Language comprehenders mentally represent the shapes of objects. *Psychological Science, 13* (2), 168–171.

Index

A la Recherche du Temps Perdu (Proust), 134–135
Ackerman, J., 27–28, 33, 117
activated metaphoricity, 12, 16
  co-text and, 216
  motion and, 63
  signalling, foregrounding, and, 67–69
  strong, gesture and, 46
  in teaching, 73
adults, 51–52, 77, 88, 92–93, 216–217, 222
  music represented by, 89–92, 95–101
  number represented by, 89–90, 92–93
  relational structure preferred by, 78–79
  time represented by, 89–91, 93–94
  valence represented by, 89–91, 94–95
adults, older, 51–52, 102–103
advertisements, 181–183
affect, positive and negative
  brightness and, 29, 155–156
  up-down orientation and, 156, 210–211
affection, warmth as, 26, 39
affirmation, negation and, 33–34
Aikhenvald, A., 198
Akpinar, E., 40
Alibali, M., 6–7, 44, 48, 55, 202–203
Almohammadi, A., 80–81
altered minds, 150–152
Amazonians, 200
Ambody, N., 32
American English, 80
American Sign Language (ASL), 132–134
analogical reasoning ability, 178–179, 220
analytic thinkers, holistic thinkers and, 177–178, 219–220
animistic intuition, 82
anorexia, 110–113, 121, 217
anosognosia, 59–60
apraxia, 136
Arabic, 87–88, 194
ASD. *See* autistic spectrum disorders
ASL. *See* American Sign Language

Asperger syndrome, 174–175
  in *The Curious Incident of the Dog in the Night-Time*, 169–170
  with metaphor, difficulties in, 170–171, 173
  with metaphor, proficiency in, 172–173, 219
  metaphor in, contradictory findings on, 169–170, 173–174
  primary metaphor and, 173–174
Astonishing Splashes of Colour (Morrall), 124–137
autistic spectrum disorders (ASD), 173–175
  in *The Curious Incident of the Dog in the Night-Time*, 169–170
  with metaphor, difficulties in, 151–152, 169–173
  with metaphor, proficiency in, 172–173, 219
  metaphor in, contradictory findings on, 151–152, 169–170, 173–174
Aymara, 194–195

Bakker, S., 85
Bardolph, M., 35
Bargh, J., 26
Barsalou, L. W., 35–36
Basque, 195–196
behavioural studies, evidence from, 22
  eye tracking studies in, 24
  front-back orientation in, 22–24
  importance as weight in, 27–28
  limitations of, 32–33, 36–37
  morality as cleanliness in, 21, 27
  moving time, moving ego in, 23–24
  time and space in, 22–24
  up-down orientation in, 24–25
  as warmth, emotional closeness and affection in, 26
Benton, J., 27
bereavement, 150–155, 219
Bergen, B., 6
Berger, J., 40
Berlusconi, Silvio, 114
Birdsell, B., 183–184

blending, metaphorical, 160, 177–178
Blending Theory, 160
blindness, 52. *See also* sight, synaesthesia and
    other senses impacted negatively by, 128
    primary metaphors and, 130–131
    sensory advantages conferred by, 127
    sensory metaphor and, 128–131, 148–149
    temporal and spatial metaphors with, 130–131
    up-down orientation in, 131
Blomberg, J., 30–31, 65–66
bodies, different, 48–49, 105, 121–122, 217
    body shape, 106, 108–113, 121, 217, 222
    disabled, 109, 128–129, 222
    gendered, 52, 105–106, 113–121, 217–218
    handedness, 106–108, 121, 134, 217
body, nation as, 186, 196
body consciousness, 180, 220
Body Consciousness Questionnaire, 180
body posture, depression and, 156
body shape, 106, 222
    in anorexia, 110–113, 121, 217
    dys-appearance in, 110
    height, 108–109, 121, 217–218
    weight, 109–113, 121, 217
body-object interaction ratings, 4
Boers, F., 26
Bonino, Emma, 114
Borobudur monument, 188–189
Boroditsky, L., 23–24, 47, 186–187, 194
Bouba and Kiki effect, 126, 197
Boulenger, V., 35
Bowes, A., 60
Brazil, 199
    Portuguese language of, 80, 131–132
    sign language of, 134
    speech communities of, love in, 193
Brdar, M., 28
British Civil Servant, workplace described by,
    55–56
Brown, R., 17
Buddhism, 188–189
Burgess, M., 158–162
Buxbaum, L., 136

Cable, D. M., 108–109
Cacciari, C., 58
Caers, E., 186
Calbris, G., 44
Cameroon, 198–199
cancer, 150
Cantonese, 102, 209–212
Cao, Y., 187–189
Caramazza, A., 36
cardiac habituation/dishabituation method, 83
Cardillo, E. R., 57–58

career of metaphor hypothesis, 56–57
Casasanto, D., 23, 29, 156
    embodied simulation hypothesis critiqued
        by, 35–36
    on handedness, 107–108, 134
    HMMT of, 18–19, 201–202
Chandler, J., 27–28
Chang, C. T., 181–182
Charteris-Black, J., 114–115, 137
Chartres cathedral, 188–189
Cheng, Y. Y., 27
children, 51–52, 77–81, 88, 92–93, 216–217.
    See also infants
    conflation by, 17, 79
    music represented by, 89–90, 92, 95–102
    number represented by, 89–90, 92–93
    primary metaphors and, 79–81, 103–104,
        216–217
    relational structure of, 78–79
    resemblance metaphors and, 80–81
    time represented by, 89–94
    valence represented by, 89–90, 92, 94–95
Chinese, 200
    Cantonese, 102, 209–212
    literature, 82–83
    Mandarin, English compared with, 194, 201
    on nation as body, 196
    time and, 18, 194, 201
Chiou, W. B., 27
Christianity, 188–189, 221
    Eastern Orthodox, fasting in, 189
    Roman Catholic Church, 176
    transubstantiation, 176
Chrysikou, E., 107
Churchill, Winston, 152
Cienki, A., 15, 45–46, 206–207
Citron, F. M., 59
Classen, C., 199–200
cleanliness
    morality as, 21, 27
    predisposition towards, 180–181
cline, embodied metaphor on, 214–215
Clore, G., 180–181
cognition, embodied, 3
    as continuum, theories of, 9
    emotion in, 8
    empirical evidence for, 4–8
    in everyday language, 7
    in eye tracking studies, 7–8
    4E approach and, 9–10
    gesture providing evidence for, 5–7
    neurological evidence and, 36
    perceptual systems theory and, 4
    somatic markers in, 8
    as unconscious and conscious, 8–9

cognition, need for, 181–183, 220
cognitive style, 177–178, 219–220
Cognitive Styles Analysis (CSA), 177
cognitive unconscious, 8–9
Coker, E. M., 156–157
cold analogies, 58–59
communicative dynamism, 7, 55
communicative purpose, 70–72, 75–76
    persuasion, 71–72
    in teaching, 72–73
communicative stress, 203, 206, 208, 223
conceptual metaphors, primary metaphors and,
    11
concretised metaphors, 70, 110–113, 217
conflation
    in anorexia, 111, 217
    by children and infants, 17, 79
    in depression, 157, 159
    of source and target domains, 79–80, 110,
        217, 222
    in synaesthesia, 141
conscientiousness, 179–180, 220
contextual factors, 54–56, 69, 215–216
    emotional, 62
    genre, 51, 56, 69–73, 75–76
    immediate context, 50
    register, 51, 56, 69, 73–76
co-text, 215–216
Coulson, S., 35
creativity, 183–184, 224
crime, attitudes towards, 186–187, 220–221
cross-cultural variation, 50, 192–193, 212–213,
    223–224
    bodily-based word-colour associations and,
        208–213
    body as source domain in, 195–197
    in children, primary metaphor and, 80–81
    in cross-sensory metaphor, 84–85, 197–201,
        221–222
    HMMT and, 201–202
    of magnitude representation, 87–88
    pitch in, 197–198
    second language and, 53, 201–208,
        210–213, 221–222, 224
    in senses, hierarchy of, 198–200
    in time and space metaphors, 193–195,
        221–222
cross-domain mappings, 10–11, 78–91, 216
cross-linguistic variation. *See* cross-cultural
    variation
cross-sensory mappings, 126–127
    emotion in, 126–127
    in English, smell and, 135
    synaesthesia and, 140, 143–145, 147–149,
        218

cross-sensory metaphor
    cardiac habituation/dishabituation study of,
        83
    cross-cultural variation in, 84–85, 197–201,
        221–222
    in infants, 81–85
    motion and, 84
    in pitch, 197–198
    senses, hierarchy of, and, 198–200
    in South America, 199–200
CSA. *See* Cognitive Styles Analysis
cultural artefacts, in primary metaphor, 18–19
cultural metaphor, embodied, 193
*The Curious Incident of the Dog in the Night-
    Time* (Haddon), 169–170

Damasio, A., 8
De Beauvoir, Simone, 105–106
De Grauwe, S., 210
De Sousa, H., 102
deafness, 131–132
    sensory advantages conferred by, 127
    sensory metaphor and, 131–134
    sign languages and, 52, 124, 132–134
Death before Birth project, 158–162
Deignan, A.
    on genre and register, 69
    piano-playing example of, 11–12, 70–71
    T'ai Chi example of, 13–14, 70–71
    teaching example of, 72–73
del (heart-stomach), 195–196
depression, 150–152, 155–157, 174–175
    after bereavement, 152–155, 219
    body posture and, 156
    clinical and subclinical, 155–156
    conflation in, 157, 159
    after pregnancy loss, 1, 151, 157–162, 219
    in Southern Sudanese refugees, 156–157
Desai, R., 34–35
Desana Indians, 199
Despot, K., 164
Dijkstra, K., 156
disability, 222
    as metaphor, 128–129
    up-down orientation and, 109
discourse community, 70–71
distance. *See* proximity
divided self
    in pregnancy loss, 161–162, 219
    in schizophrenia, 167–169, 219
Dolscheid, S., 84–85, 197–198, 202
domains, source and target, 16, 68, 177
    cognitive style and, 177–178
    conflation of, 79–80, 110, 217, 222
    cross-domain mappings of, 10–11, 78–91, 216

gesture and, 67, 73, 207
motion in, 63
signalling, foregrounding, and, 67
source, body as, 195–197
in stress, merging of, 174–175
time, space, and, 82–83, 195
Dowker, A., 200
Dudschig, C., 210–211
Duffy, S. E., 66, 179–180
Dutch, 197–198, 202
dynamic/developmental view, of embodied
metaphor, 50
dys-appearance, bodily, 110

Eastern Orthodox Christianity, 189
The Economist, 186
EEG. *See* electroencephalogram
El Refaie, E., 42
electroencephalogram (EEG), 47–48, 208
embodied cognition. *See* cognition, embodied
embodied metaphor. *See specific topics*
embodied simulation hypothesis, 35–36
emotion, 58–63, 75–76
in blindness, up-down orientation of, 131
as context, 62
creativity, embodied metaphor, and, 224
in cross-sensory mappings, 126–127
in embodied cognition, 8
empathy, metaphor, and, 60
gesture and, 62–63
hot and cold analogies of, 58–59
metaphor processing triggering, 59
motion and, 38–39, 64–65, 215, 223
novelty and, 59–61, 150, 215, 223
primary metaphors evoking, 61
RMET and, 60
sensory activation and, 59–60
stressful, difficulty perceived in, 155
valence of, 63
emotional closeness, warmth as, 26
emotional intimacy, proximity as, 38–39
emotional memory, 134–135
empathy
metaphor, emotion, and, 60
RMET, 60
synaesthesia and, 141–142
Enckell, H., 110, 112
energy flow metaphors, 164
English, 1–2, 31, 183–184
American, Brazilian Portuguese and, 80
Arabic, Hebrew, and, 87–88
Cantonese and, word-colour associations in,
209–212
gesture in, native speakers using,
204–206

Greek speakers compared with, 201–202
Mandarin Chinese compared with, 194, 201
as second language, 202–208
smell and cross-sensory mappings in, 135
time in, 18, 23–24, 87–88, 179–180
exbodied mind, 6
externally-driven variation, 185
ideology and politics, 186–187, 190–191,
196, 220–221
religious and spiritual beliefs, 176, 187–191,
220–221
eye tracking studies
in behavioural studies, evidence from, 24
embodied cognition in, 7–8

Faber, P., 14
Fainsilber, L., 58–59
Farsi, 195–198, 202
fasting, 189
Fauconnier, G., 177
Faust, M., 151, 170–171, 173
feature mapping, 78–91
Feist, M. I., 66, 179–180
Fetterman, A. K., 23
fictive motion, 29–31
neurological evidence for, 35
perspective and, 65–66
field, of register, 73–74
Figueras Bates, C., 112
film, 41–42
Flynn, Nick, 129
fMRI. *See* functional Magnetic Resonance
Imaging
football (soccer), 109
foregrounding, signalling and, 66–69, 75–76
4E approach, 9–10, 15–16
front-back orientation, 22–24
Fuhrman, O., 201
Fuller, D., 158–162
functional Magnetic Resonance Imaging
(fMRI), 33–35, 57–58
Fuoli, M., 55–56

Gamez-Djokic, V., 34
gender, 52, 113, 223
body difference and, 105–106, 113–121,
217–218
De Beauvoir on, 105–106
distance metaphors and, 115–116, 121
male perspective dominant in, 105–106, 113,
217–218
in metaphor, production of, 113–115
primary metaphors, response to, and,
117–119
social stereotypes in, 119

gender (cont.)
  vertical hierarchy metaphor and, 117–121,
    181, 217–218
generalized magnitude representation. *See*
  magnitude representation
genre, 56, 69, 75
  communicative purpose of, 70–73, 75–76
  discourse community of, 70–71
  staging of, 70, 73
Gentner, D., 78–79
German, as second language, 210
Germany, 193
gesture
  activated metaphoricity and, 46
  changes in, studies on, 46–47
  communicative stress and, 203, 206, 208
  EEG in studying, 47–48, 208
  for embodied cognition, evidence from,
    5–7
  emotion and, 62–63
  evidence from, 5–7, 42–48
  Gesture-for-Conceptualization Hypothesis,
    5–6, 43, 202–203, 206
  Gestures as Simulated Action Framework,
    6–7, 44, 55, 202–203
  Gibbs and, 31, 42, 48, 71
  motion and studies of, 63
  moving time and moving ego with, 47
  native English speakers using, 204–206
  primary metaphors and evidence from, 44–46
  resemblance metaphors and, 11–13
  in schizophrenia, 163–167
  second language speakers using, 202–208
  source and target domains with, 67, 73, 207
  spoken, studies of, 48
  in sports, 71
  time and space in, 47, 194–195
Gibbs, R. W., 2, 40–41, 50
  on cancer, experiences with, 150
  on embodied cognition, 3
  gesture and, 31, 42, 48, 71
  primary metaphor development study of, 80
Giessner, S. R., 109
Gijssels, T., 35–36
Gino, F., 28–29
Gold, R., 170–171, 173
Goldberg, A. E., 59
Goldberg, R. F., 124–125
Goschler, J., 114
Grady, J. E., 17, 38–40
Greek speakers, 201–202
grief. *See* depression
grounding by interaction hypothesis, 36
The Guardian, 186
Gullberg, M., 203

Haddon, Mark, 169–170
Haidt, J., 27
handedness, 106–107, 121, 134, 217
  empirical evidence on, 107
  of politicians, data on, 107–108
  valence and, 107–108
Harber, K., 155
hardness, difficulty as, 39–40
Hatano, G., 82
Hausa, 200
heart-stomach *(del)*, 195–196
Hebrew, 82–83, 87–88, 194
height, 108–109, 121, 217–218
Hierarchical Mental Models Theory (HMMT),
    18–19, 201–202
Himba, 197
HMMT. *See* Hierarchical Mental Models
  Theory
Hodder, A., 71–72
holistic thinkers, analytic thinkers and,
    177–178, 219–220
homogeneity, 48–49, 214
horror movies, 41–42
Horton, W. S., 60
Hostetter, A. B., 6–7, 44, 48, 55, 202–203
hot analogies, 58–59
Houghton, D., 71–72
Hubbard, E., 138–139
Huber, Francois, 129
Huette, S., 7–8
Hurtienne, J., 102–103
Hussey, K., 113–114
Hutchinson, S., 118–119

Ibáñez, A., 47–48, 208
Ibarretze-Antuñano, I., 195–196
ideology, 186–187, 190–191, 196, 220–221
idioms, embodied, 31
imagers, verbalisers and, 177–178, 219–220
Implicit Association Test, 184–185
Inagi, K., 82
Inca, 199
infants, 51–52, 77
  conflation by, 17, 79
  cross-sensory metaphor in, 81–85
  feature mapping of, 78–91
  magnitude representation in, 81, 87
  personification metaphor in, 81–82
internally-driven individual differences, 50–53,
    176–177, 185, 190–191, 219–220
  analogical reasoning ability, 178–179, 220
  body consciousness, 180, 220
  cleanliness, 180–181
  in cognition, need for, 181–183, 220
  cognitive style, 177–178, 219–220

conscientiousness, 179–180, 220
creativity, 183–184
in power, need for, 181, 220
psychopathy, 184–185, 220
intrinsic and co-textual features, 51, 54–55. *See also* co-text
emotion as, 58–63, 75–76
motion as, 63–65, 75–76
novelty as, 56–58, 75–76
perspective, 65–66, 75–76
signalling and foregrounding, 66–69, 75–76
Ishihara, M., 86–87
It's a Knockout, 55–56

Jamalian, A., 46–47
Jasmin, K., 107–108
Johansson-Falck, M., 40–41, 55–68
Johnson, C., 17
Johnson, M., 8–9, 48–49, 105, 124, 177, 214
Jospin, Lionel, 44
Jostmann, N. B., 27–28
Judge, T. A., 108–109

Kaneko, M., 132–133
Kapsiki, 198–199
Kasirer, A., 172–173
Katz, A. N., 60, 113–114
Kenett, Y. N., 151
Khrushchev, Nikita, 192
Kita, S., 5–6, 43, 202–203, 206, 208
Kleege, Georgina, 129–130
Köhler, W., 126, 197
Kok, K., 15
Kouchaki, M., 28–29
Kövecses, Z., 2–3, 177
Kuberska, K., 158–162

Lacey, S., 33
Ladewig, S. H., 67–68
Lakens, D., 25
Lakoff, G., 8–9, 48–49, 105, 124, 177, 214
Langston, W., 24–25
Larkin, Philip, 11
Leonardelli, G. J., 26
Lewkowicz, D. J., 83
Li, H., 187–189
Liljenquist, K., 21
linguistic evidence
corpus-based, 40–41
for primary metaphors, 38–40
Littlemore, J., 55–56, 158–162
piano-playing example of, 11–12, 70–71
T'ai Chi example of, 13–14, 70–71
teaching example of, 72–73

long-term memory, 225
Lossifova, R., 130–131
Louwerse, M., 7, 118–119
love, 193
Low, S. M., 157
Lynott, D., 26

Macbeth effect, 21
Maglio, S., 32
magnitude representation, 86–87
cross-cultural studies of, 87–88
in infants, 81, 87
theory of generalized, 85–86, 138
Mahon, B., 36
Mairs, Nancy, 109
malleability, of different embodied metaphors, 223
Mandarin Chinese, 194, 201
Marmolejo-Ramos, F., 130–131
Mashal, N., 172–173
Matlock, T., 115–116
Matthews, J., 115–116
McGuinness, S., 158–162
McNeill, D., 7, 42–43
Meier, B., 29, 155–156, 184–185, 188, 210–211
Merabet, L., 127
metaphtonymy, 72, 182
Meteyard, L., 9
methodology, development of, 224–225
metonymy, 16–17, 71–72, 109–110, 182–183, 224–225
Mian, 194
Miles, L. K., 22–23
MIP. *See* Pragglejaz Group Metaphor Identification Procedure
mirror neurons, 5–6, 64
Mittelberg, I., 6, 70
modal specificity, 35–36
modality switching cost, 125
mode, of register, 73–75
morality, as cleanliness, 21, 27
Morrall, Claire, 124–137
motion, 75–76
activated metaphoricity and, 63
cross-sensory metaphor and, 84
emotion and, 38–39, 64–65, 215, 223
fictive, 29–31, 35, 65–66
in gesture studies, 63
moving time, moving ego, 23–24, 47, 179–180, 220
in religious beliefs, proximity and, 188–189, 221
time, space, and, 22–24, 63–64, 179–180, 195, 220

Mould, T., 164–165
moving time, moving ego versus, 23–24, 47,
    179–180, 220
Müller, C., 46, 167
    on activated metaphoricity, 12, 16, 46,
        67–69, 216
    on experiential, metaphor as, 16
    on metaphoricity, awakening of, 73, 75
music, evidence from, 41–42
music, representation of, 89–90, 101–102
    major and minor chords, 91–92, 99–101
    pitch, 91–92, 95–96, 197–198
    staccato and legato, 91–92, 96–100
Muslims, 188, 221
Musolff, A., 193, 196

Nadeau, J. W., 152–153
Namibia, 197
narrative, 94–95
nation, body as, 186, 196
naturally-occurring data, evidence from,
    37–38
    in film, 41–42
    gestural, 42–48
    linguistic, 38–41
    in music, 41–42
    in political cartoons, 42
negation, affirmation and, 33–34
nerves, 157
neural embodiment, 8–9
neurological studies, evidence from, 33–35
    embodied cognition and, 36
    fictive motion in, 35
    fMRI, 33–35, 57–58
    limitations of, 35–38
    modal specificity in, 35–36
    negation and affirmation in, 33–34
    synaesthesia in, 138
    TMS, 58
    up-down orientation in, 35
Nigeria, 198–199
novelty, 56–58, 75–76, 174, 225
    career of metaphor hypothesis and, 56–57
    discourse community and, 70
    emotion and, 59–61, 150, 215, 223
    fMRI data on, 57–58
    TMS study on, 58
number, representation of, 89–90, 92–93
Núñez, R., 194–195

Ohala, J. J., 48
Okita, S., 82
Olofson, E. L., 172
ontological metaphor, 164–165
Orange is the New Black, 11

Ortony, A., 58–59
Özçalişkan, Ş., 195

pain, 136–137
Pascuale-Leone, A., 127
path metaphors, 40–41
perceived embodiment, 209–210, 213
perceptual systems theory, 4
Perlman, M., 48
personification metaphor, 81–82
perspective, 65–66, 75–76
persuasion, 71–72, 75–76
Philosophy in the Flesh (Lakoff and Johnson,
    M.), 48–49
piano-playing, 11–12, 70–71
pitch. See music, representation of
political cartoons, 42
political positioning, 186–187, 190–191, 196,
    220–221
Popova, Y., 82–83
power
    need for, 181, 220
    up-down orientation and, 25, 220
Pragglejaz Group Metaphor Identification
    Procedure (MIP), 164
preferential looking paradigm, 84–85
pregnancy loss, 1, 151, 158–159, 161–162. See
    also bereavement
    Death before Birth research project on,
        158–162
    divided self in, 161–162, 219
    as isolating, 157–158
    with mind and body, relationship in, 161–162
    time and, 159–162, 219
presidential elections, US, 107–108
primary metaphor, 10–11
    ASD, Asperger syndrome, and, 173–174
    blindness and, 130–131
    children and, 79–81, 103–104, 216–217
    conflation and, 17, 79–80
    cross-cultural variation and, 80–81
    cross-domain mappings and, 10–11
    cultural artefacts role in, 18–19
    deafness and, 131–132
    in depression, 153–157, 174–175
    emotion evoked by, 61
    fully-embodied account of, 16–17
    gender and response to, 117–119
    gestural evidence for, 44–46
    linguistic differences and, 80–81
    linguistic evidence for, 38–40
    origin of, theories on, 16–19
    resemblance metaphors and, 13–14, 61,
        80–81, 173–174

sensory impairments and, 124, 131
    usage-based accounts of, 17–18
production, metaphorical, 113–115
Protestant Church, 176
Proust, Marcel, 134–135
proximity
    emotional intimacy as, 38–39
    gender and, 115–116, 121
    in religious beliefs, motion and, 188–189,
        221
    resemblance as, 29
psychopathy, 184–185, 220
psychotherapy, 157, 164

Quechua, 200

Ramachandran, V., 138–139
Reading the Mind in the Eyes Test (RMET), 60
refugees, Southern Sudanese, 156–157
register, 56, 69, 75–76
    field of, 73–74
    mode of, 73–75
    tenor of, 73–75
relational structure, 78–79
religious beliefs, 176, 190–191, 220–221
    commonality, variation in, 189–190
    fasting, 189
    movement, proximity metaphors in,
        188–189, 221
    religious buildings in, 188–189
    up-down orientation and, 187–189
resemblance, proximity as, 29
resemblance metaphors
    children and, 80–81
    enacted, 13
    gesture and, 11–13
    primary metaphors and, 13–14, 61, 80–81,
        173–174
response codes, 86–87
Richardson, D., 30
Richardson, P., 188–189
Riding, R. J., 177
rigidity-chaos semantic continuum, 151
Rinaldi, L., 130–131
RMET. See Reading the Mind in the Eyes
    Test
road metaphors, 40–41
Robinson, M. D., 23, 29, 155–156, 188,
    210–211
Roman Catholic Church, 176
Rowland, Beth, 150

Saffran, E., 136
San Roque, L., 198
satellite-framed languages, 195

schizophrenia, 164–165, 174–175
    divided self metaphor in, 167–169, 219
    gesture in, 163–167
    with metaphor, difficulties in, 151–152,
        163–164
    metaphor use in, 164–165
    in psychotherapy, 164
    study on, 165–169, 219
Schnall, S., 27, 155
Schneider, I. K., 27–28
Schubert, T., 25, 119–120
Schwartz, L., 82
second language speakers, 53, 201, 221–222,
    224
    bodily-based word-colour associations in,
        210–213
    of English, 202–208
    of German, 210
    gestures used by, 202–208
    HMMT and, 201–202
    of Mandarin, time and, 201
    up-down orientation and, 210–211
The Second Sex (De Beauvoir), 105–106
secrets, as burden, 155
Selbom, M., 184–185
Semino, E., 114, 136–137
    piano-playing example of, 11–12, 70–71
    T'ai Chi example of, 13–14, 70–71
    teaching example of, 72–73
senses, hierarchy of, 198–200
sensory impairments
    other senses impacted negatively by,
        128
    primary metaphors and, 124, 130–131
    sensory advantages conferred by, 127
    sensory metaphors and, 123–124, 127–134,
        137, 148–149, 218
sensory metaphor, 52, 123–125. See also cross-
    sensory metaphor
    blindness and, 128–131, 148–149
    cross-sensory mappings in, 126–127
    deafness, sign languages, and, 131–134
    modality switching cost in, 125
    sensory impairments and, 123–124,
        127–134, 137, 148–149, 218
    synaesthesia and, 124, 138–148, 218
    tactile disadvantage in, 125
Sharifian, F., 193, 195–196
Shaw, M., 164
Shelley, C., 58–59
Shen, Y., 82–83
Sherman, G., 180–181
Shintel, H., 48
sight, synaesthesia and, 142–143
Sight Unseen (Kleege), 129–130

sign languages, 52, 124, 132–134
    ASL, 132–134
    Brazilian, 134
    sensory metaphor and, 131–134
    Spanish, 134
signalling, foregrounding and, 66–69, 75–76
Siqueira, M., 80, 131–132, 134
Skårderud, F., 110–113
Slepian, M. L., 32, 155
Slobin, D., 42–43
smell
    in Amazonian culture, 200
    in English, cross-sensory mappings and, 135
    in Kapsiki culture, 198–199
    synaesthesia and, 144–146
    taste and, 134–135
soccer (football), 109
social media, 61
soft-assembled metaphors, 50
somatic marker hypothesis, 8
somatization, 156–157
sound, synaesthesia and, 143–144
source domain. See domains, source and target
South America, cross-sensory metaphor in,
    199–200
Southern Sudanese refugees, 156–157
space, 82–83, 216
    in blindness, time and, 130–131
    cross-cultural variation in, time and,
        193–195
    eye tracking studies on time and, 24
    in gesture, time and, 47, 194–195
    motion and time in, 22–24, 63–64, 179–180,
        195, 220
    moving time, moving ego, 23–24, 47,
        179–180, 220
    perspective shaping time and, 66
    satellite-framed, verb-framed languages and,
        195
    in second language speakers, time and, 201
    in spatial responses, time and, 63–64
    STEARC effect, 86–87
Spanish sign language, 134
spatial-temporal association of response codes
    (STEARC effect), 86–87
Spence, C., 126–127
staging, 70, 73
STEARC effect. See spatial-temporal
    association of response codes
Stec, K., 188–189
Stefanowitsch, A., 114
Storch, A., 198
Straube, B., 163–164
Sutton-Spence, R., 132–133
Sweetser, E., 188–189, 194–195, 198

synaesthesia, 52, 124–139
    associations in, motivated and non-arbitrary,
        138
    cross-sensory mappings and, 140, 143–145,
        147–149, 218
    empathy and, 141–142
    kinds of, 137–138
    neurologically rooted, 138
    sensory metaphor and, 124, 138–148, 218
    sight and, 142–143
    smell and, 144–146
    sound and, 143–144
    taste and, 146–147
    touch and, 147–148

tactile disadvantage, 125
Tag, S., 55–68, 167
T'ai Chi, 13–14, 70–71
Talmy, L., 30
Taoists, 188
target domain. See domains, source and target
taste, 134–135, 146–147
Taub, S., 132–133
Tay, D., 157
teaching, 72–73
temporal, embodied metaphor as, 50
tenor, of register, 73–75
Thagard, P., 58–59
Thatcherite-era UK, 186
Theory of Mind deficit, 171–173
Thibodeau, P. H., 186–187
time, 50
    adults representing, 89–91, 93–94
    in blindness, space and, 130–131
    children representing, 89–94
    Chinese speakers and, 18, 194, 201
    cross-cultural variation in, 193–195,
        221–222
    in English, 18, 23–24, 87–88, 179–180
    eye tracking studies on space and, 24
    in gesture, space and, 47, 194–195
    motion and, 22–24, 63–64, 179–180, 195,
        220
    moving through, space and, 22–24
    moving time, moving ego, 23–24, 47,
        179–180, 220
    perspective and, 66
    pregnancy loss and, 159–162, 219
    in satellite-framed and verb-framed
        languages, 195
    second language speakers and, 201
    in spatial responses, space and, 63–64
    STEARC effect, 86–87
TMS. See Transcranial Magnetic Stimulation
touch, 136, 147–148

Transcranial Magnetic Stimulation (TMS), 58
transubstantiation, 176
traumatic events, 52, 222
Trope, Y., 32
Tuck, P., 55–56
Turkewitz, G., 83
Turner, M., 177
Turner, S., 55–56, 158–162
Tversky, B., 46–47, 87–88, 90, 194

United Kingdom (UK), 55–56, 186
United States (US). *See* presidential elections, US
universality, prevalence of, 2–3
up-down orientation
    behavioural evidence on, 24–25
    in blindness, of emotions, 131
    disability and, 109
    gender and, 117–121, 181, 217–218
    neurological evidence on, 35
    positive and negative affects in, 156, 210–211
    power and, 25, 220
    in psychopathy, 184–185, 220
    religious beliefs and, 187–189
    second language speakers and, 210–211
Ureña, J-M., 14
US (United States). *See* presidential elections, US

valence
    adults representing, 89–91, 94–95
    children representing, 89–90, 92, 94–95
    of emotion, 63
    handedness and, 107–108
    narrative and representation of, 94–95
Van Beek, W. E. A., 198–199
Van Quaquebeke, Niels, 109

verbalisers, imagers and, 177–178, 219–220
verb-framed languages, 195
vertical hierarchy. *See* up-down orientation
Viberg, Å., 198
Vidali, A., 128–129

Waist High in the World (Mairs), 109
Walker, P., 84
Wang, C., 200
Wang, Q., 127
warmth
    affection as, 26, 39
    emotion and analogies of, 58–59
    emotional closeness as, 26
Weak Central Coherence (WCC) theory, 171
Wehling, E., 33–34
weight
    body, 109–113, 121, 217
    difficulty and guilt as, 28–29
    importance as, 27–28
Wheeler, K., 6
Wilcox, P., 133–134
Williams, L., 26
Wilson, N., 31
Winchester, D., 189
Winter, B., 41–42, 44, 125, 135
Woodin, G., 63
word-colour associations, bodily-based
    second language speakers using, 210–213
    universality of, 208–210, 212–213
Wygant, D. B., 184–185

Yen, C. T., 181–182
Yu, N., 82–83

Zanolie, K., 25
Zhong, C. B., 21, 26–27
Zlatev, J., 30–31, 65–66